The Last Stroke for World Empire
Great German Tank attack in
the final advance to the Marne

Painting by the German artist,
Prof. Hugo Ungewitter

THE GREAT EVENTS

OF

THE GREAT WAR

A COMPREHENSIVE AND READABLE SOURCE RECORD OF THE
WORLD'S GREAT WAR, EMPHASIZING THE MORE IMPORTANT
EVENTS, AND PRESENTING THESE AS COMPLETE NARRATIVES
IN THE ACTUAL WORDS OF THE CHIEF OFFICIALS AND MOST
EMINENT LEADERS

NON-PARTISAN   NON-SECTIONAL   NON-SECTARIAN

PRESENTING DOCUMENTS FROM GOVERNMENT ARCHIVES AND
OTHER AUTHORITATIVE SOURCES, WITH OUTLINE NARRATIVES,
INDICES, CHRONOLOGIES, AND COURSES OF READING ON SOCIO-
LOGICAL MOVEMENTS AND INDIVIDUAL NATIONAL ACTIVITIES

EDITOR-IN-CHIEF

CHARLES F. HORNE, Ph.D.

DIRECTING EDITOR

WALTER F. AUSTIN, LL.M.

With a staff of specialists

VOLUME VI

❦ ❦

𝔑𝔞𝔱𝔦𝔬𝔫𝔞𝔩 𝔄𝔩𝔲𝔪𝔫𝔦

CONTENTS

VOLUME VI—1918

THE YEAR OF VICTORY

vii

ILLUSTRATIONS

VOLUME VI

1918
THE YEAR OF VICTORY

AN OUTLINE NARRATIVE OF

THE WINNING OF THE WAR

BY CHARLES F. HORNE

THE year of victory! In 1918, the fifth year of combat, the Great War reached its tremendous climax and heroic close. The Allies rescued civilization from destruction, rescued Democracy from that State Absolutism of Prussia which had seemed the most overpowering of all forms of government. Moreover, the rescue was accomplished with dramatic suddenness at the instant when all hope seemed failing, accomplished in that one last desperate effort which precedes despair. History will never record a moment more tense with anxiety than that in which the American troops checked the Germans in their great June advance toward Paris. No reversal of the tidal wave of world-wide battle had ever been one-half so stupendous as that in which the United Allies swept back the entire German army from July until November, and kept them retiring at ever-increasing speed until the Armistice.

Americans may forever remember with just pride the glory of their part in the achievements of 1918. Yet there are some among them who have blindly overestimated America's triumph and have thus sunk back into a complacent ignoring of other nations, an idle boasting that, having beaten the world's greatest military power, they could repeat the deed with ease, if Germany or another were ever again so mad as to defy them. This, of course, is a complete misreading of their real part in the War. Upon them devolved the proud fortune of striking the final blow; but they struck at an antagonist already exhausted by many blows far mightier than theirs. The effort they made was full of sturdy promise; but in performance their deeds were still small when compared with the achievements by which Britain, France and Russia had held back the foe, or the still more stupendous effort by which Germany had matched these three powers at once. It is an open question whether they alone, unprepared as they were, could have outfought the feeblest of these four desperate and determined nations.

By the spring of 1918, however, the strength of all the European powers was ebbing fast. The terrific drain of the past four years had brought them all close upon exhaustion, bankruptcy, starvation. The value of the support they were to receive from America's military aid was still an unanswered riddle for the future. Hence the outcome of the War loomed grimly doubtful. Russia, with her lower civilization and her cruder form of absolutism in government, had been the first Power to break beneath the strain; and her complete military downfall had increased enormously the danger of defeat to the Allies. Germany was now relieved from all military effort in the East. Austria, though terribly weakened, had still strength to support her Balkan allies, to hold conquered Rumania in check, and even to threaten Italy, exhausted by the anarchistic disaster of the preceding year. Thus Germany, for the first time since 1914, was able to turn all her forces westward against France and Britain. These two had withstood her every previous assault. Could they withstand one more, the heaviest of all, wherein their great foe's united armies were all to gather in one last and most terrific blow?

On the other hand, even Germany could not hide from herself the fact that this blow must be her last. She was straining her resources to the uttermost. Beyond this year and this assault, there could be no more heaping up of great masses of ammunition, no more feeding of enormous armies. The alternative of victory was no longer more battles, more piling of "cannon-fodder" into the maw of slaughter. The alternative now would be a complete military breakdown, followed by surrender or else by anarchy and all the mad massacre that rides in fellowship with despair.

So the real German dictator, General Ludendorff, now gave his ultimatum to the shifting series of shadowy Imperial Chancellors who had superseded Bethmann-Hollweg. This ultimatum was soon known to the public of Germany and of the world. Ludendorff declared that if he were given all the men and all the munitions Germany could still gather, he could smash this Franco-British line. It would cost, he estimated, 400,000 men; but Paris would be captured and France be broken. So Germany would be victorious before the summer—and before the Americans could be ready.

There was the real issue! Could America send across the seas enough men, enough competent fighting men, to offset the new and mighty reënforcement of German veterans gathered from the Russian front? This seemed to Europe tragically uncertain. Britain was still very strong, and very resolute to fight; but she had passed the zenith of her power. France, with the loss of half her fighting men, continued strong only in her heroic spirit. Her sons could be relied on to maintain the struggle until the last man fell. But was that strength sufficient?

Then it was that the President of the United States stood forth in the world-crisis, as the world's leader. The uncertainty of victory upon either side in Europe, and the certain approach of anarchy from every side, had led to much talk of peace. Britain and France were even grudgingly prepared to abate something of their former demands, though making peace with the German autocracy was like trying to live with a double-ended poison snake, which talked and struck from both ends at once. Then, on January 8th of 1918, President Wilson announced his famous "fourteen points," which when summarized into one, meant that justice to all the fighting peoples was the only basis on which the United States would sheathe the sword she had unwillingly drawn. The clear, high words had a tremendous influence. They raised the Allies' cause to be the World's cause. They gave Europe new heart and courage. They were adopted by every one of the Allied governments; and Woodrow Wilson became the acknowledged leader and spokesman of this first real "league of nations." [1]

[1] See § I, "The Fourteen Points of Peace," Wilson, Hertling, etc.

THE RUSSIAN PEACE WITHOUT PEACE

Even Germany approved the "fourteen points," at least in words, for to refuse approval to such high thoughts would have been for any man an open confession of wickedness. But at heart the German leaders had as yet no intent of admitting their injustice, or of making restitution for their crimes. Their triumph over Russia had so much encouraged them that they still dreamed of being the leaders, and ultimately the despots, of the world. Hence they paltered with peace talk in the West, while in the East they prepared for devouring helpless Russia.

The armistice which Germany had made with the Bolshevist rulers of Russia in the preceding December called for a peace convention to be held at Brest-Litovsk, the former Russian fortress city now held by the Germans. When the convention met, there appeared before it in January of 1918 the representatives of a new country, previously unknown to the general world. This was the Ukraine, or Ukrainia, comprising the rich grain lands of southwestern Russia, whose people had always been known as "little Russians," and whose chief center was the very ancient Russian holy city of Kiev. Some Ukrainian leaders, upheld by Germany's military support, now declared Ukrainia an independent state, separate from Bolshevist Russia and bound to Germany by close ties of alliance and commercial dependence. In effect Ukrainia was to become a German province.[1]

The Bolshevist rulers were here caught in a trap of their own making. They had declared that every community had the right to frame its own government. They could not therefore protest against the Ukraine's doing so. They acknowledged Ukrainia's independence. But then there immediately followed further German demands. Finland, in the north, must also be separated from Russia; so must Poland; so must all the western regions which German troops had already seized, the districts known as Lithuania and Esthonia and Courland and Livonia. In short, all the richest and most populous parts of western Russia, right up to the very edge of Petrograd itself, were to be formed into small, sepa-

[1] See § II, "Creation of the Ukraine," by Vinichenko, Lenine, etc.

rate states, which were nominally to select their own forms of government. But the new governments were to be established under the direction and control of the German governors and German troops who were in possession of the entire region—and who obviously intended to remain so. This, Germany called a "peace without annexations."

There was of course an element of grim farce in the way Germany thus turned against the Bolshevists their own proclamation, and wrenched from them all their richest lands in the name of "freedom." To the Allies it showed manifestly how little Germany had meant by her surface acquiescence in the "fourteen points," and how completely she intended to twist each one, by some hypocritical turn, to her own enrichment and enlargement. With such a foe, force and only force could insure justice. So, presently, Mr. Wilson spoke for the Allies once more in his celebrated speech of April 6th, declaring that Germany should now be met with "Force to the uttermost." Even though Germany might break western Europe as she had broken Russia, America would still fight on, upholding universal justice as against all the slave armies Germany might drag from her tortured new dominions.

Neither did the Bolshevists themselves yield easily to Germany's iron demands. They protested; they argued; and when the German military leaders at Brest-Litovsk stopped argument with grim, contemptuous commands, the Bolshevist leaders adopted the fantastic policy of simply quitting the peace conference, declaring that Russia was at peace anyway, though she would accede to none of Germany's demands—beyond that of the Ukraine's independence. The Bolshevists seem to have thought, or hoped, that Germany, content with keeping the lands she already held, would at least leave Petrograd alone, and so enable them to "save their face" with the Russian people, to whom they had promised an equal peace. At least they could now say that they had signed no unequal peace; and they still hoped for an uprising in their favor among the German masses.

German militarism was, however, far too strong to leave the opportunity, even had there been the desire, for a revolt in Germany; and the German leaders had no intent of letting Russia off so vaguely. If the two countries were not at peace, they were at war. So the German generals marched their troops further onward into Russia—unopposed; for the Bolshevist army was still of such type that, while eagerly slaughtering thousands of helpless civilians at home, it was as unwilling as it was incompetent to fight a well armed foe.[1]

Under pressure of this renewed German invasion, which began in February, the Bolshevist rulers abandoned their defiant attitude. They again met the German peace commissioners, yielded everything that had been demanded, and agreed also to pay to Germany a heavy money "indemnity." The first installment of this was soon afterward paid; the final peace treaty was signed on March 3rd; and Germany was left to absorb the newly created border states as best she might. In her proclamations she represented herself to these peoples as their noble benefactor, bringing to them the inestimable advantage of studying German "Kultur" and of holding their lives and fortunes subject to the mercy of some Prussian "junker" instead of a Russian Czar.

Forlorn Rumania, left isolated by the Russian and the Ukrainian peace, was also compelled to sign a treaty which placed her helpless in Germany's power, ruled by the able German general, Mackensen, who had already half-conquered her. The only Ally forces that remained in the East were two. At Salonika and Monastir, the combined army of British, French and Serbian troops still upheld the Greeks in their wavering defiance of exhausted Bulgaria and Austria. And in Asia, British forces held Bagdad and Jerusalem, and could push onward, almost at will, against the exhausted, starving and despairing Turks. Germany's allies thus continued to pay, by their increasing and utter ruin, the full price for all her Russian triumph.

THE TREMENDOUS GERMAN DRIVE IN THE WEST

Against this eastern background of intrigue and conquest, massacre and desolation, such as the world had not known through all the centuries of modern civilization, against this was to be pictured the great final drama of battle in the

[1] See § III, "Bolshevism Bows to Germany," Trotsky, Czernin, etc.

West. The great Ludendorff had made all his preparations,
and on March 21st he launched Germany's final "thrust for
victory." He proclaimed that this was to be the vastest,
the most rigorously continued, and in the end the most glorious for Germany, of all world battles; it was to be called the
"Kaiser-battle." For this assault, Ludendorff had carefully
culled from all his regiments their best fighting soldiers,
and he had united these in new regiments as "shock troops."
He could thus rely on his new regiments for a most powerful
attack; yet the policy was almost suicidal in its recklessness.
If once these shock troops were all expended in the desperate
battle, what strength could be expected from the other weakened regiments! The device made clear that this was indeed
the relentless desperation of a final blow.

How near that desperation came to victory is still an
awesome vision to the peoples who escaped. For four
months, from mid-March to mid-July, the great Kaiser-battle
raged, while the whole civilian world watched in breathless
expectation this struggle which must decide the fate of every
human soul among us all. Generals on either side may have
been earlier confident as to the final issue; but as to the rest
of the world, not until after the 18th of July, when the last
great German assault had crumbled before Rheims and the
great Foch counter-attack had been successfully launched
against the "Marne salient," not until then could we say with
easier breath that the end was in sight, that with God's good
grace the victory would be ours.

Let us follow the steps of this stupendous battle. It
consisted of four, or perhaps we should reckon them five,
separate German assaults, each stupendous in itself, each followed by a period of renewed preparation, and each launched
against a different sector of the Ally line.

That first Ludendorff assault of March 21st has been
called the Battle of Picardy. It was directed against the
British army along a front of over fifty miles in Picardy,
the region where the great Battle of the Somme had been
fought in 1916 and had forced the Hindenburg Retreat of
1917. Along all this line there now broke forth the heaviest
bombardment of the War, followed by the fierce charge of

the German "shock troops." Ludendorff's hope, as he himself has told us, was to break through the British lines at the northern end of his attack, near Arras, and thus separate the chief force of the Britons from their comrades and their French allies to the south. Thus the Britons could be quickly crowded back upon the Channel ports, crushed into helpless disorder in this restricted space, and even annihilated. After that the victorious Germans would turn upon the French and capture Paris.[1]

Fortunately for the Allies, the strongly guarded British lines at Arras held firm against the utmost German effort. There came a break, however, farther south, where the extreme end of the British line joined the French army. Here the "Fifth British Army" under General Gough had been extended in thin formation over a considerable space, and under the continued beating of the German thunderstorm the thin line snapped. Sweeping through the gap, the Germans rushed down the valley of the Somme, and soon recovered all the region they had resigned in the former Hindenburg Retreat. Unfortunately for themselves, their previous devastation of this region had been so complete that it was now an utter wilderness, a morass of mud, offering extraordinary difficulty to their advance and to the bringing forward of supplies. So their own previous thoroughness now proved their undoing. Their great leader afterward said that he would sooner have broken through the Ally line in any other place whatever. His very success became a trap by luring him to more costly effort.

The advance of his exhausted troops grew slower and slower. The Allies attacked them desperately from either side; and by March 28th the line in front of the Germans had formed again. On that day they captured the French city of Montdidier; but that marked the apex of their advance in this "Battle of Picardy." On the same day their last huge assault on Arras, their original goal, broke down with tremendous losses. This was probably the heaviest single day of fighting in the entire War.

The narrow escape of the Allied forces from a complete

---

[1] See § IV, "Opening of the Kaiserbattle," by Haig, Ludendorff, etc.

and crushing defeat in this first assault, the unexpected snapping of the sturdily held British line, led to one great forward step in the Ally plans. General Foch was made Commander-in-Chief with full authority over all the forces on the Western front. This step had been urged by the American authorities from the first; but the British had refused thus to subordinate themselves. Their prime minister, Lloyd George, had risked his whole popularity by urging it. Now the obvious necessity shook even British pride; and the American general, Pershing, set them a gallant example. In the hour of disaster, he publicly offered all his American troops, untrained as most of them still were, to be used in this extremity in whatever way the French commander wished, either as an army or as individual companies and regiments to be brigaded under French or British generals and to lend reënforcement wherever needed. This splendid sacrifice of America's individuality may have exerted the last pressure needed; for now the British army rulers yielded their opposition. On April 3rd, Marshal Foch assumed control over what was for the first time one vast united army directed by a single brain toward a single purpose. Thus Ferdinand Foch, Frenchman, Catholic, a professor once dismissed from a military college, came into command of the greatest single army ever gathered in the world.[1]

Foch knew well that the mighty Kaiser-battle had as yet passed only its initial stage. He made hasty realignment of his troops. The fighting meanwhile continued every day, though in less tremendous fashion. Then no sooner had the Germans readjusted themselves than they struck again with all their strength. This second huge outburst of destruction began on April 9th, and has been called the Battle of the Lys. In it Ludendorff resumed his original plan, to drive against the Britons in the north and sweep them back upon the Channel coast. Since he had failed at Arras, he tried now further north along the Lys River, just to the south of Ypres.

The Battle of the Lys was almost a duplicate of that of Picardy. This time it was a Portuguese regiment that gave

[1] See § VI, "Foch Assumes Supreme Command," Lloyd George, etc.

way, overwhelmed by the massed thousands of the Germans. Through the gap thus made, the foe swept down the valley of the Lys River, surrounding and capturing Armentières with its British garrison, and storming Messines Ridge, which the British had so brilliantly won the year before. Soon the Germans had regained all the ground they had lost in the great 1917 Battle of Flanders, and were threatening Ypres with complete encirclement. On April 12th the British chief commander, Haig, issued his frank and startling appeal to his men, declaring that they were fighting with their "backs to the wall," and that any further loss of ground would mean irremediable disaster.[1]

But that ground was not lost. General Foch rushed French troops to the Britons' aid; and again the gap was closed. Again the German blow had reached the limit of its power. So tremendous had been the slaughter of the German "cannon-fodder" in this desperate attack that they could not even hold the ground they had won. During the first week of May, British counter-attacks pressed them back from their furthest advance, although still leaving them closer to Ypres and the Channel than they had ever won before.

During the momentary lull of the last days of April, while the soldiers everywhere hardened their resolution and gathered strength for the next giant clash, the younger officers of the British navy achieved what was perhaps the most spectacular deed of the War, the blocking of the Zeebrugge harbor. This Belgian port and also that of Ostend, had been converted into submarine bases, the nearest bases from which the U-boats could creep out upon the Ally ships. On April 23rd, in a most dashing raid, the Allies destroyed the port of Zeebrugge by smashing its breakwaters and sinking old cement ships in the harbor, which was thereafter useless. In similar fashion they raided Ostend, sinking an old warship in its channel mouth, and partly blocking that port as they had wholly blocked Zeebrugge. This came as an almost final blow to the German U-boat power, which had been steadily waning since America's entrance into the War.[2]

---

[1] See § VII, "Britain with Back to the Wall," by Haig, Gaedke, etc.
See § VIII, "The Zeebrugge Affair," Carpenter, Von Tirpitz, etc.

The third great blow of the Kaiser-battle, the Battle of the Aisne, was launched by Ludendorff on May 27th. Twice now he had struck at the British lines and broken them, but failed of power to follow up the first success. Now he turned his attention to the south. Perhaps the French reënforcements sent by Foch to the Britons' aid had left the French line feeble. So the Germans now struck southward from their line along the *Chemin des Dames,* sweeping across the Aisne River, where they had fought their first defensive fight in 1914. Now for the second time they were rushing onward toward the Marne.[1]

This was the supreme German effort of the War. The shock troops seemed to burst through the French line even more readily than through that of Britain. In four days they drove forward over forty miles. They reached and crossed the Marne. They pushed westward down its valley toward Paris. They were within less than forty miles of the metropolis, and there was no large force between them and that splendid goal. Was France to perish after all? The scant reënforcements near at hand were rushed hastily forward from every source. Was this to be the end? It was not; for there, at the very apex of the attack, on June 1st, at Château-Thierry (shăt-ō'-tē-ā-rē), on the Marne, the Germans met the American vanguard.[2]

German generals have since explained that Paris was not their real objective in this drive, that they sought rather to force their way southward across the Marne, and so to separate Rheims and the French armies to the east of it from Paris and the armies further west. But the fact remains that in this effort the Germans had unexpectedly won dangerously near to Paris, that it seemed almost in their grasp, and that their troops upon the spot began pushing eagerly toward it. The French troops around Château-Thierry began withdrawing, true to their stern policy of slaying as many Germans as possible but saving their own men by retreat at whatever cost to the neighboring country. When, however, the counsel to withdraw reached the American com-

[1] See § X, "The Chief Blow of the Kaiserbattle," by Berthaut, Von Schriebershofen, etc.

[2] See § XII, "Château-Thierry," by Kahn, Daniels, etc.

mander, General Bundy, he made the now famous comment, "My men would not understand such an order. Americans do not retreat." And he held his line.

That was the supreme moment of the Great War. At last the Germans were to meet face to face in decisive battle those Americans who had journeyed half across the earth to fight them. In not unequal numbers the two clashed, the stern, full manhood of Autocracy against the glowing, eager youth of Democracy. For miles along the line they met, not only at Château-Thierry but at Vaux (vō), at Belleau (bell-ō) Wood, at Torchy (tor-shē), at Bouresches (boo-rĕsh). These are all names to be forever treasured by Americans. At every one of these sanctified spots, Democracy more than held its own. The German shock troops were slowly driven back. Farther north and farther east their advance was held up by French and by Italian troops; but the apex of their drive was broken by the Americans. By June 7th the Champagne Battle had definitely failed of its purpose. It had only driven a third wedge into the Ally line without dividing it in twain.

Almost immediately afterward the Germans delivered two further assaults which should perhaps be reckoned as part of this third great battle. They attempted to widen the "Marne salient," this deep gash in the Ally line, by attacking in turn its two basic angles. On June 9th they launched a tremendous drive against its northern front, advancing from the region they had won in March around Montdidier. For this attack, however, General Foch was fully prepared; and it broke down completely, with enormous German losses. Then on June 18th the Germans attacked the southern buttress of the wedge, the fortress city of Rheims. This attack was as futile and almost as costly as the preceding one. The German generals had again to pause, to take stock of their losses, and to reorganize.

Presumably by this time Ludendorff knew that the great battle had been decided against him. His check along all the line, in this third effort to break through, had been decisive. His thousands of regiments of shock troops had been almost annihilated. Nevertheless he made one more giant effort, the fourth and last assault, the mighty *Friedensturm* or Peace-battle, as the Germans called it because of their general's promise that it should conquer peace at last.

The Peace-battle was begun on July 15th. Its immediate commander was the Prussian Crown Prince, and its direction of attack was southward all along the Marne from Château-Thierry to Rheims and eastward beyond Rheims. Hence it is sometimes called the second battle of the Marne. Along this front of sixty miles, almost a million Germans rushed forward in this last attack. General Foch expected them, was ready for them. At Château-Thierry the Americans checked them sharply. Between there and Rheims the Germans drove back some Italian troops and almost encircled Rheims. Its fall was menacingly near. But farther eastward beyond Rheims, the Germans met frightful defeat. The French general, Gouraud, had devised a new method of meeting them with machine guns and blocking their attacks, a method so effective that the Crown Prince's troops melted away like snow under the July sun. The slaughter was awful; and within three days the Germans had abandoned the entire *Friedensturm* as hopeless.[1]

On the fourth day, July 18th, Foch launched his great counter-offensive which continued until the end of the War. But before following that glorious march to victory we must note briefly what had been happening in other fields.

AIR RAIDS AND REPRISALS

All through the spring aërial raids had been continued on either side with ever increasing skill and power, until at length the German Kaiser made public proposal that both sides should abandon these. This offer from the men who had counted on winning the war with their Zeppelins and who had maintained aërial raiding for almost a year before the Allies began retaliating, was an open confession that the German leaders believed they had hopelessly lost their supremacy in the air, and that Germany was now suffering more than her opponents from the raids.

Paris, which had grown hardened to these aërial attacks, was now startled by a new sensation. Soon after the great

[1] See § XV, "Germany's Last Effort," by Gouraud, Hesse, etc.

German advance began in March, the French capital was
suddenly bombarded by an immense "long distance" cannon,
hurling a shell through the air some seventy miles, whereas
twenty-five miles had previously been the very farthest limit
of bombardment. So amazingly unexpected was this new
German device that for a time men doubted the existence
of such a cannon and sought to explain the coming of the
mysterious projectiles in some other way. Of course from
such a distance there was no chance of aiming the gun;
it was just pointed toward Paris in a general way, and the
shells were fired to fall where they might. Thus the bombardment did comparatively little injury, while it roused
French anger to a sterner hardness than ever.[1]

ANARCHY IN THE EAST

Outside of France, the chief Ally centers of interest lay
in eastern Europe, in Italy, and in the United States. In
the East, both Russia and Austria had presented new problems with the advancing year. When Bolshevist Russia had
definitely accepted the German peace, the land became dangerously like a German province. Freed Teuton prisoners
took an active rôle in its armies and assemblies. The German government had only to demand the surrender of any
supplies it wished, or to take possession of whatever was
denied it. Of course exhausted and distracted Russia had
comparatively little produce left to give; but she did possess
considerable military stores previously loaned her by the Allies for use in the common cause. More important still, she
possessed millions of ignorant and hungry men, who might
easily be induced to join a German army. German officials became prominent everywhere in Russia. They toiled
indeed in the cause of order and of renewed industry, but
of German order and of an industry that was both German and military.

In fact, there now ensued between German militarism
and Russian anarchy a peculiar and in some phases not unequal struggle. As part of the nominal peace, a Russian
envoy settled in Berlin. He was an eager Bolshevist, and

[1] See § IV, "Most Tremendous of War Inventions," by Ambassador
Sharp, General Rohne.

with him came a long train of Bolshevist supporters well
supplied with money and with the typical Bolshevist literature, full of impassioned denunciation of "capital" and impossible extravagance of promises for a poor man's paradise. There was in Germany much bitter discontent for such
extravagant appeals to work upon; and if Autocratic Germany had crushed Russia, Bolshevik Russia was not now
without influence in weakening Autocratic Germany. In
fact, more than one German writer since the War, unwilling
to admit the overwhelming military victory of the Allies,
has ascribed his country's defeat almost wholly to the "weakening of the Will to Victory" caused by the spread of the Bolshevist propaganda.

In this new Russian situation the Allies were sorely puzzled as to how to treat their former ally. To Czaristic Russia they had in 1914 pledged friendship and support. The
Democratic Russia which replaced it in March, 1917, had
received new and stronger pledges, in which the United States
had also joined. But to Bolshevist Russia the Allies owed
nothing. Its leaders had not even been in Russia or been
recognized as Russians when the mutual pledges had been
given. Moreover, the Bolshevists had repudiated every former pledge and declared themselves the enemies of every
other government in the world, accusing all of being "capi-
talistic" and declaring themselves the only "friends of the
people," those people who were perishing in agony by the
hundred thousand under Bolshevism's blind and brutal law-
lessness.

Ought the great Democratic doctrine that every civilized
people had the right of "self-determination" of their form
of rule, be accepted by the Allies as extending even to this
Russian "no rule" and mob-massacre of all its nobler elements? Should the Ally governments stand passive and
watch the destruction of all civilization extend abroad from
anarchistic Russia, as it had threatened to extend from autocratic Germany? Bolshevism was not itself content with
"self-determination." It challenged the whole world to war.
It eagerly spread everywhere its delusive propaganda, calling
for world-revolution, for the annihilation of every form of

education, culture and wealth, except Lenine's, and for the destruction of all established governments and all existing religions.

Tentatively, hesitantly, the Ally governments began to reach out the hand of interference within Russia. Wherever any Russians themselves rallied and declared a preference for order rather than disorder, for law and justice rather than dull prejudice and red injustice, there the Allies lent aid to the new parties opposing Bolshevism. The first definite step of this sort was taken in April, 1918, when the United States and Japan landed forces at Vladivostok, the chief Siberian port on the Pacific, to protect from Bolshevist seizure or destruction the large Ally supplies which had been sent there for Democratic Russia. The Bolshevists, it should be remembered, had repudiated all the debts of the former government, so certainly they had no claim upon the supplies those debts had purchased.[1]

With Ally support, Siberian Russia soon shook itself free of the Bolshevists and declared its independence of them. In similar fashion the Allies lent assistance to northern Russia. Ally troops, including some from the Unted States, were landed at Archangel, the chief port of Europe's Arctic coast, and there aided the forming of a "Peasants' Government of Northern Russia" with Archangel as its capital. In southern Russia, the Cossacks repudiated Bolshevist rule, and allied themselves with the Ukraine. Thus in every direction there gradually formed a resisting front, limiting the extension of the Bolshevist domain, or sometimes actively driving it back toward Petrograd and Moscow, its chief centers.

To the aid of these frontiers of resistance against the spreading anarchy, there came another force, one of the very strangest of all time, the "army without a country," the Czecho- (check-o) Slavs. This remarkable army had its origin in the Austrian Empire. There the subject nations had grown increasingly desperate; for the Austrians and Hungarians had perforce tightened the reins of tyranny under the pressure of Austrian defeat and approaching starvation. The strongest of these subject people were the Bohemians,

[1] See § XIV, "Siberian Independence," Ackerman, Bakhmeteff, etc.

who with their neighboring related peoples have now become known as the Czecho-Slavs. These Czecho-Slavs had always wished to fight upon the Allies' side rather than that of the Teutons. Hence there had gradually grown up in Russia a Czecho-Slav division in the Russian army. This began with some of the Slavs of Russian birth, but in the later years was built up largely of Slav prisoners captured from the Austrian army. Many of these eagerly joined Russia and turned their arms against their former oppressors. This Czecho-Slav division, at the time of Russia's military breakdown in 1917, furnished almost the only troops who still would fight. Austria had proclaimed them traitors, and executed any who were captured. Hence surrender to the Teutons meant for them now sure death. As the disintegration of Russia continued, these Czecho-Slavs drew ever closer together under officers of their own choosing, until they formed an army of their own.

When the Bolshevists made peace with Germany, the Czecho-Slavs refused to be included in this peace. They asked to be transferred to some Ally country where they might still continue the fight which had become to them an inescapable battle for independence or for death. The Bolshevist leaders tried to beguile the Czecho-Slavs with kindly words and then disarm them, tried, it would seem, to secure their surrender to the Teutons and to destruction. At any rate, the Czecho-Slavs believed this; and turning their arms against the Bolshevists, they fought their way across all Russia to Siberia, and onward through Siberia till they reached touch with the Allies. Thus they achieved at last the most remarkable march and battle and escape in all history.[1]

ITALY'S VICTORY OVER AUSTRIA

If we turn from this Russian turmoil to look more closely to the Austrian Empire's increasing misery, we find her subject nations growing ever more vehement and desperate in defiance. It was not a lustful anarchy which here fought against autocracy; the revolting masses formed an earnest and intelligent democracy. Those Czechs (checks) who

---

[1] See § IX, "Odyssey of the Czecho-Slavs," by Nosek, Masaryk, etc.

could escape from Austria had formed in Paris a national government of their own; and this proclaimed the Czecho-Slavic independence and democratic form of government. A remnant of Jugo- (yugo) Slavs, or southern Slavs from the regions around Serbia, also proclaimed, from Paris, their defiance of Austria, and their resolve to achieve democracy.

In Italy, too, democracy had once more regained full ascendancy. The nation rallied slowly, painfully and heroically from the anarchistic breakdown of its army in 1917. All through the spring of 1918 the Italian army was patiently built up again, until it grew so strong that, as we have noted, some of its regiments were loaned to France to strengthen the resistance against Ludendorff.

Meanwhile Germany had been constantly urging the Austrians to aid her great French assault by renewing their attack on Italy. Austria's rulers had grown heartily disgusted with the entire war and were awake to the stern fact that a German victory was likely to be fully as destructive to them as was an Ally one. Hence they were by no means eager for further battle. Their new young Emperor Charles even made secret peace overtures to the Allies, too secret and too timorous to be effective.

When at last the Austrians felt they could delay attack no longer, they began on June 15th a double assault along the Italian front. One Austrian advance came from the mountain region of the Alps. It struck at the French and British forces which had been aiding Italy since the previous fall, and which now held the advanced posts of honor and of danger. They beat back the Austrian attack at once.

Meanwhile an even larger Austrian army was being hurled against the Italian line along the lower Piave (pee-ah-ve) River, in the neighborhood of Venice. Some hundred thousands of Austrians forced the passage of the Piave; but beyond that the Italians held firm, and presently Nature came impressively to their aid. Torrential rains so swelled the Piave as to make its passage temporarily impossible. The Austrians who had crossed were left without sufficient supplies, the Italians attacked them again and again, and threw them into utter confusion. Those who could not flee

back across the river were killed or captured. The total Austrian loss approached three hundred thousand. This was the chief Austrian disaster on the western front, the chief Italian victory of the War, a fitting prelude to the greater Ally victories which were to follow.[1]

HOW AMERICA PREPARED

Meanwhile what had the United States been doing to aid the approaching triumph? Pershing's generous offer to Marshal Foch in March, that the American troops would fight wherever needed, had been typical of the Americans' whole attitude. They were in the War not to profit, nor to boast, nor to show their prowess, but to crush the German monster by whatever manly means they could, and so restore peace to the suffering world. Europe was amazed by the whole-souled devotion with which Americans turned their entire thought and energy to "war work"; and the results were such as not even mighty Germany had achieved. So rapidly did the number of fully-drilled, fully-equipped American troops increase in France that Pershing's offer of March had placed a quarter of a million men at Marshal Foch's disposal. Even as early as this, his forces were the reserve which helped to block the Ludendorff drive.

By May, the Americans in France were a great army, and on May 28th, just at the opening of Ludendorff's third drive, they were set to fight their first battle all by themselves. This was a small affair as battles were then measuring, an attack by some five thousand men to capture the town of Cantigny, near Montdidier, where the first mighty German attack had ended. Yet the storming of Cantigny might well be quoted as a model battle. Their officers planned it out as they would have planned a football contest, and their men went into it in the same spirit. Each soldier knew exactly what he had to do—and did it. And they took Cantigny and hurled back the ensuing German counter-attacks with the precision of clock-work, or rather with the yet more beautiful accuracy of human intelligence, when self is wholly subordinated to the achieving of a higher purpose.[2]

[1] See § XIII, "Austria's Breakdown," Kervarec, Von Hoetzendorf.
[2] See § XI, "Europe's Cry for Help," by Clemenceau, Orlando, etc.

The French generals watched that Cantigny assault with keenest anxiety. Were the Americans as yet first class soldiers, troops who could be equally trusted with the French and British? When, upon the Cantigny success, there followed immediately the victory of the sterner battles of unexpected necessity at Château-Thierry and at Belleau Wood, General Foch knew that victory was in his hands. He had now three great armies to depend upon, instead of two. The two had been reeling back almost exhausted; the third was fresh with all the vitality of untried youth. When Foch launched his great counter-attack on July 18th, he started it along the line that reached from Cantigny to Belleau and he started it with an equal mingling of French troops and Americans.

THE ALLIES' DRIVE TO VICTORY

So we come to that stupendous Ally advance, the final campaign of the War. The surge of troops swept onward as steadily, as successfully, as ever the German shock-troops had in the Kaiser-battle. And the lines *never fell back again*. On that first day, July 18th, American and French troops advanced some six miles. Two American divisions fighting in the line just south of the city of Soissons (swahsŏn) were the spearhead of the attack. Theirs had been the honor of checking Germany at Château-Thierry. Theirs was now at Soissons, the yet greater honor of forcing her to begin her final retreat. Ludendorff poured in all possible reenforcements to aid his yielding troops, but within a week the Germans had been driven back from across the Marne and were hurriedly evacuating the entire salient they had captured in their great assault of May.[1]

The forcing of the foe from that salient was soon left almost entirely to the Americans. Those were glorious days! They fought heroically at Fère (fair), at Fismes (feem), and in the deadly valley of the Vesle (văl) River, where they began to meet the heavy artillery from the old German main defense line along the *Chemin des Dames*. Not until late August was that salient wholly empty of the still desperately resisting foe.

[1] See § XVI, "The Beginning of the End," by Foch, Buchan, etc.

Then suddenly on August 8th, Foch struck elsewhere along the line. He had been marshaling both French and British divisions, and some Americans also, for this second great offensive. It was in the north, along the old Somme Valley region, and was entrusted mainly to British troops. So once more these heroes fought their way back over the same old ground. And now for the first time there became evident the decreasing morale of the German troops, that decrease of individual resistance which Ludendorff's policy of the "shock-troops" had made inevitable. In fact Ludendorff himself has called that day of August 8th the blackest of the War. Some of his retreating regiments shouted curses at their leaders, and even cursed the reënforcements which, by hurrying forward to replace the retreaters, were thus prolonging the War.

The rapid advance with which the Britons now drove their way up the Somme was an impressive contrast to their bitterly fought progress in the huge battle of 1916. Then, as the German cartoons had suggested, they had won each day scarce ground enough to lay out the graves of the fallen. Now, they advanced by miles and miles. Before the end of August, French and British troops had regained practically all the ground lost in all the Kaiser-battle. They were once more facing the old established Hindenburg Line of 1917.

More than that, on August 26th, the Canadians, fighting under a British army commander, made the first break in the Hindenburg Line itself. Germany had deemed that line impregnable.[1] Her leaders simply dared not tell the public it was gone. If German battle announcements had been deceptive before, they now became absolutely false. A deluded people struggled on at home, unconscious of how closely their approaching doom was now enfolding them.

There was no pause in the great battle during early September. While the British still pushed on across the northern end of the Hindenburg line, and the French assailed it from the south, Foch suddenly launched his third great blow farther east, beyond Verdun. This was the wiping out of the St. Mihiel (sŏn mē-yĕl) salient, in which the Germans had

[1] See § XVII, "Breaking the Hindenburg Line," by Hindenburg, etc.

been firmly entrenched since 1914. It was the first major action entrusted wholly to the United States troops, and it was one of the most, perhaps *the* most, completely successful, fully rounded and technically perfect operation of the War.[1]

The American soldiers had now been released to a large extent from that voluntary service under other generals to which General Pershing had generously surrendered them during the terrible need of the Kaiser-battle. He had been able for the first time to form an American Army. To this Marshal Foch had entrusted a large portion of the Ally line east of Paris, including the region around St. Mihiel. Here on September 12th, along a front of over twenty miles, more than two hundred thousand United States soldiers suddenly attacked both sides of the salient. On that first day, they broke through the German lines on each side of the salient; and in the morning of the second day the American troops from the two sides met at Vigneulles, in the middle of the salient, enclosing within their lines, and afterward capturing, all the troops who had not yet found time to escape.

Small respite was given the successful American army after St. Mihiel. Now that this last dangerous German salient was wiped out, Foch was ready for his final general advance. No scattered blows now! On September 26th the Allies' whole line from the English Channel to St. Mihiel was launched forward all at once. The eager Belgian troops who had so long held the dreary seacoast rushed back across their own home land. Aided by French troops they, on September 30th, temporarily seized the Belgian city of Roulers. South of them came the smashing British advance, aided by United States troops and Canadians. On October 2nd the British armies captured Armentières, and the Germans began a hurried evacuation of Lille, the metropolis and chief center of their four years' power in northern France. South of the British came the stern French armies; and on October 1st they seized St. Quentin (sŏn-kän-tŏn). An old prophecy had said that when St. Quentin was regained, France would be cleared of her foes. There was no question now that the Germans were going; the only doubt

[1] See § XVIII, "St. Mihiel," by Frederick William and Pershing.

was as to whether their crumbling front would enable them to escape without utter disaster.

Meanwhile the hardest advance of all had been this time entrusted to the Americans. From Verdun and St. Mihiel they were to advance northward up the Meuse River Valley and through the Argonne forest. This forest had been deliberately abandoned by the French in Joffre's first retreat of 1914; but so dense and craggy were its tangled depths that no foe had ever yet fought a passage through the Argonne to victory. The desperate achievement had been tried in earlier wars, and again repeatedly in this war by both French and Germans. But the defensive advantages of the wilderness had ever proved invulnerable. Let the boys from the western world break through it if they could![1]

They did. From September 26th onward for four weeks they fought their way through the Argonne against the main strength of the German army. Germany realized that defeat here would shut off her troops from their chief supply line from home by way of Metz, and would leave them enclosed, with their backs pinned against the rough Belgian highlands and forests. So her best remaining troops were now marshaled against the Americans. In vain! The men fought with an impassioned firmness that carried them through everything. The price of victory was cruelly high, but they paid it all. They were well aided by General Gouraud's French troops to their west; and on October 16th the Americans captured Grand Pré, the city beyond the Argonne. On October 26th they broke the last German line of defense; and on November 6th they seized the heights above the city of Sedan. That blocked the Germans' escape southward by way of Metz. Their main line of communication with Germany was definitely smashed.[2]

By this time the advance of the British in the north and of the French in the center had become almost equally successful. In the first days of November the whole Belgian seacoast was reoccupied by the Belgian troops, and the British were at the gates of Ghent. On November 2nd the Brit-

---

[1] See § XXI, "Storming the Argonne," by Pershing, Marwitz, etc.
[2] See § XXIV, "The Final Ally Drive," by Maurice, Foch, etc.

ish seized Valenciennes; and by November 8th the whole German center was retreating in wild haste before the French. Unless the Germans made good speed, they were likely to be entrapped from both the north and south by the Britons and Americans.

THE CRUMBLING OF THE CENTRAL POWERS

There is no disputing that in those last days of the Ally drive, the German soldiers as a whole no longer battled with their former energy. In some sections, as in the Argonne, they still fought gallantly, but there was no longer any great center of command to keep them all at their best. The confusion of retreat had left each division dependent on its own commanders, or even on the temper of its own soldiers; and these were most of them no longer in a fighting mood. Despair was upon them.

The breakdown of Teutonic power, when it came, had proven more swift and more complete than the most optimistic of the Allies had dared to hope. 1918 had opened so disastrously that the utmost the Ally leaders expected from its closing months was the restoration of the balance in their favor. They expected the Foch drive to push slowly onward until winter checked its power. Everywhere men were preparing for another winter of grim endurance. 1919 was to be the year of final effort and of victory.

Suddenly, however, in those glorious days of September, each of Germany's fellow-culprits was separately beaten down. They had long been but empty shells, upheld only by the strength she lent them. And now Germany herself was reeling. At last the German people knew that they stood alone, and that the end was near. What wonder that German soldiers were no longer willing to die for the lost Hohenzollern madness of world-ownership!

Bulgaria had been the first of the Central Powers to collapse and to surrender. The Allied army, so long held on the defensive at Salonika, had at length secured complete Greek coöperation. Thus, no longer fearful of treachery in the rear, it was enabled to begin on September 15th a general advance against the Bulgarian lines. The resistance was feeble; for Germany could lend the Balkans no assistance now. On September 21st, a dashing Serbian charge broke the line of Bulgarian communications. After that the only Ally difficulty was to keep up with the fleeing foe. On September 30th the French occupied the old Serbian capital of Uskub; and on that day the Ally commander, General D'Esperey, accepted from Bulgaria her offer of unconditional surrender. Bulgaria's army was dispersed, and her king fled the country.[1]

Thereafter the Austrian and other troops holding northern Serbia and Montenegro retreated rapidly before the Allies. On October 30th all Montenegro was freed; and on November 3rd the Serbians triumphantly reëntered Belgrade. What awful sufferings had been theirs since they had fled from their capital three years before!

Turkey was the second of the falling Central Powers to surrender. The British forces under General Allenby in the Holy Land, aided by their Arab allies, broke the last shred of Turkish resistance in Asia at the battle of Rafat, on September 18th. Pressing promptly forward, Allenby seized Damascus on September 30th. He then captured the Turko-German bases of supply; and the Turks in Constantinople entreated peace on any terms to save themselves and their people from complete destruction. An armistice amounting to unconditional surrender was granted them on October 30th.[2]

Meanwhile Austria had also felt the closing grip of the Allies. The Italian army, aided by British and French divisions and one United States regiment, began its final advance against the opposing Austrian forces on October 24th. The Austrians had no heart left for this last battle. They knew that Bulgaria and Turkey were broken, and that Germany was breaking fast. For a day, the Austrian soldiers vigorously resisted the Italian charge along the Piave River; then they gave way completely. The Italians pursued them with cavalry. On October 31st the Austrians begged an armistice on any terms. On November 3rd, having first

[1] See § XIX, "Bulgaria's Downfall," Venizelos, King Ferdinand, etc.
[2] See § XX, "Fall of Turkey" by Allenby, Sultan Mohammed, etc.

seized the great seaport of Trieste, Italy granted the armistice on terms which meant that Austria also dismissed her army and placed herself unconditionally at the Allies' mercy.[1]

Some similar armistice, upon less costly terms, Germany had been seeking for a month before. On September 30th, Kaiser William issued an "Imperial Decree" announcing that henceforth the Reichstag was to be a real parliament, and that Imperial Chancellors were to rule subject to its will. In not very convincing evidence of this, he dismissed his latest Chancellor and himself appointed another, Prince Max of Baden, who was reputedly opposed to militarism. We know now that this step was only taken because Generals Hindenburg and Ludendorff had both declared that peace was necessary, and the German leaders thought that Prince Max and a nominally representative parliament could secure better terms than the militarists.

Prince Max at once appealed to President Wilson, declaring that he wished to arrange peace on the basis of Wilson's "fourteen points." The United States government, however, steadily refused to be beguiled by further German pretense. President Wilson pointed out that the new government of Germany looked too nearly similar to the old, and that the only armistice the Allies could venture to allow would be one that left Germany defenseless and entirely incapable of suddenly changing her government back to the old one and renewing the contest. The Allies would stand by the "fourteen points," but meant to establish themselves in such a position that they alone should decide what those points might mean in practice; and Germany must submit to this interpretation. Thus in plainest words Wilson said that the Allies wholly mistrusted Germany's sudden repentance, and would grant her no armistice which did not include a complete military surrender.

At the beginning of October, Germany haughtily declared such a surrender impossible. Before the end of the month, however, increasing disaster made her change her tone. On October 24th, the Socialist leader Haase asserted openly in

[1] See § XXII, "Austria's Breakdown," by Diaz, Sapelli, etc.

the Reichstag that militarism had ended in hopeless failure, and that the German Empire must end, and be replaced by a Republic. On October 27th, General Ludendorff resigned his dictatorial command. At the beginning of November, the government planned to send out the German fleet to strike a blow in the desperate hope that the fleet might by some fortunate chance be successful, and restore the balance of power. But on November 3rd, the sailors at Kiel mutinied, and refused to be thus sent to slaughter in a blind effort to save the Hohenzollern government. The red flag of Socialistic, and even of anarchistic, defiance began to be waved everywhere in Germany.[1]

Facing now the utter disruption of their government from within, the German leaders consented to military surrender, that is, they sent commissioners to meet General Foch in the field, and ask him for terms. These commissioners reached Foch on November 8th, and learned that the only terms he offered them were such as would make Germany absolutely helpless. The commissioners sought to argue and bargain, but Foch refused to listen or even to delay his attack while they planned some new evasion. Immediately thereafter, November 9th, Kaiser William abdicated and fled to Holland. His last hope was lost in Foch's determined attitude.[2]

On the same day Berlin was seized by revolutionaries, who included soldiers, sailors and civilians. Herr Scheidemann, the Socialistic leader, became the chief guide of the people; and when he announced the downfall of the Empire, the masses agreed to leave to Scheidemann and his colleagues the forming of a republican government. The cautious German people were as little eager for Russian anarchy as they were for further Prussian militarism.

Under pressure of these changes at home, the German commissioners to Foch signed before daybreak on November 11th the armistice he had dictated. Revolutionary Germany submitted herself wholly to the Allies, protected only by their assurance that in reorganizing the world they would follow

[1] See § XXII, "Awakening of the German People," by Bussche, Liebknecht, etc.

[2] See § XXV, "Germany a Republic," Prince Max, the Kaiser, etc.

President Wilson's "fourteen points." These included "self-government" even for Germany. The armistice was put promptly into effect at the eleventh hour of that eleventh day of the eleventh month of 1918.[1]

At that moment the Allied troops were everywhere pressing victoriously forward; and there have since been embittered patriots in every Ally land who have voiced a regret that our leaders granted any armistice at all, that they did not command the troops to go on fighting until every German was fleeing or was slain, and the united Ally flags were waving in Berlin. Such a course, however, would not only have been to value a somewhat empty glory above a very heavy cost in human life and suffering; it would also have increased a hundredfold the danger of engulfing the entire universe in anarchy.

Exhausted France might easily have broken under the further strain; so might socialistic Italy. Moreover, the new Germany that had just been born, revolutionary Germany, seething with new passions, furious, universally suspicious, and still equipped with the weapons of the former Germany, would have been a desperate antagonist if driven to join fortunes with anarchistic Russia. From such a possible contest, not with the tumbling German Empire, but with all the forces of anarchy and starvation and despair gathering in mad union through all the world, from such a hideous contest heaped in unendurable load upon an already staggering civilization, our leaders wisely saved us.

From a military standpoint the Great War was over. It ended with that armistice of November 11, 1918. It ended with all of Germany's fellow conspirators completely crushed, with France clear of the foe, Americans and Frenchmen crossing the German border, and Britons and Belgians sweeping rapidly through Belgium. The German military colossus was broken, we may say with confident hope, forever. The cost to Europe had been terrible, immeasurable; but the victory was complete. The Great War had achieved its purpose.

[1] See § XXVI, "The Armistice," by Foch, Hindenburg, Wilson, etc.

THE "FOURTEEN POINTS" OF PEACE

AMERICA ESTABLISHES THE BASIS FOR THE WORLD'S RECONSTRUCTION

JANUARY 8TH

WOODROW WILSON   GEORG, COUNT VON HERTLING
ARTHUR BALFOUR   BARON DE BROQUEVILLE

Through all the year 1917 there had been talk of peace. Always, however, the German standpoint was that Germany must emerge from the War with larger territory and greater power than before, that is, that she must emerge as an acknowledged victor and without blame either for opening the War or for her methods of conducting it. The Allies, on the other hand, were equally determined to force from Germany not only a restitution of all the lands she and her allies had seized, but also such recompense as might be possible for all the slaughter of civilians which had everywhere followed upon the victories of the Central Powers.

In July of 1917 the German Reichstag made its first decided stand against the extreme "war-party" of the Kaiser and his generals. It refused to vote war supplies until the long controlling Imperial Chancellor, Bethmann-Hollweg, resigned office, and a new Chancellor of presumably less warlike tendency supplanted him. Having won its way in this, the Reichstag on July 19th passed a resolution declaring, on one side, that Germany had been driven into the War by the Allies, but on the other, that Germany desired no "forced acquisitions of territory." Unfortunately the Reichstag did not really speak for the German Government, which continued to seek a peace of expansion.

In August of 1917, the Pope issued from Rome an appeal to both sides to end the War by mutual concessions. He suggested as the basis of peace that each side should forego all claim for damages, and that each should restore all territory. This seemed to Western Europe and America an impossible solution, as it gave back to Germany all her colonies, left her in possession of Alsace, and freed her and her allies from all retribution for the Belgian, Serbian, Armenian and other massacres. Thus, in effect, it left Germany where she had been at the opening of the War, only with an infinitely stronger control over Austria and Turkey, whereas it left the rest of the world with many regions ravished, ruined and forever hopelessly impoverished by the German methods of desolation.

President Wilson responded to the Papal note on August 27th; and the other Allies promptly announced that they accepted his reply as their own. He had become the spokesman of the great world league. The central thought of his decisive rejection of the Papal proposal was expressed in the following words:

"The object of this war is to deliver the free peoples of the world from the menace and the actual power of a vast military establishment controlled by an irresponsible Government which, having secretly planned to dominate the world, proceeded to carry the plan out without regard either to the sacred obligations of treaty or the long-established practices and long-cherished principles of international action and honor; which chose its own time for the war; delivered its blow fiercely and suddenly; stopped at no barrier either of law or of mercy; swept a whole continent within the tide of blood—not the blood of soldiers only, but the blood of innocent women and children also and of the helpless poor; and now stands balked but not defeated, the enemy of four-fifths of the world. This power is not the German people. It is the ruthless master of the German people.

"To deal with such a power by way of peace upon the plan proposed by His Holiness the Pope would, so far as we can see, involve a recuperation of its strength and a renewal of its policy; would make it necessary to create a permanent hostile combination of nations against the German people, who are its instruments; and would result in abandoning the new-born Russia to the intrigue, the manifold subtle interference, and the certain counter-revolution which would be attempted by all the malign influences to which the German Government has of late accustomed the world. Can peace be based upon a restitution of its power or upon any word of honor it could pledge in a treaty of settlement and accommodation?

"The test, therefore, of every plan of peace is this: Is it based upon the faith of all the peoples involved or merely upon the word of an ambitious and intriguing Government, on the one hand, and of a group of free peoples, on the other? This is a test which goes to the root of the matter; and it is the test which must be applied.

"We cannot take the word of the present rulers of Germany as a guarantee of anything that is to endure, unless explicitly supported by such conclusive evidence of the will and purpose of the German people themselves as the other peoples of the world would be justified in accepting. Without such guarantees treaties of settlement, agreements for disarmament, covenants to set up arbitration in the place of force, territorial adjustments, reconstitution of small nations, if made with the German Government, no man, no nation could now depend on."

These decisive words put a temporary end to peace proposals. America would not abandon the War without accomplishing the purpose for which she had begun it; and Britain and France, encouraged by her firmness, were ready to uphold her despite the Russian breakdown.

The opening of the peace-conference between Russia and the Central Powers at Brest-Litovsk in December, 1917, brought the general peace question up for new discussion. On Christmas day Germany, or rather the Austrian Prime Minister, Count Czernin, speaking for all the Central Powers, proposed that all the world should join the Brest-Litovsk conference. But in the pride of victory over Russia the Central Powers now offered as the peace basis terms even more triumphantly German than before.

Naturally the Allies had no thought of yielding to these terms; and the incident would have been a minor one, had it not called forth President Wilson's celebrated speech of January 8, 1918, in which he named definitely the "fourteen points" on which alone would the United States consent to peace. Once more his words were accepted by the Allies. The "fourteen points," soon supplemented by their summary in "five points" in President Wilson's speech of February 11th, became the enduring basis of the Allies' demands. Upon these points, and their development as caused by the events of 1918, peace was ultimately established by the Allies' victory.

We give here both the "fourteen" and the "five" points as announced by President Wilson, and also the responses made by the German Chancellor of the moment, the aged Bavarian statesman, Georg, Count von Hertling. We present also the official British and official Belgian commentaries upon von Hertling's words. These were expressed for Britain by her Secretary of Foreign Affairs and former Prime Minister, Hon. Arthur Balfour, and for Belgium by her noted Minister of Foreign Affairs, Baron de Broqueville. The reader should note also the comments of Count Czernin, Austria's Prime Minister, as given in a later section of our volume, in his discussion of the Russian peace.

C. F. H.

BY WOODROW WILSON

From the Address delivered to Congress, January 8, 1918

WE have entered this war because violations of right had occurred which touched us to the quick and made the life of our own people impossible, unless they were corrected, and the world secured once for all against their recurrence.

What we demand in this war, therefore, is nothing peculiar to ourselves. It is that the world be made fit and safe to live in, and particularly that it be made safe for every peace-loving nation which, like our own, wishes to live its own free life, determine its own institutions, be assured of justice and fair dealing by the other peoples of the world, as against force and selfish aggression. All the peoples of the world are in effect partners in this interest, and for our own part we see very clearly that unless justice be done to others it will not be done to us.

The program of the world's peace, therefore, is our program; and that program, the only possible one as we see it, is this:

I. Open covenants of peace, openly arrived at, after which there shall be no private international understandings of any kind, but diplomacy shall proceed always frankly and in the public view.

II. Absolute freedom of navigation upon the seas, outside territorial waters, alike in peace and in war, except as the seas may be closed in whole or in part by international action for the enforcement of international covenants.

III. The removal, so far as possible, of all economic barriers and the establishment of an equality of trade conditions among all the nations consenting to the peace and associating themselves for its maintenance.

IV. Adequate guarantees given and taken that national armaments will be reduced to the lowest point consistent with domestic safety.

V. A free, open-minded, and absolutely impartial adjustment of all colonial claims, based upon a strict observance of the principle that in determining all such questions of sovereignty the interests of the populations concerned must have equal weight with the equitable claims of the Government whose title is to be determined.

VI. The evacuation of all Russian territory, and such a settlement of all questions affecting Russia as will secure the best and freest coöperation of the other nations of the world in obtaining for her an unhampered and unembarrassed opportunity for the independent determination of her own political development and national policy, and assure her of a sincere welcome into the society of free nations under institutions of her own choosing; and, more than a welcome, assistance also of every kind that she may need and may herself desire. The treatment accorded Russia by her sister nations in the months to come will be the acid test of their good will, of their comprehension of her needs as distinguished from their own interests, and of their intelligent and unselfish sympathy.

VII. Belgium, the whole world will agree, must be evacuated and restored without any attempt to limit the sovereignty which she enjoys in common with all other free nations. No other single act will serve as this will serve to restore confidence among the nations in the laws which they have themselves set and determined for the government of their relations with one another. Without this healing act the whole structure and validity of international law is forever impaired.

VIII. All French territory should be freed and the invaded portions restored; and the wrong done to France by Prussia in 1871 in the matter of Alsace-Lorraine, which has unsettled the peace of the world for nearly fifty years, should be righted, in order that peace may once more be made secure in the interest of all.

IX. A readjustment of the frontiers of Italy should be effected along clearly recognizable lines of nationality.

X. The peoples of Austria-Hungary, whose place among the nations we wish to see safeguarded and assured, should be accorded the freest opportunity of autonomous development.

XI. Rumania, Serbia, and Montenegro should be evacuated; occupied territories restored; Serbia accorded free and secure access to the sea; and the relations of the several Balkan states to one another determined by friendly counsel along historically established lines of allegiance and nationality; and international guarantees of the political and economic independence and territorial integrity of the several Balkan states should be entered into.

XII. The Turkish portions of the present Ottoman Empire should be assured a secure sovereignty, but the other nationalities which are now under Turkish rule should be assured an undoubted security of life and an absolutely unmolested opportunity of autonomous development, and the Dardanelles should be permanently opened as a free passage to the ships and commerce of all nations under international guaranties.

XIII. An independent Polish state should be erected which should include the territories inhabited by indisputably Polish populations, which should be assured a free and secure access to the sea, and whose political and economic independence and territorial integrity should be guaranteed by international covenant.

XIV. A general association of nations must be formed, under specific covenants, for the purpose of affording mutual guaranties of political independence and territorial integrity to great and small states alike.

In regard to these essential rectifications of wrong and assertions of right we feel ourselves to be intimate partners of all the Governments and peoples associated together against the imperialists. We cannot be separated in interest or divided in purpose. We stand together until the end.

BY CHANCELLOR VON HERTLING

Summarized from his Address to the Reichstag, January 24th

(1) The negotiations at Brest-Litovsk prove "that we are quite ready to accept this proposal [President Wilson's first point, on no secret international agreements] and declare publicity of negotiations to be a general political principle."

(2) There is "no difference of opinion" with Mr. Wilson in respect to his second point, on freedom of the seas; but to realize this it would be well if the fortifications at Gibraltar, Malta, Aden, Hong-Kong, and other places should be removed.

(3) The Central Powers are "in thorough accord with the removal of economic barriers which interfere with trade in a superfluous manner" and "condemn economic war."

(4) "The idea of limitation of armaments is entirely discussable."

(5) As to colonies, "Mr. Wilson's principles will encounter some difficulties in the realm of reality," but the "reconstitution of the world's colonial possessions" will "have to be discussed in due time."

(6) In respect to evacuation of Russian territory, "we are dealing with questions which concern only Russia and the four allied [Central] Powers."

(7) "The Belgian question belongs to those questions the details of which are to be settled by war and peace negotiations (*Kriegs und Friedensverhandlungen*)."

(8) "The integrity of our territory [including Alsace] offers the only possible basis of peace discussion. The occupied parts of France are a valuable pawn in our hands;

forcible annexation forms no part of the official German policy."

(9 to 12) Mr. Wilson's points 9 to 12 touch chiefly Austria and Turkey.

(13) "It may be left to Germany, Austria-Hungary, and Poland to come to an agreement on the future constitution" of Poland.

(14) The German Government "is gladly ready, when all other pending questions have been settled, to begin the examination of the basis of . . . a bond of nations."

BY WOODROW WILSON

From the Address delivered to Congress, February 11th

After all, the test of whether it is possible for either Government to go any further in this comparison of views is simple and obvious. The principles to be applied are these:

First, that each part of the final settlement must be based upon the essential justice of that particular case and upon such adjustments as are most likely to bring a peace that will be permanent;

Second, that peoples and provinces are not to be bartered about from sovereignty to sovereignty as if they were mere chattels and pawns in a game, even the great game, now forever discredited, of the balance of power; but that—

Third, every territorial settlement involved in this war must be made in the interest and for the benefit of the populations concerned, and not as a part of any mere adjustment or compromise of claims amongst rival states; and—

Fourth, that all well-defined national aspirations shall be accorded the utmost satisfaction that can be accorded them without introducing new or perpetuating old elements of discord and antagonism that would be likely in time to break the peace of Europe and consequently of the world.

A general peace erected upon such foundations can be discussed. Until such a peace can be secured we have no choice but to go on. So far as we can judge, these principles that we regard as fundamental are already everywhere accepted as imperative, except among the spokesmen of the military and annexationist party in Germany.

BY CHANCELLOR VON HERTLING
Address to the Reichstag, February 25th

I entertain certain doubts as to the utility and success of dialogues carried on by Ministers and statesmen of belligerent countries.

Mr. Runciman in the House of Commons recently expressed the opinion that we would get much nearer peace if responsible representatives of the belligerent powers would come together in an intimate meeting for discussion. I can only agree with him that that would be the way to remove numerous intentional and unintentional misunderstandings and compel our enemies to take our words as they are meant, and on their part also to show their colors.

I cannot at any rate discover that the words which I spoke here on two occasions were received in hostile countries objectively and without prejudice. Moreover, discussion in an intimate gathering alone could lead to understanding on many individual questions which can really be settled only by compromise.

It has been repeatedly said that we do not contemplate retaining Belgium; but that we must be safeguarded from the danger of a country with which we desire after the war to live in peace and friendship becoming the object or the jumping-off ground of enemy machinations. If, therefore, a proposal came from the opposing side—for example, from the Government in Havre—we should not adopt an antagonistic attitude, even though the discussion at first might only be unbinding.

Meanwhile it does not appear as if Mr. Runciman's suggestion has a chance of assuming tangible shape, and I must adhere to the existing methods of dialogue across the Channel and ocean.

Adopting this method, I readily admit that President Wilson's message of February 11th represents, perhaps, a small step toward a mutual rapprochement. I therefore pass over the preliminary and excessively long declarations in order to address myself immediately to the four principles which, in President Wilson's opinion, must be applied in a mutual exchange of views.

The first clause says that each part of the final settlement must be based upon the essential justice of that particular case and upon such adjustments as are most likely to bring a peace that will be permanent.

Who would contradict this? The phrase, coined by the great father of the Church, Augustine, 1,500 years ago— *"justitia fundamentum regnorum"*—is still valid to-day. Certain it is that only peace based in all its parts on the principles of justice has a prospect of endurance.

The second clause expresses the desire that peoples and provinces shall not be bartered about from sovereignty to sovereignty as if they were mere chattels and pawns in a game, even the great game, now forever discredited, of the balance of power.

This clause, too, can be unconditionally assented to. Indeed, one wonders that the President of the United States considered it necessary to emphasize it anew. This clause contains a polemic against conditions long vanished, views against Cabinet politics and Cabinet wars, against mixing State territory and princely and private property, which belong to a past that is far behind us.

I do not want to be discourteous, but when one remembers the earlier utterances of President Wilson, one might think that he is laboring under the illusion that there exists in Germany an antagonism between an autocratic Government and a mass of people without rights.

And yet President Wilson knows (as, at any rate, the German edition of his book on the State proves) German political literature, and he knows, therefore, that with us Princes and Governments are the highest members of the nation as a whole, organized in the form of a State, the highest members, with whom the final decision lies. But, seeing that they also, as the supreme organs, belong to the whole, the decision is of such a nature that only the welfare of the whole is the guiding line for a decision to be taken. It may be useful to point this out expressly to President Wilson's countrymen.

Then finally at the close of the second clause the game
of the balance of power is declared to be forever discredited.
We, too, can only gladly applaud. As is well known, it was
England which invented the principle of the maintenance of
the balance of power in order especially to apply it when one
of the States on the European Continent threatened to become too powerful for her. It was only another expression
for England's domination.

The third clause, according to which every territorial settlement involved in this war must be made in the interest
and for the benefit of the populations concerned, and not as
part of any mere adjustment or compromise of claims among
rival States, is the only application of the foregoing in a
definite direction, or a deduction from it, and is therefore
included in the assent given to that clause.

Now, in the fourth clause he demands that all well-defined
national aspirations shall be accorded the utmost satisfaction
that can be accorded them without introducing new or perpetuating old elements of discord and antagonism that would
be likely in time to break the peace of Europe, and consequently of the world. Here, also, I can give assent in principle, and I declare, therefore, with President Wilson, that
a general peace on such a basis is discussable.

Only one reservation is to be made. These principles
must not be proposed by the President of the United States
alone, but they must also be recognized definitely by all
States and nations. President Wilson, who reproaches the
German Chancellor with a certain amount of backwardness,
seems to me in his flight of ideas to have hurried far in
advance of existing realities.

Certainly a League of Nations, erected upon justice and
mutual unselfish appreciation, a condition of humanity in
which war, together with all that remains of the earliest
barbarism, should have completely disappeared and in which
there should be no bloody sacrifices, no self-mutilation of
peoples, no destruction of laboriously acquired cultural values
—that would be an aim devoutly to be desired.

But that aim has not yet been reached. There does
not yet exist a court of arbitration set up by all nations for

the safeguarding of peace in the name of justice. When President Wilson incidentally says that the German Chancellor is speaking to the court of the entire world, I must, as things stand to-day, in the name of the German Empire and her allies, decline this court as prejudiced, joyfully as I would greet it if an impartial court of arbitration existed and gladly as I would coöperate to realize such ideals.

Unfortunately, however, there is no trace of a similar state of mind on the part of the leading powers in the Entente. England's war aims, as recently expressed in Lloyd George's speeches, are still thoroughly imperialistic and want to impose on the world a peace according to England's good pleasure. When England talks about peoples' right of self-determination, she does not think of applying the principle to Ireland, Egypt, or India.

Our war aims from the beginning were the defense of the Fatherland, the maintenance of our territorial integrity, and the freedom of our economic development. Our warfare, even where it must be aggressive in action, is defensive in aim. I lay especial stress upon that just now in order that no misunderstandings shall arise about our operations in the east.

After the breaking off of peace negotiations by the Russian delegation on February 10th we had a free hand as against Russia. The sole aim of the advance of our troops, which was begun seven days after the rupture, was to safeguard the fruits of our peace with Ukraine. Aims of conquest were in no way a determining factor. We were strengthened in this by the Ukrainians' appeal for support in bringing about order in their young State against the disturbances carried out by the Bolsheviki.

If further military operations in other regions have taken place, the same applies to them. They in no way aim at conquest. They are solely taking place at the urgent appeals and representations of the populations for protection against atrocities and devastation by Red Guards and other bands. They have, therefore, been undertaken in the name of humanity. They are measures of assistance and have no other character. It is a question of creating peace and order in the interest of peaceable populations.

We do not intend to establish ourselves, for example, in Esthonia or Livonia. In Courland and Lithuania our chief object is to create organs of self-determination and self-administration. Our military action, however, has produced a success far exceeding the original aim.

News was received yesterday that Petrograd had accepted our conditions and had sent its representatives to Brest-Litovsk for further negotiations. Accordingly, our delegates traveled thither last evening. It is possible that there will still be dispute about the details, but the main thing has been achieved. The will to peace has been expressly announced from the Russian side, while the conditions have been accepted and the conclusion of peace must ensue within a very short time.

To safeguard the fruits of our peace with Ukraine, our army command drew the sword. Peace with Russia will be the happy result.

Peace negotiations with Rumania began at Bucharest yesterday. It appeared necessary that Secretary von Kühlmann should be present there during the first days when the foundations were laid. Now, however, he will presumably soon go to Brest-Litovsk. It is to be remembered regarding negotiations with Rumania that we are not taking part in them alone, and are under obligation to champion the interests of our allies, Austria-Hungary, Bulgaria, and Turkey, and to see to it that a compromise is arranged there regarding any divergent desires that will possibly give rise to difficulties, but these difficulties will be overcome.

With regard to Rumania, too, the guiding principle will be that we must, and desired to, convert into friends the States with which on the basis of the success of our army we now conclude peace.

I will say a word regarding Poland, in behalf of which the Entente and President Wilson have recently appeared specially to interest themselves, as a country liberated from oppressive independence of Czarist Russia by the united forces of Germany and Austria-Hungary, for the purpose of establishing an independent State, which, in unrestricted development of its national culture, shall at the same time become a pillar of peace in Europe.

The constitutional problem—in the narrower sense the question what constitution the new State shall receive—could not, as is easily understood, be immediately decided, and is still in the stage of exhaustive discussions between the three countries concerned. A fresh difficulty has been added to the many difficulties which have in this connection to be overcome, difficulties especially in the economic domain in consequence of the collapse of old Russia. This difficulty results from the delimitation of the frontier between the new State and adjacent Russian territory. For this reason the news of peace with the Ukraine at first evoked great uneasiness in Poland. I hope, however, that with good-will and proper regard to the ethnographical conditions a compromise on the claims will be reached. The announced intention to make a serious attempt in this direction has greatly calmed Polish circles.

In the regulation of the frontier question only what is indispensable on military grounds will be demanded on Germany's part.

The Entente is fighting for the acquisition of portions of Austro-Hungarian territory by Italy and for the severance of Palestine, Syria, and Arabia from the Turkish Empire.

England has particularly cast an eye on portions of Turkish territory. She has suddenly discovered an affection for the Arabians and she hopes by utilizing the Arabians to annex fresh territories to the British Empire, perhaps by the creation of a protectorate dependent upon British domination.

That the colonial wars of England are directed at increasing and rounding out the enormous British possessions, particularly in Africa, has been repeatedly stated by British statesmen.

In the face of this policy Entente statesmen dare to represent Germany as the disturber of peace, who, in the interest of world peace, must be confined within the narrowest bounds. By a system of lies and calumny they endeavor to instigate their own people and neutral countries against the Central Powers and to disturb neutral countries with the specter of the violation of neutrality by Germany.

Regarding the intrigues recently carried on in Switzerland we never thought, nor will we think, of assailing Swiss neutrality. We are much indebted to Switzerland. We express gratitude to her, Holland, the Scandinavian countries, and Spain, which by her geographical position is exposed to especial difficulties, and no less to the extra-European countries which have not entered the war, for their manly attitude in that, despite all temptations and oppressions, they preserve their neutrality.

The world yearns for peace and desires nothing more than that the sufferings of war under which it groans should come to an end. But the Governments of the enemy States contrive ever anew to stir the war fury among their peoples.

Our people will hold out further, but the blood of the fallen, the agonies of the mutilated and the distress and sufferings of the peoples will fall on the heads of those who insistently refuse to listen to the voice of reason and humanity.

BY ARTHUR BALFOUR
Address to the British Parliament, February 27th

Many questions must be settled at the peace conference, but the question of Belgium is the best touchstone of the honesty of purpose of Central European diplomacy, and especially of German diplomacy. There is only one course for the offending nation in this case, namely, unconditional restoration and reparation.

When was Belgium the jumping-off ground of enemy machinations and why should Germany suppose it is going to be? Belgium has been the victim, not the author, of these crimes, and why should she be punished because Germany is guilty? Germany always had in mind new territorial, commercial or military conditions which would prevent Belgium from taking an independent place among the nations, which Germany and ourselves were pledged to preserve.

What we have to consider is how far von Hertling's lip service to President Wilson's four propositions really is exemplified by German practice.

I could understand a German taking a different view from the view of the French, British, Italian, or American Government, but not a German discussing the principles of essential justice and saying: "There is no question of Alsace-Lorraine to go before a peace conference."

Regarding President Wilson's second proposition, we have had within the last few weeks a specimen of how von Hertling interprets in action the principle he so glibly approves in theory. To take one instance only, there is the cession of Polish territory to the Ukraine. We would like to know how the Germans came to make this gross violation of their principle.

Coming to the third proposition, von Hertling says, with justice, that the doctrine of the balance of power is a more or less antiquated doctrine. He further accuses England of being the upholder of that doctrine for purposes of aggrandizement. That is a profoundly unhistorical method of looking at the question. Great Britain has fought time and again for the balance of power, because only by fighting could Europe be saved from the domination of one overbearing and aggressive nation.

If von Hertling wants to make the balance of power antiquated, he can do it by inducing his countrymen to abandon that policy of ambitious domination which overshadows the world at this moment.

As to President Wilson's third and fourth principles: Consider for a moment how von Hertling desires to apply the principle that the interest and benefit of the populations concerned should be considered in peace arrangements. He mentions three countries he wishes to see restored to Turkey, namely, Armenia, Palestine, and Mesopotamia.

Does any one think that this would be to the interest and benefit of the populations concerned? Von Hertling accuses us of being animated with purely ambitious designs when we invaded Mesopotamia and captured Jerusalem. I suppose he would say that Russia was similarly moved when she occupied Armenia. But when Turkey went to war she picked a quarrel with us for purely ambitious purposes. She was promised by Germany the possession of Egypt. Would the interest and happiness of the population of Egypt be best conserved by Turkish conquest of Egypt?

The Germans in the search for the greatest happiness of these populations would have restored Egypt to the worst rule the world has ever known. They would have destroyed Arab independence and abandoned Palestine to those who had rendered it sterile all these centuries.

How could any one preach seriously a profession of faith about the interests of populations after this evidence of the manner in which von Hertling desires to see it carried out? If the Reichstag had any sense of humor it must surely have smiled when it heard the Chancellor dealing in that spirit with the dominating doctrine of every important German statesman, soldier, and thinker for two generations at least.

So much for the four principles which Mr. Holt says von Hertling accepts, and which he thinks the British Government is backward in not accepting. I hope my short analysis may have convinced him that there are two sides to that question.

I cannot, however, leave von Hertling without making some observation upon the Russian policy which he defines. That also is a demonstration of German methods. He tells us the recent arrangements with Russia were made on the urgent appeal of the populations for protection against the Red Guard and other bands, and, therefore, undertaken in the name of humanity.

We know that the East is the East and the West is the West and that the German policy of the West is entirely different from the German policy of the East. The German policy in the East recently has been directed toward preventing atrocities and devastation in the interest of humanity, while German policy in the West is occupied entirely in performing atrocities and devastations. Why this difference of treatment of Belgium on one side and other populations on the other? I know of no explanation, except that

Germany pursues her methods with remorseless insistency and alters or varies the excuse she gives for her policy.

If she invades Belgium, it is military necessity; if Courland, it is in the interest of humanity. It is impossible to rate very high the professions of humanity, international righteousness and equity in regard to those populations which figure so largely in the speeches. I am quite unable to understand how anybody can get up in the Reichstag and claim that Germany is waging a defensive war.

I am convinced that to begin negotiations, unless you see your way to carry them through successfully, would be to commit the greatest crime against the future peace of the world, and, therefore, while I long for the day when negotiations may really begin, negotiations which must have preparations for the bringing of ideas closer together, I do believe I should be doing an injury to the cause of peace if I encourage the idea that there is any use in beginning these verbal negotiations until something like a general agreement is apparent in the distance and until the statesmen of all the countries see their way to that broad settlement, which, it is my hope, will bring peace to this sorely troubled world.

BY BARON DE BROQUEVILLE

Official Belgian Statement of February 28th

The Belgian Government's views are known and have not changed. It affirmed them quite recently. In its answer to the Holy See on December 24th the Belgian Government said:

"The integrity of the metropolitan and colonial territory; political, economic and military independence without condition or restriction; reparation for damages and guarantees against repetition of the aggression of 1914 are the indispensable conditions for a just peace as far as Belgium is concerned."

The Belgian Government has already declared and repeated that it will not discuss peace except in consort with the powers which guaranteed its independence and which have fulfilled their obligations toward Belgium.

CREATION OF THE NEW STATE, THE UKRAINE

THE WAR'S FIRST PEACE TREATY AND THE BREAKING UP OF RUSSIA

FEBRUARY 9TH

PRESIDENT VINICHENKO   NICOLAI LENINE

THE UKRAINIAN PEACE TREATY

DR. VON KUHLMAN   CHARLES, EMPEROR OF AUSTRIA

The first people to break definitely away from ancient Russia, and set themselves up on her territory as an independent State, were the Ukrainians. The Finns and other border peoples soon followed them. The word Ukraine indeed means borderland, and the Ukrainians, lying along the southwest border of Russia, are a Slavic people, but were never genuinely Russian. They have a language of their own, and form a different Christian sect from the Russians, having long been known religiously as Uniates and racially as Little Russians. Just as Russia had striven to rouse discontent against Austria among the subject peoples of Galicia, so Austria had sought to stir up against Russia these Ukrainians.

When Russia became a republic in 1917 the movement for a separate Ukrainian Government gathered strength, and in July the Russian Government recognized the National Socialistic Council or Rada of the Ukraine, and accepted the Ukraine as a sort of independent State within the Russian union. This Rada had been set up by Austrian aid, but it made at least an outward effort to free itself from Austrian influence; and in August of 1917 President Vinichenko and the other leaders of the Rada all declared themselves wholly independent of their Teutonic friends.

When, in November, Russia turned to Bolshevism, its leaders soon clashed with the Ukrainians, who were Socialists but not Bolsheviks. On November 20th Vinichenko issued the following noted proclamation announcing Ukrainia's policy, her faith and her desire to remain self-governing under the Russian roof. By December the Ukraine found itself at civil war with the Bolshevists, who accused it, as shown in the following "ultimatum" by Lenine, of aiding the other Russian parties in opposition to the Bolshevists.

Hence the Ukrainians came as a separate nation to Brest-Litovsk, and entreated Teutonic protection against the Bolshevists. This was readily granted them. Indeed, the world is never likely to know very surely how much the entire movement for Ukrainian independence had been fostered by Teutonic agents. At all events, on February 9th, at Brest-Litovsk, the Central Powers signed a treaty with Ukrainia, and afterward compelled the Bolshevists to accept it.

18

This was the first peace treaty arising from the War, and was consequently received by the people of the Central Powers with much rejoicing. It was of course a thoroughly Teutonic treaty, that is to say, the Ukraine pledged itself to supply the Central Powers with large amounts of grain and to aid them in other ways which brought Ukrainia to the verge of being a Teutonic ally. Indeed, the Ukrainian leaders promised more than they could perform. Teuton armies traversing the Ukraine found it impossible to gather the expected foodstores from the exhausted country. During the remainder of 1918 the Ukraine suffered from Teutonic plunder and massacre quite as much as did the other Russian borderlands. Its lot was almost as tragic as that of Poland or Rumania. The fate of these three nominally independent dependents of Germany was in truth far more than enough to warn any other country against accepting from the Teutons this peace of subservience which was more terrible than war. C. F. H.

BY PRESIDENT VINICHENKO
Proclamation of November 20, 1917, by the Ukrainian Rada or National Socialistic Council

UKRAINIAN people and all peoples of the Ukraine! An hour of trials and difficulties has come for the land of the Russian Republic. In the north in the capitals (Petrograd and Moscow) a bloody internecine struggle is in progress. A Central Government no longer exists, and anarchy, disorder, and ruin are spreading throughout the State.

Our country also is in danger. Without a strong, united, and popular Government, Ukrainia also may fall into the abyss of civil war, slaughter, and destruction.

People of Ukrainia, you, together with the brother peoples of Ukrainia, have entrusted us with the task of protecting rights won by struggle, of creating order and of building up a new life in our land. And we, the Ukrainian Central Rada, by your will, for the sake of creating order in our country and for the sake of saving the whole of Russia, announce that henceforth Ukrainia becomes the Ukrainian National Republic. *Without separating from the Russian Republic,* and preserving its unity, we take up our stand firmly on our lands that with our strength we may help the whole of Russia, and that the whole Russian Republic may become a federation of free and equal peoples.

Until the Ukrainian Constituent Assembly meets, the whole power of creating order in our lands, of issuing laws, and of ruling, belongs to us, the Ukrainian Central Rada, and to our Government—the General Secretariat of Ukrainia.

Having strength and power in our native land, we shall defend the rights of the revolution, not only in our own lands, but in all Russia as well.

Therefore we announce: To the territory of the National Ukrainian Republic belong the lands where the majority of the population is Ukrainian: Kiev, Podolia, Volhynia, Tchernigov, Poltava, Kharkov, Yekaterinoslav, Kherson, Tauris (without the Crimea). The further delimitation of the frontiers of the Ukrainian National Republic, viz., the addition of part of Kursk, Kholm, Voronez, and the neighboring provinces and districts, where the majority of the population is Ukrainian, is to be settled according to the organized wishes of the peoples.

To all the citizens of these lands we announce: Henceforth in the territory of the Ukrainian National Republic the existing rights of ownership to the lands of large proprietors and other lands not worked by the owners which are fit for farming, and also to lands belonging to the royal family, to monasteries, to the Crown and to the Church, are abolished. Recognizing that these lands are the property of the whole working people, and must pass to the people without compensation, the Ukrainian Central Rada instructs the General Secretary for Land Questions to work out immediately a law for the administration of these lands by Land Committees, chosen by the people, until the meeting of the Ukrainian Constituent Assembly.

The labor question in the Ukrainian National Republic must immediately be regulated. For the present we announce: In the territory of the National Ukrainian Republic henceforth *an eight hours' day* is ordained in the factories and workshops.

The hour of trial and danger which all Russia and our Ukrainia is now experiencing necessitates the proper regulation of labor, and a fair distribution of food supplies and a better organization of work. Therefore, we instruct the General Secretary for Labor, together with representatives of labor, to establish from to-day State control over production in Ukrainia, respecting the interests both of Ukrainia and also the whole of Russia. For four years on the front blood has been shed, and the strength of all the peoples of the world has been wasting away. By the wishes and in the name of the Ukrainian Republic we, the Ukrainian Central Rada, firmly insist on the establishment of peace as soon as possible. For this end we make resolute efforts to compel, through the Central Government, both allies and enemies to enter immediately upon peace negotiations.

Likewise we shall insist that at the Peace Congress the rights of the Ukrainian people in Russia and outside Russia shall not be infringed in the treaty of peace. But until peace comes, every citizen of the Republic of Ukrainia, together with the citizens of all the peoples of the Russian Republic, must stand firmly in their positions both at the front and in the rear.

Recently the shining conquests of the revolution have been clouded by the reëstablishment of the death penalty. We announce: Henceforth in the lands of the Republic of Ukrainia *the death penalty is abolished.* To all who are imprisoned and arrested for political offenses hitherto committed, as well as those already condemned or awaiting sentence, and also those who have not yet been tried, full amnesty is given. A law will immediately be passed to this effect.

The courts in Ukrainia must be just and in accordance with the spirit of the people.

With this aim we order the General Secretary for Judicial Affairs to make every attempt to establish justice and to execute it according to rules understood by the people.

We instruct the General Secretary for Internal Affairs as follows: To make every effort to strengthen and extend the rights of local self-government, which shall be the organs of the highest local administrative authority, and until the establishment of the closest connection with the organs of revolutionary democracy, which are to be the best foundation of a free democratic life. Also in the Ukrainian National Republic all the liberties won by the Russian revolution are to be guaranteed, namely, freedom of the press, of speech, of religion, of assembly, of union, of strikes, of inviolability of person and of habitation, the right and the possibility of using local dialects in dealing with all authorities.

The Ukrainian people, which has fought for many years for its national freedom and now has won it, will firmly protect the freedom of national development of all nationalities existing in Ukrainia. Therefore, we announce that to the Great Russian, Jewish, Polish, and other peoples of Ukrainia we recognize national personal autonomy for the security of their rights and freedom of self-government in questions of their national life, and we instruct our General Secretary for Nationality Questions to draw up in the near future a measure for national personal autonomy.

The food question is the foundation of the power of the State at this difficult and responsible moment. The Ukrainian National Republic must make every effort to save itself both at the front and in those parts of the Russian Republic which need our help.

Citizens! In the name of the National Ukrainian Republic in federal Russia, we, the Ukrainian Central Rada, call upon all to struggle resolutely with all forms of anarchy and disorder, and to help in the great work of building up new State forms, which will give the great and powerful Russian Republic health, strength, and a new future. The working out of these forms must be carried out at the Ukrainian and all-Russian Constituent Assemblies.

The date for the election of the Ukrainian Constituent Assembly is fixed for January 9, 1918, and the date for its summoning January 22, 1918.

A law will be immediately published regulating the summoning of the Ukrainian Constituent Assembly.

BY NICOLAI LENINE

Ultimatum of December 17, 1917, recognizing the already existing war
with the Ukraine

The Russian Socialist Government, by the voice of the Soviet of the people's commissaries, once more confirms the independent national rights of all the nationalities that were oppressed by the Czarist-Great Russian bourgeoisie, even to the point of recognizing the right of these nationalities to separate themselves from Russia. Consequently, we, the Soviet of the commissaries of the people, recognize the right of the Ukrainian People's Republic to separate itself entirely from Russia and to enter into pourparlers with the Russian Republic on the subject of the determination of federal or other mutual relations to be established between the two republics.

All that concerns the national rights and the independence of the Ukraine we, the commissaries of the people, freely recognize without any limits or conditions.

As regards the bourgeois Republic of Finland, which is still bourgeois, we will not make a gesture toward restricting its national rights or toward interfering with the independence of the Finnish people. We will not make a movement against the national independence of any people belonging to the Russian Federation.

Nevertheless, we accuse the Rada of Ukraine of the fact that, under cover of phrases and declarations regarding national independence, it has given itself over to a systematic bourgeois policy, under which neither the Rada nor the Soviets of Ukrainia are willing to recognize the action of our Soviet over their country. Among other things, the Rada has refused to call immediately the Soviets of Ukrainia in a general assembly, as they demand.

This double-faced policy, which deprives us of the possibility of recognizing the Rada as authorized representative of the laboring masses (exploited as they are by the Ukrainian Republic), has latterly reached a point where it has practically annihilated every possibility of accord with us. This attitude in the beginning disorganized the front. Through its manifestos addressed to the Ukrainian troops at the front, the Rada destroyed its unity and provoked division at a time when unity was possible only by following the path of systematic accord between the Governments of the two republics.

In the second place, the Rada has been guilty of dispersing the troops in the Ukraine that were faithful to the Soviets.

In the third place, the Rada is lending assistance to the plots of Kaledine by taking its stand against the influence of the Soviets and by meddling effectively with the autonomous rights of the Don and Kuban Provinces. By sheltering the counter-revolutionary movement of Kaledine, and by running counter to the will of the great mass of Cossack workmen in allowing the armies favorable to Kaledine to pass through the Ukraine, and at the same time refusing such passage to the armies hostile to that General, the Rada is opening the way to an unheard-of treason against the revolution.

By supporting the worst enemies of the national independence of the peoples of Russia—the Cadets and the partisans of Kaledine—the Rada may oblige us to declare war upon it; and this we would do without any hesitation, even if that institution were formally recognized as representing incontestably the entire population of the independent and bourgeois Republic of the Ukraine.

For the reasons given, the Council of The People's Commissaries, calling to witness the Ukrainian People's Republic, submits to the Rada the following questions:

1. Does the Rada promise to renounce in future all action for the disorganization of the common front?

2. Does the Rada promise to refuse in future to permit the passage over Ukrainian territory of any troops going into the region of the Don, the Urals, or elsewhere, and never to permit such passage without first having obtained the authorization of our Generalissimo?

3. Does the Rada promise to lend assistance to the armies of the revolution in the struggle against the counter-revolutionary forces of the Cadets and of Kaledine?

4. Does the Rada promise to put an end to the attempts to crush the armies of the Soviet and of the Red Guard in the Ukraine, and return their arms, immediately and without delay, to those from whom they have been taken?

In case a satisfactory reply has not been received within twenty-four hours, the Soviet of the People's Commissaries *will consider the Rada in a state of war with the influence of the Soviet in Russia and in the Ukraine.*

BY PRESIDENT VINICHENKO
Appeal presented by the Ukraine to the conference at Brest-Litovsk
on January 10, 1918

1.   The entire democracy of the Ukrainian State is striving for the termination of the war, for peace throughout the
entire world, and a general peace between all the belligerent
States.

2.   The peace which is to be concluded between all the
powers must be democratic and must assure to every people,
even the smallest, full and unlimited national self-determination.

3.   In order to render possible the real expression of the
people's will, proper guarantees must be given.

4.   Any annexation that means annexation by force or
the surrender of any portion of territory without the consent of its population is therefore inadmissible.

5.   Any war indemnities, without regard to the form
given them, are from the standpoint of the interests of the
working classes also inadmissible.

6.   In conformity with regulations to be drawn up at the
peace congresses, material assistance must be given to small
nations and States which in consequence of the war have suffered considerable losses or devastations.

7.   The Ukrainian Republic, which at present occupies
the Ukrainian front on its own territory and is represented
in all international affairs by its Government, whose duty is
the protection of the Ukrainian people's interests and which
acts independently, must, like other powers, be allowed to
participate in all peace negotiations, conferences, and congresses.

8.   The power of the (Petrograd) Council of Commissioners does not extend to the whole of Russia, and therefore
not to the Ukrainian Republic.   Any eventual peace resulting from negotiations with the powers waging war
against Russia can therefore be binding for the Ukraine only
if the terms of this peace are accepted and signed by the
Government of the Ukraine Republic.

9.   In the name of all Russia only such a Government
(and it must be an exclusively Federal Government) can

conclude peace as would be recognized by all the republics
and regions of Russia possessing a State organism. If, however, such a Government cannot be formed in the near future,
then this peace can only be concluded by the united representatives of those republics and regions.

Firmly adhering to the principle of a democratic peace,
the Secretariat General is also striving for the speediest
possible attainment of this general peace, and attaches great
weight to all attempts which can bring its realization nearer.
The Secretariat therefore considers it imperative to have
its representatives at the conference, while at the same time
it hopes that a final solution of the peace question will be
reached at an international congress.   VINICHENKO,
President of the Secretariat.

PEACE TREATY BETWEEN THE CENTRAL POWERS AND THE
UKRAINE, SIGNED FEBRUARY 9, 1918, AND LATER
ACCEPTED ALSO BY BOLSHEVIK RUSSIA

Whereas, the Ukrainian People has, in the course of
the present world war, declared its independence, and has
expressed the desire to establish a state of peace between
the Ukrainian People's Republic and the Powers at present
at war with Russia, the Governments of Germany, Austria-
Hungary, Bulgaria, and Turkey have resolved to conclude
a Treaty of Peace with the Government of the Ukrainian
People's Republic; they wish in this way to take the first
step towards a lasting world peace, honorable for all parties,
which shall not only put an end to the horrors of war, but
shall also conduce to the restoration of friendly relations
between the peoples in the political, legal, economic, and intellectual spheres.

To this end the Plenipotentiaries of the above-mentioned
Governments have met together at Brest-Litovsk for the in-
ception of peace negotiations, and have agreed upon the following points: ARTICLE I

Germany, Austria-Hungary, Bulgaria, and Turkey of
the one part, and the Ukrainian People's Republic of the
other part, declare that the state of war between them is at

an end. The contracting parties are resolved henceforth to live in peace and amity with one another.

ARTICLE II

(1) As between Austria-Hungary of the one part, and the Ukrainian People's Republic of the other part, in so far as these two Powers border upon one another, the frontiers which existed between the Austro-Hungarian Monarchy and Russia prior to the outbreak of the present war will be preserved.

(2) Further north, the frontier of the Ukrainian People's Republic, starting at Tarnograd, will in general follow the line Bilgoray, Szczebrzeszyn, Krasnostav, Pugashov, Radzin, Miedzyzheche, Sarnaki, Melnik, Vysokie-Litovsk, Kameniec-Litovsk, Prujany, and Vygonovsk Lake. This frontier will be delimited in detail by a mixed commission, according to the ethnographical conditions and after taking the wishes of the inhabitants into consideration.

(3) In the event of the Ukrainian People's Republic having boundaries coterminous with those of another of the Powers of the Quadruple Alliance, special agreements may be come to thereupon at a later date.

ARTICLE III

The evacuation of the occupied territories shall begin immediately after the ratification of the present Treaty of Peace.

The manner of carrying out the evacuation and the transfer of the evacuated territories shall be determined by the Plenipotentiaries of the interested parties.

ARTICLE IV

Diplomatic and consular relations between the contracting parties shall commence immediately after the ratification of the Treaty of Peace.

Provision for the admission of consuls on the widest scale possible on both sides is held over for special agreements.

ARTICLE V

The contracting parties mutually renounce repayment of their war costs, that is to say, their State expenditure for the prosecution of the war, as well as payment for war damages, that is to say, damages sustained by them and their nationals in the war areas through military measures, including all requisitions made in enemy territory.

ARTICLE VI

Prisoners of war of both parties shall be permitted to return home, in so far as they do not desire, with the approval of the State in whose territory they shall be, to remain within its territories or to proceed to another country. Questions connected with this will be dealt with in the separate treaties provided for in Article VIII.

ARTICLE VII

It has been agreed as follows with regard to economic relations between the contracting parties, viz. :

The contracting parties mutually undertake to enter into economic relations without delay and to organize the exchange of goods on the basis of the following stipulations [here follow details which by a supplementary commercial treaty placed the Ukraine under German control] :

ARTICLE VIII

The establishing of public and private legal relations, the exchange of prisoners of war and interned civilians, the amnesty question, as well as the question of the treatment of merchant shipping in the enemy's hands, shall be settled by means of separate Treaties with the Ukrainian People's Republic, which shall form an essential part of the present Treaty of Peace, and, as far as practicable, come into force simultaneously therewith.

ARTICLE IX

The agreements come to in this Treaty of Peace shall form an indivisible whole.

ARTICLE X

For the interpretation of this Treaty, the German and Ukrainian text shall be authoritative for relations between Germany and the Ukraine; the German, Hungarian, and Ukrainian text for relations between Austria-Hungary and the Ukraine; the Bulgarian and Ukrainian text for relations between Bulgaria and the Ukraine; and the Turkish and Ukrainian text for relations between Turkey and the Ukraine.

FINAL PROVISION

The present Treaty of Peace shall be ratified. The ratifications shall be exchanged in Vienna at the earliest possible moment.

The Treaty of Peace shall come into force on its ratification, in so far as no stipulation to the contrary is contained therein.

In witness whereof the Plenipotentiaries have set their hands and seals to the present Treaty.

Executed in quintuplicate at Brest-Litovsk on the 9th day of February, 1918.

[Here follow signatures.]

BY RICHARD VON KUHLMAN
Address of February 9, 1918, as Chairman of the Brest-Litovsk Conference

Gentlemen, none of you will be able to close his eyes to the historical significance of this hour at which the representatives of the four allied powers are met with the representatives of the Ukrainian People's Republic to sign the first peace attained in this world war. This peace, signed with your young State, which has emerged from the storms of the Great War, gives special satisfaction to the representatives of the allied delegation. May this peace be the first of a series of blessed conclusions; peace blessed both for the allied powers and for the Ukrainian People's Republic, for the future of which we all cherish the best wishes.

RESPONSE BY ALEXANDER SEVERYUK, FOR THE UKRAINE

We state with joy that from this day peace begins between the Quadruple Alliance and Ukrainia. We came here in the hope that we should be able to achieve a general peace and make an end of this fratricidal war. The political position, however, is such that not all of the powers are met here to sign a general peace treaty. Inspired with the most ardent love for our people, and recognizing that this long war has exhausted the cultural national powers of our people, we must now divert all our strength to do our part to bring about a new era and a new birth. We are firmly persuaded that we conclude this peace in the interests of great democratic masses, and that this peace will contribute to the general termination of the Great War.

BY CHARLES, EMPEROR OF AUSTRIA-HUNGARY
Address of February 14, 1918

To My Peoples: Thanks to God's gracious aid, we have concluded peace with Ukrainia. Our victorious arms and the sincere peace policy which we pursued with indefatigable perseverance have shown the first fruit of a defensive war waged for our preservation.

In common with my hard-tried peoples, I trust that after the first conclusion of peace, which is so gratifying an event for us, a general peace will soon be granted suffering humanity.

Under the impression of this peace with Ukrainia, our glance turns with full sympathy to that aspiring young people in whose heart first among our opponents the feeling of neighborly love has become operative, and which, after bravery exhibited in numerous battles, also possessed sufficient resoluteness to give expression by deed before the whole world to its better conviction.

It thus has been the first to leave the camp of our enemies in order, in the interest of the speediest possible attainment of a new and great common aim, to unite its efforts with our strength.

Having from the first moment I mounted the throne of my exalted forefathers felt myself one with my peoples in the rocklike resolve to fight out the struggle forced upon us until an honorable peace was reached, I feel myself so much the more one with them in this hour in which the first step has now been taken for the realization of this aim. With admiration for and affectionate recognition of the almost superhuman endurance and incomparable self-sacrifice of my heroic troops, as well as of those at home who daily show no less self-sacrifice, I look forward with full confidence to the near and happier future.

May the Almighty bless us further with strength and endurance, that, not only for ourselves and our faithful allies, but also for entire humanity, we may attain a final peace!

BOLSHEVISM BOWS TO GERMANY

TEUTON ARMIES FORCE RUSSIA TO ACCEPT THEIR PEACE TERMS

FEBRUARY 15TH-MARCH 3RD

LEON TROTSKY   NICOLAI LENINE
SIR GEORGE ASTON   COUNT VON HERTLING
OTTOKAR, COUNT CZERNIN

The Russian Bolshevist leaders who in 1917 promised to bring peace to the poor Russian masses, spoke partly deceived and partly deceiving. A military peace with Germany they may have thought they could achieve; but a permanent peace with any other party or government whatsoever was beyond possibility for men of their purpose and their character. As to character, they displayed no least regard for truth or fair dealing or for the rights of any one except themselves. They were wholly lacking in the spirit of compromise without which all social organization becomes impossible. As to purpose, they meant to create class-hatred and class-war over all the world, until only they themselves should remain alive, as rulers of the most evil and dull and embruted of all classes. They were as set, as ever were the German war lords, or as ever Lucifer himself had been, to rule the universe, or else to ruin it.

They believed, or more probably they pretended to believe, that Germany would grant them an equal peace. When they met her in conference at Brest-Litovsk in January of 1918, they soon realized that under a thin pretense of words she was determined to take from Russia all her western provinces. The head of the Russian peace delegates was Leon Trotsky, the former New York student and agitator. He raged against the German demands, and finally on February 10th withdrew his delegates altogether, declaring that Russia would sign no such treaty; she would simply stop fighting and expect the Germans to do the same.

To German solidness and stolidness of purpose, such an hysterical defiance offered merely further opportunity for conquest. Without a treaty, she was still at war; and promptly on February 10th her troops everywhere advanced, taking possession of more and more Russian territory, unopposed. In face of this unyielding resoluteness, the Bolshevist leaders weakened and on February 28th announced their readiness to sign Germany's treaty—though Trotsky continued protesting to the end.

The actual treaty was signed on March 3rd. It compelled Russia to acknowledge the complete independence of Ukrainia and Finland, to resign all authority over Poland, Courland and Lithuania, which

31

were to be made into such States as Germany might decide, and to withdraw all Bolshevik troops from the Russian provinces of Esthonia and Livonia, leaving the people there to select their own government while under the control of German troops. Turkey also was rewarded at Russia's expense by receiving the border provinces of the Caucasus, thus giving the Turks some millions more of Armenians to massacre.

More important than all these cessions, from the War standpoint of the Allies, was the fact that Russia was immediately to free her Teuton war prisoners. This meant the nominal restoration of over a million men to the Teuton armies. Actually, however, only a fraction of these prisoners reëntered the War. They scattered over Russia, aiding in its disruption, aiding in Germanizing its spirit, or, as in the remarkable case of the Czecho-Slav army, taking independent action of their own.

Another result of the Russian and Ukrainian treaties was the forcing of a similar treaty upon Rumania (March 5th). Shut off from all western aid, Rumania could not possibly stand out alone against the Teuton forces. The country retained a nominal independence but disbanded its armies, gave its supplies and munitions to the Teutons, and was policed and held to obedience by Teuton troops.

We give here the Bolshevist official statements as to the Brest-Litovsk treaty, and the explanations of both Trotsky and Lenine. Then comes the Ally viewpoint from General Sir George Aston, a noted British military writer. Then, in contrast, comes the official Teuton rejoicing, as voiced by the German and Austrian figure-heads of the moment, the German Imperial Chancellor, Georg, Count von Hertling, and the Austro-Hungarian Foreign Minister, Ottokar, Count Czernin.

RUSSIAN OFFICIAL ANNOUNCEMENT DESCRIBING THE FIRST CONFERENCE AT BREST-LITOVSK, ISSUED JANUARY 23, 1918

LEON TROTSKY, the Bolshevist Foreign Minister, addressing the conference, declared that "the position of the Austro-Germans is now absolutely clear." Continuing, the Foreign Minister said:

"Germany and Austria seek to cut off more than 150,000 square versts from the former Polish Kingdom of Lithuania, also the area populated by the Ukrainians and White Russians, and, further, they want to cut into territory of the Letts and separate the islands populated by the Esthonians from the same peoples on the mainland. Within this territory Germany and Austria wish to retain their reign of military occupation, not only after the conclusion of peace with Russia, but after the conclusion of a general peace. At the same time the Central Powers refuse not only to give any explanation regarding the terms of evacuation, but also refuse to obligate themselves regarding the evacuation.

"The internal life of these provinces lies, therefore, for an indefinite period in the hands of these powers. Under such conditions any indefinite guarantees regarding the expression of the will of the Poles, Letts, and Lithuanians is only of an illusory character. Practically it means that the Governments of Austria and Germany take into their own hands the destiny of these nations."

Trotsky declared that he was glad now that the Central Powers were speaking frankly, stating that General Hoffmann's conditions proved that the real aims were builded on a level quite different from that of the principles recognized on December 25th, and that real or lasting peace was only possible on the actual principle of self-definition.

"It is clear," Trotsky declared, "that the decision could have been reached long ago regarding peace aims if the Central Powers had not stated their aims differently from those expressed by General Hoffmann."

Dr. Richard von Kuhlman, German Secretary for Foreign Affairs, replied to Trotsky, declaring in principle that General Hoffmann's aims were the same as those advanced at Chistmas. Throughout the negotiations, he said, the Germans had kept in view the ethnological boundaries, but also the actual boundaries of the old Russian Empire. The Central Powers intended to permit free self-definition, and he scoffed at the theory that the presence of troops would prevent this. Regarding evacuation, Dr. von Kuhlman said that it must be taken up with the newly born self-defined Governments.

"If General Hoffmann expresses the terms more strongly," said Dr. Kuhlman, "it is because a soldier always expresses stronger language than diplomats. But it must not be deduced from this that there is any dissension between us regarding the principles, which are one whole and well thought out."

Dr. Kuhlman consented to Trotsky's request for a postponement of the conference, declaring, however, that it would be much pleasanter if they could finish the negotiations at once, as the former recess brought about many misunderstandings.

BY LEON TROTSKY

Proclamation of February 10, 1918, declaring the War ended without
a peace treaty

The peace negotiations are at an end. The German capitalists, bankers, and landlords, supported by the silent co-operation of the English and French bourgeoisie, submitted to our comrades, members of the peace delegations at Brest-Litovsk, conditions such as could not be subscribed to by the Russian revolution.

The Governments of Germany and Austria possess countries and peoples vanquished by force of arms. To this authority the Russian people, workmen and peasants, could not give its acquiescence. We could not sign a peace which would bring with it sadness, oppression, and suffering to millions of workmen and peasants.

But we also cannot, will not, and must not continue a war begun by Czars and capitalists in alliance with Czars and capitalists. We will not and we must not continue to be at war with the Germans and Austrians—workmen and peasants like ourselves.

We are not signing a peace of landlords and capitalists. Let the German and Austrian soldiers know who are placing them in the field of battle and let them know for what they are struggling. Let them know also that we refuse to fight against them.

Our delegation, fully conscious of its responsibility before the Russian people and the oppressed workers and peasants of other countries, declared on February 10th, in the name of the Council of the People's Commissaries of the Government of the Federal Russian Republic to the Governments of the peoples involved in the war with us and of the neutral countries, that it refused to sign an annexationist treaty. Russia, for its part, declares the present war with Germany and Austria-Hungary, Turkey, and Bulgaria at an end.

Simultaneously, the Russian troops have received the following order for complete demobilization on all fronts.

Military Order

No military operations must again take place. The beginning of a general demobilization on all fronts is decreed. I order the issue of instructions on the front for the withdrawal of the troops from the first lines and for their concentration in the rear, and, further, for their dispatch to the interior of Russia, in accordance with the general plan for demobilization. For the defense of the frontier some detachments of younger soldiers must be left.

I beg our soldier comrades to remain calm and await with patience the moment of the return of each detachment to its home in its turn. I beg that no effort be spared to bring into the stores all artillery and other military equipment which cost milliards of the people's money.

Remember that only systematic demobilization can be carried out in the shortest time, and that systematic demobilization alone can prevent interference with the sending of food supplies to those detachments which remain for a certain period on the front.

BY NICOLAI LENINE

Address of February 23rd, urging acceptance of the Teutonic Terms

The German reply offers peace terms still more severe than those of Brest-Litovsk. Nevertheless, I am absolutely convinced that to refuse to sign these terms is only possible to those who are intoxicated by revolutionary phrases. Up till now I have tried to impress on the members of the party the necessity of clearing their minds of revolutionary cant. Now I must do this openly, for unfortunately my worst forebodings have been justified.

Party workers in January declared war on revolutionary phrases, and said that a policy of refusal to sign a peace would perhaps satisfy the craving for effectiveness—and brilliance—but would leave out of account the objective correlation of class forces and material factors in the present initial moment of the Socialist revolution. They further said that if we refused to sign the peace then proposed more crushing defeats would compel Russia to conclude a still more disadvantageous separate peace.

The event proved even worse than I anticipated, for our retreating army seems demoralized and absolutely refuses to fight. Only unrestrained phrasemaking can impel Russia at this moment and in these conditions to continue the war, and I personally would not remain a minute longer either in the Government or in the Central Committee of our party if the policy of phrasemaking were to prevail.

This new bitter truth has revealed itself with such terrible distinctness that it is impossible not to see it. All the bourgeoisie in Russia is jubilant at the approach of the Germans. Only a blind man or men infatuated by phrases can fail to see that the policy of a revolutionary war without an army is water in the bourgeois mill. In the bourgeois papers there is already exaltation in view of the impending overthrow of the Soviet Government by the Germans.

We are compelled to submit to a distressing peace. It will not stop revolution in Germany and Europe. We shall now begin to prepare a revolutionary army, not by phrases and exclamations, as did those who after January 10th did nothing even to attempt to stop our fleeing troops, but by organized work, by the creation of a serious national, mighty army.

Their knees are on our chest, and our position is hopeless. This peace must be accepted as a respite enabling us to prepare a decisive resistance to the bourgeoisie and imperialists. The proletariat of the whole world will come to our aid. Then we shall renew the fight.

BY GENERAL SIR GEORGE ASTON

In November, 1917, the party identified with M. Lenine, afterwards known as the Bolshevists or Bolsheviks, took up the reins of government at Petrograd, and on the 21st they proposed an immediate armistice on all Fronts to bring about a democratic peace without annexations or indemnities. In December, a Bolshevist delegation, headed by Trotsky, abandoned Russia's treaty obligations with Allied Powers, and entered into separate peace negotiations with representatives of the Central Powers at Brest-Litovsk. I am tempted to use a quotation from Clausewitz, as a clew to German

policy in the events leading up to and during the course of
these negotiations. He wrote that Russia "can only be subdued by its own weakness, and by the effects of internal dissension. In order to strike these vulnerable points in its
political existence, the country must be agitated to its very
center." Those words must have been written by Clausewitz
about a hundred years ago, and all German General Staff
officers have been brought up on them ever since!

On the 1st of December the Germans agreed to stop all
hostilities against the Russians on the Eastern Front. Cunning, *for the time,* was thought to pay better than violence.
Two days afterwards negotiations for an armistice were begun at the Headquarters of Prince Leopold of Bavaria, who
commanded the German armies on that Front. The armistice
was extended to the Rumanians on the 9th of December.
Peace negotiations were opened at Brest-Litovsk. The Germans immediately took advantage of the situation to improve
their strategical position. Now that "very inexpensive"
declarations would serve the purpose formerly fulfilled by
armies in the East, hordes of troops were hurried across to
strike blows in the southwest and in the west against the
menacing armies of Russia's Allies, who had remained stanch
to their obligations.

Then the Bolshevists began to bombard the whole world
through the Petrograd Wireless Station with high-sounding
phrases and peace propaganda, of which the burden was contained in the words "no forcible annexations." The Germans carried on their military movements. The Ukrainians
sent their own delegates to the "peace" conference, thus rendering the position of Rumania still more hazardous. The
delegates assembled, and at Christmas time Count Czernin,
the Austro-Hungarian Minister, was put up to make the dramatic announcement that the Quadruple Alliance favored
an immediate general peace "without forcible acquisitions of
territory and without war indemnities." Troop movements
to the advantage of the Central Powers went on. Cunning
was used to *camouflage* projected violence, while Russia, in
accordance with the advice of Clausewitz, was being subdued

"by her own weakness, and by the effects of internal dissension."

The Russian delegates scored a moral victory by proving the worthlessness of the "no annexations" formula; when that formula was put to the test, it appeared that German troops were to retain their grip over provinces wrested from Russia, and the opinion of the population upon their future fate was to be expressed at the point of German bayonets. The Bolshevists struggled to prolong the discussions in the vain hope that the people of Germany would be influenced by the barrage of high-sounding phrases put up by the Petrograd Wireless Station, and in the still vainer hope that, if so influenced, a population with no voice in the policy of their country, saturated with the falsehoods of their rulers, and controlled by the machine guns of the military party, would have any chance whatever of affecting the situation.

After a short visit to Petrograd, Trotsky's deputation returned to Brest on the 7th of January. The Germans, in his absence, had seized upon the opportunity to confer with the Ukrainians separately, and had laid the seeds of the separate Ukraine peace which subsequently had such far-reaching results. The pitiful farce was soon brought to a conclusion. At the right moment General Hoffmann, representing the military party, and really dominating the whole conference, threw off the mask of conciliation and fair dealing, and only allowed force—the military situation, vastly improved during the intervening weeks—to count in the discussions. The conspicuous successes gained by the Italians against the Austrians had been annulled, the plans for the great Kaiser-Battle on the Western front had been drawn up, and troops set free from the East were being massed to take part in it. Trotsky managed to drag on the negotiations for a time. Early in February a separate peace was forced upon the Ukraine, on terms facilitating the plunder of that province for the advantage of the population of Germany and Austria. On the 11th of February Petrograd wireless announced that the Russian negotiators had failed to gain any respite from their pitiless opponents; the German and

Austrian Governments desired to possess countries and peoples vanquished by force of arms.

While unable to sign a peace, the Bolshevists could not continue the War. They *demobilized the remnants of the Russian army,* and so lay at the mercy of their enemies.

The German purpose had so far been fulfilled by the cunning of the "very inexpensive" verbal acceptance of the "no annexations or indemnities" meaningless jargon. Violence was reverted to. The Germans broke the armistice, advanced further into Russian territory, murdering and devastating as they went, until, on the 3rd of March, they forced a "peace" treaty, exacted at the point of the bayonet, upon the Bolshevist delegates at Brest. They robbed Russia of her Baltic provinces and of territory extending all the way to the Black Sea and along its eastern shores. These territories carry a population of about 60,000,000, and without their resources and their seaports the remainder of the Russian population will be in imminent danger of starvation.

After this "glorious" example of the fruitful results of peace negotiations conducted upon German lines, the next step was to enter at once into "peace" negotiations with pro-German delegates hastily summoned from Finland, a country with which Germany was not understood to be at war! The mask was thrown off at last. Count Hertling announced gloatingly in the Reichstag that "economic development in every direction" had been the German war aim "from the beginning," and the Kaiser rejoiced publicly in the "rich future" likely to result from the Hohenzollern sharp-sword policy. Robbery of weak neighbors was the new ideal set before a nation hitherto told that they had gone to war to defend their beloved Fatherland.

Rumania still held out for a time. Her fine army was threatened on all sides—by Bulgaria on the south, by Austro-Hungarian and German forces in the west and north. The territory of her late Ally, Russia, was no longer available for retreat in an easterly direction, and the Russian army within her borders had degenerated into an undisciplined and pillaging mob. She was forced by Mackensen, the German General, into negotiating for peace as the price

for continuing the armistice. Again the German sword
rattled in its scabbard. She was forced to *demobilize her
army* as a condition for further respite.
Meanwhile the German "wily one" was not inactive.
Every peace treaty has been the germ from which has developed a whole host of supplementary treaties and agreements, all stipulating for advantages in the "economic development in every direction" of German commerce. By
seizing control of communications and of harbors every step
has been taken to secure the continuance of these advantages. But markets accessible by land are not enough. The
situation on the Baltic was secured; greedy eyes were then
cast upon the Black Sea. The next step was to provide further for German economic expansion by the simple method
of expanding the boundaries of provinces which had come
under German control under the terms of "peace" forced
upon Russia. A "German-Ukraine" army pushed beyond
the Ukraine boundaries into the Crimea.
All this has resulted from the peace conferences at Brest-
Litovsk.

BY COUNT VON HERTLING
Congratulatory Address to the Reichstag on March 19, 1918

Hypocrisy has become second nature to the enemy, whose
untruthfulness is made worse by its brutality. Every attempt
at calm explanation and every real deliberation must fail,
when the enemy, at the very moment he is laying a heavy
hand on a neutral country, dares to speak of a policy guided
by complete unselfishness. The treaty with Russia contains
no conditions disgraceful to Russia, if the provinces breaking away from Russia say it is in accordance with their own
wish and the wish is accepted by Russia.
Courland and Lithuania have long been united to Germany politically, economically, and militarily. Livonia and
Esthonia are the eastern frontier fixed by the treaty, but we
hope that they also will have close and friendly relations
with Germany; not, however, to the exclusion of their
friendly relations with Russia. Poland is not mentioned in
the treaty, and we shall endeavor to see if it is possible to

live in stable and good-neighborly relations with the new State.

If the Reichstag adopts the treaty, peace on the whole eastern front will be restored, as I announced February 24th; but among the Entente Powers there is not the least inclination to finish this terrible war. The responsibility for bloodshed will be upon the heads of those who wish continuation of the bloodshed.

Russia proposed that all the belligerents enter into peace negotiations. We and our allies accepted the proposals and sent delegates to Brest-Litovsk. The powers until then allied with Russia remained aloof. The course of the negotiations is known to you. You remember the endless speeches, which were intended not so much for the delegates there assembled as for the public at large, and which caused the desired goal of an understanding to recede into the distance. You remember the repeated interruptions, the rupture and the resumption of the negotiations. The point had been reached where "yes" or "no" had to be said, and on March 3rd peace was concluded at Brest-Litovsk. On March 16th it was ratified by a competent assembly at Moscow.

If in the telegram from Washington it was thought fit to express to the Congress assembled at Moscow the sympathy of the United States at a moment when, as it says, the German power obtruded itself, in order to bring success to the battle for freedom, then I put that calmly aside with the rest.

We have not for a moment contemplated, and do not contemplate, opposing the justified wishes and endeavor of Russia to be liberated. As I said on November 29th, we desire for that sorely tried land a speedy return to a peaceful and orderly state of affairs, and we deeply deplore the terrible conditions which have made their appearance in many places.

The Russian treaty contains no conditions whatever which dishonor Russia, no mention of oppressive war indemnities, no forcible appropriations of Russian territory. A number of the border States have severed their connection with the Russian State in accordance with their own will, which was recognized by Russia. In regard to these States we adopt the standpoint formerly expressed by me, that under the mighty protection of the German Empire they can give themselves political form corresponding with their situation and the tendency of their kultur, while at the same time, of course, we are safeguarding our own interests.

BY COUNT CZERNIN

Public Address of April 2, 1918

With the signing of peace with Rumania the war in the east is ended. Three treaties of peace have been signed— with Petrograd, Ukraine, and Rumania. One principal section of the war is thus ended.

Before discussing the separate peaces which have been signed, and before going into details, I wish to return to the statements of the President of the United States wherein he replied to the speech I made before the delegations on January 24th. In many parts of the world Mr. Wilson's speech was regarded as an attempt to drive a wedge between Vienna and Berlin. I do not believe that, because I have much too high an opinion of Mr. Wilson's statesmanship to suspect him of such a train of thought.

According to my impressions, Mr. Wilson does not want to separate Vienna from Berlin. He does not desire that, and knows that it is impossible.

He perhaps thinks, however, that Vienna presents more favorable soil for sowing the seeds of a general peace. He has perhaps said to himself that the Austro-Hungarian Monarchy has the good fortune to have a monarch who genuinely and honorably desires a general peace, but that this monarch will never be guilty of a breach of faith; that he will never make a shameful peace, and that behind this monarch stand 55,000,000 souls.

I imagine that Mr. Wilson says to himself that this closely knit mass of people represents a force which is not to be disregarded and that this honorable and firm will to peace with which the monarch is imbued and which binds him to the peoples of both States is capable of carrying a great idea in the service of which Mr. Wilson has also placed himself.

President Wilson's four points are a suitable basis upon which to begin negotiating about a general peace. The question is whether or not Mr. Wilson will succeed in uniting his allies upon this basis.

God is my witness that we have tried everything possible to avoid a new offensive. The Entente would not have it. A short time before the beginning of the offensive in the west M. Clemenceau inquired of me whether and upon what basis I was prepared to negotiate. I immediately replied, in agreement with Berlin, that I was ready to negotiate, and that as regards France I saw no other obstacle for peace than France's desire for Alsace-Lorraine.

The reply from Paris was that France was willing to negotiate only on that basis. There was then no choice left.

The gigantic struggle in the west has already begun. Austro-Hungarian and German troops are fighting shoulder to shoulder as they did in Russia, Serbia, Rumania, and Italy. We are fighting united for the defense of Austria-Hungary and Germany. Our armies will show the Entente that French and Italian aspirations to portions of our territory are Utopias which will be terribly avenged.

The explanation of this attitude of the Entente Powers, which verges on lunacy, is to a great extent to be sought in certain domestic events here, to which I shall return later. Whatever may happen, we shall not sacrifice German interests any more than Germany will desert us. Loyalty on the Danube is not less than German loyalty. We are not fighting for imperialist or annexationist ends, either for ourselves or for Germany, but we shall act together to the end for our defense, for our political existence and for our future.

The first breach in the determination of our enemies to war has been driven by the peace negotiations with Russia. That was a break-through by the idea of peace.

It is a symptom of childish dilettantism to overlook the close relationship of the various peace signatures with each other. The constellation of enemy powers in the east was like a net. When one mesh was cut through the remaining meshes loosened of their own accord.

We first gave international recognition to the separa- tion of Ukraine from Russia, which had to be accomplished as an internal affair of Russia. Profiting from resultant circumstances which were favorable to our aims, we con- cluded with the Ukraine the peace sought by that country.

This gave the lead to peace with Petrograd, whereby Rumania was left standing alone, so that she also had to conclude peace. So one peace brought another, and the desired success, namely, the end of the war in the east, was achieved.

The peace concluded with Rumania, it is calculated, will be the starting point of friendly relations. The slight frontier rectifications which we receive are not annexations. Wholly uninhabited regions, they serve solely for military protection. To those who insist that these rectifications fall under the category of annexations and accuse me of incon- sistency, I reply that I have publicly protested against hold- ing out a license to our enemies which would assure them against the dangers of further adventures.

From Russia I did not demand a single meter, but Ru- mania neglected the favorable moment. The protection of mercantile shipping in the lower Danube and the guarding of the Iron Gate are guaranteed by the extension of the frontier to the heights of Turnu-Severin, by leasing for thirty years a valuable wharf near this town, together with a strip along the river bank at an annual rental of 1,000 lei, and, finally, by obtaining the leasing rights to the islands of Ostrovo, Marecorbu, and Simearu, and the transfer of the frontier several kilometers southward in the region of the Petroseny coal mine, which better safeguards our posses- sions in the Szurdok Pass coal basin.

Nagy-Szeben and Fogaras will receive a new security frontier of an average width of from 15 to 18 kilometers at all passes of importance, as, for instance, Predeal, Bodz, Gyimes, Bekas, and Tolgyes. The new frontier has been so far removed to Rumanian ground as military reasons require.

The rectification east of Czernowitz has protected that city against future attacks.

At the moment when we are successfully endeavoring to renew friendly and neighborly relations with Rumania, it is unlikely that we would open old wounds, but every one knows the history of Rumania's entrance into the war and will admit that it was my duty to protect the monarchy against future surprises of a similar kind.

I consider the safest guarantee for the future, international agreements to prevent war. In such agreements, if they are framed in binding form, I should see much stronger guaranties against surprise attacks by neighbors than in frontier rectifications, but thus far, except in the case of President Wilson, I have been unable to discover among any of our enemies serious inclination to accept this idea. However, despite the small degree of approval this idea receives, I consider that it will be realized.

Calculating the burdens with which the States of the world will emerge from the war, I vainly ask myself how they will cover military expenditures if competition in armaments remains unrestricted. I do not believe that it will be possible for the States after this war adequately to meet the increased requirements due to the war. I think, rather, that financial conditions will compel the States to enter into a compromise regarding the limitation of armaments.

This calculation of mine is neither idealistic nor fantastic, but is based upon reality in politics in the most literal sense of the word. I, for my part, would consider it a great disaster if in the end there should be failure to achieve general agreements regarding the diminution of armaments.

It is obvious that in the peace with Rumania we shall take precautions to have our interests in the questions of grain, food supply, and petroleum fully protected. We shall further take precautions that the Catholic Church and our schools receive the state of protection they need, and we shall solve the Jewish question. The Jew shall henceforth be a citizen with equal rights in Rumania.

The irredentist propaganda, which has produced so much evil in Hungary, will be restrained and, finally, precautions will be taken to obtain indemnification for the injustice innocently suffered by many of our countrymen owing to the war.

We shall strive by means of a new commercial treaty and appropriate settlement of the railway and shipping questions to protect our economic interests in Rumania.

Rumania's future lies in the east. Large portions of Bessarabia are inhabited by Rumanians, and there are many indications that the Rumanian population there desires close union with Rumania. If Rumania will adopt a frank, cordial, friendly attitude toward us we will have no objections to meeting those tendencies in Bessarabia. Rumania can gain much more in Bessarabia than she lost in the war.

In concluding peace with Rumania and Ukraine, it has been my first thought to furnish the monarchy with foodstuffs and raw materials. Russia did not come into consideration in this connection owing to the disorganization there.

We agreed with Ukraine that the quantity of grain to be delivered to the Central Powers should be at least 1,000,-000 tons. Thirty cars of grain and peas are now en route, 600 cars are ready to be transported, and these transports will be continued until the imports are organized and can begin regularly. Larger transports are rendered possible by the peace with Rumania, which enables goods to be sent from Odessa to Danube ports.

We hope during May to undertake the first large transport from Ukraine. While I admit that the imports from Ukraine are still small and must be increased, nevertheless our food situation would have been considerably worse had this agreement not been concluded.

From Rumania we will obtain a considerable surplus of last year's harvest. Moreover, about 400,000 tons of grain, peas, beans, and fodder must be transported via the Danube. Rumania must also immediately provide us with 800,000 sheep and pigs, which will improve our meat supply slightly.

It is clear from this that everything will be done to obtain from the exploitation of the regions which peace has opened for us in the east whatever is obtainable. The difficulties of obtaining these supplies from Ukraine are still considerable, as no state of order exists there. But with the good-will of the Ukrainian Government and our organization we will succeed in overcoming the difficulties.

An immediate general peace would not give us further advantages, as all Europe to-day is suffering from lack of foodstuffs. While the lack of cargo space prevents other nations from supplying themselves, the granaries of Ukraine and Rumania remain open to the Central Powers.

The forcible annexation of foreign peoples would place difficulties in the way of a general peace, and such an extension of territories would not strengthen the empire. On the contrary, considering the grouping of the monarchy, they would weaken us. What we require are not territorial annexations, but economic safeguards for the future.

We wish to do everything to create in the Balkans a situation of lasting calm. Not until the collapse of. Russia did there cease to exist the factor which hitherto made it impossible for us to bring about a definite state of internal peace in the Balkans.

We know that the desire for peace is very great in Serbia, but Serbia has been prevented by the Entente Powers from concluding it. Bulgaria must receive from Serbia certain districts inhabited by Bulgarians. We, however, have no desire to destroy Serbia. We will enable Serbia to develop, and we would welcome closer economic relations with her.

We do not desire to influence the future relations between the monarchy and Serbia and Montenegro by motives conflicting with friendly, neighborly relations. The best state of egoism is to come to terms with a beaten neighbor, which leads to this : My egoism regarding Austria-Hungary is that after being conquered militarily our enemies must be conquered morally. Only then is victory complete, and in this respect diplomacy must finish the work of the armies.

Since I came into office I have striven only after one aim, namely, to secure an honorable peace for the monarchy and to create a situation which will secure to Austria-Hungary future free development, and, moreover, to do everything possible to insure that this terrible war shall be the last one for time out of mind. I have never spoken differently. I do not intend to go begging for peace, or to obtain it by entreaties or lamentations, but to enforce it by our moral right and physical strength. Any other tactics, I consider, would contribute to the prolongation of the war.

I must say, to my regret, that during the last few weeks and months much has been spoken and done in Austria that prolongs the war. Those who are prolonging the war are divided into various groups, according to their motives and tactics. There are, first, those who continuously beg for peace. They are despicable and foolish. To endeavor to conclude peace at any price is despicable, for it is unmanly, and it is foolish because it continuously feeds the already dying aggressive spirit of the enemy. The desire for peace of the great masses is natural as well as comprehensible, but the leaders of the people must consider that certain utterances produce abroad just the opposite effect from what they desire.

Firmly relying on our strength and the justice of our cause, I have already concluded three moderate but honorable peace treaties. The rest of our enemies also begin to understand that we have no other desire than to secure the future of the monarchy and of our allies, and that we intend to enforce this and can and will enforce it. I shall unswervingly prosecute this course and join issue with any one who opposes me.

The second group of war prolongers are the annexationists. It is a distortion of fact to assert that Germany has made conquests in the east. Lenine's anarchy drove the border people into the arms of Germany. Is Germany to refuse this involuntary choice of foreign border States?

The German Government has as little desire for oppressions as we, and I am perfectly convinced that neither annexationists nor weaklings can prevent forever a moderate and honorable peace. They delay it, but they cannot prevent it.

The hopes of our enemies of final victory are not merely based on military expectations and the blockade. They are based to a great extent on our interior political conditions and on certain political leaders, not forgetting the Czechs.

Recently we were almost on the point of entering into negotiations with the Western Powers, when the wind suddenly
veered round and, as we know with certainty, the Entente
decided it had better wait, as parliamentary and political
events in our country justified the hope that the monarchy
would soon be defenseless.

Czech troops are now criminally fighting against their
own country, and we must unite against this high treason.
The government is quite ready to proceed to the revision
of the Constitution, but this will not be helped by those who
hope through the victory of the Entente to gain their ends.
If we expel this poison, a general honorable peace is nearer
than the public imagines, but no one has the right to remain
aside in this last decisive struggle.

OPENING OF THE MIGHTY "KAISERBATTLE"

GERMANY SMASHES THE BRITISH LINE, BUT IS CHECKED AT ARRAS

MARCH 21ST

MARSHAL HINDENBURG   SIR DOUGLAS HAIG
GUSTAVE BABIN   GENERAL VON ARZ
GERMAN AND AMERICAN OFFICIAL REPORTS

The great spring attack which was to be Germany's supreme effort for victory had been fully expected by the Allies; and they had taken every possible precaution against it. Their lines were as strong as military science could make them. Both sides were waiting only for the ending of the winter weather. Germany indeed struck before winter had fled. She struck too soon; but with the United States' strength in France increasing so rapidly, the German leaders felt they could not wait. Even as it was, the Americans checked them in June, before their battle was quite won.

In their first effort, of March 21st, the Germans struck upon a wide front of about fifty miles extending from Arras southward. Their real hope, as General Ludendorff has since stated, was to break through at Arras; but here the British were in great force and resisted every assault, hurling the Germans back with tremendous losses.

South of Arras, however, in the region of the Somme River the British line was less strongly held. This was the district which the Germans were supposed to be least likely to attack, since they themselves had reduced it to utter ruin in their "Hindenburg retreat." Hence during the winter the British forces had extended their line and taken over from the French the defense of this desolated district, thus enabling the French to concentrate in the southern regions which seemed more dangerously exposed. Thus the Germans found in the Somme district only a single widely extended British army, the Fifth Army, under General Gough.

This army gave way under the pressure of overwhelming numbers, was beaten back day after day, and was soon separated from the strong British forces at Arras on the north, and from the French along the Oise River in the south. But the natural difficulties of the season and the ruined land so delayed the German advance, that the British army was never quite surrounded or enclosed. On the north the British general, Carey, gathered a hurried force of men from every source and blocked the gap which had opened there. On the south, the French in large numbers and brilliant valor fought their way northward until they had closed the still more open break through which the Germans were making their main advance. Thus by March 26th the chief danger was averted. The Germans were far in advance of their former posi-

50

tions but a new line had been drawn in front of them, and they were themselves almost exhausted. They did not immediately accept their check. On March 28th they drove the new formed French line farther back and captured Montdidier, the apex of their advance. But so heavy were their losses that they made no further great advances. The "Battle of Picardy," as the Allies called it, or the first drive in the great "Kaiserbattle," was definitely over by about April 5th. It had cost each side perhaps a quarter of a million casualties. The Germans lost most in their desperate frontal attacks; but the breaking of the British line resulted in the capture of many thousand Britishers, ninety thousand was the German claim. So the two sides suffered not unequally.

As to the result of the battle upon the spirit of the contenders, the Allies were startled indeed that their supposedly impregnable line had been so swiftly broken. In all their three years of assault the Allies themselves had gained no such large advance. The German civilian population was much encouraged; but the German leaders knew well that beneath their seeming success lay really—failure. Their position on the field was no better than before; and they had lost weeks of time and many thousands of their best fighting men that they could ill afford to lose.   C. F. H.

BY MARSHAL HINDENBURG

From his Memoirs

SHORTLY before we left Spa His Majesty issued the Order for the first great battle. I will quote the material portion of this order in full to save a detailed description of our plans. By way of explanation I may remark that the preparations for the great battle are indicated by the rubric "Michael," and that the day and hour of the attack were only inserted when we knew for certain that our preparations were complete.

MAIN HEADQUARTERS,
10-3-18.

BY HIS MAJESTY'S ORDERS:

1. The Michael attack will take place on the 21.3. The first attack on the enemy's lines is fixed for 9.40 A. M.

2. The first great tactical objective of the Crown Prince Rupprecht's Army Group is to cut off the English in the Cambrai salient and reach the line Croisilles (southeast of Arras)—Bapaume-Péronne. If the attack of the right wing (Seventeenth Army) proceeds favorably, this army is to press on beyond Croisilles.

The further task of this Army Group is to push forward in the general direction of Arras-Albert, keep its left wing on the Somme at Péronne, and intensifying its pressure on the right wing compel the retirement of the English front facing the Sixth Army also, and release further German troops from trench warfare for the general advance.

3. The German Crown Prince's Army Group will first gain the line of the Somme south of the Omignon stream (this flows into the

Somme south of Péronne) and the Crozat Canal (west of La Fère).
By pushing on rapidly the Eighteenth Army (right wing of the Crown
Prince's Army Group) is to secure the crossing of the Somme and
the Canal.

The tension in which we had left Spa in the evening of
March 18th had increased as we arrived at our new headquarters at Avesnes. The beautiful bright weather of
early spring which we had been enjoying had changed.
Violent rain-storms swept over the country. They did full
justice to the nickname which the French had given to
Avesnes and its neighborhood. In themselves clouds and
rain were by no means unwelcome to us in these days.
They would probably shroud our final preparations. But
aad we really any grounds for hoping that the enemy had
not got wind of what we were about? Here and there the
hostile artillery had been particularly wide-awake and lively.
But the firing had then died down. From time to time
enemy airmen at night had tried to observe the most important of our roads with the help of light-balls and turned
their machine-guns on all suspected movements. But all
this supplied no definite data on which to answer the question: "Can our surprise succeed?"

The reinforcements earmarked for the attack entered
the assembly trenches in the final few nights; the last
trench-mortars and batteries were brought up. The enemy
did not interfere to any appreciable extent! At different
points parties volunteered to drag heavy guns right up to
our wire and there conceal them in shell-holes. We believed that we ought to be venturesome if we could thereby
guarantee that the attacking infantry should have artillery
support in their passage through the whole enemy defensive
system. No hostile counter-measures hindered this preparatory work.

The weather was stormy and rainy almost the whole
day on March 20th. The prospects for the 21st were uncertain. Local mist was probable. But at midday we decided definitely that the battle should begin in the morning
of the following day.

The early morning hours of March 21st found the
whole of Northern France, from the coast to the Aisne,

shrouded in mist. The higher the sun mounted into the sky the thicker the fog became. At times it limited the range of vision to a few yards. Even the sound waves seemed to be absorbed in the grey veil. In Avesnes we could only hear a distant indefinite roll of thunder coming from the battlefield, on which thousands of guns of every calibre had been belching forth fury since the early morning.

Unseeing and itself unseen, our artillery had proceeded with its work. It was only our conscientious preparation which offered any guarantee that our batteries were being really effective. The enemy's reply was local, fitful and of varying violence. It looked as if he were groping about for an unseen enemy rather than systematically fighting a troublesome foe.

It was therefore still uncertain whether the English were not fully prepared with their defence and expecting our attack. The veil which hid everything did not lift. About 10 A.M. our brave infantry advanced into the very heart of it. At first we received only vague reports, recitals of objectives reached, contradictions of previous reports, recalls. It was only gradually that the atmosphere of uncertainty cleared and we were in a position to realise that we had broken through the enemy's first line at all points. About midday the mist began to dissolve and the sun to triumph.

By the evening hours we were able to piece together a definite picture of what had been accomplished. The armies on the right wing and the centre of our battle front were to all intents and purposes held up in front of the enemy's second position. The army on the left had made immense progress beyond St. Quentin. There was no doubt that the right wing was faced with the stoutest opposition. The English had suspected the danger which was threatening them from the north and brought up all their available reserves to meet it. On the other hand the left wing had had relatively the easiest task, apparently as the result of a wholesale surprise. In the north our losses had been larger than we expected; otherwise they were in accordance with anticipation.

The results of the day seemed to me satisfactory. Such was also the opinion of the General Staff officers who had followed the troops and were now returning from the battlefield. Yet only the second day could show whether our attack would now share the fate of all those which the enemy had made upon us for years, the fate of finding itself held up after the first victorious break-through.

The evening of the second day saw our right wing in possession of the second enemy position. Our centre had even captured the third enemy line, while the army on the left wing was in full career and now miles away to the west. Hundreds of enemy guns, enormous masses of ammunition and other booty of all kinds were lying behind our lines. Long columns of prisoners were marching eastwards. The destruction of the English troops in the Cambrai salient could not be achieved, however, as, contrary to our expectations, our right wing had not pushed on far and quickly enough.

The third day of the battle made no change in the previous impressions of the course of events; the heaviest fighting was on our right wing, where the English defended themselves with the greatest obstinacy and were still maintaining themselves in their third line. On the other hand we had gained more ground in our centre and also on the left wing. This day the Somme had been reached south of Péronne, and indeed crossed at one point.

In view of the brilliant sweep of our attack to the west, a sweep which put into the shade everything that had been seen on the Western Front for years, it seemed to me that an advance on Amiens was feasible. Amiens was the nodal point of the most important railway connections between the two war zones of Central and Northern France (the latter being mainly the English sphere of operations) which had the line of the Somme as a definite boundary. The town was thus of very great strategic importance. If it fell into our hands, or even if we succeeded in getting the town and its neighborhood under effective artillery fire, the enemy's field of operations would be cleft in twain and the tactical break-through would be converted into a strategical wedge, with England on one side and France on the other. It was possible that the strategic and political interests of the two countries might drift apart as the result of such a success. We will call these interests by the names of Calais and Paris. So forward against Amiens!

We did indeed go forward, and with giant strides. And yet it was not quick enough for active imaginations and glowing wishes. For we had to fear that the enemy also would realise the peril in which he now stood, and would do everything in his power to avert it. English reserves from the northern wing, French troops drawn from the whole of Central France were hastening to Amiens.

The evening of the fourth day saw Bapaume in our hands. Péronne and the line of the Somme south of it was already well behind our leading divisions. We were once more treading the old Somme battlefield. For many of our men it was rich in proud, if serious memories, and for all who saw it for the first time it spoke straight to the heart with its millions of shell-holes, its confused medley of crumbling and overgrown trenches, the majestic silence of its desolate wastes and its thousands of graves.

Whole sections of the English front had been utterly routed and were retiring, apparently out of hand, in the direction of Amiens. It was the progress of the army on our right wing which was first held up. To get the battle going again at this point we attacked the hills east of Arras. The attempt only partially succeeded, and the action was broken off. Meanwhile our centre had captured Albert. On the seventh day our left wing, guarding against French attacks from the south, pressed forward through Roye to Montdidier.

The decision was therefore to be sought more and more in the direction of Amiens. But here also we found the resistance stiffening, and our advance became slower and slower. The hopes and wishes which had soared beyond Amiens had to be recalled. Facts must be treated as facts. Human achievements are never more than patchwork. Favorable opportunities had been neglected or had not always been exploited with the same energy, even where a splendid goal was beckoning. We ought to have shouted into the ear of every single man: "Press on to Amiens. Put in your last ounce. Perhaps Amiens means decisive victory. Capture Villers-Brétonneux whatever happens, so that from its heights we can command Amiens with masses of our heavy artillery!" It was in vain; our strength was exhausted.

The enemy fully realised what the loss of Villers-Brétonneux would mean to him. He threw against our advancing columns all the troops he could lay hands on. The French appeared, and with their massed attacks and skilful artillery saved the situation for their Allies and themselves.

With us human nature was urgently voicing its claims. We had to take breath. The infantry needed rest and the artillery ammunition. It was lucky for us that we were able to live to a certain extent on the supplies of the beaten foe; otherwise we should not even have been able to cross the Somme, for the shattered roads in the wide shell-hole area of the first enemy position could only have been made available after days of work. Even now we did not give up all hope of capturing Villers-Brétonneux. On April 4, we made another attempt to drive the enemy from the village. The first reports of the progress of our attack on that day were very promising, but the next day brought a reverse and disillusionment at this point.

Amiens remained in the hands of the enemy, and was subjected to a long-range bombardment which certainly disturbed this traffic artery of our foe but could not cut it.

The "Great Battle" in France was over!

BY SIR DOUGLAS HAIG

Official Report of July, 1918

On the 19th of March my Intelligence Department reported that the final stages of the enemy's preparations on the Arras-St. Quentin front were approaching completion, and that from information obtained it was probable that the actual attack would be launched on the 20th or 21st of

March. On our side our dispositions to meet the expected offensive were as complete as the time and troops available could make them.

The front of the Fifth Army, at that date commanded by General Sir H. de la P. Gough, extended from our junction with the French just south of Barisis to north of Gouzeaucourt, a distance of about forty-two miles. Over 10 miles of this front between Amigny Rouy and Alaincourt were protected by the marshes of the Oise River and Canal, and were therefore held more lightly than the remainder of the line; but on the whole front of this Army the number of divisions in line only allowed of an average of one division to some 6,750 yards of front. The Third Army, under the command of General the Hon. Sir J. H. G. Byng, K.C.B., K.C.M.G., M.V.O., held a front of about 27 miles from north of Gouzeaucourt to south of Gavrelle. The average length of front held by each division in line on the Third Army front was about 4,700 yards.

In all at least sixty-four German divisions took part in the operations of the first day of the battle, a number considerably exceeding the total forces composing the entire British Army in France. The majority of these divisions had spent many weeks and even months in concentrated training for offensive operations, and had reached a high pitch of technical excellence in the attack.

To meet this assault the Third Army disposed of eight divisions in line on the front of the enemy's initial attack, with seven divisions available in reserve. The Fifth Army disposed of fourteen divisions and three cavalry divisions, of which three infantry divisions and three cavalry divisions were in reserve. The total British force on the original battle front, therefore, on the morning of the 21st of March was twenty-nine infantry divisions and three cavalry divisions, of which nineteen infantry divisions were in line.

Launched on a front of about fifty-four miles on the 21st of March, the area of the German offensive spread northwards on the 28th of March, until from La Fère to beyond Gavrelle some sixty-three miles of our former line were involved. On this front a total of seventy-three German divisions were engaged during March against the Third and Fifth Armies and the right of the First Army, and were opposed in the first place by twenty-two British infantry divisions in line, with twelve infantry divisoins and three cavalry divisions in close reserve.

As soon as it became evident that the enemy had thrown practically the whole of his striking force against this one battle front, it became both possible and necessary to collect additional reserves from the remainder of my front, and hurry them to the battlefield. Plans previously drawn up to meet such an eventuality were put into execution at once, and before the end of March, by which date the principal German effort had been broken, a further force of eight British divisions was brought south and sent into the fight.

Shortly before 5 a. m. on the 21st of March a bombardment of great intensity, with gas and high explosive shell from all natures of artillery and trench mortars, was opened against practically the whole fronts of the Fifth and Third Armies from the Oise to the Scarpe River, while road centers and railways as far back as St. Pol were engaged by high velocity guns. Violent bombardments were opened also on the French front in wide sectors east and northeast of Rheims, and on portions of the British front between the Scarpe River and Lens. Our positions from south of the La Bassée Canal to the River Lys were heavily shelled with gas, and battery areas between Messines and the Ypres-Comines Canal were actively engaged. Dunkirk was bombarded from the sea.

The hour of the enemy's assault varied in different sectors, but by about 9.45 a. m. a general attack had been launched on a battle front of fifty-four miles between the Oise and the Sensee Rivers. Later in the day, as visibility improved, large numbers of low-flying aëroplanes attacked our troops and batteries.

Favored by a thick white fog, which hid from our artillery and machine gunners the S.O.S. signals sent up by our outpost line, and in numbers which made loss of direction impossible, the attacking German infantry forced their way into our foremost defensive zone. Until 1 p. m. the fog made it impossible to see more than 50 yards in any direction, and the machine guns and forward field guns which had been disposed so as to cover this zone with their fire were robbed almost entirely of their effect. The detachments holding the outpost positions were consequently overwhelmed or surrounded, in many cases before they were able to pass back information concerning the enemy's attack.

The attack being expected, reserves had been brought forward and battle stations manned. On all parts of the battle front garrisons of redoubts and strong points in the forward zone held out with the utmost gallantry for many hours. From some of them wireless messages were received up to a late hour in the day, giving information of much value. The losses which they were able to inflict upon the enemy were undoubtedly very great and materially delayed his advance. The prolonged defense of these different localities, under conditions which left little hope of any relief, deserves to rank among the most heroic actions in the history of the British Army.

So intense was the enemy's bombardment that at an early hour our communications were severed, and so swift was his advance under the covering blanket of the mist that certain of our more advanced batteries found the German infantry close upon them before they had received warning from their own infantry that the expected attack had been launched. Many gallant deeds were performed by the personnel of such batteries, and on numerous occasions heavy losses were inflicted on bodies of hostile troops by guns firing over open sights at point-blank range.

During the morning reports were received that the enemy had penetrated our front line opposite La Fère, and had also broken into our forward positions north of the Bapaume-Cambrai road, and opposite Lagnicourt and Bullecourt. The first indication that the progress made by him was developing a serious aspect was the news that at noon German infantry were entering Ronssoy. This meant that in this sector the attack had already reached and penetrated a considerable distance into the second defensive belt which constituted our battle positions.

The enemy's success at this point was followed up vigorously. Templeux-le-Guerard fell into his hands shortly afterwards, while the villages of Hargicourt and Villeret, attacked simultaneously in flank and rear, were practically surrounded, and were entered about midday.

Thereafter the enemy was held up by the resistance of our troops in the rear defenses of the battle zone, greatly assisted by the very gallant action of the 24th Division in Le Verguier and the 21st Division at Epehy, on the two flanks of his advance. Both these divisions held out throughout the day against repeated attacks delivered in great strength, and killed large numbers of the enemy. In this fighting, parties of German troops who had entered Peizière on the northern outskirts of Epehy were driven out by our infantry, with the assistance of tanks, which on this and many subsequent occasions did valuable and gallant work.

At midday the enemy's infantry had reached the first line of our battle positions in strength on practically the whole front of his attack, except at the Flesquières salient, where his assaults were not pressed with the same weight as elsewhere. Save in the neighborhood of Ronssoy, however, and at certain other points in a less serious degree, our battle positions themselves had not been entered, while at numerous localities in front of them fierce fighting was taking place around strong points still occupied by our troops.

The most serious progress made by the enemy during this part of the struggle was on the right, south of St. Quentin. At Fargnier, having reached the eastern portion of the village by 4 p. m., during the remainder of the day his troops pressed on to the Crozat Canal and captured Quessy. North of this point the 18th Division, reënforced by troops of the 2nd Cavalry Division, still held their battle positions intact, though threatened on both flanks by the enemy's progress at Quessy and at Benay, and successfully restored the situation in the neighborhood of Ly-Fontaine by a counter-attack. Many of the strong points in the forward zone on the front of this division were also holding out, though surrounded. Wireless messages from their gallant defenders were received as late as 8.30 p. m., and rifle fire was heard in their vicinity until midnight.

At the end of the first day, therefore, the enemy had made very considerable progress, but he was still firmly held in the battle zone, in which it had been anticipated that the real struggle would take place. Nowhere had he effected that immediate break-through for which his troops had been training for many weeks, and such progress as he had made had been bought at a cost which had already greatly reduced his chances of carrying out his ultimate purpose.

In view of the progress made by the enemy south of St. Quentin, the thinness of our line on that front, and the lack of reserves with which to restore the situation in our battle positions, the Fifth Army Commander decided on the evening of March 21st, after consultation with the G.O.C., IIIrd Corps, to withdraw the Divisions of that Corps behind the Crozat Canal. The movement involved the withdrawal of the 36th Division, on the right of the XVIIIth Corps, to the line of the Somme Canal.

The enemy's advance south and north of the Flesquières salient rendered a withdrawal by the Vth Corps and by the 9th Division on its right necessary also. Orders were accordingly issued to the Divisions concerned for a line to be taken up, as a first stage, along the high ground known as Highland Ridge, and thence westwards along the Hindenburg Line to Havrincourt and Hermies.

The Second Day of the Battle

On the morning of the 22nd of March the ground was again enveloped in thick mist, under cover of which the enemy renewed his attacks in great strength all along the line. Fighting was again very heavy, and short-range fire from guns, rifles, and machine guns caused enormous losses to the enemy's troops. The weight of his attack, however, combined with the impossibility of observing beforehand and engaging with artillery the massing of his troops, enabled him to press forward.

In the south the enemy advanced during the morning as far as the line of the canal at Jussy, and a fierce struggle commenced for the passage of the canal, his troops bringing up trench mortars and machine guns, and endeavoring to cross on rafts under cover of their fire. At 1 p. m. he succeeded in effecting a crossing at Quessy, and made progress during the afternoon in the direction of Vouel.

To the south and north the progress of the German infantry continued. Constantly attacked from almost every direction, Le Verguier fell into the enemy's hands at about 10 a. m., after a most gallant defense. On the left bank of the Cologne River the capture of Ste. Emilie was followed by the fall of Villers Faucon, and both Roisel and Epehy were threatened with envelopment from the rear.

Accordingly, our troops about Roisel were withdrawn during the afternoon under orders, the enemy making no attempt to interfere, and were directed to reorganize behind the line of our third defensive belt between Bernes and Boucly. Later in the afternoon the troops of the 21st Division in Epehy also fell back under orders, though with more difficulty, as parties of hostile infantry were west of the village. To the north the 9th Division held their battle positions practically intact until the late afternoon, when they were withdrawn under orders to the rear line of defense between Nurlu and Equancourt. This retirement also was made with great difficulty.

The Break Through at St. Quentin

With Maissemy already in the enemy's hands, the fall of Le Verguier greatly weakened the defense of the center of the Fifth Army. The rear line of our battle positions was held during the morning, in spite of unceasing pressure from large hostile forces, but as the day wore on the great concentration of German divisions attacking west of St. Quentin had its effect. During the early afternoon our troops east of Holnon Wood were forced to withdraw from their battle zone trenches; while after repulsing heavy attacks throughout the morning, the 30th Division were again attacked during the afternoon and evening and compelled to give ground. Our troops, fighting fiercely and continuously, were gradually forced out of the battle zone on the whole of this front, and fell back through the 20th Division and the 50th Division holding the third defensive zone between Happencourt, Villeveque and Boucly, in the hope of reorganizing behind them.

By 5.30 p. m. the enemy had reached the third zone at different points, and was attacking the 50th Division heavily between Villeveque and Boucly. Though holding an extended front of some 10,500 yards, the division succeeded in checking the enemy's advance, and by a successful counterattack drove him temporarily from the village of Coulaincourt. At the close of the engagement, however, the troops of the 50th Division about Poeuilly had been forced back, and by continued pressure along the south bank of the Omignon River the enemy had opened a gap between their right flank and the troops of the 61st Division, under command of Major-General C. J. Mackenzie, C.B., and of the 20th Division farther south. *At this gap, during the late afternoon and evening, strong bodies of German troops broke through the third defensive zone about Vaux and Beauvois.*

All available reserves at the disposal of the Fifth Army had already been thrown into the fight, and except for one French division and some French cavalry in the IIIrd Corps area, no further support was within reach of the fighting line. There remained, therefore, no course open but to fall back on the bridgehead positions east of the Somme.

The Crossing at Ham

In the course of the withdrawal to the Somme on March 23rd, a gap occurred in our line in the neighborhood of Ham, and the enemy, following closely upon our troops, entered the town during the early morning. Before midday bodies of German infantry, though at first only in small numbers, succeeded in crossing the river about Ham and Pithon, where the bridges had not been completely destroyed. In the afternoon these forces increased in strength, gradually pressing back our troops, until a spirited counterattack by troops of the 20th and 61st Divisions about Verlaines restored the situation in this locality. To the east of this point, heavy fighting took place around Ollezy, which the 36th Division regained and held until a late hour, and around Aubigny and Brouchy, both of which villages, however, fell into the enemy's hands before night.

Farther north, the withdrawal to the west bank of the Somme was carried out successfully during the morning and early afternoon, effectively covered by troops of the 50th Division. By 3.15 p. m. all troops were across the river, and the bridges for the most part destroyed.

The Northern Front Firm

Meanwhile, very heavy fighting had been taking place on the northern portion of the battle front. The enemy pressed closely upon our troops, as they withdrew to the line of the ridge running from north of Péronne to Nurlu and Equancourt. Heavy attacks developed at an early hour between these two places.

On the Third Army front, where our resources were greater, the enemy was held in check, though he gained possession of Le Bucquière and Beugny after a prolonged struggle. In this fighting the 9th Battalion Welsh Regiment, 19th Division, greatly distinguished itself in the defense of Beugny, which it held till dusk, thereby enabling the other battalions of its brigade in position to the north of the village to extricate themselves successfully from what would otherwise have been a hopeless situation.

No less than six separate attacks, in two of which the enemy brought up cavalry and guns, were repulsed by the 124th Brigade of the 41st Division. The fighting in this sector of the front was very severe, but here and at all points north of the Bapaume-Cambrai Road our line was maintained. About 3.30 p. m. the enemy again attacked five times from the direction of Vaulx and five times from Beaumetz-lez-Cambrai, and on each occasion was repulsed.

At the junction of the Third and Fifth Armies the situation was less satisfactory, and as the day wore on it became critical. During the morning, the divisions of the Vth Corps had proceeded with their withdrawal, and, covered by rearguards who were heavily engaged, had fallen back from the

The Kaiser in Command
A widely circulated German picture
of the Kaiser at Headquarters on the
Flanders Front, directing the Kaiser-
battle from his private train

Painting by F. Schwarmstadt

Auf der Fahrt
Zur Flandr. Front April 1918
F.Schwormstädt

Metz-en-Couture salient to the defenses of the third zone about Ytres. The left of the VIIth Corps, however, had been withdrawn under orders during the morning from the Nurlu positions to the line of the Canal du Nord, north of Moislains. As the result of this movement, a gap was formed between the flank divisions of the two corps, and this gap the enemy rapidly exploited. Though vigorous efforts were made to reëstablish touch both by the 47th Division, under command of Major-General Sir G. F. Gorringe, and by a brigade of the 2nd Division, they were unsuccessful. The right of the Vth Corps was forced back by pressure from the southeast first to the neighborhood of Four Winds Farm, south of Ytres, where troops of the 47th Division made a gallant stand in the open until nightfall, and later to a position east of Rocquigny.

The divisions of the VIIth Corps, after heavy fighting during the afternoon, were forced back west of Péronne, and across the line of the River Tortille to the high ground about Bouchavesnes and Government Farm, south of Sailly-Saillisel. At dusk, however, the line was still in movement. Small parties of the enemy searched constantly for gaps, and, having found them, bodies of German infantry pressed through in force and compelled our troops to make further withdrawals.

The Extension of the French Front

From the time when the indications of an offensive on my front first became definite I had been in close touch with the Commander-in-Chief of the French Armies. On different occasions, as the battle developed, I discussed with him the situation and the policy to be followed by the Allied Armies. As the result of a meeting held in the afternoon of the 23rd of March, arrangements were made for the French to take over as rapidly as possible the front held by the Fifth Army south of Péronne, and for the concentration of a strong force of French divisions on the southern portion of the battle front.

For my own part, after consultation with the First and Second Army Commanders, General Sir H. S. Horne and

General Sir H. C. O. Plumer, concerning the situation on the fronts of their Armies and the possibilities of attacks developing there also, I arranged for the formation from the troops under their command of a special force of reserve divisions for action as occasion might demand. Measures were also taken to permit of the employment of the Canadian Corps for counter-attack, in the event of the enemy succeeding in piercing my front.

In this connection I desire to express my deep appreciation of the complete unselfishness with which the needs of their own fronts were at all times subordinated by the Army Commanders to the more pressing demands of the battle. A variety of considerations made it necessary for me at this date to draw particularly heavily upon the resources of the Second Army. All my demands were met by the Second Army Commander in the most helpful and disinterested spirit.

The Retreat Across the Somme Battlefield

During the night of March 23rd-24th the situation on the battle front remained unchanged as far south as the neighborhood of Ytres. Beyond that point divisions and brigades had lost touch in the course of their frequent withdrawals, and under the constant pressure of the enemy the rearward movement continued. At dawn German infantry had already reached Bus, Lechelle, and Le Mesnil-en-Arrouaise, and during the morning of March 24th entered Saillisel, Rancourt, and Cléry. It became necessary to order the evacuation of Bertincourt, and gradually to swing back the right of the Third Army in conformity with the movement farther south. To the north of Bertincourt, though the enemy gained possession of Mory in the early morning after continuous fighting throughout the night, our troops substantially maintained their positions, the Guards Division in particular beating off a succession of heavy attacks.

The enemy's advance at the junction of the Third and Fifth Armies was not made without heavy sacrifice. *In the retirement of our troops there was no panic of any sort.*

Units retreated stubbornly from one position to another as they found them turned and threatened with isolation; but at many points fierce engagements were fought, and wherever the enemy attempted a frontal attack he was beaten off with loss.

During the early part of the morning troops of the 17th Division drove off four attacks east of Barastre, and the 47th Division held the village of Rocquigny from sunrise until well into the afternoon, beating off all attacks with rifle and machine-gun fire, until the enemy worked round their flank between Rocquigny and Le Transloy and forced them to withdraw.

South of this point, however, the enemy pressed forward rapidly through the gap which he had made, and succeeded in isolating a part of the South African Brigade, 9th Division, near Marrières Wood, north of Cléry. These troops maintained a most gallant resistance until 4.30 p. m., when they had fired off all their ammunition, and only about 100 men remained unwounded. Early in the afternoon German infantry entered Combles, and having gained the high ground at Morval, were advancing towards Les Bœufs. Their continued progress threatened to sever the connection between the Fifth and Third Armies, and the situation was serious.

The withdrawal of the right and center of the Third Army was carried out during the afternoon and evening in circumstances of great difficulty, as on the right flank bodies of German infantry were already between our troops and the positions to which they were directed to fall back. In this withdrawal valuable service was rendered by twelve machine guns of the 63rd Division Machine Gun Battalion, in Les Bœufs. These guns held up the enemy's advance from Morval at a critical period, firing 25,000 rounds into the enemy's advancing masses, and by their action enabling their division to reach the position assigned to it.

The Situation South of the Somme

South of the Somme the situation was less satisfactory. The greater portion of the defensive line along the river and canal had been lost, and that which was still held by us was endangered by the progress made by the enemy north of the Somme. All local reserves had already been put into the fight, and there was no immediate possibility of sending further British troops to the assistance of the divisions in line.

On the other hand, the French forces engaged were increasing steadily, and on this day our Allies assumed responsibility for the battlefront south of the Somme, with general control of the British troops operating in that sector. The situation still remained critical, however, for every mile of the German advance added to the length of front to be held, and, while the exhaustion of my divisions was hourly growing more acute, some days had yet to pass before the French could bring up troops in sufficient strength to arrest the enemy's progress.

During the night the enemy had gained possession of Guiscard, and in the early morning of March 25th, strongly attacked the Allied positions on the wooded spurs and ridges east and northeast of Noyon. The position of the French and English batteries north of the Oise Canal became hazardous, and they were accordingly withdrawn across the canal at Appilly. Dismounted troops of the Canadian Cavalry Brigade actively assisted in covering this withdrawal, which was successfully completed at 1 p. m. Shortly afterwards another heavy attack developed in this sector and was checked after hard fighting. At the close of this engagement, troops of the 18th Division retook the village of Babœuf by a brilliant counter-attack, capturing 150 prisoners. Early in the fight French armored cars rendered valuable service and killed a number of the enemy.

Meanwhile the enemy's progress south and west of Guiscard had continued, and that night his troops entered Noyon. The French and British troops to the east of the town were therefore ordered to withdraw southwards across the Oise, and by the morning of March 26th this had been successfully accomplished.

On the Fifth Army front, also, fighting had recommenced at an early hour on March 25th. Hostile attacks at Licourt and to the south of it widened the gap between the XVIIIth and XIXth Corps and the enemy entered Nesle, forcing the French and British troops back to the high ground on the south bank of the Ingon River, southwest of the town. To the south of this point his troops crossed the Libermont Canal, while to the north the right of the XIXth Corps was slowly pushed back in the direction of Chaulnes. March-elepot was burning, but our troops at midday were reported to be still holding the line of the canal east of Villers Carbonnel and Barleux.

In view, however, of the situation to the south, and the progress made by the enemy on the right bank of the Somme west of Péronne, it was impossible for this position to be maintained. Accordingly, our troops were gradually withdrawn during the evening to the general line Hatten-court-Estrées-Frise, the 39th Division delivering a counter-attack south of Biaches to cover the withdrawal in that area.

A gap still existed between the XVIIIth and XIXth Corps west of Nesle, and the Germans had already reached Liancourt Wood, when the 61st Brigade of the 20th Division, which had hitherto been engaged with the 36th Division farther south, was brought up in busses to the neighborhood of Liancourt. Though reduced to some 450 rifles in its previous fighting, the brigade successfully held up the enemy's advance and made it possible for the remainder of its division to withdraw unmolested through Roye on the morning of the 26th of March.

Carey's Force

The whole of the troops holding the British line south of the Somme were now greatly exhausted, and the absence of reserves behind them gave ground for considerable anxiety. As the result of a conference held by the Fifth Army Commander on the 25th of March, a mixed force, including details, stragglers, schools personnel, tunneling companies, Army troops companies, field survey companies, and Canadian and American engineers, had been got together and organized by General Grant, the Chief Engineer to the Fifth Army. On the 26th of March these were posted by General Grant, in accordance with orders given by the

Fifth Army Commander, on the line of the old Amiens defenses between Mezières, Marcelcave, and Hamel. Subsequently, as General Grant could ill be spared from his proper duties, he was directed to hand over command of his force to General Carey.

Except for General Carey's force there were no reenforcements of any kind behind the divisions which had been fighting for the most part continuously since the opening of the battle. In consideration of this fact, and the thinness of our fighting line, the Fifth Army Commander did not deem it practicable for our troops to attempt to maintain the Hattencourt-Frise positions if seriously attacked. Accordingly, orders had been given on the night of the 25th of March that, in the event of the enemy continuing his assaults in strength, divisions should fall back, fighting rearguard actions, to the approximate line Le Quesnoy-Rosières-Proyart. This line was intended to link up with the right of the Third Army at Bray.

The Attempt to Sever the Allied Armies

On the morning of the 26th of March the enemy recommenced his attack in strength southwestwards and westwards from Nesle, in the double hope of separating the French and British Armies and interfering with the detraining arrangements of our Allies by the capture of Montdidier.

Heavy attacks developed also about Hattencourt, in the neighborhood of the St. Quentin-Amiens road, and at Herbecourt. Under the pressure of these assaults our divisions commenced to withdraw slowly in accordance with orders to the line indicated above. This was taken up successfully and maintained, a number of hostile attacks during the afternoon and evening being beaten off by counter-attacks in which local commanders displayed great energy and initiative.

As the British forces retired westwards, however, the French troops on their right were gradually forced back in a southwesterly direction beyond Roye, leaving a gap between the French and British Armies of which the enemy took immediate advantage. To fill this gap, the 36th and

30th Divisions, which on the previous day had been withdrawn to rest, were put once more into the battle and speedily
became involved in heavy fighting about Andechy and to the
north of that place. Though the enemy had penetrated
behind them and had taken Erches, the troops of the 36th
Division at Andechy maintained a most gallant resistance
until the afternoon of the 27th of March, thereby playing
no small part in preventing the enemy from breaking through
between the Allied Armies.

On this part of the battle front a very gallant feat of
arms was performed on this day by a detachment of about
100 officers and men of the 61st Brigade, 20th Division, at
Le Quesnoy. The detachment was detailed to cover the withdrawal of their Division, and successfully held the enemy at
bay from early morning until 6 p. m. at night, when the
eleven survivors withdrew under orders, having accomplished their task.

At the end of the day, although the enemy's thrust west
of Roye had pressed back our right somewhat beyond the
positions to which it had been intended to withdraw, the
British forces south of the Somme were in touch with the
French, and the general line, Guerbigny—Rouvroy-en-San-
terre—Proyart, had been taken up successfully.

The Northern Advance Stopped

Meanwhile, north of the Somme the battle was entering
upon its final stages; though the enemy's effort was not yet
fully spent and his troops were still capable of powerful
attacks.

During the morning of March 26th our troops continued
the taking up of the Ancre line without much interference
from the enemy, but between Hamel and Puisieux the situation was not yet clear. A gap still existed in this area between the Vth and IVth Corps, through which bodies of
German infantry worked their way forward and occupied
Colincamps with machine guns. These machine guns were
silenced by a section of field artillery of the 2nd Division,
which gallantly galloped into action and engaged them over
open sights.

Farther south, the Bray-sur-Somme—Albert line had been taken up successfully on the night of March 25th-26th, and fighting of a minor character occurred during the morning, particularly at Meaulte, where troops of the 9th Division beat off a strong attack. Owing, however, to a misunderstanding, the Bray-sur-Somme—Albert line was regarded by the local commander as being merely a stage in a further retirement to the line of the Ancre, south of Albert. Accordingly, on the afternoon and evening of March 26th, the withdrawal was continued, and when the higher command became aware of the situation the movement had already proceeded too far for our former positions to be reestablished.

By the time the withdrawal had been stopped the right of the Third Army rested on the Somme about Sailly-le-Sac; while the Fifth Army still held the south bank of the Somme north of Proyart, about five miles farther east. The left flank of the Fifth Army, therefore, was dangerously uncovered, being protected merely by the natural obstacle of the river and an improvised force of 350 men with Lewis guns and armored cars which had been sent up to hold the crossings.

The Fight for the Rosières Line

South of the Somme, meanwhile, the enemy had recommenced his attacks at about 8.30 a. m. on the greater part of the Fifth Army front and against the French. The line occupied by our troops at this time, had it been maintained, would have preserved Amiens from serious bombardment, and orders were issued that every effort was to be made to hold our positions. In the fighting which followed troops of all divisions, despite the weakness of their numbers and the tremendous strain through which they had already gone, displayed a courage and determination in their defense for which no praise can be too high.

At 10 a. m. the 8th Division at Rosières had already repulsed a heavy attack, and the enemy was pressing hard against our positions in the neighborhood of Proyart. The results of the unfortunate withdrawal from Bray now became apparent. The enemy was not slow to take advantage of the position held by him along the north bank of the Somme in the rear of our troops, and in spite of our efforts to destroy or hold the river crossings, began to pass strong parties of infantry to the south bank at Cerisy.

Being heavily attacked in front and with bodies of the enemy established south of the river in their immediate rear, our troops at Proyart and to the north were compelled to fall back. The enemy gained Framerville, Proyart, and Morcourt, and endeavored to advance southwards behind our line.

In view of the absence of reserves behind this front other than the composite force already referred to, the situation was serious. A counter-attack by the 66th Division restored the situation about Framerville, and at nightfall our troops were still east and north of Harbonnières, whence our line ran northwestwards to Bouzencourt.

South of Harbonnières, the 8th Division held the village of Rosières against all attacks and killed great numbers of the enemy. South of this point, as far as Arvillers, troops of the 24th, 30th, and 20th Divisions maintained their positions substantially unchanged throughout the day, though beyond their right flank the enemy passed Davenscourt and captured Montdidier.

The Amiens Defenses

During the night of March 27th-28th, parties of the enemy worked their way southwards from Morcourt and Cerisy and entered Bayonvillers and Warfusee-Abancourt, astride the main Amiens road. Our troops east of these places were seriously endangered, and in the early morning of March 28th were directed to withdraw to the line Vrely-Marcelcave. Our line from Marcelcave to the Somme was manned by Carey's Force, with the 1st Cavalry Division in close support. During the evening the enemy concentrated heavy artillery fire on Marcelcave, and forced these troops to withdraw a short distance to the west of the village.

The position of our troops at Arvillers and Vrely, however, in the deep and narrow salient between the Avre and

Luce Rivers, was rapidly becoming untenable. The enemy was pushing southwards from Guillaucourt, and beyond our right flank had entered Contoire and was pressing the French troops back upon Hangest-en-Santerre. A gallant attempt by troops of the 61st Division to regain Warfusee-Abancourt and lighten the pressure from the north proved unsuccessful, and in the course of the afternoon and evening our troops fell back through the 20th Division, which during the evening was disposed on the line Mezières-Demuin. At nightfall we held approximately the Amiens defense line on the whole front south of the Somme from Mezières to Ignaucourt and Hamel.

The nature of the fighting on the southern portion of the battle front where our troops had been engaged for a full week with an almost overwhelming superiority of hostile forces had thrown an exceptional strain upon the Fifth Army Commander and his Staff. In order to avoid the loss of efficiency which a continuance of such a strain might have entailed, I decided to avail myself of the services of the Staff of the Fourth Army, which was at this time in reserve. General Sir H. S. Rawlinson, who had but recently given up the command on appointment to Versailles, accordingly returned to his old Army, and at 4.30 p. m. on this day assumed command of the British forces south of the Somme. At the same time the construction of new defense lines made necessary by the enemy's advance called for the appointment of an able and experienced Commander and Staff to direct this work and extemporize garrisons for their defense. I accordingly ordered General Gough to undertake this important task.

The Attack on Arras

Meanwhile, between 7 and 8 a. m. on the morning of March 28th fighting of the most intensity had broken out north of the Somme from Puisieux to northeast of Arras. Finding himself checked on the northern flank of his attack, the enemy on this day made a determined effort to obtain greater freedom for the development of his offensive, and struck in great force along the valley of the Scarpe at Arras.

This development of the battle, which had been foreseen as early as March 23rd, involved the right of the XIIIth Corps on the right of the First Army, and represented a considerable extension of the original front of attack. A German success in this sector might well have had far-reaching effects. There is little doubt that the enemy hoped to achieve great results by this new stroke, and that its failure was a serious setback to his plans.

After a bombardment of great violence three fresh German divisions advanced to the assault along the north bank of the Scarpe River and were supported in their attack by the two German divisions already in line. According to captured documents, the enemy's immediate object was to gain the general line Vimy—Bailleul—St. Laurent—Blangy, when three special assault divisions were to carry the Vimy Ridge on the following day. Immediately south of the Scarpe four German divisions were engaged, to two of which were assigned the tasks of capturing Arras, and the heights overlooking the town. This assault was supported by powerful attacks, in which eleven hostile divisions were engaged, along our whole front southwards to beyond Bucquoy. Still farther south, as far as Dernancourt, strong local attacks were delivered at different points. The methods followed by the enemy on this occasion were the same as those employed by him on the 21st of March, but in this instance the thick fog which had played so decisive a part on that day was absent. In consequence, our artillery and machine guns were given every opportunity to engage the German infantry both when assembling and while advancing to the attack, and the heaviest losses were inflicted on them by our fire.

Immediately prior to the assault, masses of German infantry with artillery in rear of them were observed drawn up in close formation on Greenland Hill, and were shelled by our artillery. North of the Scarpe, about Rœux, great execution was done at point-blank range by single guns which we had placed in forward positions close up to our front line. The enemy's infantry in this sector are reported to have advanced almost shoulder to shoulder in six lines, and on the whole front our machine gunners obtained most favorable targets.

The weight and momentum of his assault and the courage of his infantry, who sought to cut their way through our wire by hand under the fire of our machine guns, sufficed to carry the enemy through the gaps which his bombardment had made in our outpost line. Thereafter, raked by the fire of our outposts, whose garrisons turned their machine guns and shot at the enemy's advancing lines from flank and rear, and met by an accurate and intense fire from all arms, his troops were everywhere stopped and thrown back with the heaviest loss before our battle positions.

A second attack launched late in the afternoon north of the Scarpe, after a further period of bombardment, was also repulsed at all points. At the end of the day our battle positions astride the Scarpe were intact on the whole front of the attack, and in the evening successful counter-attacks enabled us to push out a new outpost line in front of them. Meanwhile, the surviving garrisons of our original outpost line, whose most gallant resistance had played so large a part in breaking up the enemy's attack, had fought their way back through the enemy, though a party of the 2nd Battalion, Seaforth Highlanders, 4th Division, remained cut off at Rœux until successfully withdrawn during the night.

On the southern portion of his attack, the enemy's repulse was, if possible, even more complete than on the new front east of Arras. Attacks on the Guards Division and on the 31st Division were defeated after all-day fighting. The 42nd Division drove off two attacks from the direction of Ablainzevelle, and the 62nd Division with an attached brigade of the 4th Australian Division also beat off a succession of heavy attacks about Bucquoy with great loss to the enemy.

Less important attacks at different points between Hebuterne and Dernancourt were in each case repulsed, and led to the capture of a number of prisoners by our troops.

With this day's battle, which ended in the complete defeat of the enemy on the whole front of his attack, the first stage of the enemy's offensive weakened and eventually closed on the 5th of April. During these days hostile pressure continued south of the Somme, and after much fierce and fluctuating fighting in this area, accompanied by a number of strong local attacks also on the northern portion of the battle front, the enemy on the 4th and 5th of April made final unsuccessful efforts to overcome the resistance of the Allies. These attacks, however, though formidable, lacked the weight that had made his earlier successes possible, while the strength of the Allied positions increased from day to day.

It has been seen that in the Somme battle, by the end of March, in addition to some ten German divisions engaged against the French, a total of seventy-three German divisions were engaged and fought to a standstill by forty-two British infantry divisions and three cavalry divisions.

Finally, I am glad to acknowledge the ready manner in which American engineer units have been placed at my disposal from time to time, and the great value of the assistance they have rendered. In the battles referred to in this dispatch American and British troops have fought shoulder to shoulder in the same trenches, and have shared together in the satisfaction of beating off German attacks. All ranks of the British Army look forward to the day when the rapidly growing strength of the American Army will allow American and British soldiers to coöperate in offensive action.

AMERICAN ASSOCIATED PRESS REPORT
On General Sanderson Carey's employment of U. S. and Canadian engineers

A disastrous-looking gap appeared in the 5th Army south of Hamel in the later stages of the opening battle. The Germans had crossed the Somme at Hamel and had a clear path for a sweep southwestward.

No troops were available to throw into the opening. A brigadier general was commissioned by General Gough, commander of the 5th Army, to gather up every man he could find and to "hold the gap at any cost." The general called upon the American and Canadian engineers, cooks, chauffeurs, road workmen, anybody he could find; gave them guns, pistols, any available weapon, and rushed them into the gap in trucks, on horseback, or on mule-drawn limbers.

A large number of machine guns from a machine-gun school near by were confiscated. Only a few men, however, knew how to operate the weapons, and they had to be worked by amateurs with one "instructor" for every ten or twelve guns. The Americans did especially well in handling this arm.

For two days the detachment held the mile and a half gap. At the end of the second day the commander, having gone forty-eight hours without sleep, collapsed. The situation of the detachment looked desperate.

While all were wondering what would happen next, a dusty automobile came bounding along the road from the north. It contained Brigadier General Carey, who had been home on leave and was hunting for his headquarters.

The general was commandeered by the detachment and he was found to be just the commander needed. He is an old South African soldier of the daredevil type. He is famous among his men for the scrapes and escapades of his schoolboy life as well as for his daring exploits in South Africa.

Carey took the detachment in hand and led it in a series of attacks and counter-attacks which left no time for sleeping and little for eating. He gave neither his men nor the enemy a rest, attacking first on the north, then in the center, then on the south—harassing the enemy unceasingly with the idea of convincing the Germans that a large force opposed them.

Whenever the Germans tried to feel him out with an attack at one point, Carey parried with a thrust somewhere else, even if it took his last available man, and threw the Germans on the defensive.

The spirit of Carey's troops was wonderful. The work they did was almost supernatural. It would have been impossible with any body of men not physical giants, but the Americans and Canadians gloried in it. They crammed every hour of the day full of fighting. It was a constantly changing battle, kaleidoscopic, free-for-all, catch-as-catch-can. The Germans gained ground. Carey and his men were back at them, hungry for more punishment. At the end of the sixth day, dog-tired and battle-worn, but still full of fight, the detachment was relieved by a fresh battalion which had come up from the rear.

BY GUSTAVE BABIN

France's part in the Battle

The Great German offensive was launched on March 21st. It had been preceded by a heavy bombardment extending from La Fère to Arras, and from the Oise River to the Scarpe. Perhaps even at the very moment of attack the German High Staff still hesitated between launching their assault southward toward Paris or northward against the English Channel. The yielding of the British line under General Gough in the south, fixed their purpose. The southern road leading along the valley of the Oise River opened to them. Their great dream of French conquest, broken in 1914, began to soar again.

The German forces advanced by way of the narrow corridor formed between the valley of the Oise and Nesle. Almost every division which was engaged passed along that avenue. Coming first by this path, they hurled themselves in masses on the British right wing. They succeeded here more rapidly perhaps than they themselves had hoped.

Those who attacked to the northward were the least fortunate. They encountered there a heavy resistance. Their objective on the first day was the Somme River in the neighborhood of Ham, an advance of about seventeen kilometers. Bursting forth from St. Quentin, they found that, by the first evening, they had only advanced four kilometers, after tremendous effort; they had only reached to Savy, whose woods they had destroyed in their preceding retreat and whose venerable college they had brutally ravaged.

Their heaviest blow, as I have said, was that delivered against General Gough, with twelve German divisions. Six of these had held the front line between St. Quentin and the Oise. Six more now came to aid them. By the 25th of

March, this number had been largely increased. Germany poured her strength against this point of least resistance. In all, before March 30th, she had 28 divisions pushing forward by this route toward Montdidier. These were her best troops, her shock-divisions.

This was the force which the French troops had to encounter when on March 22nd they were summoned to the rescue of the retreating British right. Add to this the fact that the enemy was maneuvering in a region which he knew as well as we, and which he had systematically devastated. He had shrewdly chosen his own field of battle, easily accessible to him by the roads and railways which he had prepared. Moreover, he possessed constantly the tremendous advantage of acting on the inner lines of a salient, so that he could quickly correct an error, replace a broken regiment, and move always more rapidly than we.

Over all these obstacles French valor, French genius, triumphed, as it had triumphed at the Marne, on the Yser, on the Somme, and at Verdun. In vain did the foe hurl into the fiery furnace division after division beyond counting, and engage in a struggle as savage as it was desperate. His redoubtable artillery could not follow swiftly enough for a rapid advance. His general, von Hutier, had plenty of leisure to reflect upon the fate of von Kluck, who for a moment had held the same dream, before he let fall the reality and attempted to seize the shadow. One may naturally suppose that von Hutier was resolved not to fall into the same error. But to wipe from the military map such a morsel as the Capital of France is not an easy matter, even if one dares attempt the venture.

On the morning of March 21st, the right of the British Army, where it was in touch with the French lines, was violently attacked. The twelve German divisions were animated by a terrible energy, because their chiefs had assured them that this was the final and supreme effort. The British held them well at first, held them back all day. So well were they checked that the President of France that evening returned to Paris after a day of anxiety; and he said, "It has been a great check for Germany."

Yet, at the very hour when it seemed possible to speak thus with all confidence, General Gough, fearing that he could no longer resist the endless masses that were being poured against him, gave orders to his troops, toward eleven o'clock at night, to fall back upon the Crozat Canal. There he hoped to pause and again check the foe. But troops that retreat are not easily regathered and rearranged in a new line. True, the feat had been accomplished at the Marne! But that has been well said to have been a miracle.

On March 23rd, the Germans, having again failed to advance further north, crossed the Somme at Ham. The extreme right of the British Army was in danger of being surrounded, as the foe could easily advance from Ham to Nesle. A new retreat by the British right was now necessary. A sort of seesaw was thus established. The first retreat of the extreme right on March 22nd had forced the northern divisions to withdraw beyond Ham. This in its turn forced a new withdrawal on the southern divisions.

During March 22nd one French army corps had been made ready to help the British. The possibility of our lending aid had been already considered, but the case had not seemed to require it. Now, however, with the loss of the Crozat Canal, prompt aid was absolutely necessary. On the 23rd this first French corps closed with the enemy. Four more divisions were hastened to the danger point. The motor transport and the railroad rivaled each other in their speed and zeal. The troops were thrown into the fight as they arrived, the first lines sheltering the unloading of the rest.

Events swept dizzily onward. When General Pétain, commanding these forces, received his orders, he was told to join the British on the line of the Crozat Canal and to aid them in holding it. But on the morning of the 23rd came the Germans' successful passage of the Somme at Ham; and from there they marched southwestward. The next arriving French division was sent to meet them there, while the earlier divisions, already advancing eastward to the canal, were deflected to meet the new attack from the north. Here we were soon engaged in magnificent combat. In the after-

noon an overwhelming German attack drove in the remainder
of the British line from the east, and those exhausted Britons
withdrew behind our lines.

On the morrow, the 24th, the enemy again attacked in
force, marching down the valley of the Oise with his left
wing touching the river bank. He increased the pressure
of his enormous masses. He forced his way down the valley to Viry and to Chauny. We on our side brought up
another division to increase our resistance. The British
troops, scattered now, and without higher command, fought
admirably at many points along the front. In the night they
were officially placed under the orders of the French commanding general.

On the afternoon of the 24th, the foe drove down from
the north along the route from Ham to Noyon. His num-
berless troops fought their way on "shoulder to shoulder,
breast to breast." Our divisions had scarcely had time to
form in line; yet they met the German push with magnificent
vigor. Only step by step could the foe advance. To the
northward, on the other hand, there was a new British withdrawal; that evening the enemy crossed the Somme all along
the line above Ham.

On the 25th, the Germans directed two great attacks
against Noyon, the one coming from the north, the other
from the east. General Humbert, commanding our army at
this point, reënforced this pivotal position with a new division. The defense of the city gradually became impossible
and its evacuation was decided upon. The retreat was accomplished during the night without attack from the enemy.
The divisions which lay south of Noyon in the Oise withdrew to the south bank of the river; those on the high ground
to the west of Noyon fell back further to the westward to
keep in touch with the British on the north.

The next day General Humbert issued this proclamation
of highest military spirit: "The enemy, equally with ourselves, is much wearied. We have now a powerful artillery.
Our troops are defending the very heart of France. The importance of their task will point out to them their duty."

The important thing for us was to hold the heights south

of Noyon and so retain control of this pivotal position. It was the hinge upon which our forces must swing in order to continue to hold possession of the south bank of the Oise.

On the morning of the 26th the drive of the enemy recommenced along all of our front; but his chief effort was directed particularly against the region around Noyon, of which he fully recognized the importance. There are to the west of the city two heights of unequal altitude, the mountain of Porquericourt and Mont Renaud, the two constituting a solid mass of defense barring the road to Compiegne. The enemy knew well that we would hold these to the uttermost; so, advancing his forces beyond Noyon, he redoubled his efforts to become master of these heights. There our artillery mowed the enemy down by whole companies, the main attack being directed against Mont Renaud. It remained permanently in our hands.

In the afternoon of the 26th the German effort seemed directed more toward the north. Our reconnoissances revealed large movements of his troops advancing from his original lines toward the British forces at Roye. These forces seemed also endeavoring to encircle our left wing either to surround us, or to advance on Paris. But fighting foot by foot our armies were extended westward to meet each westward advance of the foe. In vain, that evening, did the Germans make one more desperate attack to break this line. Our machine guns met them at every point. The route to Paris was thenceforth closed. The enemy had to seek some other goal. Noyon had fallen, but our army remained firm and unshaken.

All the next day, the 27th, the enemy continued to test our line from Noyon to the south of Roye, as if seeking to find a passage through our lines. A new French army was by now hurrying along the railways to fill the vacant space between our forces and the broken British front. This army took the field to the west of Montdidier adjoining the left of our army, which until then had upheld battle.

Here there was to be another dramatic moment. The foe found an open gap between Roye and Montdidier, and attempted to penetrate between the sections of the rapidly arriving new army. Our men were detrained with a celerity and accuracy and a steadiness most impressive. Even while the enemy attacked our general was constructing his army, checking them with cavalry while he placed his rapidly arriving artillery.

By the 28th this new army was also fully prepared. Its line held firm. We were once more fixed, established; our forces were in full touch with the British army. On the 29th we began our counter-attacks.

BY GENERAL VON LUDENDORFF
Official Report of March 21st to 28th

When the drum-fire on the morning of March 21st had poured forth its thick sheaves of shot, the barrels of the cannon were red hot.[1] In the battery positions the powder smoke of the shots had thickened the fog to such an extent that one could not see from one gun to another. The attacking artillery fired the number of shots planned in the thick fog, but the objectives and the time of the firing were so exactly calculated that the attack remained independent of the weather. The first English position has disappeared, and in its place there extends a wide and desolate crater-field. Everywhere there are the remains of wire entanglements, broken-down shaft entrances, and destroyed blockhouses. At most places the battered-in trenches were overrun, and the survivors came rushing towards the Germans minus their weapons and with their hands in the air.

At other places the English are defending themselves with great stubbornness. Near Epéhy, for example, they defended the edge of the village until the evening. Farther south, however, Lempire, Ronssoy, Hargicourt, Villeret, and Pontru have been taken. The storming troops, with indescribable energy, overran the crater-field and are now storming beyond the chains of hills west of the captured villages, of which the fields and meadows have long since been transformed into desolate steppes. The English sought to make a stand in the artillery position. The ground favored them; but their artillery was too much overcome to support

[1] The guns could not have been loaded had this been the case.

their infantry effectively. The German batteries, on the other hand, pressed forward. The fire continued to be directed on the crater-land, whilst the pioneers were building a road through the wilderness of mire, and on the first day of attack the artillery followed up the storming troops. At many points the artillery protecting position was broken through. Even in the declining evening the loftily situated ruins of Templeux, with the whole of the strongly constructed quarries, were taken.

The second day also began with a thick fog. Its impenetrable veil favored the English retirement. The German attacking artillery, which was brought forward over the crater zone, had at first small objectives. The fire of the English guns of heavy caliber barred the few crossings through the miry field. But German field batteries galloped between the towers of smoke. They were thus able closely to support the infantry attack. At 7 o'clock the firing began against the second British position. Hardly an hour later the triple wire entanglements protecting it were broken through. The fog continued beyond midday. The infantry stormed farther into the field of mist. Afterwards, in unceasing pursuit, it followed the artillery. At midday companies which had pushed forward had already reached Roisel. Fighting continued desperately around the station. Numerous guns were captured here. At the same time English detachments continued to hold out on the heights south of Templeux. Their machine-gun fire struck the German advancing troops in the flanks, but not for long. Before our storming waves, advancing over the chains of hills, rises the English Army. Close bands of prisoners are streaming backwards. In the roads field grays are followed by chains of reserves and columns. The enemy retreats to his third position. North of the Cologne Brook their wire entanglements were reached even before nightfall.

Bright sunshine favored the progress of the German offensive between the Scarpe and the Oise on the second day's fighting. On the whole front of attack the German infantry, determined upon victory, unceasingly pressed forward. The German artillery fire had produced its effect. The strong

obstacles which had been prepared during many months
were destroyed. The English trenches were transformed
into graves, which were full of dead. Whilst the first lines
in places were only thinly occupied, the English offered a
brave resistance in their second position, which was broken
down in a desperate struggle. The dugouts had to be taken
in hard hand-to-hand fighting. Here the superiority of the
German infantry showed itself in the best light. Unexpectedly commenced and extremely effective, German artillery
preparation only allowed the counter-effect of the English
to be brought into action gradually. The German losses were
thus surprisingly light.

In the captured second English position many closely-
massed counter-attacks had to be warded off, two of which,
supported by tanks, took place in the evening of March 21st
in the region of Doignies, after the capture of the village
of Vaulx-Vraucourt. Sixteen tanks were destroyed by artillery and infantry fire and trench mortar fire. The English suffered unusually heavy losses during their fruitless
counter-attacks. The booty and number of prisoners are
continually increasing. A single German regiment captured
30 guns near Monchy. In the advance beyond the heights
south of Maissemy, German storming troops encountered
enemy batteries. After three of them had been blown up,
an additional one was destroyed before our troops passed
farther on.

On the whole front our battle aviators participated successfully in the fighting, bombs being freely dropped on the
railway stations of Chaulnes, Roye, and Noyon. Good hits
on arriving trains, as well as great explosions at the station
of Compiègne, were observed. Further strong explosions
in the direction of Behagnies confirmed the excellent effect of
our long-distance fire, which was well supported by our artillery aviators.

The decision in the Monchy-Cambrai-St. Quentin-La
Fère battle was brought about by a surprise overrunning
of the third position. South of Bernes, the English, on
March 22nd, had sent forward fresh forces from Amiens
into these positions. The troops had scarcely reached these

positions, and their machine guns had not been fetched forward, when they were surprised by the German attack. On the 23rd the mist lifted earlier than on the preceding days, and the English gave way over the whole front. It is true that their rearguards defended every hilly ridge, but in a short time they were driven out of every new position they took up. The superiority of the German leaders and troops made itself felt to the full. The English artillery sacrificed itself in order to cover the retreat. Their batteries moved back only a few hundred yards before the German storming waves. In raging, rapid fire they shot away their munitions, and then attempted to limber up and to drive away. Under our shrapnel and machine-gun fire numerous batteries could not be got away, whilst others were captured with their teams. The counter-attacks made by the tanks helped just as little. Gun and mine-thrower fire put most of them out of action before they had got properly working. One tank, which broke out into the German infantry line, was rendered harmless by the clever deed of a non-commissioned officer, who sprang upon the tank and killed the crew by means of revolver shots fired through the air-hole in the covering of the tank.

South of Péronne, on the Somme, we advanced. At the same time other detachments pressed forward towards Péronne and to the north of it. Here the English undertook counter-attacks from the town. Their companies, however, fled when the Germans stormed towards them. Péronne is in flames. What the French, after careful work, had built up after the evacuation of the town by the Germans, the English destroyed before their retreat.[2] But the retreat was over-hasty, and rich booty remained behind on every hand. Automobiles with English staffs left the town shortly before the Germans arrived. Between the retreating columns the tanks traveled, which no longer dared to make fresh attacks. German battle-plane squadrons accompanied the retreat. Their machine-guns and bombs brought death and confusion. British airmen did not accept battle, and flew away as soon as they saw the German chaser airmen.

[2] This is untrue.

On the battlefield between the Scarpe and the Oise, within a period of three days from the 21st to the 23rd instant, the English Army suffered the greatest defeat in British history. The successes achieved in the great victory are such as have not been nearly approached by the Entente since the beginning of the battle of positions in the western theater. The English offensive near Arras in April, 1916, was made on a front 12 miles wide; the Anglo-French attack on the Somme in July, 1916, was made on double that width; the French attacked on the Aisne in 1917 on a width of 24 miles. The English big attack, prepared for months in Flanders, never exceeded a space of 18 miles, and the whole of the territorial gains of almost half a year's fighting only amounted to 36 square miles. In the three days' battle in the west, the Germans made a territorial gain of 700 square miles.

On March 24th, the Crown Prince Rupprecht of Bavaria, with the armies of Generals Otto von Below and von der Marwitz, again defeated the enemy in the tremendous struggle near Bapaume. General Kühne broke through the strong positions of the enemy to the northeast of Bapaume in bitter fighting; the troops of General Grünert and General Staabs, coming from the east and southeast, drove the enemy back via Ypres and Sailly. The stubborn enemy resistance, which had been reënforced with French forces, was broken in violent battles. Freshly brought-up troops and numerous tanks threw themselves against our advancing troops along the roads leading from Bapaume to Cambrai and Péronne. They could not bring about a decision in favor of the enemy. In the evening, defeated, they streamed back again in a westerly direction.

During the course of a night battle, Bapaume fell into the hands of the victors. Hot fighting developed for the possession of Combles and the heights situated to the west. The enemy was defeated. English cavalry attacks broke down. We are now standing to the north of the Somme, in the middle of the former Somme battlefield. .

The German Crown Prince, with the army of General von Hutier, forced a passage across the Somme below Ham.

His victorious troops, in bitter fighting, mounted to the west of the Somme. Violent counter-attacks by English infantry and cavalry broke down with sanguinary losses. The town of Nesle was taken by storm this evening.

Between the Somme and the Oise the troops which penetrated across the Crozat Canal have, late in the evening of the 23rd, taken by storm the strongly-fortified and stubbornly-defended positions on the western bank of the canal. In hot fighting the English, French and Americans were thrown back through the pathless wooded country via La Neuville and Villequier-Aumont. The attack continued yesterday. French infantry and cavalry divisions, which were brought forward for counter-thrust, were thrown back with sanguinary losses. In restless pursuit, General von Conta and General von Gayl pressed after the retreating enemy. Guiscard and Chauny were captured in the evening. We bombarded the fortress of Paris with long-range guns.

The enemy casualties are unusually heavy. The tremendous booty which fell into our hands from the 21st cannot yet be estimated. More than 45,000 prisoners have been ascertained, many more than 600 guns, thousands of machine guns, tremendous quantities of munitions and implements, great stores of supplies and pieces of clothing.

In continuation of the great battle in France our troops on March 25th achieved fresh successes. English divisions brought up from Flanders and Italy with the French threw themselves against our troops in desperate attacks. They were defeated. The armies of General Otto von Below and General von der Marwitz have finally maintained themselves in Ervillers after a hot and fluctuating battle, and in their advance against Achiet-le-Grand, captured the villages of Bihucourt, Biefvillers, and Grevillers. They captured Irles and Miraumont and have crossed the Ancre. English troops freshly brought forward attacked violently on a wide front from the direction of Albert. The enemy was driven back after a bitter struggle.

We crossed the Bapaume-Albert road, near Courcelette and Pozières. To the south of Péronne, General von Hofacker has forced a passage across the Somme, and has taken by storm the height of Maisonnette, which was so hotly contested in the Somme battle of 1916, as well as the villages of Biaches and Barleux. Strong enemy counter-attacks wore themselves out before our lines.

The army of General von Hutier, after hard fighting, drove the enemy back near Marchelepot and Hattencourt across the Péronne-Roye railway. The tenaciously defended Etalon was wrested from the French and English.

Our signal service has taken a prominent share in the successes which we have achieved. Laboring untiringly, they rendered possible the coöperation between the units fighting next to one another, and gave the leaders the assurance of being able to guide the battle into the desired channels.

Railway troops, which first carried out the tremendous advance from the beginning of the fighting without any friction, and who are now coping with the traffic behind the front, are working ceaselessly on the reconstruction of the destroyed railways.

Since the beginning of the battle 93 enemy aëroplanes and six captive balloons have been brought down.

The booty in guns has increased to 963. Over 100 tanks are lying in the captured positions.

On the rest of the Western front the artillery battles continued, increasing on the Lorraine front to great strength. We continued the bombardment of the fortress of Paris.

From the other theaters of war there is nothing new to report.

First Quartermaster-General
von Ludendorff.

BY FREIHERR VON ARZ

Statement of April 2nd, by Austria's chief general in France

Among other things, the wound of our enemies in the west is so deep to-day that it can never heal again. I should be telling a lie if I said that the latest German successes surprised me; of these victories I was confident. The splendid leadership of the great masters of war, Hindenburg and Ludendorff, who have known their own aim, the depth and thoroughness of the German mind, and the high moral earnestness of the German soldiers were sufficient guarantee for success to the onlooker acquainted with the circumstances. The change from trench to active warfare makes the superiority of the German Army appear still more conspicuous. When the barbed-wire defenses are left some miles behind, and the maneuvers take place in the open field, then the alertness and experience of the non-commissioned officers, who have been trained by years of instruction during peace, and our thoroughly trained General Staff get their reward. Millions of fighters can be raised out of the soil, but it is not so easy to obtain even a fraction of the necessary leaders of all ranks. The facts we must keep before us when judging of the position on the western front. The German company and battalion commanders are a hundred times better than the English, and in that form an important guaranty of success.

The victorious and confident feelings of the German troops had not suffered any change by reason of the bad weather, the cold and rain which set in on March 27th. Against the wet and cold they were protected by the huge quantities of booty, consisting of coats, jackets and canvas, which they had found, while the rich lots of foodstuffs, which were found everywhere piled up in the British army depots, most advantageously supplemented their own rations. These unexpectedly large supplies have enabled many of the troops to live completely on what they find, so that their own supplies can be saved for a later period.

THE MOST TREMENDOUS OF GERMAN WAR INVENTIONS

THE LONG DISTANCE BOMBARDMENT OF PARIS

MARCH 23RD-MAY

WILLIAM G. SHARP   GENERAL ROHNE

The bombardment of Paris from behind the German line was timed to open with the great military attack of the Kaiserbattle. Thus a double purpose was intended, first to add to the confusion, terror and even despair which the Germans hoped would result from their attack, and second to obscure the source of the bombardment. With the artillery everywhere at fullest discharge and with the French Army fully engrossed in immediate battle, the site of the huge guns directed against Paris might long remain a mystery.

In fact, however, the French observers located the three monster cannon with admirable skill and promptitude; and managed before very long to batter them into uselessness. Moreover, the French people refused to be terrified by this blind and not really very destructive assault upon their capital. Paris suffered no more than London had previously suffered from the Zeppelin raids. In short, the great German guns were very spectacular, but very ineffective.

Their one best shot was that here described by the U. S. Ambassador in Paris at the time, Mr. William Sharp. It plunged through the roof of the church of St. Gervais during the church service on Good Friday, March 29th, and killed almost a hundred people, mostly women and children. Among the few men slain was the Secretary of the Swiss Legation. Considering the fact that the members of the Swiss Legation were Germany's best friends—her only open friends—in Paris during the War, the result of the bombardment could scarcely have made more manifest the recklessly indiscriminate character of the German attacks upon civilians. Here was no warning, no pretense even of confining war to the armed forces. The Germans themselves knew there was no military value to their new gun. They were simply following their old policy of "frightfulness."

We cull a brief explanation of the character of the gun from the accounts of Germany's chief artillery authority, General Rohne; and that the impression made upon the Ally world may be understood, we quote also a news report of the time.

CHARACTERISTICS OF THE GERMAN LONG RANGE GUN

The German long range guns used in bombarding Paris were constructed from worn out 15-inch, 45-caliber naval guns, mounted on concrete emplacements. The converted guns were of two parts; the main section was 98.5 feet long, and the forward section 19.7 feet. The 15-inch gun was bored out, and a heavy uniformly-rifled tube 8.26 inches in diameter inserted, 42.3 feet of this tube projecting beyond the muzzle of the gun. Over this projecting portion a hoop was shrunk. The muzzle section, 23.6 feet in length, was screwed to the end of this hoop tube. This forward tube was unrifled and was probably added to impart additional lineal velocity and better align the axis of the projectile with that of the bore of the gun. The reliners used in this gun were of such a thickness that when worn out they could be rebored to 9.3 inches, and then to 9.93 inches. Up to the time the firing on Paris ceased, at least one of the seven guns constructed had been rebored and was firing 9.3-inch projectiles.

A comparison of the general characteristics of this gun with our 14-inch naval gun, model 1920, is shown below.

Source of information: Ordnance Department.

Comparison of German Long Range Gun and American 14″ Navy Gun

	German 8.26″	American 14″ Navy	German gun in per cent of U. S. Navy gun
Muzzle Energy, foot tons	467,250	85,750	545
Range, yards	132,000	39,000	338
Length, feet	118.2	59.7	198
Weight, pounds	318,000	180,395	176
Muzzle Velocity, feet per sec	4,760	2,800	170
Elevation, degrees (maximum)	55	38	145
Chamber Pressure, lbs. per sq. in	44,000	40,000	110
Length of Projectile, feet	3.44	5.09	68
Accuracy Life, rounds	50	250	20
Weight of Projectile, pounds	264	1,400	19

AIR SERVICE

German L 72 Built to Bomb New York City

The German rigid airship L 72 shown in the picture was built especially for the purpose of bombing New York City, having been designed for a non-stop voyage of 9,500 miles. It would have carried 4½ tons of bombs. The big dirigible, which is 19 feet longer than the Capitol at Washington, lacked but three days of completion when the armistice was signed. It is now in the possession of France.

Characteristics of the L 72

Length	770 feet	Cruising distance	9,500 miles
Height	95 feet	Maximum speed	62 M.P.H.
Width	88 feet	Gasoline capacity	11,000 gallons
Capacity	2,470,000 cu. ft.	Engines, six	240 H.P. Maybach
Lifting power. total	85.75 tons	Total horse power	1,440

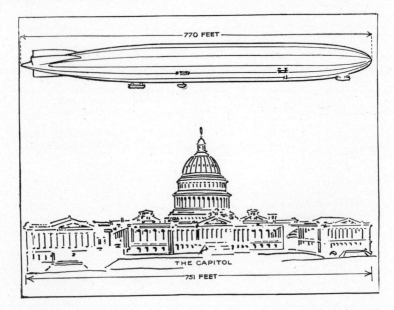

THE CAPITOL

U. S. REPORT FROM AMBASSADOR SHARP

Washington, April 3rd.

THE Secretary of State has received from Ambassador Sharp in Paris a graphic report of his visit to the scene of the horrible tragedy which occurred on the afternoon of Good Friday in a church by the explosion of a German shell projected from far back of the enemy lines a distance of more than seventy miles. The appalling destruction wrought by this shell is, as the Ambassador remarked, probably not equaled by any single discharge of any hostile gun in the cruelty and horrors of its results.

In no other one spot in Paris, even where poverty had gathered on that holy day to worship, could destruction of life have been so great. Nearly a hundred mangled corpses lying in the morgues, with almost as many seriously wounded, attested to the measure of the toll exacted. Far up to the high, vaulted arches, between the flying buttresses well to the front of the church, is a great gap in the wall, from which fell upon the heads of the devoted worshipers many tons of solid masonry. It was this that caused such a great loss of life.

As the Ambassador entered the church, where but a few hours before had been gathered the worshipers, he could easily picture the scene that followed the explosion. The amount of débris, remaining just as it fell on the floor, covered the entire space between the lofty columns supporting the arches at each side. Only a miracle could have saved from death or serious injury those who escaped the falling mass. The scene was that of some horrible shambles, and it was not until well into the night that all the bodies were recovered. Upon the floor in many places could still be seen the blood of the victims, among whom were many prominent and well-to-do people.

The Ambassador called to express his sympathy to his Swiss colleague, whose lifelong friend, the Secretary of the Swiss Legation, was killed while leaving the church. The Minister was deeply affected as he spoke of the great loss to him through the Secretary's death. The Secretary was

well known in Washington, where he served with the Swiss
Legation from 1902 to 1904, and was very highly esteemed
by all who knew him.

In conclusion, Mr. Sharp says that the exceptional circumstances under which this tragedy occurred, both as to
the sacred character of the day and the place, have greatly
aroused the indignation of the people of Paris toward an
enemy who seeks to destroy human life without regard to
the immunities prescribed by the laws of civilization and
humanity, and, instead of terrorizing the people, shells of
the great cannons, as well as the bombs dropped from the
German airplanes, only serve to strengthen the resolve of
the French to resist, to the last man if necessary, the invasion of such a foe.

BRITISH PRESS REPORT

This date (Saturday, March 23rd) was marked by a
new departure in warfare. Paris was startled by a heavy
shell falling in the town at 7.30 a. m. It was followed by
others at intervals of about 20 minutes for some few hours.
The effects of the bombardment were entirely without military importance, the only results being some destruction
of property and the killing and wounding of a number of
harmless citizens, including many women and children. On
the 24th, Palm Sunday, Paris was again shelled, and Good
Friday was also singled out as an appropriate day for the
work of destruction. On the latter date the churches of
Paris would be filled with worshipers, and there would be
a grand opportunity for repeating on land the brave deed
achieved in sinking the *Lusitania* on the sea. A church was
struck, part of the roof blown in, with the result that 76
persons were killed and 90 wounded, of whom a large proportion were women and children. On March 30th the victims numbered 8 dead and 90 wounded, but with these two
exceptions the casualties were limited to quite small numbers,
rarely over one, for each shell fired. At the beginning of
May the bombardment ceased for a time.

It did not take long to discover where the guns were
stationed, and within a few hours from the time the bom-

bardment began it was located by French aviators behind the St. Gobain Forest, not far from La Fère. A few days later the positions of two others were ascertained. All three gun emplacements were on the reverse slope of a wooded hill known as the Mont de Joie, between the Laon-La Fère railway and the Laon-La Fère road, where they were hidden by the trees. It was an outlying spur of the hill-mass of St. Gobain. A line drawn from Fourdrain to Couvron and Aumencourt would run through the center of the position of the three gun-pits arranged approximately in the form of an equilateral triangle, the apex of which pointed towards Paris. They were all well under the crest line. Each installment consisted of a concrete pit in the shape of a long and deep trench, to which a line of railway ran back to the Laon-La Fère railway line. At the front end of each a concrete platform was constructed on which the gun carriage rested. This was carefully covered by branches of trees which, combined with the neighboring wood, served to protect the position as much as was possible from view. When a big gun was fired a number of 17 cm. guns in its neighborhood were simultaneously let off so as to cover the sound of the larger explosion, and whenever the French aviators were seen approaching, the anti-aircraft guns were brought into action and volumes of smoke also discharged to render observation difficult. Except at the time of discharge the gun was not elevated, its long-chase being kept down to avoid detection. Accommodation for the gun crews was provided in a bomb-proof dugout, which was connected with the gun-pit by a deep trench.

The distance from the big guns to the French lines was about six miles; the French heavy guns were some two miles farther back. A range of eight miles is long for accurate practice, but on the fourth day (*i.e.,* March 26th) a shell fell into one of the gun cuttings and rendered the gun useless. It must be remembered that unless a shell dropped actually in the trench or on the gun it would not do much harm. Artillery fire and bombs from the air were continuously directed on the position.

It was not till May 3rd that a very clear atmosphere allowed continuous observation. It was then seen that only one gun was in action and the concentrated fire of the French heavy guns would appear to have silenced it. From that day forward no shell fell on Paris till May 27th, by which time the gun had been repaired.

BY GENERAL ROHNE

The huge "super-guns" used by us in the bombardment of Paris were one of our chief triumphs of the War. Had they been completed at an earlier stage, they could have been directed against England equally with France, and might well have proved the decisive factor in forcing a peace upon our foes. As it was, their destructive fire caused widespread panic in the French capital. Many thousands of people fled from Paris, and the party which was seeking for an immediate, honorable peace became much stronger. The damage done to the French fortifications was not large; but the damage to the city itself was considerable, and the damage to the enemy *morale* was extreme.

These guns had a range of over seventy miles, gaining this enormous advance over all earlier cannon by the tremendous initial velocity of their discharge. The highest velocity previously imparted to a shell at the moment of its leaving the cannon muzzle did not reach 3,000 feet per second; the velocity attained by the new guns was 4,800 feet per second, an increase of over 60 per cent. The shell itself weighed 330 pounds, a light weight in comparison with some which have been used in shorter guns; but 330 pounds of concentrated explosives is quite sufficient to work untold destruction. To this velocity of flight, we added a high angle of fire, with the result that the projectile soared high above the lower levels of the atmosphere, and found at the top of the curve of its flight so little air-resistance that it was practically traveling in a vacuum. This explains the length of its flight; and when it fell, the increasing speed generated by the height of the fall, gave it a weight and power of destruction that made it as destructive as would have been a much larger, slower shell.

FOCH GIVEN SUPREME COMMAND

AMERICA LEADS THE WAY TO THE COMPLETE UNION OF THE ALLIES' FORCES

APRIL 3RD

GENERAL JOHN PERSHING   DAVID LLOYD GEORGE

A main element in the winning of the War, definitely recognized as such by all the Ally governments, was the union of all the military forces under General Foch. This step was hurriedly and informally taken on the actual field of battle when the British line was breaking under the pressure of the Kaiserbattle. There was a hasty meeting of statesmen and generals at the town of Doulens, just back of the battle-line; and immediate control over all the scattered and intermingled Ally soldiers was given to the great French commander. The formal authorization of the step came later. General Foch's actual commission dated from April 3rd, and the various Ally governments confirmed it individually at later dates.

This step, which France had long desired and Britain and Italy had opposed, was carried through largely by the insistence of the American authorities, and under the impulse of the noble step taken by General Pershing, when he had voluntarily subordinated himself and all his troops to the French general's command. The yielding of the other Allies would, however, have been impossible had there not been a General Foch. In a way he stood to the Allies as General Washington had once stood to the thirteen American colonies. They all trusted him and were sure he would guard the interests of all as highly as he guarded his own. Foch had proven himself by years of service. He was the one general in whom all armies and all governments had confidence. It was to him rather than to France that the Allies yielded precedence. He stood undisputedly the foremost of men in proven military ability and loyalty to the great cause of Civilization.

BY GENERAL PERSHING
From his Official Report of September, 1919

IN the latter part of January, 1918, joint note No. 12, presented by the military representatives with the supreme war council, was approved by the council. This note concluded that France would be safe during 1918 only under certain conditions, namely:

"(a) That the strength of the British and French troops

in France are continuously kept up to their present total strength and that they receive the expected reënforcements of not less than two American divisions per month."

The first German offensive of 1918, beginning March 21st, overran all resistance during the initial period of the attack. Within eight days the enemy had completely crossed the old Somme battlefield and had swept everything before him to a depth of some fifty-six kilometers. For a few days the loss of the railroad center of Amiens appeared imminent. The offensive made such inroads upon French and British reserves that defeat stared them in the face unless the new American troops should prove more immediately available than even the most optimistic had dared to hope. On March 27th the military representatives with the' supreme war council prepared their joint note No. 18. This note repeated the previously quoted statement from joint note No. 12, and continued:

"The battle which is developing at the present moment in France, and which can extend to the other theaters of operations, may very quickly place the Allied armies in a serious situation from the point of view of effectives, and the military representatives are from this moment of opinion that the above-detailed condition can no longer be maintained, and they consider as a general proposition that the new situation requires new decisions.

"The military representatives are of opinion that it is highly desirable that the American Government should assist the allied armies as soon as possible by permitting in principle the temporary service of American units in allied army corps and divisions. Such reënforcements must, however, be obtained from other units than those American divisions which are now operating with the French, and the units so temporarily employed must eventually be returned to the American army.

"The military representatives are of the opinion that from the present time, in execution of the foregoing, and until otherwise directed by the supreme war council, only American infantry and machine-gun units, organized as that government may decide, be brought to France, and that all agreements or conventions hitherto made in conflict with this decision be modified accordingly."

The Secretary of War, who was in France at this time, General Bliss, the American military representative with the supreme war council, and I at once conferred on the terms of this note, with the result that the secretary recommended to the President that joint note No. 18 be approved in the following sense:

"The purpose of the American Government is to render the fullest coöperation and aid, and therefore the recom-mendation of the military representatives with regard to the preferential transportation of American infantry and machine-gun units in the present emergency is approved. Such units, when transported, will be under the direction of the commander-in-chief of the American Expeditionary Forces, and will be assigned for training and use by him in his discretion.

"He will use these and all other military forces of the United States under his command *in such manner as to render the greatest military assistance,* keeping in mind always the determination of this government to have its various military forces collected, as speedily as their training and the military situation permit, into *an independent American army,* acting in concert with the armies of Great Britain and France, and all arrangements made by him for their temporary training and service will be made with that end in view."

When, on March 21, 1918, the German army on the western front began its series of offensives, it was by far the most formidable force the world had ever seen. In fighting men and guns it had a great superiority, but this was of less importance than the advantage in morale, in experience, in training for mobile warfare, and in unity of command. Ever since the collapse of the Russian armies and the crisis on the Italian front in the fall of 1917, German armies were being assembled and trained for the great campaign which was to end the war before America's effort could be brought to bear. Germany's best troops, her most successful generals, and all the experience gained in three years of war were mobilized for the supreme effort.

The first blow fell on the right of the British armies, including the junction of the British and French forces. Only the prompt coöperation of the French and British general headquarters stemmed the tide. The reason for this objective was obvious and strikingly illustrated the necessity for having some one with sufficient authority over all the Allied armies to meet such an emergency. The lack of complete coöperation among the Allies on the western front had been appreciated and the question of preparation to meet a crisis had already received attention by the supreme war council. A plan had been adopted by which each of the Allies would furnish a certain number of divisions for a general reserve to be under the direction of the military representatives of the supreme war council of which General Foch was then the senior member. But when the time came to meet the German offensive in March these reserves were not found available and the plan failed.

This situation resulted in a conference for the immediate consideration of the question of having an Allied commander-in-chief. After much discussion during which my view favoring such action was clearly stated, an agreement was reached and General Foch was selected. His appointment as such was made April 3rd and was approved for the United States by the President on April 16th. The terms of the agreement under which General Foch exercised his authority were as follows:

"Beauvais, April 3, 1918.

"General Foch is charged by the British, French, and American Governments with the coördination of the action of the allied armies on the western front; to this end there is conferred on him all the powers necessary for its effective realization. To the same end, the British, French, and American Governments confide in General Foch the strategic direction of military operations.

"The commander-in-chief of the British, French, and American armies will exercise to the fullest extent the tactical direction of their armies. Each commander-in-chief will have the right to appeal to his government, if in his opinion his army is placed in danger by the instructions received from General Foch."

The grave crisis precipitated by the first German offensive caused me to make a hurried visit to General Foch's headquarters at Bombon, during which all our combatant forces were placed at his disposal. The acceptance of this offer meant the dispersion of our troops along the Allied front and a consequent delay in building up a distinctive American force in Lorraine, but the serious situation of the Allies demanded this divergence from our plans.

ADDRESS OF GENERAL PERSHING TO GENERAL FOCH
The offer to subordinate American forces, made at Bombon on March 28th

I have come to tell you that the American people will hold it a high honor that their troops should take part in the present battle. I ask you to permit this in my name and in theirs. At the present moment there is only one thing to do, to fight. Infantry, artillery, aëroplanes—all that I have I put at your disposal—do what you like with them. More will come—in fact, all that may be necessary. I have come expressly to tell you that the American people will be proud to take part in this, the greatest and most striking battle of history.

BY DAVID LLOYD GEORGE
Statement issued by the British Prime Minister, March 30, 1918

For the first few days after the German Army had launched upon our lines an attack unparalleled in its concentration of troops and guns the situation was extremely critical. Thanks to the indomitable bravery of our troops, who gradually stemmed the enemy advance until reënforcements could arrive and our faithful Ally could enter into the battle, the situation is now improved. The struggle, however, is still only in its opening stages, and no prediction of its future course can yet be made.

From the first day the War Cabinet has been in constant session and in communication with Headquarters and with the French and American Governments. A number of measures have been taken in concert between the Governments to deal with the emergency.

The enemy has had the incalculable advantage of fighting as one army. To meet this the Allies have, since the battle began, taken a most important decision.

With the cordial coöperation of the British and French Commanders-in-Chief, General Foch has been charged by the British, French, and American Governments to coördinate the action of the Allied Armies on the Western front.

In addition to the action taken to meet immediate needs of the moment, it will be necessary to bring into operation certain measures which have long been in contemplation should a situation such as the present arrive.

It is clear that, whatever may happen in this battle, the country must be prepared for further sacrifices to insure final victory. I am certain that the nation will shrink from no sacrifice which is required to secure this result, and the necessary plans are being carefully prepared by the Government and will be announced when Parliament meets.

Further Statement of the Prime Minister on April 9th

It has become more obvious than ever before that the Allied Armies were suffering from the fact that they were fighting as two separate armies, and had to negotiate support with each other. Valuable time was thus lost. And yet the inherent difficulties were tremendous. There were national prejudices, national interests, professional prejudices, traditions. The inherent difficulties of getting two or three separate armies to fight as one were almost insurmountable, and it could only be done if public opinion in all the countries concerned insisted upon it as the one condition of success.

A few days after the battle commenced, not merely the Government, but the Commanders in the field—we had not merely the Field Marshals, but all the Army Commanders present—were so convinced—and the same thing applied to the French, they were so convinced—of the importance of more complete strategic unity, that they agreed to the appointment of General Foch to the supreme direction of the strategy of all the Allied Armies on the Western front. May I just say one word about General Foch? It is not merely that he is one of the most brilliant soldiers in Europe. He is a man who, when we were attacked and were in a similar plight at the first battle of Ypres, rushed the French Army there by every conceivable expedient—omnibuses, cabs, lorries, anything he could lay his hands upon—he crowded French Divisions through, and undoubtedly helped to win that great battle. There is no doubt about the loyalty and comradeship of General Foch. I have no doubt that this arrangement will be carried out not merely in the letter, but in the spirit. It is the most important decision that has been taken in reference to the coming battle.

There are three functions which a Generalissimo wields —the strategical, the tactical, and the administrative. What does the administrative mean? It means the control of the organization, the appointment and dismissal of officers and generals, and that is a power which it is difficult or almost impossible to give to a general of another country with a national army. Therefore, in spite of all the arrangements made, unless there be not merely good will, but the knowledge that the public in France, Great Britain and America will assist in coördination and in supporting the authorities in the supreme strategical plans chosen by the Governments, and in any action they may take to assert their authority, any arrangements made will be futile and mischievous.

I make no apology for dwelling at some length upon this point. I have always felt that we are losing value and efficiency in the Allied Armies through lack of coördination and concentration. We have sustained many disasters already through that, and we shall encounter more unless this defect in our machinery is put right. Hitherto I regret that every effort at amendment has led to rather prolonged and very bitter controversy, and these difficulties, these great inherent difficulties, were themselves accentuated and aggravated. There were difficulties of carrying out plans, and other obstacles, and, what is worse, valuable time is lost. I entreat the nation as a whole to stand united for a united control of the strategical operations of our armies at the front.

BRITAIN FIGHTS "WITH BACK TO THE WALL"

BATTLE OF THE LYS, THE SECOND BLOW OF THE KAISER-BATTLE

APRIL 9TH-30TH

MARSHAL HINDENBURG   SIR ARTHUR CURRIE
SIR DOUGLAS HAIG   GENERAL VON GAEDKE

If Germany had seemed approaching a great victory in her first blow in the Kaiserbattle, she seemed even nearer to decisive triumph in her second mighty blow. This was delivered against the British in the Lys valley, just south of Ypres. It began on April 9th, and by the 11th the British forces were so shaken that General Haig issued the noted appeal to his army which opens our present article. In it he told them frankly that their position was desperate, and each man must die where he fought, rather than retreat. In similar fashion the Canadian general, Sir Arthur Currie, appealed to his Canadian corps, which played a gallant part throughout the battle.

These spirited words met the success they deserved. The British troops held firm. General Foch sent a French army to their aid, and ultimately the German advance was checked. Some small forces of Americans also took part in the widespread confused resistance, and General Haig makes special mention of their valiant service.

Tactically this battle has been called "General Ludendorff's one mistake." Started, as the great German chieftain himself has said, merely to weaken and confuse the Allies, it had in its opening stages secured this result to a truly staggering degree. But Ludendorff seems to have been tempted by this initial success into an effort to make this in itself the main, decisive battle. He would crush the British completely, here and now. For this purpose he abandoned his successful attacks by "infiltration," that is, by searching for weak spots through which to penetrate and so encircle the stronger positions and cut them off from their bases. Instead, he returned to the earlier German method of mass attacks, hurling huge forces directly against the British line in the hope of "smashing through." In these tactics he failed; or perhaps as Ludendorff was not in person on the field, we should lay the blame on the actually commanding generals, von Quast, south of the Lys, and von Armin, on the north. At any rate, on April 12th the mass attacks of the Germans took the place of subtler maneuvers, and the battle of the Lys became for them a bloody and most costly failure. They had previously won considerable ground; they won now a little more, enough to enable them to talk of the battle as a victory. But its end left the general position along the whole

104

west front just about as it had been a month before—and American aid was one month nearer at hand. As the historian Buchan, whose general estimate of the battle we quote, has said of this attack, "It all but destroyed the British Army; but it saved the Allies' front, and in the long run gave them the victory."

BY MARSHAL HINDENBURG

IN winter the low-lying area of the Lys river-valley was to a large extent flooded, and in spring it was often nothing but a marsh for weeks on end—a real horror for the troops holding the trenches at this point. North of the Lys the ground gradually rose, and then mounted sharply to the great group of hills which had its mighty pillars at Kemmel and Cassel.

It was perfectly hopeless to think of carrying out such an attack before the valley of the Lys was to some extent passable. In normal circumstances of weather, we could only expect the ground to become dry enough by the middle of April. But we thought we could not wait until then to begin the decisive conflict in the West. We had to keep the prospects of American intervention steadily before our eyes. Notwithstanding these objections to the attack, we had the scheme worked out, at any rate in theory. In this working out we provided for the eventuality that our operation at St. Quentin would compel the enemy's leaders to withdraw large reserves from the group in Flanders to meet our break-through there.

This eventuality had materialized by the end of March. As soon as we saw that our attack to the west must come to a standstill, we decided to begin our operations on the Lys front. An inquiry addressed to the Army Group of the Crown Prince Rupprecht elicited the reply that, thanks to the dry spring weather, the attack across the valley of the Lys was already feasible. The enterprise was now taken in hand by the Army Headquarters Staff and the troops with amazing energy.

On April 9, the anniversary of the great crisis at Arras, our storm troops rose from their muddy trenches on the Lys front from Armentières to La Bassée. Of course they were not disposed in great waves, but mostly in small detachments and diminutive columns which waded through the morass which had been upheaved by shells and mines, and either picked their way towards the enemy lines between deep shell-holes filled with water or took the few firm causeways. Under the protection of our artillery and trench-mortar fire, they succeeded in getting forward quickly in spite of all the natural and artificial obstacles, although apparently neither the English nor the Portuguese, who had been sandwiched in among them, believed it possible. Most of the Portuguese troops left the battlefield in wild flight, and once and for all retired from the fighting.

It must be admitted that our exploitation of the surprise and of the Portuguese failure met with the most serious obstacles in the nature of the ground. It was only with the greatest difficulty that a few ammunition wagons were brought forward behind the infantry. Yet the Lys was reached by the evening and even crossed at one point. Here again the decision was to be expected only in the course of the next few days. Our prospects seemed favorable. On April 10th Estaires fell into our hands and we gained more ground north-west of Armentières. On the same day our front of attack was extended to the region of Wytschaete. We again stormed the battered ruins of the much-fought-for Messines.

The next day brought us more successes and fresh hopes. Armentières was evacuated by the enemy and we captured Merville. From the south we approached the first terrace of the great group of hills from which our opponent could see our whole attack and command it with his artillery. From now on progress became slower. It soon came to a stop on our left wing, while our attack in the direction of Hazebrouck was slowly becoming paralysed. In our centre we captured Bailleul and set foot on the hills from the south. Wytschaete fell into our hands, but then this first blow was exhausted.

The difficulties of communication across the Lys valley which had to be overcome by our troops attacking from the south had been like a chain round our necks. Ammunition could only be brought up in quite inadequate quantities, and it was only thanks to the booty the enemy had left behind on the battlefield that we were able to keep our troops properly fed.

Our infantry had suffered extremely heavily in their fight with the enemy machine-gun nests, and their complete exhaustion threatened unless we paused in our attack for a time. On the other hand, the situation urgently exacted an early decision. We had arrived at one of those crises in which the continuation of the attack is extremely difficult, but when the defence seems to be wavering. The release from such a situation can only come from a further attack and not by merely holding on.

We had to capture Mount Kemmel. It had lain like a great hump before our eyes for years. It was only to be expected that the enemy had made it the key to his positions in Flanders. The photographs of our airmen revealed but a portion of the complicated enemy defence system at this point. We might hope, however, that the external appearance of the hill was more impressive than its real tactical value. We had had experiences of this kind before with other tactical objectives. Picked troops which had displayed their resolution and revealed their powers at the Roten-Turm Pass, and in the fighting in the mountains of Transylvania, Serbian Albania and the Alps of Upper Italy, might once more make possible the seemingly impossible. A condition precedent to the success of our further attacks in Flanders was that the French High Command should be compelled to leave the burden of the defence in that region to their English Allies. We therefore first renewed our attacks at Villers-Brétonneux on April 24th, hoping that the French commander's anxiety about Amiens would take precedence of the necessity to help the hard-pressed English friends in Flanders. Unfortunately this new attack failed. On the other hand, on April 25th the English defence on Mount Kemmel collapsed at the first blow. The loss of this pillar of the defence shook the whole enemy front in Flanders. Our adversary began to withdraw from the Ypres salient which he had pushed out in months of fighting in

1917. Yet to the last Flemish city he clung as if to a jewel which he was unwilling to lose for political reasons.

But the decision in Flanders was not to be sought at Ypres, but by attacking in the direction of Cassel. If we managed to make progress in that quarter, the whole Anglo-Belgian front in Flanders would have to be withdrawn to the west. Just as our thoughts had soared beyond Amiens in the previous month, our hopes now soared to the Channel Coast. I seemed to feel how all England followed the course of the battle in Flanders with bated breath. After that giant bastion, Mount Kemmel, had fallen, we had no reason to flinch from the difficulties of further attacks. We must have Cassel at least! From that vantage point the long-range fire of our heaviest guns could reach Boulogne and Calais. Both towns were crammed full with English supplies, and were also the principal points of debarkation of the English armies. The English army had failed in the most surprising fashion in the fight for Kemmel. If we succeeded in getting it to ourselves at this point, we should have a certain prospect of a great victory.

If no French help arrived, England would probably be lost in Flanders. Yet in England's dire need this help was once more at hand. French troops came up with bitter anger against the friend who had surrendered Kemmel, and attempted to recover this key position from us. It was in vain. But our own last great onslaught on the new Anglo-French line at the end of April made no headway.

On May 1st we adopted the defensive in Flanders, or rather, as we then hoped, passed to the defensive for the time being.

Twice had England been saved by France at a moment of extreme crisis. Perhaps the third time we should succeed. If we reached the Channel Coast we should lay hands directly on England's vital arteries. In so doing we should not only be in the most favorable position conceivable for interrupting her maritime communications, but our heaviest artillery would be able to get a portion of the South Coast of Britain under fire. The mysterious marvel of technical science, which was even now sending its shells into the

French capital from the region of Laon, could be employed against England also.

BY SIR DOUGLAS HAIG

His "Backs to the Wall" appeal to his troops, issued as the "Order of the Day" on April 11th

There is no other course open to us but to fight it out. Every position must be held to the last man; there must be no retirement. With our backs to the wall, and believing in the justice of our cause, each one of us must fight on to the end. The safety of our homes and the freedom of mankind depend alike upon the conduct of each one of us at this critical moment.

BY GENERAL SIR ARTHUR CURRIE

His appeal to his Canadian troops entering the battle

Looking back with pride on the unbroken record of your glorious achievements, asking you to realize that to-day the fate of the British Empire hangs in the balance, I place my trust in the Canadian Corps, knowing that where Canadians are engaged there can be no giving way. Under the orders of your devoted officers in the coming battle you will advance or fall where you stand facing the enemy.

To those who fall I say, "You will not die, but step into immortality. Your mothers will not lament your fate, but will have been proud to have borne such sons. Your names will be revered for ever and ever by your grateful country, and God will take you unto Himself."

Canadians, in this fateful hour I command you and I trust you to fight as you have ever fought, with all your strength, with all your determination, with all your tranquil courage. On many a hard-fought field of battle you have overcome this enemy. With God's help you shall achieve victory once more.

BY SIR DOUGLAS HAIG
Official report of July, 1918

The possibility of a German attack north of the La Bassée Canal, for which certain preparations appeared to have been carried out, had been brought to my notice prior to the 21st of March. Indications that preparations for a hostile attack in this sector were nearing completion had been observed in the first days of April, but its extent and force could not be accurately gauged.

There were obvious advantages for the enemy in such a course of action. In the first place, the depth of his advance on the southern portion of the battle front had left him with a long and dangerously exposed flank between Noyon and Montdidier. The absence of properly organized communications in the battle area made this flank peculiarly vulnerable to a counter-stroke by the French. To prevent this, and preserve the initiative in his hands, it was essential that he should renew his attack without delay.

In the second place, the heavy and prolonged struggle on the Somme had placed a severe strain on the forces under my command and had absorbed the whole of my reserves. Further, to meet the urgent demands of the battle, I had been forced to withdraw ten divisions from the northern portion of my line, and to replace them by divisions exhausted in the Somme fighting, which had only just been made up with reënforcements recently sent out from home. The divisions thus withdrawn had been taken chiefly from the Flanders front, where, in a normal year, the condition of the ground could be relied upon to make offensive operations on a large scale impossible before May at the earliest.

In consequence of these different factors, the bulk of the divisions in front line in the northern battle, and in particular the divisions which on the 9th of April held the portion of my front between the Portuguese sector and the Ypres-Comines Canal, had already taken part in the southern battle. It must be remembered that before the northern battle commenced forty-six out of my total force of fifty-eight divisions had been engaged in the southern area.

Arrangements for the relief of the Portuguese divisions, which had been continuously in line for a long period and needed rest, were therefore undertaken during the first week of April, and were to have been completed by the morning of the 10th of April. Meanwhile, other divisions which had been engaged in the Somme fighting, and had been withdrawn to rest and reorganize, were moved up behind the Lys front. Arrangements had already been made for the evacuation of the salient at Passchendaele should circumstances require it, a measure which would both upset any preparations which the enemy might have made for an offensive there and economize a few troops for use elsewhere.

The persistence of unseasonably fine weather and the rapid drying up of the low-lying ground in the Lys Valley enabled the enemy to anticipate the relief of the 2nd Portuguese Division. On the night of the 7th of April, an unusually heavy and prolonged bombardment with gas shell was opened along practically the whole front from Lens to Armentières. At about 4 a. m. on the 9th of April the bombardment recommenced with the greatest intensity with both gas and high explosive shell.

The enemy's attack in the first instance was launched on the northern portion of the front of General Sir H. S. Horne's First Army, held by the XIth and XVth Corps. On the 10th of April the right of General Sir H. C. O. Plumer's Second Army, held by the IXth Corps, was also involved.

At about 7 a. m. on the 9th of April, in thick fog which again made observation impossible, the enemy appears to have attacked the left brigade of the 2nd Portuguese Division in strength and to have broken into their trenches. A few minutes afterwards, the area of attack spread south and north. Shortly after 7 a. m. the right brigade of the 40th Division reported that an attack had developed on their front, and was being held, but that machine gunners near their right-hand post could see the enemy moving rapidly through the sector to the south of them.

Communication with the divisions in line was difficult,

but during the morning the situation cleared up, and it became apparent that a serious attack was in progress.

South of the Portuguese sector, the 55th Division was heavily attacked on its whole front, and by 10.30 a. m. its left brigade had been forced back from its outpost line. The main line of resistance was intact and a defensive flank was formed facing north between Festubert and a strong point just south of Le Touret, where touch was established later with troops of the 51st Division.

Throughout the remainder of the day, the 55th Division maintained its positions against all assaults and by successful counter-attacks captured over 750 prisoners. The success of this most gallant defense, the importance of which it would be hard to overestimate, was due in great measure to the courage and determination displayed by our advanced posts. These held out with the utmost resolution, though surrounded, pinning to the ground those parties of the enemy who had penetrated our defenses, and preventing them from developing their attack. Among the many gallant deeds recorded of them, one instance is known of a machine gun which was kept in action although the German infantry had entered the rear compartment of the "pill-box" from which it was firing, the gun team holding up the enemy by revolver fire from the inner compartment.

To the north of the positions held by the 55th Division the weight and impetus of the German attack overwhelmed the Portuguese troops, and the enemy's progress was so rapid that the arrangements for manning the rear defenses of this sector with British troops could scarcely be completed in time.

The 1st King Edward's Horse and the 11th Cyclist Battalion, indeed, occupied Lacouture, Vieille Chapelle, and Huit Maisons, and by their splendid defense of those places enabled troops of the 51st and 50th Divisions to come into action east of the Lawe River between Le Touret and Estaires. East of Estaires our troops found the enemy already in possession of the right bank of the river, and touch between the 50th and 40th Divisions could not be established. After heavy fighting the right of the 40th Division was forced back upon the Lys, and early in the afternoon withdrew across the river at Bac St. Maur.

The remainder of the 40th Division, reënforced by troops of the 34th Division, established themselves in a position covering the approaches to Erquinghem and Armentières, between Fort Rompu on the Lys and our old front line northeast of Bois Grenier. Here they successfully maintained themselves, although the line was not readily defensible and was constantly attacked. In the fighting very gallant service was rendered by the 12th Battalion, Suffolk Regiment, 40th Division, who held out in Fleurbaix until the evening, though heavily attacked on three sides.

During the afternoon troops of the 51st and 50th Divisions (chiefly composed of drafts hurriedly sent up to join their regiments) were heavily engaged east of the Lawe River and were gradually pressed back upon the river crossings. The enemy brought up guns to close range and in the evening crossed at Estaires and Pont Riqueul, but in both cases was driven back by counter-attacks. At the end of the day the bridgeheads were still held by us as far east as Sailly-sur-la-Lys.

In the course of the night our troops at Estaires and in the sector to the south were withdrawn to the left bank of the Lawe and Lys Rivers, after sharp fighting about Pont Riqueul. The bridges across both rivers were blown up, though, as had been the case in the Somme battle, in some instances their destruction was incomplete.

Early in the morning of the 10th of April, the enemy launched heavy attacks covered by artillery fire about the river crossings at Lestrem and Estaires, and succeeded in reaching the left bank at both places; but in each case he was driven back again by determined counter-attacks by the 50th Division.

The enemy continued to exercise great pressure at Estaires, and fierce street fighting took place, in which both sides lost heavily. Machine guns, mounted by our troops in the upper rooms of houses, did great execution on his troops as they moved up to the attack until the machine guns were knocked out by artillery fire. In the evening the

German infantry once more forced their way into Estaires, and after a most gallant resistance the 50th Division withdrew at nightfall to a prepared position to the north and west of the town.

East of Estaires the enemy had already crossed the Lys in strength, with artillery in close support of his infantry, and by the evening had pressed back our troops to a position north of Steenwerck. Thereafter, the arrival of British reënforcements for the time being held up his advance.

The Attack at Messines

Meanwhile, after an intense bombardment of our front and support lines and battery areas between Frelinghien and Hill 60, strong hostile attacks had developed at about 5.30 a. m. in this sector also.

The outpost positions of the 25th and 19th Divisions in line north of Armentières and east of Messines were driven in, and during the morning the enemy worked his way forward under cover of mist along the valleys of the Warnave and Douve Rivers, on the flanks of our positions in Ploegsteert Wood and Messines. By midday he had gained Ploegsteert Village, together with the southeastern portions of Ploegsteert Wood, and had captured Messines. North of that village the area of attack extended during the afternoon as far as the north bank of the Ypres-Comines Canal. In this new sector the enemy carried our forward positions as far as Hollebeke, pushing back our line to the crest of the Wytschaete Ridge.

Messines was retaken early in the afternoon by the South African Brigade, 9th Division. During the night this division cleared Wytschaete of parties of German troops. North of Hollebeke our positions astride the Ypres-Comines Canal were substantially unchanged, and on this front the 9th Division killed great numbers of the enemy.

The Withdrawal from Armentières

The enemy's advance north of Armentières made the position of the 34th Division in that town very dangerous. Though it had not yet been attacked on its own front, its available reserves had already been heavily engaged in protecting its southern flank. As the northern flank also had now become exposed, it was decided to withdraw the division to the left bank of the Lys. The early stages of the movement were commenced shortly after midday. Though the operation was closely followed up by the enemy and pressed by him on all sides, it was carried out with great steadiness and in good order, and by 9.30 p. m. had been completed successfully. All the bridges across the river were destroyed.

On the morning of the 11th of April the enemy recommenced his attacks on the whole front, and again made progress. Between Givenchy and the Lawe River the successful resistance of the past two days was maintained against repeated assaults. Between Locon and Estaires the enemy, on the previous evening, had established a footing on the west bank of the river in the neighborhood of Fosse. In this area and northwards to Lestrem he continued to push westwards, despite the vigorous resistance of our troops.

At Estaires, the troops of the 50th Division, tired and reduced in numbers by the exceptionally heavy fighting of the previous three weeks, and threatened on their right flank by the enemy's advance south of the Lys, were heavily engaged. After holding their positions with great gallantry during the morning, they were slowly pressed back in the direction of Merville.

The enemy employed large forces on this front in close formation, and the losses inflicted by our rifle and machine-gun fire were unusually heavy. Our own troops, however, were not in sufficient numbers to hold up his advance, and as they fell back and their front gradually extended, gaps formed in the line. Through these gaps bodies of German infantry worked their way forward, and at 6 p. m. had reached Neuf Berquin. Other parties of the enemy pushed on along the north bank of the Lys Canal and entered Merville. As it did not appear possible to clear the town without fresh forces, which were not yet available, it was decided to withdraw behind the small stream which runs just west of the town. This withdrawal was successfully carried out during the evening.

Though our troops had not been able to prevent the enemy's entry into Merville, their vigorous resistance, combined with the maintenance of our positions at Givenchy and Festubert, had given an opportunity for reënforcements to build up our line in this sector. As troops of the 3rd, 4th, 5th, 31st, 61st, and 1st Australian Divisions began to arrive, the southern portion of the battle front gradually became steady. Time was still required, however, to complete our dispositions, and for the next two days the situation in this area remained critical.

The Thrust Towards Hazebrouck

Meanwhile, a situation which threatened to become serious had arisen north of Merville. At about 8 a. m. the enemy attacked in great strength on a front extending from south of the Estaires-Vieux Berquin Road to the neighborhood of Steenwerck. After very heavy fighting he succeeded in the afternoon in overcoming the resistance of our troops about Doulieu and La Becque, forcing them back in a northwesterly direction. As the result of this movement, a gap was formed in our line southwest of Bailleul, and bodies of the enemy who had forced their way through seized Outtersteene and Merris.

In the evening a brigade of the 33rd Division, with a body of Cyclists, a Pioneer battalion, and every available man from schools and reënforcement camps, came into action in this sector. On their left, troops of the 25th, 34th, and 49th Divisions, though heavily attacked, maintained their positions to the south and southeast of Bailleul, and before midnight our line had been reformed.

Next day, the enemy followed up his attacks with great vigor, and the troops of the 29th and 31st Divisions, now greatly reduced in strength by the severe fighting already experienced, and strung out over a front of nearly 10,000 yards east of the Forêt de Nieppe, were once more tried to the utmost. Behind them the 1st Australian Division was in process of detraining, and the troops were told that the line was to be held at all costs, until the detrainment could be completed.

During the morning, which was very foggy, several determined attacks, in which a German armored car came into action against the 4th Guards Brigade on the southern portion of our line, were repulsed with great loss to the enemy. After the failure of these assaults, he brought up field guns to point-blank range, and in the northern sector with their aid gained Vieux Berquin. Everywhere, except at Vieux Berquin, the enemy's advance was held up all day by desperate fighting, in which our advanced posts displayed the greatest gallantry, maintaining their ground when entirely surrounded, men standing back to back in the trenches and shooting to front and rear.

In the afternoon the enemy made a further determined effort, and by sheer weight of numbers forced his way through the gaps in our depleted line, the surviving garrisons of our posts fighting where they stood to the last with bullet and bayonet. The heroic resistance of these troops, however, had given the leading brigades of the 1st Australian Division time to reach and organize their appointed line east of the Forêt de Nieppe. These now took up the fight, and the way to Hazebrouck was definitely closed.

The performance of all the troops engaged in this most gallant stand, and especially that of the 4th Guards Brigade, on whose front of some 4,000 yards the heaviest attacks fell, is worthy of the highest praise. No more brilliant exploit has taken place since the opening of the enemy's offensive, though gallant actions have been without number.

The action of these troops, and indeed of all the divisions engaged in the fighting in the Lys Valley, is the more noteworthy because, as already pointed out, practically the whole of them had been brought straight out of the Somme battlefield, where they had suffered severely, and had been subjected to a great strain. All these divisions, without adequate rest and filled with young reënforcements which they had had no time to assimilate, were again hurriedly thrown into the fight, and, in spite of the great disadvantages under which they labored, succeeded in holding up the advance of greatly superior forces of fresh troops. Such an accomplishment reflects the greatest credit on the youth of Great Britain, as well as upon those responsible for the training of the young soldiers sent out from home at this time.

The Struggle for Neuve Eglise

On the afternoon of the 12th of April sharp fighting had taken place in the neighborhood of Neuve Eglise, and during the night the enemy's pressure in this sector had been maintained and extended. By the morning of the 13th of April his troops had forced their way into the village, but before noon were driven out by troops of the 33rd and 49th Divisions by a most successful counter-attack in which a number of prisoners were taken.

In the course of this day, also, a succession of heavy attacks were driven off with great loss to the enemy by the 33rd and 34th Divisions about Méteren and La Crèche. In the evening further attacks developed on this front and at Neuve Eglise. The pressure exercised by the enemy was very great, and bodies of German infantry, having forced their way in between La Crèche and Neuve Eglise, began a strong encircling movement against the left of the 34th Division north and east of the former village. During the early part of the night our troops maintained their positions, but before dawn on the 14th of April withdrew under orders to a line in front of the high ground known as the Ravelsburg Heights between Bailleul and Neuve Eglise, the enemy having been too severely handled to interfere.

At Neuve Eglise the enemy again forced his way into the village, and heavy and confused fighting took place throughout the night. A party of the 2nd Battalion Worcestershire Regiment maintained themselves in the Mairie until 2 p. m. on the 14th of April, and during the morning of this day other troops of the same division were reported to have cleared the village with bombs. The enemy persisted in his attacks, however, and by midnight Neuve Eglise was definitely in his possession. Other attacks delivered on the 14th of April between Neuve Eglise and Bailleul and southeast of Méteren were repulsed.

On the morning of the 15th of April the 19th Division

repulsed hostile attacks about Wytschaete. Late in the afternoon fresh assaults in great strength, in which the Alpine Corps and two other fresh German divisions were engaged, developed against Bailleul and the Ravelsburg Heights. After heavy fighting the enemy gained a footing on the eastern end of the high ground, and, though driven back by a counter-attack, reëstablished his position there and worked west along the ridge. By 7 p. m. the whole of it was in his possession, and the retention of Bailleul itself became very difficult. Two hours later, hostile infantry forced their way into the town, and our troops, who were being heavily attacked from the east and south, were compelled to fall back to positions between Méteren and Dranoutre.

The Arrival of French Troops

The constant and severe fighting on the Lys battle front, following so closely upon the tremendous struggle south of Arras, had placed a very serious strain upon the British forces. Many British divisions had taken part both in the northern and southern battles, while others had been engaged almost continuously from the outset of the German offensive. I had represented the state of affairs to General Foch, Commanding-in-Chief the Allied Forces, and had pointed out to him the necessity of relief for the British troops and their need of an opportunity to rest and refit. General Foch had complied with my request without delay. Certain French forces were moved to the north, and by this date were already in position close behind the British front in Flanders.

The First Attacks on Kemmel

At different times on the 16th of April a number of strong local attacks were made by the enemy on the Méteren-Wytschaete front, which were for the most part repulsed with heavy loss to him. At Méteren and Wytschaete, however, he succeeded in penetrating our positions, and after much rather confused fighting established himself in both villages. Counter-attacks delivered during the evening by British and French troops failed to eject him, though at

Wytschaete a battalion of the 9th Division reached the eastern edge of the village, and our line was ultimately established close up to its western and northern outskirts.

These attacks were followed on the morning of the 17th of April by a determined attempt on the part of the enemy to capture the commanding feature known as Kemmel Hill. The assault was launched after a preliminary bombardment of great intensity, and was accompanied by strong attacks in the Méteren and Merris sectors.

The enemy's attacks in the Kemmel sector were pressed with great determination, but ended in his complete repulse at all points, his infantry being driven out by counter-attacks wherever they had gained a temporary footing in our line. The attacks at Méteren and Merris were also beaten off with heavy loss.

On this day also the enemy launched a strong assault upon the right of the Belgian Army about the Ypres-Staden Railway. This attack, the object of which was to capture Bixschoote and advance beyond the Yser Canal, ended in complete failure, and left over 700 prisoners in the hands of our Allies.

On the 18th of April the enemy made a fresh effort to overcome our resistance on the southern flank of his attack. After a heavy bombardment which at Givenchy is reported to have exceeded in intensity even the bombardment of April 9th, his infantry attacked on nearly the whole front from Givenchy to west of Merville. At Givenchy and Festubert they succeeded at certain points in entering our positions, but after severe and continuous fighting, lasting throughout the day, the troops of the 1st Division regained by counter-attacks practically the whole of their original positions. Elsewhere the enemy failed to obtain even an initial success, being repulsed with exceedingly heavy loss at all points.

For nearly a week following the failure of these attacks the battle on the Lys front died down, though sharp fighting of a minor character took place from time to time at different points, particularly in the neighborhood of Festubert where a strong point known as Route "A" Keep changed hands more than once before remaining finally in our possession. Further west, the 4th Division, in coöperation with the 61st Division, carried out a series of successful local operations north of the La Bassée Canal, resulting in the capture of some hundreds of prisoners and a considerable improvement of our positions between the Lawe and the Clarence Rivers.

During this period, also, the French troops which had already come into line in the neighborhood of Méteren and opposite Spanbroekmolen, gradually relieved the British troops between these two points, and by the morning of the 21st of April had taken over the whole of the Kemmel sector.

The Capture of Kemmel Hill

Operations on the southern front were followed on the 25th of April by a renewal of the enemy's attacks in great strength north of the Lys.

Following upon a very violent bombardment, at about 5 a. m. the enemy attacked the French and British positions from Bailleul to the Ypres-Comines Canal with nine divisions, of which five were fresh divisions and one other had been but lightly engaged. The main object of the attack was the capture of Kemmel Hill by a direct assault upon the French, combined with an attack upon the British right south of Wytschaete, aimed at turning the British right flank and separating it from the French. At that date the British right flank lay on the Messines-Kemmel road, at a point about halfway between Kemmel and Wytschaete.

After very heavy fighting, the German infantry worked their way round the lower slopes of the high ground, and at 10 a. m. had succeeded in capturing Kemmel Village and Hill; though elements of French troops held out until a late hour on the hill and in the village.

The weight of the attack in the British sector fell on the 9th Division and attached troops of the 49th Division, who at 7 a. m. were still holding their positions about Wytschaete intact, though heavily engaged. Fierce fighting continued in this neighborhood for some hours later, and great numbers of Germans were killed by rifle and machine-gun

fire at short range. Later in the morning the right of the
9th Division was forced to fall back fighting stubbornly to
Vierstraat, but at 1 p. m. our troops still held the Grand
Bois north of Wytschaete.

In the afternoon the attack spread northwards along the
front held by the 21st Division. By the evening our troops
had been gradually pushed back from their forward positions, and held a line running from Hill 60 to Voormezeele,
when it passed north of Vierstraat to our junction with the
French about La Clytte. The Allied line had not been broken,
and reënforcements were hurrying up.

Next day fighting continued fiercely. In the early morning a very gallant counter-attack by the 25th Division, undertaken in conjunction with the French, penetrated into
Kemmel Village, taking over 300 prisoners. Our troops
then found themselves exposed to heavy machine-gun fire
from the flanks, and were unable to maintain their positions.
Later in the morning the enemy renewed his attacks in
strength, but, in spite of repeated efforts, was only able to
make small progress at certain points.

Successful counter-attacks were carried out also by the
French, in the course of which the village of Locre was recaptured in a very gallant action.

The capture of Kemmel Hill seriously threatened our
position in the Ypres salient, the communications and southern defenses of which were now under direct observation by
the enemy, while his continued progress to the northwest
in the Voormezeele sector would make the extrication of
troops east of Ypres most hazardous. A further readjustment of our lines in the salient was accordingly carried out
on the night of the 26th-27th of April, our troops withdrawing to the general line Pilckem-Wieltje-west end of
Zillebeke Lake-Voormezeele.

On the 28th of April local fighting took place in the neighborhood of Locre and Voormezeele without material change
in the situation; but on the following day, encouraged by
the capture of Kemmel Hill, the enemy made a determined
effort to improve his success.

After a bombardment of exceptional intensity, which

started at 3.10 a. m., a series of strong attacks were launched about 5 a. m. against the French and British positions from west of Dranoutre to Voormezeele. Very heavy fighting rapidly developed on the whole of this front, and ended in the complete repulse of the enemy with the heaviest losses to his troops.

At Locre and to the north of that village the enemy made desperate attempts to overcome the resistance of our Allies and gain possession of the high ground known as the Scherpenberg. At one time parties of his troops entered Locre, and penetrated to the cross-roads between the Scherpenberg and Mont Rouge; but in both localities successful French counter-attacks drove him out after bitter fighting.

On the British front the positions were strongly attacked between 5 a. m. and 5.30 a. m. On the failure of these attacks, bodies of German infantry advanced at 6 a. m. in mass formation, with bayonets fixed, against the 49th Division, and were repulsed with the heaviest losses. The 25th Division was again attacked at 8.35 a. m., and during the morning repeated attacks were made without result on this division and the 49th Division. At all points the attack was pressed vigorously with massed bodies of troops, and the losses suffered by the German infantry were very great. Throughout the whole of the fighting our infantry and artillery fought magnificently, and in more than one instance our troops went out to meet the German attack and drove back the enemy with the bayonet.

At the end of the day, except for a small loss of ground about Voormezeele, our line was intact, and the enemy had undergone a severe and decided check.

In concert with this operation, the Belgian positions astride the Ypres-Staden Railway were again attacked, and once more vigorous counter-strokes by Belgian troops promptly ejected the German infantry from such ground as had been gained by them in their first assault. Here also the enemy's failure was complete.

On the 30th of April the French retook Locre early in the morning, but beyond this no infantry action of importance took place, and the month closed with the enemy definitely held on both the southern and the northern battle fronts.

In the Lys battle, up to the end of April, the enemy engaged against the British forces a total of 42 divisions, of which 33 were fresh and nine had fought previously on the Somme in March. Against these 42 German divisions, 25 British divisions were employed, of which eight were fresh and 17 had taken a prominent part in the preceding battle.

Our Allies

I cannot close this report without paying my personal tribute to the ready and effective assistance given me by the French and Belgian Higher Command in the course of the Somme and Lys battles. Reference has already been made to the schemes for mutual coöperation and assistance between the French and British Armies which formed so important a part of the Allied plan for the year's campaign. These schemes have been carried out with absolute loyalty. The support rendered by French troops south of the Somme and north of the Lys, and by Belgian troops in taking over the responsibility for the greater part of the line previously held by British troops north of Ypres, has been of incalculable value.

I desire also to express my appreciation of the services rendered by the Portuguese troops who had held a sector of my front continuously throughout the winter months, and on the 9th of April were called upon to withstand the assault of greatly superior forces.

Finally, I am glad to acknowledge the ready manner in which American Engineer Units have been placed at my disposal from time to time, and the great value of the assistance they have rendered. In the battles referred to in this Dispatch, American and British troops have fought shoulder to shoulder in the same trenches, and have shared together in the satisfaction of beating off German attacks. All ranks of the British Army look forward to the day when the rapidly growing strength of the American Army will allow American and British soldiers to coöperate in offensive action.

BY GENERAL VON GAEDKE

The defense of the battle by the standard German military critic

The beginning of the German offensive was regarded by Britons as evidence of the haste with which the German High Command was trying to end the war. This only shows ignorance of the conditions necessary for military success. Every High Command must naturally endeavor to end the war as quickly as their strength permits. It would be a breach of their most sacred duty if they tried to do otherwise, for war is always so great an evil that it cannot be ended quickly enough. It follows, therefore, that it is necessary to attack, because the offensive alone can bring a victorious peace, independent of the will of the enemy. Trench warfare means the indefinite prolongation of the war with all its injuries and disadvantages. This necessity was bitterly felt for years, so long as we had to divide our forces between East and West. With us, it was only a measure of necessity: for the British and French it was a sign of impotence. Through all these years, in countless attacks, they have rightly endeavored to get rid of trench warfare and restore open fighting, but all their attempts broke down against the unshatterable wall of the resistance of our troops.

Hindenburg always dictates the methods of fighting. The enemy has to follow his lead, presumably even when he retreats, and as long as this is the case there is no question of a standstill in any sense. The enemy is obliged to use his reserves wherever Hindenburg wishes. This is the most striking feature of the present period of the fighting—the enemy has yet attempted no strategic counter-attack. Hindenburg's first positions have hypnotized the enemy Command: all they seem capable of doing is to rush up one division after another and place them wherever the German pressure seems greatest. Our enemies are incapable, apparently, of any original thought; they adopted the ideas of Hindenburg and Ludendorff in constructing their trenches.

Further, we are informed that the whole country as far as and even beyond Paris consisted of lines of trenches, one behind the other, and they had used more barbed wire than in a whole year previously.

THE "ZEEBRUGGE AFFAIR"

THE MOST BRILLIANT NAVAL EXPLOIT OF THE WAR

APRIL 22ND

LIEUTENANT J. K. BELL and CAPTAIN ALFRED CARPENTER
BRITISH ADMIRALTY NARRATIVE
STATEMENTS OF ADMIRALS VON TIRPITZ AND SCHEER

For six months the British naval chiefs were planning an attack upon the German U-boat bases on the Belgian coast, Zeebrugge and Ostend. So close had become the combined British and American blockade against the U-boats, so many were the watchful "destroyers" ever patrolling the dangerous North Sea, that U-boats which started from a German port seldom got far enough to do much damage before they were detected and hunted back to harbor or destroyed. Only by a sudden pounce from the Belgian ports could the U-boats successfully reach the English Channel and prey upon the constant sea-traffic there. So Zeebrugge and Ostend were to be blocked, if the thing was in any way possible.

The work was done, and thoroughly, chiefly by the venture of April 22nd, popularly known as the "Zeebrugge Affair." But as this first raid, while blocking the Zeebrugge channel was less successful at Ostend, a second raid was directed at Ostend on May 10th. This more nearly, though not quite completely, achieved its purpose.

The officer in direct command of the chief attacking ship at Zeebrugge, Captain Carpenter, here tells his own story—or has it told in an interview by Lieutenant J. Keble Bell, a standard British author better known by his pen-name of Keble Howard. Its vivid picture is then expanded and confirmed by the official narrative issued by the British Admiralty. Not often does official Britain let itself be stirred to poetical reports; but there is an emotional quality in this whole dashing exploit that fairly compels perfervid language. It has been widely accepted as the most brilliant naval exploit of the War. German officials have naturally discussed it but little; but we give here two somber admissions of its weight. Von Tirpitz was the champion and director of unrestrained U-boat attacks. Scheer was the admiral in command of the great Jutland fight and generally regarded as Germany's ablest naval officer.

BY J. KEBLE BELL

Introducing Captain Carpenter's own narrative

L ET me, first of all, try to tell you the story of Zeebrugge as I extracted it, not without difficulty, from several of the leading spirits of that enterprise. This is no technical story. Elsewhere you will find the official narrative issued by the Admiralty to the Press, and that contains, as all good official documents do, names, ranks, dates, times, and movements.

I lay claim to no such precision. It is my proud yet humble task to bring you face to face, if I can, with the men who went out to greet what they regarded as *certain death* —bear that in mind—in order to stop, in some measure, the German submarine menace, and to prove yet once again to all the world that the British Navy is the same in spirit as it was in the days of Nelson and far down the ages.

These men went out on the eve of St. George's Day, 1918, to do those two things—the one utilitarian, the other romantic. They went out to block the Bruges Canal at Zeebrugge—to stop that mouth which for so long past has been vomiting forth its submarines and its destroyers against our hospital ships, and our merchant vessels, and the merchant vessels of countries not engaged in this war. They blocked it so neatly, so effectively, that it will be utterly useless as a submarine base for—I long to tell you the opinion of the experts, but I may not—many months to come.

This shall be proved for you as we proceed. Now let me explain, very briefly, the nature of the task which the Navy set itself. You imagine Zeebrugge, perhaps, as a long and dreary breakwater, flanked by flat and sparsely populated country, with a few German coastguards dotted about, and a destroyer or two in the offing. I am certain that that is the mental picture most of us had of Zeebrugge— if we had one at all.

Now conceive instead a crowded fortress. Conceive a garrison of no less than one thousand men ever on the breakwater. Figure to yourself, at every possible coign of vantage, guns of mighty caliber, destroyers lurking beneath the Mole on the harbor side, searchlights at all points, and great land guns in the distance ready to pulverize any hostile craft that dares to show its nose within miles.

Picture all that as vividly as you can, and then ask yourself the question: "Would it be possible to storm Zeebrugge so successfully that block-ships could be sunk in the very mouth of the Canal and seal it up?" How would you have set about it? With a huge force of cruisers? No, for the enemy must be taken by surprise. The action must be swift, cunning, and sure. The enemy must not be warned, or your one object, the blocking of the Canal, will be lost.

It took Lord Jellicoe and Sir Roger Keyes six long and anxious months to perfect their plan, with the chance that the secret, at any moment, might slip out. But it was perfect at last, and the secret had not slipped out. Next they wanted a number of men—picked men with special qualities —who would be ready and eager to die if only this amazing coup might be achieved. Last of all they wanted a night on which all the conditions—the wind, the weather, the light —should be in their favor. They did not get that, but they went in, none the less, and did the job.

What would you say if you heard, some fine morning, that an almost obsolete German cruiser had come and leant up against the wall of Dover Harbor, that two German officers had calmly sat astride the wall in the course of their business, that some German sailors had landed on the wall and chased our gunners away from their guns, and that, in the meantime, three quite obsolete German ships, filled with concrete, had been sunk in the mouth of the harbor and blocked it? What in the world would you say?

I think you would at first refuse to believe it. Then, when some official communication lent color to the story, you would tear your hair, declare that all was lost, and utter extremely unpleasant things about the British Forces and those in charge of them.

Yet this is precisely what happened at Zeebrugge. There is nothing more gallant in the annals of the British Navy. Not one man expected to come back. There is nothing more successful in the annals of the British Navy. They did to the full just what they hoped and had planned to do.

"Some people," said Captain Carpenter, "have called this affair audacious. That isn't the word I should use for it."

"What word would you use?"

"Impertinent," he replied, laughingly. "Just imagine this Armada of smoke-boats, motor launches, ferry-boats, obsolete submarines, and ancient cruisers laden with concrete, headed by the old *Vindictive,* setting out in broad daylight to attack the mighty fortress of Zeebrugge."

"In broad daylight!" I exclaimed.

"Certainly. We timed ourselves to reach the Mole by midnight, so, owing to our slow speed, we had to do three hours of the oversea passage in daylight."

"How were the men? Excited?"

"Oh, no; quite calm, and immensely relieved to be at it at last. Well, so soon as it got dark, it *was* dark! We could hardly see a thing, and when the smoke-boats got to work, pouring out great waves of dense smoke at regular intervals, which the light northeast wind carried right across the Mole and the harbor, pitch doesn't describe it!"

"What about the mine-field?"

"H'm! Anyway, we dodged it. My job, you understand, was to get alongside the Mole, land my Marines, help *Iris* and *Daffodil* to do the same, stay there drawing the fire of the batteries and diverting attention while the block-ships got into the Canal and sunk themselves, then get the Marines back on board, shove off, and clear out as quickly as possible. Incidentally, of course, we meant to put out of action as many Huns as was convenient by fire from our guns. You've seen the picture of the fighting-top? That was filled with Marines armed with Lewis guns. They did capital work. I'll come to that later.

"We got pretty near the Mole before they saw us, and then the fun began! Up went the star-shells, the guns began blazing, and we went pell-mell for the old Mole like that." A savage dig at the model with his cane. "I had intended to fetch up just here"—he indicated a spot on the exterior of the great wall pretty near the head of it—"but actually came in here"—a little further inland.

"We'd had things called 'brows' constructed—a sort of light drawbridge with a hinge in the middle. These were lowered away, but the current was so strong against the Mole, and the *Vindictive* bounced up and down so nimbly, that the men had the devil of a job to drop the ends of these brows on the wall.

"All this time, naturally enough, the Huns were blazing at us with everything they'd got. If you have a look at the *Vindictive* in the morning, you'll soon see what they were doing to us. We were just swept with fire from two sides. Even before the party could begin to land, Colonel Elliot and Captain Halahan, poor chaps, who were in charge of that part of the business, were killed.

"The *Iris* went ahead of me and came alongside the Mole just here"—a little nearer the shore end. "They tried to hang on with their grapnels, but couldn't quite manage it, so Lieut.-Commander Bradford and Lieut. Hawkins scrambled ashore and sat on the parapet, trying to fix the grapnels. They were both killed.

"In the meantime, owing to the difficulty of securing to the Mole when alongside, I ordered the *Daffodil* to continue pushing, according to plan, so as to keep us in position. This was a pity, because she was full of men, and they couldn't land to help with the fighting. Eventually, some of them scrambled across the *Vindictive* and landed that way.

"The wind had changed about fifteen minutes before we came alongside the Mole; all the smoke had cleared off and the harbor was plain to the eye. That helped the Huns to pot at us, and they took fine advantage of it. The din, as you can guess, was terrific, and I think they got the old *Vindictive* in every visible spot.

"Suddenly the thing happened for which we had been, semi-consciously, waiting. There was a tremendous roar, and up went a huge tower of flame and débris and bodies into the black sky! My fellows cheered like mad, for they knew what it meant. Sandford had got home beneath the viaduct with his ancient submarine and touched her off. I never saw such a column of flame! It seemed a mile high!

"I must tell you a curious feature of this affair. As he approached the Mole they got the searchlights on to him and began firing at him. That was a nasty position, because she was stuffed full of explosives, and also had a big quantity of petrol on board. But when they saw him still coming on, and dashing straight at the Mole, they stopped firing and simply gaped. I suppose they thought he was mad.

"Anyway, they paid for their curiosity. On the viaduct itself there were a whole lot of Huns—masses of them. There they stood, staring at Sandford in his submarine. The searchlights lit them up. Then, presently, came the explosion, and bang went the whole lot to glory! They must have been the most surprised Huns since the war started.

"All this time, of course, a lot of other things were happening. Many of the seamen and Marines had landed on the Mole and were making fine play with the astonished Germans. Some went right to the head of the Mole and found the guns deserted. One gun, I must tell you, had not even been uncovered, which is clear proof that the garrison was taken by surprise. Others were chasing the enemy all down the Mole towards the viaduct, which they were never to cross, and some went into the shed I told you about and dealt with such people as they found.

"The men in the fighting-top were also doing fell work. All along the Mole, you see, and close under the fifteen-foot parapet, there are dug-outs or funk-holes. At first the Huns popped into these, but by-and-by it occurred to them that they would certainly be found and spitted if they stayed there, so the bright idea occurred to them of nipping across the Mole and dropping down the side into their own destroyers lying there. An excellent scheme but for our fellows in the fighting-top, who picked them off with their Lewis guns as they ran.

"Those chaps in the fighting-top had to pay for it, though, in the end. They were attracting a lot of attention, and the Huns were constantly trying to drop a shell amongst them. They succeeded at last, I'm sorry to say, and laid out every man jack but one—Sergeant Finch. He was wounded badly, but dragged himself out from under the bodies of his pals and went on working his little gun until he couldn't work it any longer.

"Now we come to the block-ships. We saw *Thetis* come steaming into the harbor in grand style. She made straight for the opening to the Canal, and you can imagine that she was a blaze of light and a target for every big thing they could bring to bear. She was going toppingly, all the same, when she had the rotten luck to catch her propeller in the defense-nets. Even then, however, she did fine work. She signaled instructions to the *Intrepid* and *Iphigenia,* and so they managed to avoid the nets. It was a gorgeous piece of coöperation!

"And, by the way, I'm not at all sure that *Thetis* won't give even more trouble to the enemy than the other two. I told you something, I think, about the tendency of the harbor to silt up. Well, *Thetis* is lying plump in the channel that must always be kept clear of silt. The consequence is that the silt will collect all round her and over her, and I doubt whether she will *ever* be removable.

"To get back to the other block-ships. In went *Intrepid,* and in after her went *Iphigenia.* They weren't content, you know, to sink themselves at the mouth of the Canal. That was not the idea at all. They had to go right in, with guns firing point-blank at them from both banks, sink their ships, and get back as best they could. And they did it. They blocked that Canal as neatly and effectively as we could have wished in our most optimistic moments, and then, thanks to the little motor-launches, which were handled with the finest skill and pluck, the commanders and men got back to safety. To-morrow I'll show you some aëroplane photographs which are due in from France, and you'll see for yourself how beautifully *Intrepid* and *Iphigenia* are lying.

"As soon as we saw that the block-ships were sunk we knew that our job was done. Now came the most ticklish part of the business—to get away. Up to this point we had been protected, so far as our hull was concerned, by the Mole. We knew that, directly we left the Mole, we should be in for it.

"The signal arranged for the men to reëmbark was a long blast from *Vindictive's* siren. But that had gone with a lot of other tackle, so we did the best we could with *Daffodil's* little hooter. (Ferry passengers across the Mersey must know it well.) It wasn't much of a hoot, but the fellows heard it, and made for the scaling-ladders.

"This was the Hun's chance. The fire turned on those chaps as they clambered up the ladders, most of them trying to carry a dead or wounded pal, was awful. Talk about heroism! Every man was a hero! You must ask some of them who actually landed to tell you about that. Wonderful!

"We got them aboard at last, and stayed to make certain that nobody was left behind. Then we shoved off from the Mole, which had had enough of us for one night, and made for home at our best speed. Instantly the big shore-guns and everything else vicious blazed away, but the very wind which had turned against us when we arrived now stood our friend. We worked all our smoke-boxes like mad, and the smoke saved us. They landed some shells home, of course, and a lot of poor fellows in the *Iris* were killed by one shell just as they were leaving the Mole. But most of the stuff aimed at the *Vindictive* fell short, thank God, and we finally ran out of range.

"It was a good fight. I think the Huns saw their ending that night."

BRITISH ADMIRALTY STATEMENT

The objectives were the canal of Zeebrugge and the entrance to the harbor of Ostend. Three cruisers, *Intrepid, Iphigenia* and *Thetis,* each duly packed with concrete and with mines attached to her bottom for the purpose of sinking her, *Merrimac*-fashion, in the neck of the canal, were aimed at Zeebrugge; two others, similarly prepared, were directed at Ostend. The old cruiser *Vindictive,* with two ferry-boats, *Iris* and *Daffodil,* was to attack the great half-moon Mole which guards the Zeebrugge Canal, land bluejackets and marines upon it, destroy what stores, guns, and Germans she could find, and generally create a diversion while the blockships ran in and sank themselves in their appointed place. Vice-Admiral Keyes, in the destroyer *Warwick,* commanded the operation.

There had been two previous attempts at the attack, capable of being pushed home if weather and other conditions had served. The night of the 22nd offered nearly all the required conditions, and at some fifteen miles off Zeebrugge the ships took up their formation for the attack. *Vindictive,* which had been towing *Iris* and *Daffodil,* cast them off to follow under their own steam; *Intrepid, Iphigenia,* and *Thetis* slowed down to give the first three time to get alongside the Mole; *Sirius* and *Brilliant* shifted their course for Ostend; and the great swarm of destroyers and motor craft sowed themselves abroad upon their multifarious particular duties. The night was overcast and there was a drift of haze; down the coast a great searchlight swung its beams to and fro; there was a small wind and a short sea.

From *Vindictive's* bridge, as she headed in towards the Mole with her faithful ferry-boats at her heels, there was scarcely a glimmer of light to be seen shorewards. Ahead of her, as she drove through the water, rolled the smoke-screen, her cloak of invisibility, wrapped about her by the small craft. The northeast wind moved the volume of it shoreward ahead of the ships; beyond it, the distant town and its defenders were unsuspicious; and it was not till *Vindictive,* with her bluejackets and marines standing ready for the landing, was close upon the Mole that the wind lulled and came away again from the southwest, sweeping back the smoke-screen and laying her bare to the eyes that looked seaward.

There was a moment immediately afterwards when it seemed to those in the ships as if the dim coast and the hidden harbor exploded into light. A star shell soared aloft, then a score of star shells; the wavering beams of the search-lights swung round and settled to a glare; the wildfire of gun flashes leaped against the sky; strings of luminous green beads shot aloft, hung and sank; and the darkness of the night was supplanted by the nightmare daylight of battle fires. Guns and machine guns along the Mole and batteries ashore woke to life, and it was in a gale of shelling that *Vindictive* laid her nose against the thirty-foot high concrete side of the Mole, let go an anchor, and signed to *Daffodil* to shove her stern in. *Iris* went ahead and endeavored to get alongside likewise.

The fire, from the account of everybody concerned, was intense. While ships plunged and rolled beside the Mole in an unexpected send of sea, *Vindictive* with her greater draught jarring against the foundation of the Mole with every plunge, they were swept diagonally by machine-gun fire from both ends of the Mole and by heavy batteries ashore. Commander A. F. B. Carpenter (afterward Captain) conned *Vindictive* from her open bridge till her stern was laid in, when he took up his position in the flame-thrower hut on the port side. It is marvelous that any occupant of the hut should have survived a minute, so riddled and shattered is it. Officers of *Iris,* which was in trouble ahead of *Vindictive,* describe Captain Carpenter as "handling her like a picket-boat."

Vindictive was fitted along the port side with a high false deck, whence ran the eighteen brows, or gangways, by which the storming and demolition parties were to land. The men were gathered in readiness on the main and lower decks. The gangways were lowered, and scraped and rebounded upon the high parapet of the Mole as *Vindictive* rolled; and the word for the assault had not yet been given when both leaders of the assault were killed by the machine-gun fire which swept the decks.

"The men were magnificent." Every officer bears the same testimony. The mere landing on the Mole was a perilous business; it involved a passage across the crashing, splintering gangways, a drop over the parapet into the field of fire of the German machine guns which swept its length, and a further drop of some sixteen feet to the surface of the Mole itself. Many were killed and more were wounded as they crowded up to the gangways; but nothing hindered the orderly and speedy landing by every gangway.

The lower deck was a shambles as the Commander made the rounds of his ship; yet those wounded and dying raised themselves to cheer as he made his tour. The crew of the howitzer which was mounted forward had all been killed; a second crew was destroyed likewise; and even then a third crew was taking over the gun. In the stern cabin a firework expert, who had never been to sea before, was steadily firing great illuminating rockets out of a scuttle to show up the lighthouse on the end of the Mole to the block ships and their escort.

The *Daffodil,* after aiding to berth *Vindictive,* should

have proceeded to land her own men, but now Commander Carpenter ordered her to remain as she was, with her bows against *Vindictive's* quarter, pressing the latter ship into the Mole.

Iris had troubles of her own. Her first attempts to make fast to the Mole ahead of *Vindictive* failed, as her grapnels were not large enough to span the parapet. Two officers climbed ashore and sat astride the parapet trying to make the grapnels fast till each was killed and fell down between the ship and the wall.

Iris was obliged at last to change her position and fall in astern of *Vindictive,* and suffered very heavily from the fire. A single big shell plunged through the upper deck and burst below at a point where fifty-six marines were waiting the order to go to the gangways. Forty-nine were killed and the remaining seven wounded. Another shell in the ward-room, which was serving as sick bay, killed four officers and twenty-six men. Her total casualties were eight officers and sixty-nine men killed and three officers and a hundred and two men wounded.

The storming and demolition parties upon the Mole met with no resistance from the Germans, other than the intense and unremitting fire. The geography of the great Mole, with its railway line and its many buildings, hangars, and store-sheds, was already well known, and the demolition parties moved to their appointed work in perfect order. One after another the buildings burst into flame or split and crumpled as the dynamite went off.

A bombing party, working up towards the Mole extension in search of the enemy, destroyed several machine-gun emplacements, but not a single prisoner rewarded them. It appears that upon the approach of the ships, and with the opening of the fire, the enemy simply retired and contented themselves with bringing machine guns to the shore end of the Mole. And while they worked and destroyed, the covering party below the parapet could see in the harbor, by the light of the German star-shells, the shapes of the block ships stealing in and out of their own smoke and making for the mouth of the canal.

Thetis came first, steaming into a tornado of shell from the great batteries ashore. All her crew, save a remnant who remained to steam her in and sink her, had already been taken off her by the ubiquitous motor launches, but the remnant spared hands enough to keep her four guns going. It was hers to show the road to *Intrepid* and *Iphigenia,* who followed.

She cleared the string of armed barges which defends the channel from the tip of the Mole, but had the ill-fortune to foul one of her propellers upon the net defense which flanks it on the shore side. The propeller gathered in the net and rendered her practically unmanageable; the shore batteries found her and pounded her unremittingly; she bumped into a bank, edged off, and found herself in the channel again, still some hundreds of yards from the mouth of the canal, in a practically sinking condition. As she lay she signaled invaluable directions to the others, and here her commander blew the charges and sank her. A motor launch raced alongside and took off her crew. Her losses were five killed and five wounded.

Intrepid, smoking like a volcano and with all her guns blazing, followed; her motor launch had failed to get alongside outside the harbor, and she had men enough for anything. Straight into the canal she steered, her smoke blowing back from her into *Iphigenia's* eyes, so that the latter, blinded and going a little wild, rammed a dredger with a barge moored beside it, which lay at the western arm of the canal. She got clear though, and entered the canal pushing the barge before her. It was then that a shell hit the steam connections of her whistle, and the escape of steam which followed drove off some of the smoke and let her see what she was doing.

The commander of the *Intrepid* placed the nose of his ship neatly on the mud of the western bank, ordered his crew away, and blew up his ship by the switches in the chartroom. Four dull bumps was all that could be heard; and immediately afterwards there arrived on deck the engineer, who had been in the engine-room during the explosion and reported that all was as it should be.

The commander of *Iphigenia* beached her according to arrangement on the eastern side, blew her up, saw her drop nicely across the canal, and left her with her engines still going to hold her in position till she should have bedded well down on the bottom. According to latest reports from air observation, the two old ships with their holds full of concrete are lying across the canal in a V position; and the work they set out to do has been accomplished. The canal is effectively blocked.

The whole harbor was alive with small craft. As the motor launches cleared the canal, and came forth to the incessant geysers thrown up by the shells, rescuers and rescued had a view of yet another phase of the attack. The shore end of the Mole consists of a jetty, and here an old submarine, loaded with explosives, was run into the piles and touched off, her crew getting away in a boat to where the usual launch awaited them.

Officers describe the explosion as the greatest they ever witnessed—a huge roaring spout of flame that tore the jetty in half and left a gap of over 100 feet. The claim of another launch to have sunk a torpedo-boat alongside the jetty is supported by many observers, including officers of the *Vindictive,* who had seen her mast and funnel across the Mole and noticed them disappear.

Where every moment had its deed and every deed its hero, a recital of acts of valor becomes a mere catalog. "The men were magnificent," say the officers; the men's opinion of their leaders expresses itself in the manner in which they followed them, in their cheers, in their demeanor to-day while they tidy up their battered ships, setting aside the inevitable souvenirs, from the bullet-torn engines to great chunks of Zeebrugge Mole dragged down and still hanging in the fenders of the *Vindictive.* The motor launch from the canal cleared the end of the Mole and there beheld, trim and ready, the shape of the *Warwick,* with the great silk flag presented to the Admiral by the officers of his old ship, the *Centurion.* They stood up on the crowded decks of the little craft and cheered it again and again.

While the *Warwick* took them on board, they saw *Vin-*

dictive, towed loose from the Mole by *Daffodil,* turn and make for home—a great black shape, with funnels gapped and leaning out of the true, flying a vast streamer of flame as her stokers worked her up—her, the almost wreck—to a final display of seventeen knots. Her forward funnel was a sieve; her decks were a dazzle of sparks; but she brought back intact the horseshoe nailed to it, which had been presented to her commander.

Meantime the destroyers *North Star, Phœbe,* and *Warwick,* which guarded the *Vindictive* from action by enemy destroyers while she lay beside the Mole, had their share in the battle. *North Star,* losing her way in the smoke, emerged to the light of the star-shells, and was sunk. The German *communiqué,* which states that only a few members of the crew could be saved by them, is in this detail of an unusual accuracy, for the *Phœbe* came up under a heavy fire in time to rescue nearly all. Throughout the operations monitors and the siege guns in Flanders, manned by the Royal Marine Artillery, heavily bombarded the enemy's batteries.

The wind that blew back the smoke-screen at Zeebrugge served us even worse off Ostend, where that and nothing else prevented the success of an operation ably directed by Commodore Hubert Lynes, C.M.G. The coastal motor boats had lit the approaches and the ends of the piers with calcium flares and made a smoke-cloud which effectually hid the fact from the enemy. *Sirius* and *Brilliant* were already past the Stroom Bank buoy when the wind changed, revealing the arrangements to the enemy, who extinguished the flares with gunfire.

The *Sirius* was already in a sinking condition when at length the two ships, having failed to find the entrance, grounded, and were forced therefore to sink themselves at a point about four hundred yards east of the piers, and their crews were taken off by motor launches.

May 11, 1918.

The *Sirius* lies in the surf some two thousand yards east of the entrance to Ostend Harbor, which she failed so gallantly to block; and when, in the early hours of yesterday morning, the *Vindictive* groped her way through the smoke-screen and headed for the entrance, it was as though the old fighting-ship awoke and looked on. A coastal motor-boat had visited her and hung a flare in her slack and rusty rigging; and that eye of unsteady fire, paling in the blaze of the star-shells or reddening through the drift of the smoke, watched the whole great enterprise, from the moment when it hung in doubt to its ultimate triumphant success.

The planning and execution of that success had been entrusted by the Vice-Admiral, Sir Roger Keyes, to Commodore Hubert Lynes, C.M.G., who directed the previous attempt to block the harbor with *Sirius* and *Brilliant*.

There was no preliminary bombardment of the harbor and the batteries as before the previous attempt; that was to be the first element in the surprise. A time-table had been laid down for every stage of the operation; and the staff work beforehand had even included precise orders for the laying of the smoke barrage, with plans calculated for every direction of wind. The monitors, anchored in their firing-positions far to seaward, awaited their signal; the great siege batteries of the Royal Marine Artillery in Flanders—among the largest guns that have ever been placed on land-mountings—stood by likewise to neutralize the big German artillery along the coast; and the airmen who were to collaborate with an aërial bombardment of the town waited somewhere in the darkness overhead. The destroyers patrolled to seaward of the small craft.

The *Vindictive,* always at that solemn gait of hers, found the flagship's light-buoy and bore up for where a coastal motor-boat was waiting by a calcium flare upon the old position of the Stroom Bank buoy. Four minutes before she arrived there, and fifteen minutes only before she was due at the harbor mouth, the signal for the guns to open was given. Two motor-boats dashed in towards the ends of the high wooden piers and torpedoed them. There was a machine-gun on the end of the western pier, and that vanished in the roar and the leap of flame and débris which called to the guns. Over the town a flame suddenly appeared high in air, and sank slowly earthwards—the signal that the aëroplanes had seen and understood; and almost coincident with their first bombs came the first shells whooping up from the monitors at sea. The surprise part of the attack was sprung.

The surprise, despite the Germans' watchfulness, seems to have been complete. Up till the moment when the torpedoes of the motor-boats exploded, there had not been a shot from the land—only occasional routine star-shells. The motor-launches were doing their work magnificently. These pocket-warships, manned by officers and men of the Royal Naval Volunteer Reserve, are specialists at smoke-production; they built to either hand of the *Vindictive's* course the likeness of a dense sea-mist driving landward with the wind. The star-shells paled and were lost as they sank in it; the beams of the searchlights seemed to break off short upon its front. It blinded the observers of the great batteries when suddenly, upon the warning of the explosions, the guns roared into action.

It was then that those on the destroyers became aware that what had seemed to be merely smoke was wet and cold, that the rigging was beginning to drip, that there were no longer any stars—a sea-fog had come on.

The destroyers had to turn on their lights and use their sirens to keep in touch with each other; the air attack was suspended, and *Vindictive,* with some distance yet to go, found herself in gross darkness.

There were motor-boats to either side of her, escorting her to the entrance, and these were supplied with what are called Dover flares—enormous lights capable of illuminating square miles of sea at once. A pistol was fired as a signal to light these; but the fog and the smoke together were too dense for even the flares. *Vindictive* then put her helm over and started to cruise to find the entrance. Twice in her wanderings she must have passed across it, and at her third turn, upon reaching the position at which she had first lost her way, there came a rift in the mist, and she saw the entrance clear, the piers to either side and the opening dead ahead. The inevitable motor-boat dashed up, raced on into the opening under a heavy and momentarily growing fire, and planted a flare on the water between the piers. *Vindictive* steamed over it and on. She was in.

The guns found her at once. She was hit every few seconds after she entered, her scarred hull broken afresh in a score of places and her decks and upper works swept. The after-control was demolished by a shell which killed all its occupants. Upper and lower bridges and chart-room were swept by bullets. The *Vindictive* laid her battered nose to the eastern pier and prepared to swing her 320 feet of length across the channel. She was soon lying at an angle of about forty degrees to the pier, and seemed to be hard and fast, so that it was impossible to bring her further round.

The engineer, who was the last to leave the engine-room, blew the main charges by the switch installed aft. Those on board felt the old ship shrug as the explosive tore the bottom plates and the bulkheads from her; she sank about six feet and lay upon the bottom of the channel. Her work was done.

BY ADMIRAL VON TIRPITZ

Far out at sea were our raiders, detached, without friends. They were getting fine results, but one after another, I told myself, they must perish for lack of coal and provisions, for there were no revictualing ports. The same thing that handicapped our raiders was occurring in a large sense on land through England's artifices. She had just shaken the club over the Swiss and they issued a ban on our exports. Holland did likewise.

Von Tirpitz's Official Report of April 24th

During the night of April 22-3rd an enterprise of the British naval forces against our Flanders bases, conceived on a large scale and planned regardless of sacrifice, was frustrated.

After a violent bombardment from the sea, small cruisers, escorted by numerous destroyers and motorboats, under cover of a thick veil of artificial fog, pushed forward near Ostend and Zeebrugge to quite near the coast, with the intention of destroying the locks and harbor works there.

According to the statements of prisoners, a detachment of four Companies of the Royal Marines was to occupy the Mole of Zeebrugge by a *coup de main*, in order to destroy all the structures, guns, and war material on it and the vessels lying in the harbor. Only about forty of them got on the Mole. These fell into our hands, some alive, some dead. On the narrow high wall of the Mole both parties fought with the utmost fierceness.

Of the English naval forces which participated in the attack the small cruisers *Virginia* [*sic*], *Intrepid, Sirius* and two others of similar construction, whose names are unknown, were sunk close off the coast. Moreover, three torpedo-boat destroyers and a considerable number of torpedo motor-boats were sunk by our artillery fire. Only a few men of the crews could be saved by us.

Beyond damage caused to the Mole by a torpedo [*sic*] hit, our harbor-works and coast batteries are quite undamaged. Of our naval forces only one torpedo-boat suffered damage of the lightest character. Our casualties are small.

BY ADMIRAL SCHEER
Statement as quoted by General von Ludendorff

"Admiral Scheer was afterward appointed Chief of the Naval Staff. He was an unusually clear-thinking man and swift of decision. It seemed to him that the evacuation of our submarine base at Bruges [Zeebrugge is the port of Bruges] might soon become necessary. He did not, however, think that this would be necessarily fatal to our submarine campaign. The U-boats were no longer able to enter the English Channel, and were thus compelled to travel around the north of Scotland; and this would put us under the unwelcome necessity of massing all our submarine bases along the German coast. Admiral Scheer said that the building of submarines might be further speeded up, and more effective results obtained; and he asked me therefore to loan him competent workmen. This I did to some small extent, though the army could ill spare them."

THE ODYSSEY OF THE CZECHO-SLOVAKS

THE WANDERING WAR OF THE "ARMY WITHOUT A COUNTRY"

MAY-SEPTEMBER

VLADIMIR NOSEK   CHAIRMAN PROZATIMNI
THOMAS MASARYK   ROBERT LANSING

Another new country to arise in 1918 was Czecho-Slovakia. The name in itself is confusing. The Czechs are the Bohemians or North Slavs, commonly known as the Czecho-Slavs, to distinguish them from the Jugo-Slavs or South-Slavs of the Balkan States. There exist, however, contiguous to the Czechs, a people of another branch of the Slavic race, known as Slovaks; and their home, a northern district of Hungary, they have named Slovakia. As these people have united with the Czechs to form the new independent republic, its authorities have decided that both the land and the people should be called, not Czecho-Slavic as they were at first, but Czecho-Slovak.

The forming of the Czecho-Slav army in Russia, and the cause of its attempting its amazing march across Russia and Siberia, have been already told in the Outline Narrative for this volume. Their journey from Kiev in the Ukraine to Vladivostok on the Pacific coast, six thousand miles across a hostile land, has no parallel in history. The "Retreat of the Ten Thousand" Greeks under Xenophon was conducted over only a comparatively small portion of Asia Minor. It was but a schoolboy undertaking when measured against this tremendous feat triumphantly accomplished by the Czecho-Slovak army.

The outline of their effort is here given by one of their leading diplomatic representatives, M. Nosek. The detailed account of their quarrel with the Bolshevists is told officially by the man the wandering army made its executive organizer on the spot—one of the dozen Xenophons of the great march. Thomas Masaryk, the most trusted and successful leader of Czecho-Slovak affairs in Europe and America, was made first president of the new republic. He states the general position of his people.

The peculiar situation of the Czecho-Slovaks, with their land wholly in Austrian hands, but their men free either in Siberia or in the Allied lands, and ready to speak and fight, has led to many anomalies. Chief of these is that the Czecho-Slovaks were recognized as a nation even when they had no country. The United States' formal recognition of them is here given as announced in September, 1918. Their own Declaration of Independence of Austria was not issued until October 18, 1918, when it was proclaimed by Masaryk in Paris. The Teutonic breakdown enabled them to set up a government in their

144

own land in November; and the ancient Bohemian metropolis of Prague was then proclaimed the capital of Czecho-Slovakia.

BY VLADIMIR NOSEK

WHEN war broke out, the Czecho-Slavs all over the world felt it their duty to prove by deeds that their place was on the side of the Entente. The Czecho-Slavs in Great Britain, France and Russia volunteered to fight for the Allies, while in the United States of America, where there are some one and a half million Czecho-Slavs, they have counteracted German propaganda and revealed German plots intended to weaken the American assistance to the Allies.

1. In France 471 Czechs, *i.e.*, over 60 per cent., entered the Foreign Legion and greatly distinguished themselves by their bravery. The majority of them have been mentioned in dispatches and received the Military Cross. They have also won five crosses and twenty medals of the Russian Order of St. George. Their losses amount to more than 70 per cent.

Further, many Czechs living in Great Britain at the outbreak of the war joined the French Foreign Legion in France, and after His Majesty's Government allowed Czechs to volunteer for service in the British army in the autumn of 1916, practically all Czechs of military age resident in Great Britain enrolled so far as they were not engaged on munitions. In Canada, too, the Czechs joined the army in order to fight for the British Empire.

The most important part was taken, however, by the Czecho-Slavic colonies in Russia and America. In Russia, where there are large Czecho-Slavic settlements, numbering several thousand, a Czecho-Slavic legion was formed at the outbreak of the war which rendered valuable services, especially in scouting and reconnoitering. This legion grew gradually larger, especially when Czech prisoners began to be allowed to join it, and finally, under the direction of the Czecho-Slavic National Council, it was formed into a regular army. In September, 1917, it had already two divisions, and in 1918 fresh prisoners joined it, so that it counted some 100,000.

In order to be able fully to appreciate this achievement, we must remember that this was an army of volunteers, organized by the Czecho-Slavic Council without the powers of a real government. At the beginning of the war the Czecho-Slavs not only had no government of their own, but not even any united organization. And if we realize that to-day, the National Council is recognized by the Allies as the Provisional Government of Bohemia with the right of exercising all powers appertaining to a real government, including the control of an army as large as Great Britain had at the outbreak of the war, it must be admitted that the action of the Czecho-Slavs abroad was crowned with wonderful success.

In Russia the difficulties with which the National Council had to cope were especially grave, and mainly for two reasons. In the first place, the Czecho-Slavic prisoners who voluntarily surrendered were scattered all over Russia. It was extremely difficult even to get into touch with them. In addition there was a lack of good-will on the part of the old Russian Government. Thus very often these prisoners, who regarded Russia as Bohemia's elder brother and liberator, were sadly disillusioned when they were left under the supervision of German officers, and thousands of them died from starvation. Nevertheless they never despaired. Eager to fight for the Allies, many of them entered the Jugo-Slav Division which fought so gallantly in the Dobrudja. Nearly all the Czech officers in this division were decorated with the highest Russian, Serbian and Rumanian orders. Half of them committed suicide, however, during the retreat rather than fall into the hands of the enemy.

It was not until after the Russian Revolution, and especially after the arrival of Professor Masaryk in Russia in May, 1917, that the Czecho-Slavic army in Russia became a reality.

The Czecho-Slavs had been mentioned in Russian official *communiqués* of February 2, 1916, and March 29, 1917. The most glorious part was taken by the Czecho-Slavic

Brigade during the last Russian offensive in July, 1917, in which the Czechs showed manifestly the indomitable spirit that animates them. Since every Czech fighting on the side of the Entente was shot, if he was captured by the Austrians, the Czechs everywhere fought to the bitter end, and rather committed suicide than be captured by their enemies. For this reason they were justly feared by the Germans. As in the Hussite wars, the sight of their caps and the sound of their songs struck terror in the hearts of the Germans and Magyars. At the battle of Zborov on July 2, 1917, the Czechs gave the whole world proof of their bravery. Determined to win or fall, they launched an attack almost without ammunition, with bayonets and hand-grenades—and they gained a victory over an enemy vastly superior in numbers.

According to the official Russian *communiqué:* "On July 2nd, at about three o'clock in the afternoon, after a severe and stubborn battle, the gallant troops of the Czecho-Slavic Brigade occupied the strongly fortified enemy position on the heights to the west and southwest of the village of Zborov and the fortified village of Koroszylow. Three lines of enemy trenches were penetrated. The enemy has retired across the Little Strypa. The Czecho-Slavic Brigade captured 62 officers and 3,150 soldiers, 15 guns and many machine guns. Many of the captured guns were turned against the enemy."

Finally, however, when the Russians refused to fight, the Czechs had to retire as well. General Brusiloff declared: "The Czecho-Slavs, perfidiously abandoned at Tarnopol by our infantry, fought in such a way that the world ought to fall on its knees before them."

Professor Masaryk succeeded admirably in uniting and strengthening all the Czecho-Slavic forces in Russia, and in organizing a regular army of the many thousands of Czecho-Slavic prisoners there. Before the Revolution these efforts of the National Council and the Czech prisoners, who were always eager to fight for the Allies, were rendered immensely difficult by the obstacles inherent in the geographic conditions of Russia and by obstacles placed in their way by the old Russian régime.

Unfortunately now, when the Czecho-Slavs had at last succeeded after much work in realizing their plans, the Czecho-Slavic army became powerless owing to the collapse of Russia. Without ammunition, without support from anywhere, the Czecho-Slavs thought they could no more render very effective service to the Allies in the East. They decided, therefore, to go over to join their compatriots in France.

The position of our army was as follows: After the offensive of July, 1917, the Czechs retreated to Kiev, where they continued to concentrate fresh forces. At that time they numbered about 60,000, and this number had gradually increased to 80,000 by the end of 1917. They always observed strict neutrality in Russia's internal affairs on the advice of their venerable leader, Professor Masaryk. It was necessary to counsel this neutrality for the sake of our army itself, since it contained partisans of different creeds and parties, disagreement among whom might have led to its dissolution. On the whole, the Czecho-Slavs, who are an advanced nation, fully conscious of their national aspirations, remained unaffected by the misleading Bolshevist theories. The Czechs abstained throughout from interfering with Russian affairs, yet they did not wish to leave Russia as long as there was any chance for them to assist her. It was not until the shameful peace of Brest-Litovsk in February, 1918, that Professor Masaryk decided that the Czecho-Slavic army should leave Russia *via* Siberia and join the Czecho-Slavic army in France. The Bolsheviks granted them free passage to Vladivostok.

This journey of some 5,000 miles was not, however, an easy task for an army to accomplish. The troops had to move in small échelons or detachments, and concentration at the stations was prohibited. They had to procure their trains and their provisions, and they had constant trouble with the Bolsheviks, because in every district there was a practically independent Soviet Government with whom the Czechs had to negotiate. The first detachments with the generalissimo of the army, General Diderichs, at the head arrived in Vladivostok at the end of April, 1918. But the other detachments were constantly held up by the Bolsheviks and had great trouble in passing through.

They moved from Kiev via Kursk, Tambov, Penza and Samara. The two last-named towns lie on the line between Moscow and Tcheliabinsk at the foot of the Urals, whence a direct line runs across Siberia to Vladivostok.

As we have already pointed out, the Bolsheviks agreed in principle to allow our troops to leave Russia. Their commander-in-chief, General Muraviev, allowed the Czechs free passage to France on February 16th. The same concession had been granted by the Moscow Soviet. On the whole, the Czechs were on tolerably good terms with the Bolsheviks. Professor Masaryk rejected every plan directed against the Bolsheviks submitted to him even by such of their political adversaries as could not justly be called counter-revolutionaries. The Czecho-Slavic troops went still further; they actually complied with the request of the Bolsheviks and partially disarmed.

The trouble only began in May, 1918, when the Bolsheviks yielded to German intrigues and resolved to destroy our army. Already at the beginning of May the Czechs had begun to feel embittered against the Bolsheviks, because in defiance of the agreement their troops were constantly being held up by local Soviets. At Tambov, for instance, they were held up for a whole month. At Tcheliabinsk the Czechs had a serious scuffle with Magyar ex-prisoners on May 26th, and the Bolsheviks sided entirely with the Magyars, even arresting some Czecho-Slavic delegates. The Czechs simply occupied the city, liberated their comrades, and at a congress held by them at Tcheliabinsk on May 28th it was decided to refuse to surrender any more arms and ammunition and to continue transports to Vladivostok, if necessary with arms in their hands.

This was a reply to Trotsky's telegram that the Czecho-Slavs should be completely disarmed, which the Czecho-Slavs defied as they knew that another order had been issued by Trotsky simultaneously, no doubt on the instigation of Count Mirbach, saying that the Czecho-Slavic troops must be dissolved at all costs and interned as prisoners of war.

The Bolsheviks now arrested prominent members of the Moscow branch of the Czecho-Slavic National Council on the ground that they were "anti-revolutionaries." They alleged also that they had no guarantee that ships would be provided for the Czechs to be transported to France, and that the Czechs were holding up food supplies from Siberia. The Bolsheviks deliberately broke their word, and Trotsky issued an order to "all troops fighting against the anti-revolutionary Czecho-Slav brigades."

In this he said: "The concentration of our troops is complete. Our army being aware that the Czecho-Slavs are direct allies of the anti-revolution and of the capitalists, fights them well. The Czecho-Slavs are retreating along the railway. Obviously they would like to enter into negotiations with the Soviets. We issued an order that their delegates should be received. We demand in the first place that they should be disarmed. *Those who do not do so voluntarily will be shot on the spot.* Warlike operations on the railway line hinder food transports. Energetic steps must be taken to do away with this state of affairs."

The Czecho-Slavs were sorely handicapped, since they were not only almost unarmed, but were also dispersed along the trans-Siberian line in small detachments which had considerable difficulty in keeping in touch with each other. Nevertheless the fates were favorable to them. They were victorious almost everywhere, thanks to their wonderful spirit and discipline.

The first victories gained by the Czecho-Slavs over the Bolsheviks were at Penza and Samara. Penza was captured by them after three days' fighting at the end of May. Later the Czecho-Slavs also took Sysran on the Volga, Kazan with its large arsenal, Simbirsk and Yekaterinburg, connecting Tcheliabinsk with Petrograd, and occupied practically the whole Volga region.

In Siberia they defeated a considerable force of German-Magyar ex-prisoners in Krasnoyarsk and Omsk and established themselves firmly in Udinsk. On June 29, 15,000 Czecho-Slavs under General Diderichs, after handing an ultimatum to the Bolsheviks at Vladivostok, occupied the city without much resistance. Only at one spot fighting took place and some 160 Bolsheviks were killed. The Czecho-Slavs, assisted by Japanese and Allied troops, then proceeded to the north and northwest, while the Bolsheviks and German prisoners retreated to Chabarovsk.

In September the Czech and Allied troops from Vladivostok joined hands with the Czecho-Slavs from Irkutsk and western Siberia, and thus gained control over practically the whole trans-Siberian railway. By this means they have done great service to the Allies, especially to Great Britain, by defending the East against the German invaders. Furthermore, it was the Czecho-Slavs' bold action which induced Japan and America at last to intervene in Russia and for the sake of Russia, and it was their control of the Siberian railway which made such intervention possible. Let us hope that their action will lead to the regeneration and salvation of the Russian nation.

The service rendered by Czecho-Slav troops to the Allied cause was justly appreciated by the Allies. Mr. Lloyd George sent the following telegram to Professor Masaryk on September 9, 1918: "On behalf of the British War Cabinet I send you our heartiest congratulations on the striking successes won by the Czecho-Slav forces against the armies of German and Austrian troops in Siberia. The story of the adventures and triumphs of this small army is, indeed, one of the greatest epics of history. It has filled us all with admiration for the courage, persistence and self-control of your countrymen, and shows what can be done to triumph over time, distance and lack of material resources by those holding the spirit of freedom in their hearts. Your nation has rendered inestimable service to Russia and to the Allies in their struggle to free the world from despotism. We shall never forget it."

BY PROZATIMNI

Chairman of the Executive Committee of the Czecho-Slovak army
in Siberia

An authorized and verified translation of the official version of the incident given by the Temporary Executive Committee of the Czecho-Slav army, into whose hands the di-

rection of military operations and political negotiations was placed by the Assembly of Czecho-Slav Soldiers at Tcheliabinsk, May, 1918.

The principle of the neutrality of the Czecho-Slav army as regards the internal conflicts and battles of Russia was definitely expressed and recognized both in the agreement and treaty made by the Czecho-Slav National Council with the temporary government of Russia, and in that arrived at later with the government of the Ukraine Republic, the Ukraine National Council. To this principle both political and military leaders adhered firmly, and succeeded in implanting it so deeply in the minds of the soldiers that, in spite of the attempts made right and left to induce them to break it, not a single section of the army could be induced to do so.

Later, when the Ukraine National Council was defeated and gradually driven out of the governments on the eastern side of the Dnieper and later out of Kiev and the rest of the Ukraine, the commander-in-chief of the Soviet forces, Colonel Muravjof, and Mr. Kocubinsky, the minister of war of the Soviet Government of the Ukraine, recognized the strict armed neutrality of the Czecho-Slav army.

Prior to this, when on January 12, 1918, the Ukraine Central Council adopted the "Fourth Universal," which expressed the desire of the Ukraine Government to live on terms of friendship and harmony with all neighboring states, and especially with Austria, it was decided at a meeting of the Czecho-Slovak National Council, at which Professor Masaryk himself presided, to declare the Czecho-Slav army in all parts of the former Russian state as a part of the autonomous army of the Czecho-Slavs in France. This proclamation was published on February 10, 1918, after the arrival of the Bolsheviks in Kiev. Soon after that, simultaneously with the success of the peace negotiations of the delegates of the Soviet and Ukraine Governments with the representatives of the Central Powers at Brest-Litovsk, definite steps were taken to arrange for the departure of the Czecho-Slav army to the French front.

The first movement was to be the concentration of all our forces on the eastern side of the Dnieper, and this was to be carried out on the basis of an agreement made with the Ukraine-Soviet Government, which at one time planned to establish a front against the Germans in the Ukraine. In the meantime, however, the Germans began to threaten the Czecho-Slavs from both flanks, and they were obliged to retire into the territory of Great Russia. Again this retirement was made in complete agreement with the Soviet authorities in the Ukraine, an arrangement having been reached with the Czecho-Slovak National Council and the commander of the Soviet forces of the South Russian Republics, Antonov-Ovsejenko. On the basis of this agreement an order was issued to the Czecho-Slav Army Corps (No. 26, March 16, 1918) to turn over to the Soviet forces all superfluous arms and other military equipment, while Antonov on his part issued an order to all revolutionary forces of the South Russian Republics (No. 92, March 16th), from which the following is a literal extract:

"Our comrades of the Czecho-Slav Army Corps, who fought so bravely and gloriously at Zhitomir, Kieff, Grebyonka, and Bachmac, defending the way to Poltava and Kharkoff, are now leaving Ukraine territory, and are turning over to us a part of their military equipment. The revolutionary army will never forget the fraternal assistance rendered by the Czecho-Slav Army Corps in the battle of the working people of the Ukraine against the thieving bands of imperialism. The military equipment given up by the Czecho-Slavs the revolutionary army accepts as a fraternal gift."

On the basis of this agreement, Antonov consented to the departure of the Czecho-Slavs from the Ukraine, and the staff of the Soviet army of Great Russia also agreed to our departure toward the East, and issued the necessary orders to the railway officials who were to attend to the details of the transport on behalf of the Soviet Government. Agreement to our departure from Russia via Vladivostok was also expressed in telegrams sent by Lenine and Trotsky.

In Penza, however, a new set of negotiations was begun. The Council of People's Commissioners in Moscow demanded the complete disarmament of the Czecho-Slav army. As the result of the negotiations between the Czecho-Slavs and the Moscow authorities a telegram was sent from Moscow on March 26th signed by Stalin, in which a certain number of arms were to be left to each échelon to provide protection against attack by counter-revolutionists. In this same telegram the promise was made to help in every way possible the Czecho-Slavs as long as they remain on Russian territory, provided they maintain an honest and sincere loyalty. Further, the Penza Soviet was ordered to appoint reliable commissioners who were to accompany the Czecho-Slav échelons to Vladivostok, see that their unity as an organization was unimpaired, and at the same time keep the Council of People's Commissioners informed as to the progress of the transport. In this same telegram it was stated that telegrams with necessary instructions would be sent by the Council of People's Commissioners to all interested parties.

Our army maintained an honest and sincere loyalty. But meanwhile the Soviet Government proceeded to break its word at every step. The Penza Soviet named but one commissioner, who went on ahead to Vladivostok with the first échelon, and there sat down and did nothing. In spite of our repeated requests that other commissioners be named, the Penza authorities absolutely refused to do this, giving as an excuse the lack of suitable men.

The local Soviets one after another put all sorts of obstacles in our path. In Samara, but 400 versts beyond Penza, the local Soviet demanded that we give up more of our arms. These demands were repeated in Ufa, Zlatoust, Omsk, Irkutsk, Tchita, and so on all along the line. The representatives of the Czecho-Slav National Council, as well as the commanders of the various échelons, used every possible means to prevent the movement of our transports from being halted. In Samara the echelons gave up 138 rifles apiece, leaving only thirty to an échelon; in Omsk each échelon gave up a machine gun, and in Irkutsk more rifles, until there was left but twenty to an échelon. The negotiations of these loyal Soviets, being in clear opposition to the orders of the Council of People's Commissioners quoted above, often had the appearance of bargaining at the bazaar, and for the Czecho-Slav soldiers was insulting in the extreme, and had the effect of increasing every day mistrust in the Soviet Government, and in creating a disgust for them which ever grew stronger.

One great reason for this lack of confidence and disgust was the attitude assumed by the Soviet authorities, both local and central, toward those who had deserted the Czecho-Slav army and joined the ranks of the Red army. There were not many of them, and they were bad soldiers and men of weak characters. They went over to the Soviet army for mercenary reasons. The munificent salaries, the opportunities to at once assume a position of high rank, fear of the French front, petty personal spite, these were the motives that led these men to desert their comrades. Our soldiers knew these men, and were glad that they were rid of them. The Soviet Government welcomed these deserters and supported them in every way possible. At Penza the Soviet named some of these deserters as their representatives on the commission which had charge of receiving the arms given up by the Czecho-Slavs. Other deserters holding documents from the Soviet political or military authorities insisted on coming into the Czecho-Slav échelons to carry on agitations for the Red army, and to determine if we did not have some arms hidden away.

These deserters, who called themselves social revolutionists, internationalists, and communists, often declared that the holding up of our transport and all the obstacles put in our path were for the purpose of causing dissension within our ranks and gaining as many recruits as possible for the Red army. They declared that this was the reason why the Soviet Government wished a part of the troops to go by way of Archangel; that somewhere on the way in a region where no food was to be had they planned to halt us and compel us from very hunger to join their ranks.

The Czecho-Slav National Council exercised all its influence with the army to keep them from taking stock in these tales, and to induce them to keep their patience, and as good soldiers not to make any reply to the unfaithfulness and insulting behavior of the Soviet Government.

The atmosphere was therefore highly charged with electricity when the Tcheliabinsk incident occurred. At Tcheliabinsk, besides the Czecho-Slav échelons, there stood several trains filled with prisoners on their way home to Austria and Germany. The relations between the Czecho-Slav soldiers and these prisoners was good, as it was uniformly whenever they came in contact with one another on the road. The soldiers did carry on an agitation amongst them against Austrian and German imperialism, and laughed at them for returning to serve once more under Austrian and German officers. But at the same time they felt sorry for them, and often shared their food with them. On May 14th, one of these prisoners threw a piece of iron out of a train that was just leaving, wounding one of the Czecho-Slav soldiers. The soldiers immediately surrounded the car from which the iron had been thrown, and demanded that the guilty prisoner be given up to them. When this was done, they immediately killed him.

In the course of the investigation of this affair, the local Soviet called as witnesses the members of the guard which had been on duty at the station. But instead of hearing their testimony, they put these men under arrest. A deputation which was later sent by the Czecho-Slavs to demand the release of the guard was likewise put under arrest. This illegal imprisonment of their fellows was more than the soldiers in the échelons at Tcheliabinsk could stand, and, led by their commanders, they marched into the city, released their imprisoned comrades, and returned immediately to their trains. No attack by force was made, the whole proceeding was conducted in an orderly and quiet manner, hardly a shot being fired.

The local Soviet proceeded to describe this action on the part of the Czecho-Slavs in lurid colors in telegrams sent out in all directions. Believing the information thus imparted to them, the Council of People's Commissioners issued an order to disarm completely all Czecho-Slav échelons. At the same time orders were issued to the Soviets of all cities where our échelons were then located to proceed against them by force. Accordingly, almost on the same day the Soviet forces, composed for the most part of Magyar and German prisoners of war, fell upon the Czecho-Slav échelons, which were almost entirely disarmed.

At the attack made upon échelons of the Sixth Czecho-Slav Regiment at Marianovka, near Omsk, the Czecho-Slavs suffered losses amounting to ten killed and ten severely wounded. The staff of the First Regiment, whose échelon was attacked at Zlatoust, defended itself with stones against the machine guns and rifles of the Bolsheviks, but lost six men killed and ten severely wounded, and was compelled to make its way across the Urals on foot. Similarly the staff of the Second Artillery Brigades was attacked at Imokentjeska, near Irkutsk, when they had already given up their arms. Machine guns placed in the windows of the railway station opened up a heavy fire upon the Czecho-Slavs, but in spite of the fact that the men had no arms except a few hand-grenades, they succeeded in clearing the station of Bolshevist forces and in capturing their machine guns. A fourth attack was made at Serodobsk, south from Penza. All of these attacks were made on May 27th and the following two or three days immediately after the issuance of the order from Moscow to disarm the Czecho-Slavs at any cost.

Prior to these events, but after the first incident at Tcheliabinsk, the Assembly of Czecho-Slav Soldiers met for its annual meeting and decided that in view of the tense situation existing between the Soviet Government and the Czecho-Slavs, vigorous measures must be taken immediately in order to secure the rapid passage of the trains toward Vladivostok. Accordingly delegates were dispatched to all échelons with instructions to proceed ahead at any cost, and an executive committee was appointed to see that these plans were carried out. The executive committee in formulating its plans counted on the probability of an armed conflict with the Bolshevik forces, but felt confident that they would be able to force their way through to Vladivostok in spite of any resistance that might be offered by the Soviet forces.

The reason for their confidence in the successful outcome

of their new plan lay not only in the well-known weakness of
the Red army, but also in the fact of their knowledge that
the people at large were sick and tired of the Bolshevist rule,
and that therefore they would not turn a hand to help the
Bolshevists in any possible conflict with the Czecho-Slavs.
Furthermore, the Czecho-Slavs, from their intimate knowledge of political conditions throughout Russia, judged that
the feeling against the Bolshevists was strongest in the very
regions where most of their échelons were located, namely in
the Urals and western Siberia.   The executive committee,
therefore, in planning their action, took cognizance of these
facts and planned to take advantage both of the weakness of
the Red army and of the strong popular feeling against
the Bolshevists to force their way through to the East.   That
their action would be accompanied by or followed by the
overthrow of the Soviet Government and the establishment
of a new government in western Siberia never entered into
their calculations, although later, when the fall of the Soviet
Government was an accomplished fact, the Czecho-Slavs
were the first to welcome the new government and to lend
it their moral and armed support.

The plans of the executive committee for the forcing
of the passage of Vladivostok had not been thoroughly
worked out when the events of May 25th brought things
to an issue.   By its cowardly attacks upon the Czecho-Slav
échelons the Soviet Government began a warfare against
the Czecho-Slavs, the object of which was, according to
the command of Trotsky, to disarm and disband the Czecho-
Slav army corps, place them in prison camps, and there try
to enlist them in the ranks of the Red army or to put them
out at hard labor.   In short, they wished to destroy entirely the Czecho-Slav army, that important moral support
of the revolutionary movement of the Czecho-Slovakia and
the other oppressed nationalities of Austria-Hungary.

After the first order to disarm completely the Czecho-
Slav échelons, there still remained the possibility of diplomatic negotiations.   But after the attack made upon the
échelons on May 25th-26th, the soul of each soldier cried out
for revenge for the blood of their innocent comrades.   And

so there was nothing left but war, a war which has already resulted in the seizure of almost the entire Siberian Railway by the Czecho-Slavs and the fall of the Soviet Government all along the line.

The Czecho-Slavs are convinced that the action taken against them by the Soviet Government was dictated from Berlin through the German ambassador in Moscow, Count Mirbach. This conviction is based on the opinion, very widely spread throughout Russia, that the Soviet Government is the paid agent of Germany. This conviction grew stronger as repeated attempts were made to disarm the soldiers, for the men could not but see in this disarmament real danger, knowing as they did that the Central Soviet Government was really powerless, and that in most places the chief strength of their armed forces consisted in armed German and Magyar prisoners.

For example, in Omsk the commander of the forces of the Internationalists, composed of prisoners, was an Austro-Hungarian officer, a Magyar by race. This officer, Ligeti by name, had all the Czecho-Slavs and other Slavs who were serving in the Red army disarmed, so that Omsk was really in the hands of this Austro-Hungarian officer. In Ishim the Red army was composed entirely of Magyars. In Petropavlovsk the men who came to negotiate with the Czecho-Slavs in the guise of Czech communists afterward proved to be the representatives of the German section of the Internationalists. The commanding officers of the Red army were in many cases Germans and Magyars, judging by the orders and the curses in those tongues that were heard on all sides during the battles. When the échelon was attacked near Irkutsk, there was heard the command: *"Schiessen."*

The conviction that the Soviet Government wished to destroy our forces was also strengthened by the constant holding up of the transport, for which no adequate cause could be found. At first the delay was blamed upon the Amur railway, where transportation was reported to have been halted. The advance of Semenov upon Irkutsk was given as an excuse. But the Czecho-Slavs soon learned that transportation on the Amur railway had been soon resumed, while the advance of Semenov existed more in the imagination of the Soviet authorities than in reality. Amongst other excuses given was that of a lack of locomotives on the Amur road, but all the while German prisoners were being merrily transported toward the west, and there were plenty of locomotives for them.

On April 20th the people's commissioner for foreign affairs, Tchitcherin, sent the following telegram to the Siberian Soviets: "Transport German prisoners as rapidly as possible toward the west. Hold back the Czecho-Slav échelons."

It was only after a long and tedious session of negotiations that there was secured an order for the renewal of our transport toward Vladivostok. One day, about May 15th, a member of the Czecho-Slav National Council was officially informed that the trains would now be moved. On the very next day, however, he learned through private conversation with the railway officials that another order had been issued in Irkutsk to stop the movements of the Czecho-Slav trains. He finally learned that this command had issued from the commander of the Soviet forces at Irkutsk, General von Taube, a German, whose adjutant had issued the order by "mistake."

The Seventh Czecho-Slav Regiment captured a German engineer, who had been commandeered from Moscow to destroy the bridges and tunnels on the railroad beyond the Baikal. In Troitsk the commanders of the Soviet artillery were all Austrian officers.

From all these facts even an uninterested onlooker may picture to himself the news which had been spread about the Czecho-Slav army. Inasmuch as the warfare is still being carried on on all sides, it has not been possible to gather all the evidence from the Soviet offices, and unfortunately in many cases the Bolsheviks succeeded in carrying away with them or destroying all their papers before our men took possession. Later, however, there will be certainly found many proofs of the truth of the assertion made by the president of the Tcheliabinsk Soviet and the military commissioner in that town, who informed our representatives in confidence, shortly before the outbreak of hostilities, that the cause of all the acts against the Czecho-Slavs was the German ambassador at Moscow.

BY THOMAS MASARYK

Announcement issued at Washington, D. C., on July 27, 1918, by authority of the Czecho-Slovak National Council, then acting at Washington under Thomas Masaryk as president.

There have been so many promising campaigns started in Russia during the last year of which nothing more is heard that the people in this country watch with a certain lack of confidence the successes of the Czecho-Slovak forces in Siberia and Eastern European Russia.

Will they be permanent or will they come to nothing, as did the ill-fated campaigns of Korniloff, the Don Cossacks, the various Siberian governments and many others? Can the Czecho-Slovaks stand their ground, a hundred thousand men among a hundred million, and are they not themselves talking about withdrawing from Russia?

It is, of course, well known that the Czecho-Slovaks are not Russians; that they are a well organized and thoroughly disciplined force recruited from former Austrian soldiers of the Bohemian and Slovak races, who surrendered to the Russians. The Czecho-Slovak Army in Russia was created in order to fight the Germans and the Austrians, and when Russia deserted the cause of the Allies, arrangements were made by Professor T. G. Masaryk, President of the Czecho-Slovak National Council and by virtue of that Commander in Chief of the Czecho-Slovak forces, with the allied representatives in Russia and also with the Bolsheviki to march the Czecho-Slovaks out of Russia and take them to the western front.

It should be kept clearly in mind that occupation of Russian territory or the restoration of an eastern front was not thought of when these arrangements were made, in February, 1918. It was due to one of those German blunders, like the one that brought America into the war, that the Czecho-Slovaks, instead of withdrawing from Russia, are now in control of Siberia and of considerable territory west of the Urals.

Under pressure of Austrian and German demands Trotsky tried to disarm the Czecho-Slovaks and put them in prison camps, with a view of turning them over to the Austrian authorities. The Czecho-Slovaks, being attacked, had to defend themselves, and as a result found themselves in control of the greatest portion of the Trans-Siberian Railroad and the Volga River. They were like Saul, who went to seek his father's asses and found a kingdom.

Professor Masaryk was by this time in America, and the Czecho-Slovak leaders, under the changed conditions, hesitated as to their course of action. The only orders they had were to take their forces to the Pacific. They had no desire to play policemen in Russia, and they realized that their position could not be indefinitely sustained unless they were assured of a steady flow of supplies. And yet the unparalleled strategic opportunities which their position gave them made a strong appeal to their imagination. This seems evident from the fact that, instead of withdrawing from European Russia, they occupied more cities on the Volga, stretching out their detachments in the direction of the Murman Coast.

A week ago Professor Masaryk received a lengthy cable report from the leader of the Czecho-Slovak forces in which the following words are found indicative of the present desires of these men:

"In our opinion it is most desirable and also possible to reconstruct a Russia-Germany front in the east. We ask for instructions as to whether we should leave for France or whether we should stay here to fight in Russia by the side of the Allies and of Russia. The health and spirit of our troops are excellent."

Professor Masaryk has since then instructed the forces in Siberia to remain there for the present. The question, however, of staying in Russia or getting out does not depend on the Czecho-Slovaks alone. That is something which must be decided by the Allies. The Czecho-Slovak Army is one of the allied armies, and it is as much under the orders of the Versailles War Council as the French or American Army. No doubt the Czecho-Slovak boys in Russia are anxious to avoid participation in a possible civil war in Russia, but they realize at the same time that by staying where they are they may be able to render far greater services, both to Russia and the allied cause, than if they were transported to France. They are at the orders of the Supreme War Council of the Allies.

BY ROBERT LANSING

U. S. Government announcement issued by Secretary Lansing, September 3, 1918, recognizing the Czecho-Slovaks

The Czecho-Slovak peoples having taken up arms against the German and Austro-Hungarian empires, and having placed in the field organized armies, which are waging war against those empires under officers of their own nationality and in accordance with the rules and practices of civilized nations, and Czecho-Slovaks having in the prosecution of their independence in the present war confided the supreme political authority to the Czecho-Slovak National Council, the Government of the United States recognizes that a state of belligerency exists between the Czecho-Slovaks thus organized and the German and Austro-Hungarian empires.

It also recognizes *the Czecho-Slovak National Council as a* de facto *belligerent government,* clothed with proper authority to direct the military and political affairs of the Czecho-Slovaks.

The Government of the United States further declares that it is prepared to enter formally into relations with the *de facto* government thus recognized for the purpose of prosecuting the war against the common enemy, the empires of Germany and Austria-Hungary.

THE CHIEF BLOW OF THE KAISERBATTLE

GERMANY BREAKS THE FRENCH LINE ON THE AISNE

MAY 27TH-30TH

JOHN BUCHAN   MAJOR MAX VON SCHREIBERSHOFEN
GENERAL HENRI BERTHAUT

Twice had the Germans struck terrific blows against the Western front, in March and again in April; and each time the Allied line had broken and the Allies had only saved themselves by a narrow margin from complete disaster. Had the Germans still strength for another blow? Ludendorff had declared he expected to sacrifice 400,000 men; and as yet he had suffered only about that number as a total of casualties. Many of these would soon be again available. Where would the next blow fall?

It came suddenly on May 27th and in the region where it was least expected. The army of the Crown Prince struck the French defenses along the *Chemin des Dames*, the line north of the Aisne which had been won by such long fighting in the preceding year. This time the success of the Germans was even greater than before. Just as they had in a few days snatched from the British the gains of a whole year of fighting, now they snatched the same from the French. Taken by surprise, the French troops found themselves surrounded by the "infiltration" method. Thousands of them were captured; their line was broken; from the *Chemin des Dames* they retreated hurriedly southward to the Aisne, and then to the Marne. Westward they fell back on Soissons to keep touch with the British line. Then, after desperate fighting, they lost Soissons. On the night of the last of May the Paris government officials talked of a second evacuation of their capital, another flight to Bordeaux like that of 1914.

The French defense, however, now stiffened splendidly. Once more the German blow had spent its strength. The battle became equal; and for a month of attack and counter-attack both sides held firm.

BY JOHN BUCHAN

L UDENDORFF had put his hand to the plow, and there could be no turning back. The stagnation of May was not part of his plan, but a sheer necessity to enable him to fill up the gaps in his ranks. He had lost almost half a million of men—not, indeed, more than he had bargained for, but in that bargain he had assumed a success which was

still denied him. By the last week of May he had replaced
more than 70 per cent. of his losses from men returned from
hospitals and the first part of the 1920 class. He had still
a real superiority in numbers over his antagonists; he had
the strategic initiative and the priceless advantage of interior
lines. He had not changed his main purpose. He still aimed
at separating the British and French armies, and for him
the vital terrain was still the Somme. But he did not consider that the time was ripe for the final blow, and he resolved to repeat his Lys experiment, and strike first in a
different area, with the object of exhausting Foch's reserves
and stripping bare his center.

There were many inducements to this course. Repeated
blows at widely separated sections would compel the moving of Allied supports round the big outer edge of the salient;
would certainly give him local successes; and might, in the
precarious position of the Allies, supply just that finishing
stroke which would disintegrate their entire defense. He and
his colleagues had always Russia in mind. He had treated
the Russian front in this way, and by-and-by had come the
Revolution when the heart and limbs of Russia failed her.
Might not the sentimental democracies of the West be driven
down the same road? He had still some five months of cam-
paigning before him, and he did not believe that America
would prove a serious factor in the war before the winter.
His time limits were inexorable, but the allowance seemed
still sufficient.

The new terrain must be of the same type as the Lys—
that is, it must be sufficiently remote from the center to make
reënforcement difficult, and it must threaten some vital possession of the Allies. He found such an area in the Heights
of the Aisne.[1] It was the nearest point to Paris; it was a
path to the Marne; and an advance beyond that river would
cut the Paris-Chalons railways and imperil the whole French
front in Champagne. He could concentrate troops for the
attack in the angle of the salient, so that, as on March 21st,
the Allies could not guess his intention. And, having re-

---

[1] The British Staff from the month of April onward had been
confident that the next German blow would be in this area.

newed his shock troops, he could once again use the deadly
tactics of March, to which Foch as yet seemed to have found
no answer.

About the 20th of May the Army group of the Crown
Prince had mustered some forty divisions for the attempt,
twenty-five for the first wave and fifteen in reserve. The
two armies allotted to the task were : on the right, the VIIth
Army, under von Boehn ; and, on the left, the Ist Army, under
Fritz von Below. They lay between the Ailette and Rheims,
wholly to the north and east of the plateau; while on the
heights was part of the group of Franchet d'Esperey, the
French Sixth Army, under General Maistre, with only the
11th Corps of four divisions in line. On the French right
lay the British 9th Corps, which had been recently withdrawn from Flanders. It held the California Plateau and
Craonne, and extended as far south as Berméricourt, with
three divisions in line. Around Rheims lay the French Fifth
Army, with, on its right, General Gouraud's Fourth Army
extending into Champagne. The British divisions, which
were depleted and tired after their two months' struggle,
had been brought to the section to rest. The weakness of
the Allied front—seven divisions to hold a line of thirty
miles—was no fault of the High Command, but due simply
to the exigencies of the great battle. If a force is outnumbered it must be content to be thin at many points, and the
Aisne was not the only, or, so far as could be judged, the
most critical area on the western front.

We have seen that Ludendorff began the Lys battle with
an attack of nine divisions, a modest complement suitable
for a subsidiary operation. We have seen, too, that he was
gradually drawn by unexpected success into a gross expenditure of men. The new plan marked a further weakening in
the rigor of his first strategy. A thirty-mile front and
twenty-five divisions of assault were on a scale too great
for a legitimate diversion. He still held to his main plan,
but he was fumbling in his methods, and he had chosen an
ill place for one prone to temptation. For Paris lay in the
southwest beyond the forests, and the lure of a capital city

is hard to resist for the soldier, and harder for the politicians behind him.

Ludendorff employed many of the same troops, including three divisions of the Prussian Guard, as had led the assault on March 21st. Both in the secrecy of his concentration [2] and in the precision of his new tactics he far exceeded his previous record. Never, perhaps, during the whole campaign did the great German war machine move so noiselessly and so fast. On the evening of Sunday, May 26th, all was quiet in the threatened area.

At one o'clock on the morning of Monday, the 27th, a sharp bombardment began everywhere from the Ailette to the suburbs of Rheims. At four o'clock the infantry advanced, and in an hour or two had swept the French from the crest of the ridge. The odds were too desperate, and the four weak French divisions were smothered under weight of numbers and artillery. The 11th Corps early in the morning was back on the southern slopes of the heights, and by the afternoon was on the Aisne itself, five miles from its old positions. By 8 a. m. three French divisions from reserve had attempted to hold a line on the southern bank of the river covering the crossings. They were swept aside, and the vanguard of von Conta's corps crossed by the French bridges, and before nightfall had reached the Vesle: a total advance of twelve miles, and far beyond anything that had been accomplished on March 21st.

By the evening the French front ran from the Ailette, near Leuilly, by Neuville-sur-Margival to the Aisne at Condé, and then in a crescent on the southern bank by Braisne, Quincy, and Mont-Notre-Dame to south of Fismes. Large numbers of prisoners and an immense store of booty had fallen into von Boehn's hands.

At first Fritz von Below fared less well against the British 9th Corps. It was forced back to its second position, but resisted gallantly for most of the day. The 21st, between Cormicy and Berméricourt, with a French Colonial Division on its right, held its ground throughout the day.

[2] The first news of the impending attack came from prisoners taken by the French on the 26th.

The 8th, around Berry-au-Bac, stood firm till the afternoon, when the pressure on the west forced it across the river. The 50th, at Craonne, had the hardest task of all, for the retreat of the French uncovered its left flank, and it was slowly driven back to the Aisne, after making a heroic effort to recapture the Craonne plateau. That evening the line of the 9th Corps ran from Berméricourt westward through Cormicy and Bouffignereux, to link up precariously with the French northeast of Fismes.

The battle had now reached the district of the Tardenois, that upland which is the watershed between Aisne and Marne. The countryside is broken up into many hollows, but the center is open and full of excellent roads. On the west and southwest lie big patches of forest, of which the great wood of Villers-Cotterets is the chief. It is cut in the middle by the stream of the Ourcq, flowing westward, and farther east by the long and shallow valley of the Vesle. On the south it breaks down sharply to the Marne, and an enemy coming from the north by the plateau commands all the flatter southern shore.

It was Ludendorff's desire to push for the Marne at his best speed; but the difficulty lay with his flanks. So long as Soissons and Rheims held he would be forced by every day's advance into a narrowing salient. His advantage was that the French line had been completely broken, and that some days must elapse before serious resistance could be made to his triumphant center. At all costs he must broaden the salient, and on the 28th he succeeded in forcing back the containing Allied wings. On his right he drove the French to the line Venizel-Serches-Lesges, and on his left he compelled the British 9th Corps to retire to positions running well south of the Vesle by Crugny to Muizon. In the center the French were south of Lhuys and Chéry and Courville. He did more, for on his extreme right, between the Aisne and the Ailette, he captured Sancy, and won a line from Pont-St. Mard by Terny to Bray. He was now on the heights overlooking Soissons from the north and close on the town in the river flats to the east.

That day an event happened which might well have given

food for thought to the German Command. American troops had been before this date engaged in minor actions in Lorraine, but now for the first time they took part in the main battle. The 1st United States Division, brigaded with the Third French Army, attacked in the Montdidier section, and took the village of Cantigny, along with 170 prisoners. Three furious counter-attacks by the enemy failed to retake the place. It was much that a new division should thus neatly and efficiently carry out an offensive, but that they should be able to consolidate and hold their gains was a real achievement and a happy augury for the future.

On Wednesday, the 29th, the broadening of the salient began in earnest, and Soissons fell. All the day before it had been hotly shelled, and in some places set on fire; and on the morning of the 29th the enemy, strengthened by fresh divisions, pushed in from the east and entered its streets. They were driven out after severe fighting, but returned to the attack in the afternoon, and compelled the French to retire to the plateau west and south of the town. Fritz von Below, on the German left, had also increased his forces, and succeeded in pressing the British and French troops on the Allied right off the upland of St. Thierry. That day there was a general falling back everywhere, and at night the Allied line ran from La Neuvillette north of Rheims, well to the south of Crugny, south of Arcis le Ponsart, through the station of Fère-en-Tardenois, and then northwest by Cuiry-Housse, Septmonts, and Belleu, to the west of Soissons, and so to Juvigny and Pont St. Mard.

Next day the German center made a strong forward thrust. It was the second main attack of the battle, and its aims were to reach the Marne, and to destroy the two pillars of the Allied front at Soissons and Rheims. The first was immediately successful. During the morning the German vanguard appeared on the hills above the Marne between Château-Thierry and Dormans, and by the evening the enemy was in possession of some ten miles of the north bank of the river. He was less fortunate on his flanks. He failed entirely to debouch from Soissons. In the east La Neuvillette fell, and he won a foothold in Bétheny, but he was checked in front of Rheims. That night the Allied front lay from Rheims by Vrigny, Ville-en-Tardenois, and Jonquery to Dormans; then along the right bank of the Marne to just east of Château-Thierry; then northwest by Oulchy-la-Ville, Missy-au-Bois, and Tartiers to the original line at Pontoise.

The enemy had now cause to consider his position. His achievement had been brilliant—an advance of over thirty miles in seventy-two hours, the occupation of ten miles of the Marne shore, between 30,000 and 40,000 prisoners, and some 400 guns. But there were anxious elements in his success. He had used up most of the fresh divisions of the Crown Prince's reserve, and though Prince Rupprecht had twenty more, and the Duke of Wurtemberg and General von Gallwitz at least four fresh divisions to spare, it would be unwise to squander the total mass of maneuver in what had been intended as a diversion. But the position won was such that it offered no safe resting-place; the battle must be continued, or the gains must be relinquished. It is a good working rule that a salient on a formed front should not be in depth more than a third of its base. But von Boehn had far exceeded this proportion, and he found himself forced through too narrow a gate. There was nothing for it but to carry away the gate-posts—to halt the center while the flanks came into line.

The more dangerous wing was the German right, which followed roughly the high road from Soissons to Château-Thierry. If von Boehn could press out in that direction he would enlarge the borders of his salient, and, by outflanking the Soissons heights, break down that vital gate-post. Accordingly, on the morning of the 31st he performed the military operation known as "forming front to a flank." He drove back the French from the southern bank of the Oise and Aisne Canal between Guny and Noyon, and he pressed down the valley of the Ourcq as far as Neuilly St. Front. North of that point his front ran by Vierzy to Missy, and south of it through Bois-du-Châtelet and Verdilly to the northeast of Château-Thierry.

Next day, Saturday, June 1st, it was the turn of Fritz von Below, who attacked at Rheims with tanks on the left flank of the German salient and at first made ground. A French counter-attack later in the day drove him back and captured four of his tanks. Northwest of Soissons von Boehn made a half-hearted effort, and southwest of the town the French won back some ground, and checked further enemy progress down the south bank of the Aisne. On Sunday, June 2nd, both German armies made a resolute attempt to break the gate-posts. Von Below, with five divisions, attacked at Vrigny, southwest of Rheims, but failed to advance. Von Boehn drove hard against the western flank, occupied the northern part of Château-Thierry and the high riverside ground as far as Chézy-sur-Marne, and enlarged his holding farther north in the neighborhood of Chézy-en-Orzois.

But he made no progress down the Ourcq, for the French had brought up reserves in that area, and had found a line which they could defend. Just east of the great forest of Villers-Cotterets runs the little river Savières, in a deep gorge with precipitous sides. It falls into the Ourcq at Troesnes, whence an irregular line of heights stretches southward in front of Passy and Torcy. All this line, which was of some strength, was recaptured by the French by the Sunday evening, with the exception of the hamlet of Faverolles, where the Germans had still a footing. That day marked the farthest limit of von Boehn's success in this area, for, though he continued his efforts for another week, he made comparatively small progress. The Crown Prince had used forty-one divisions in the week's battle, and had practically exhausted his own reserves, but he had not drawn upon the resources of the neighboring group commanders.

The situation was still very grave, for the French line had been greatly lengthened, it bristled with vulnerable points, and there was scanty room to maneuver. Paris was dangerously near the new front, and the loss of Paris meant far more than the loss of a capital. Earlier in the campaign the great city might have fallen without bringing upon the Allies irreparable disaster. But in the past two years it was in the environs of Paris that many of the chief new munition factories had arisen. If these were lost the Allied strength would be grievously crippled, and after four years of war it was doubtful whether France had the power to replace them.

On Monday, the 3rd, there was heavy fighting around Torcy, where the Germans tried to push down the little valley of the Clignon; between Troesnes and Faverolles; and on the Chaudun plateau, southwest of Soissons, where von Boehn was endeavoring to turn the Villers-Cotterets forest by its northern end. The struggle was bitter; but the French reaction had clearly begun, and on their extreme left they recovered the southern part of the hill of Choisy, which overlooks the Oise. On the Tuesday there was a lull, and on Wednesday, the 5th, the French repulsed an attempt to cross the Oise near Mont Lagache. American troops had come into action on the western and southern side of the salient, and counter-attacked with success west of Torcy at the wood of Neuilly-la-Poterie, and defeated an attempt to ford the Marne at Jaulgonne, northeast of Château-Thierry.

On Thursday, the 6th, the Germans were forced back a mile at Torcy, and that night the British 19th Division retook the village of Bligny, eight miles to the southwest of Rheims. On the 7th the French and Americans took Neuilly-la-Poterie and Bouresches, and the French captured the important Hill 204, above Château-Thierry. Von Boehn had exhausted his strength, and had called a halt; and, according to their practice in such lulls, the Germans announced the results of their victory—55,000 prisoners and 650 guns. They were clearly preparing a blow elsewhere, and Foch waited anxiously for news of it.

It came on the morning of Sunday, the 9th, and, as had been expected, from another army. This time it was the turn of von Hutier. It had proved impossible to carry away the gate-posts by means of the two armies already engaged, so it was necessary to bring the force on their right into action. At midnight on the 8th an intense bombardment began in the Montdidier-Noyon section, and at dawn on the 9th von Hutier attacked with fifteen divisions on a front of twenty-five miles. In the next three days three more divisions were drawn in, and of the eighteen five were from the reserve of Prince Rupprecht.

The Allied front between Montdidier and Noyon had for its main feature the group of low hills south of Lassigny, between the stream of the Matz and the Oise. West of the Matz the line ran through an open country of plowland and rolling downs. East of it the front curved round the northern skirts of the hills, which were thickly wooded and rose to some 400 feet above the surrounding levels. They formed a continuous ridge except at their western end, where one summit was separated by a sharp valley, with the village of Gury at its northern end. If von Hutier could thrust down the Matz he would turn the uplands, and so get rid of the main natural obstacle between him and Compiègne. The main strategic object of Ludendorff was now to secure the front Compiègne-Château-Thierry, from which he could threaten Paris. Already his greater scheme, though not consciously relinquished, was growing dim, and the lure of the capital was overmastering him. Further, he had to release von Boehn from the awkward narrows in which he was wedged.

On most of the front of attack von Hutier failed, for there was no element of surprise, and Foch was ready for him. But in the center along the Matz there was a local success. The enemy advanced some three miles, took the isolated hill above Gury, and got as far as the village of Ressons, in the south. Next day the three miles became six, and the Germans were in Marquéglise and Elincourt, in the center; on their left they entered the Bois de Thiescourt; and on their right took the villages of Méry, Belloy, and St. Maur. The extreme French left, between Rubescourt and Courcelles, stood firm. That evening the French front ran from Mesnil St. Georges, in the west, by Le Ployron, Courcelles, Marest, Montigny, and La Bernardie, to the south of Cannectancourt.

The battle was now one of dogged resistance, and, for the enemy, slow and costly progress, very different to the Aisne action a fortnight before. But Foch could not afford to take risks, so that night he shortened his line by evacuating the salient south of Noyon, between Nampcel and Montigny. Measures were also taken for the defense of Paris should the enemy advance continue.

It was blazing June weather, the ground was bone-dry, and all the conditions favored the attackers. But a new thing had begun to appear in the campaign. The enemy continued his former tactics, but they were less successful. The French were notably quick in counter-attack, and this discomfited the shock-troops in their infiltration, for it is small use finding weak spots in a front if you are checked before you can take advantage of them. The French reserves were still scanty, and the defense was still heavily outnumbered, but the odds were not so fantastic as in March and April, and in their hundreds of thousands America was landing her troops. Already some of them had been in the line, and at Cantigny and Château-Thierry had shown their brilliant quality.

The battle-front was now gigantic, not less than 100 miles from Mesnil St. Georges to Rheims. For the remainder of the month there was a ding-dong struggle, no side gaining any real advantage, for both were near the end of their endurance. On the 11th the French retook Méry and Belloy, and advanced their line nearly two miles on a front of four between Gournay and Courcelles. Farther east they pressed back the enemy from the Matz River, and repulsed a German attack along the Ribecourt-Compiègne road. That same day, between the Ourcq and the Marne, the Americans made a fine advance at Belleau Wood, and took 300 prisoners. On the 12th the Germans had some success between Ribecourt and Marest, and took the latter village, as well as Chevincourt and Machemont and Melicocq. Just south of the Aisne they made another advance—two miles on a front of three—and reached the outskirts of Ambleny and St. Bandry. The only French gain was at Melicocq, where they won the southern bank of the Matz from Marest to the Oise.

On the 13th the enemy made a great effort between Courcelles and Méry, and again between Bouresches and Belleau, but failed utterly with heavy losses. That day von Hutier's

subsidiary operation may be said to have closed, and closed
without any serious gain. He had squandered twenty odd
divisions, and the fresh reserves left to Prince Rupprecht
were again no more than twenty. The tide of assault in the
west was slowly ebbing.

Having failed on his right flank, the Crown Prince
made a final effort on his left. On June 18th Fritz von
Below attacked at Rheims on a front of ten miles, between
Vrigny, on the southwest, and the fort of La Pompelle, on
the southeast of the city. He hoped to take Rheims, but
he underrated the defense, and used only three divisions.
The place was a vital road junction for the Allies, and,
though encircled on three sides, it had held out most stoutly
during the battle, much aided by the fact that the Allies
held the great *massif* of the Mountain of Rheims to the south
and southwest. Von Below's attempt was futile, but the
fiasco seems to have impressed the German Staff with the
necessity of a serious effort against the Mountain if they
were to make any headway beyond the Marne. Of this impression we shall presently see the fruits.

For the better part of a month silence fell on the battlefront, broken only by local attacks of the French and British,
which in every case were successful, for the enemy was holding most of his front thinly with indifferent troops. He
was preparing another blow, as all the omens indicated, and
it was likely that this blow would be his last. It was certain
that it would be on a great scale, and would be delivered
with desperate resolution, for the summer days were slipping by, and Germany waited the fulfillment of Ludendorff's
pledge.

So far, in three great actions, he had strategically failed.
He had taken heavy toll of the Allies; but he had himself
suffered colossally, and his casualties were now mounting
fast to the limit which he had named as the price of victory.
The climax of the battle—and of the war—was approaching, and Foch faced it with an easier mind; for he saw his
army growing daily as the Americans came into line, and
he could now spend more lavishly since he was sure of his
ultimate reserves. More important still, he had solved the

problem of how to meet the new German tactics, and was ready with a method of his own in which this great master of modern war had borrowed from his opponents, and glorified and transformed the borrowings.

BY MAJOR MAX VON SCHREIBERSHOFEN

A semi-official statement issued in July, 1918

For weeks the entire west front had been under a mighty tension. A great amount of puzzling and guessing had been going on in the newspapers of the Entente about the progress of the German offensive; now the tension has been relieved, the riddle is solved, the veil which had been spread over the aims of the German offensive has been lifted. The armies of von Boehn and von Below, which belong to the army group of the German Crown Prince, took the offensive between Soissons and the region north of Rheims and surprised their opponent completely.

After the first German victories on both sides of the Somme, and on the Flanders front, the newly appointed Generalissimo, General Foch, had gathered all his reserves north of Amiens to support the English front and to oppose the German advance upon Amiens and Calais. He so firmly counted upon the German offensive in this direction that he drew from the other sectors the fresh troops toward Amiens, and in their place sent the worn English divisions to relieve them. The German command had reached its objective in the attacks on the Somme and the Lys; the destruction of a part of the hostile forces and the engaging of the enemy's reserves. There was no compelling reason to continue the attack on the previous battle-grounds; for the whole offensive was not a matter of occupying a definite territory, nor of gaining a single base or fortified position, but simply of destroying the hostile forces and resources. It did not matter where this was done. If General Foch took precautionary measures against a German offensive on the Somme and near Ypres, then this gave all the more reason why the commanders of the German Army should start the combat in some other place.

It had already been declared at the beginning of the

big offensive in France, on the 21st of March, that, owing to
the character of a modern national war, it was impossible to
conquer the opponent by a single mighty blow, but rather
that his entire military and national power could only be
overcome gradually; that the operations, therefore, were consisting of a series of independent battles which need not necessarily be bound up together either as to time or place, but
which had only a common final aim, the destruction of the
enemy. In this manner the operations were conducted; first
of all, the attack on both sides of the Somme, then the advance on the Lys, and now the great offensive on the Aisne.
Even if each one of these enterprises represents an independent operation, they nevertheless form a connected whole,
and gear into each other like the ingenious work of a clock.
In their reciprocal action the brilliancy of the plan is fully
apparent.

The German attack on the 27th of May spread over a
front about 40 kilometers broad, and was directed on the
part of the army of von Boehn on the west wing against
the enemy's position on the range of hills between the Aisne
and the Ailette, on whose plateau runs the much-talked-of
Chemin des Dames; on the part of the army of von Below
on the east wing from the sector Berry-au-Bac up to and
including the range of hills of the Brimont, the attack was
directed toward the Aisne-Marne Canal. The direction of
attack of the two armies did not run parallel, but led to an
extensive action as the army of von Boehn pressed forward
from north to south, and the army of von Below from east
to west.

A hot and embittered struggle has often occurred for
the possession of the heights along the *Chemin-des-Dames.*
There the German armies had come to a halt again after
the retreat from the Marne in September, 1914, and had
successfully repulsed the attacks of General Joffre. Of the
numerous attempts by the French to pierce the German line
during the following years, the most noteworthy was the
great spring offensive of General Nivelle in April, 1917.
Not until the French had made a wedge in the German lines
in the projecting Laffaux-angle northeast of Soissons was

the German military command induced methodically to evacuate the ridge of hills along the *Chemin-des-Dames* and to withdraw beyond the Ailette. (First to second of November, 1917.) After that time the French were in possession of it, but had been unable to penetrate beyond.

An unusually difficult task was assigned to the army of von Boehn, for it had to cross the Ailette Valley under the enemy's fire, and to take the strongly fortified position on the heights by storm, from below. But owing to the extraordinary achievements of the troops, it performed its task in a brilliant manner. Already in the forenoon the position of the enemy was captured. But this was not enough. The enemy was driven back upon the Ailette; the German troops followed irresistibly; in the afternoon several crossings were gained in several places along a broad front, and the evening saw the victorious troops in possession of the hilly territory. At the same time the army of von Below had gained the crossing over the Aisne-Marne Canal, had conquered the enemy's east wing, and had considerably lightened the advance of von Boehn's army by a flank attack.

A new obstacle to the further advance of the German troops to the south presented itself in front, namely, the Vesle sector. It offered to the vanquished enemy the possibility of making a stand, and, strengthened by reserves, of presenting fresh resistance. It was, therefore, doubtful whether the German advance could be continued. But the impetuous rush of the German infantry left to the opponent no time to establish himself and to organize a defense according to plan. The forenoon of the second day of the battle saw the German troops on both sides of Fismes on the southern shore of the Vesle, in possession of the heights there. Thus this hindrance was also successfully overcome. Both wings of the armies had simultaneously worked their way forward in the direction of Soissons in the west and of Rheims in the east, and had approached the two cities to within a distance of five kilometers.

On the third day of the battle Soissons was taken and the forts of the northwest front of Rheims were captured. South of the Vesle the new front of the French which was just being formed collapsed, and the enemy was thrown back upon the Marne by the way of Fère-en-Tardenois. The number of prisoners had already increased to 45,000 on the 31st of May; the capture of war material was immense. Cannon of all kinds, inclusive of railway artillery of the heaviest caliber, were taken. Extensive munition depots, railway trains, hospitals, and aviation stations fell into our hands.

General Foch found himself in an unusually difficult position. He had collected his reserves north of Amiens and confronted the difficult question of whether he should leave them there, because he still had to count upon the possibility of a German attack on Amiens and Calais, and because he had to consider the English allies whom he could not leave to themselves. His attempt to hinder the advance of the Germans by the use of his reserves behind the Vesle sector was frustrated by the impetuous spirit of attack of our troops, who pressed on to the Marne.

As to the further development of the German operations we had to count, first of all, upon an increased use of the enemy's reserves, for the French had time to bring up troops lying at a greater distance. Moreover, the difficulties of communication with the rear, and of the bringing up of the reserves at the right time were enormous. There is a lack of great thoroughfares and railways from north to south. It was, therefore, not likely that the offensive could be carried on as speedily as in the past. We had to count rather upon its slowing down; perhaps even reckon on a pause for rest in the future. One can also see at a glance where the German command had set a limit to its goal. The German success on the Aisne was a logical consequence and development of the earlier attacks on the Somme and the Flanders front; it was a necessary step on the long road toward the gradual conquest of the enemy's national and military powers; and at the same time formed a very favorable foundation for the continuation of the operations and the gaining of the final victory.

BY HENRI BERTHAUT

The great German offensive of May 27th began on the line of the Ailette River. It extended from the forest of Pinon near Ainsy-le-Château, eastward to the neighborhood of Rheims, a distance of some thirty-five miles. The assault at the western end seemed to have for its purpose to attack our lines from two directions and so enclose within the advance our naturally strong positions along the *Chemin des Dames,* that is, the line of the Ailette River and behind that and far more important the line of the Aisne River.

It should be noted that the great southward bend in the trench line beyond Corbeny aided this purpose of the enemy by enabling him to drive in behind our line of the *Chemin des Dames.* Nevertheless, his advance would have been almost impossibly difficult if we had only taken care beforehand to fortify strongly the edge of the Paris basin. This would have given us a second line of defense parallel to the first, which extended from Corbeny southward to Rheims.

However, the main German attack met with such complete success that the foe had no need to attempt the encircling of the *Chemin des Dames* lines. On the first day of attack, he won the entire front of the Ailette, charged across it and swept over the entire length of the *Chemin des Dames,* left that behind, and even reached the Aisne River itself at several points. On the morrow he seized the Aisne along its whole length from Vailly to Berry-au-Bac.

The numerical superiority of the Germans in this attack was enormous. The French and British troops fell back fighting hard. The strong positions south of the Aisne were stormed in their turn. The retreating battle continued between the Aisne and the next river to the southward, the Vesle. Further west the original flanking attack approached toward Soissons. By the evening of the 28th the Vesle itself was crossed by the enemy at Fismes.

This time once more the German preparations which had enabled them to gain so brilliant a victory, had been accomplished with great secrecy. We must realize that they had shown remarkable skill in lulling our watchfulness to sleep. The preceding offensive to the westward had been checked. The great German salient which had for years pointed toward Soissons had been wholly reconstructed, so that its apex now lay beyond Montdidier some twenty miles further westward. One was justified in thinking that the enemy would continue his successful operations in that direction, driving his pathway southwestward above Paris or northwestward down the Somme. It was known that he had gathered mighty forces just behind this region. It was, however, precisely this gathering of strength in the very middle of the salient which had enabled him to strike in whatever direction he chose, while still concealing from us the aim of his blow.

Our lines both on the Ailette and on the Aisne were so strong that an assault against them seemed most improbable. The enemy ensnared us in a false security. His troops, it is said, were brought to the front little by little, marching only at night, hiding by day in the villages and in the woods. Thus they were able to gather unsuspected masses in the forests of Coucy and St. Gobain, and amid the wooded hills north of the Ailette. It seems also that full freedom was allowed our aviators; they were not attacked along this seemingly quiet front. They could search at will; and they discovered nothing. In brief, when the assault came the surprise was complete.

In France the loss of the *Chemin des Dames* aroused much angry protest. That of the line of the Aisne passed almost without comment; yet our real defenses lay along the Aisne. The public, however, knew only the *Chemin des Dames,* about which army reports and newspaper articles had long been speaking. The *Chemin* had been the scene of endless battle, the enemy had there resisted us most obstinately; whereas the defenses of the Aisne, being in the rear, had never been subjects of public discussion. Never before had the German been in a position to attack them, because we had so early in the war dislodged him from the south bank of the Aisne.

That a sudden, strong attack, so wholly unexpected, had caused us to lose, as in a single instant, the whole *Chemin des D'ames,* that is easily explained by the skillful tactics of the foe. The immediate fall of the strong defenses of the Aisne is less easily excusable. We can but state the facts.

On May 29th the Germans carried also the entire line of the Vesle River. Thus we had not only lost our first and second lines, but also a third line almost as strong as the second.

Next, we had to fight desperately in the streets of Soissons; and from those too we were driven by the crowding numbers of the foe. We abandoned Soissons; we fell back to the region of Fère-en-Tardenois; Rheims was threatened with encirclement. Next, Ville-en-Tardenois was attacked. Fortunately our right held firm; our soldiers could not be driven from the forests at the base of the mountain of Rheims. Our Italian allies stationed near there made also a resolute defense, and a month later they aided in driving back the enemy.

During this retreating struggle, as in the earlier one of March, the region between the two, the lower valley of the Ailette remained almost unattacked. But the advance which the Germans had now won on either side of this region compelled us to abandon it. We withdrew toward the plateau of Soissons. But, just as on our right we had been able to hold the forest of the Rheims mountain, so on our left we were able to defend the rocky forest heights of Laigue and Compiègne and Villers-Cotterets. The fighting here was bitter and not unequal. The pocket which the enemy had made in our line grew deeper, but he could not broaden it either to right or left, where we held these forest heights on either side. That was the essential point of the entire battle.

On May 31st the Germans, still deepening their pocket, reached to the Marne at Jaulgonne, south of Fère-en-Tardenois. Château-Thierry was threatened. Then we were driven back westward along the Ourcq River valley. The

foe extended his hold along the north bank of the Marne.
We evacuated Château-Thierry.[3]

During the opening days of June, the battle became more
equal. We could no longer be driven back. The German assaults against the forest of Villers-Cotterets were numerous
and powerful, but the enemy was held. He was also repelled along the Ourcq.[4] By the 4th of June his offensive
seemed exhausted. On the 5th the new line of defense was
definitely established. It stretched from Carlepont on the
north, to the Aisne River near Fontenay, then along the
border of the Villers Cotteret forest and across the Ourcq
to Bouresches, then to the Marne at Château-Thierry, and
eastward along the Marne to the border of those woods which
adjoin the forest of the mountain of Rheims.

For over a month this front was allowed to remain inactive. The calm was broken only by some minor counter-
attacks at Bouresches and around Château-Thierry.[5]

[3] This was when the Americans came forward and held the half of
Château-Thierry south of the Marne preventing the foe from crossing
the river. See later section.

[4] This also was in part the work of the Americans.

[5] Again the Americans.

EUROPE'S CRY TO AMERICA FOR INSTANT HELP

CANTIGNY, THE FIRST INDEPENDENT AMERICAN ATTACK

MAY 28TH-JUNE 2ND

GENERAL PERSHING   GEORGES CLEMENCEAU
VITTORIO ORLANDO   DAVID LLOYD GEORGE
MAJOR FREDERICK PALMER

How near Europe stood to destruction in those spring days of 1918 is best left to the Europeans themselves to tell. Note General Pershing's official authorization of the statement that a million startled citizens had abandoned Paris by early June. Read the startling appeal sent to America by the three Prime Ministers. General Foch himself had warned them that if America could not speedily come to their aid with largely increased forces, there was "immediate danger of an Allied defeat in the present campaign." To such a point of weakness and of danger had Germany's strength and persistence reduced all Europe.

Up to this time the American troops had been receiving a thorough training before being sent to the front. The Allied governments had accepted the idea that the Americans were to drill their great army during 1918, and attack with it in 1919. All aggressive plans had been postponed until then; the current year was to have been merely defensive. Now, however, it seemed startlingly clear that even the defensive could not last through the year without American help. Could America fight instantly with her half-trained troops? And could she bring more, in ever increasing numbers, to back up the relatively small number of 300,000 who had been in France by the end of March?

How well they increased their numbers General Pershing tells. As to the fighting efficiency of the men, there came at this very moment the first full, clear test—Cantigny. A Division from the former U. S. "regular army" had been thrown into the first line to aid the French and British near Montdidier, where the first break had carried the Germans in March. These Americans were directed to make a counter-attack and recapture Cantigny. They were to organize and carry out the assault wholly by themselves. Major Frederick Palmer, the noted American war-correspondent, has written a book of what he himself saw in France. His picture of that Cantigny assault is as simply clear and complete as was the assault itself. His narrative is reprinted here.

As to the effect of Cantigny upon the French, it was tremendous. General Foch suddenly saw the Americans with new eyes, and looked upon the War with a new and eager hope. It was immediately after Cantigny that he called for American troops, and he at once began

184

to employ their untrained regiments to meet the full shock of the German attack, to assume the full responsibility of France's earlier slogan, "They shall not pass!"

C. F. H.

BY GENERAL PERSHING

AT a meeting of the Supreme War Council held at Abbeville May 1st and 2nd, the entire question of the amalgamation of Americans with the French and British was reopened. An urgent appeal came from both French and Italian representatives for American replacements or units to serve with their armies. After prolonged discussion regarding this question and that of priority generally the following agreement was reached, committing the Council to an independent American Army and providing for the immediate shipment of certain troops:

"It is the opinion of the Supreme War Council that, in order to carry the war to a successful conclusion, an American Army should be formed as early as possible under its own commander and under its own flag. In order to meet the present emergency it is agreed that American troops should be brought to France as rapidly as Allied transportation facilities will permit, and that, as far as consistent with the necessity of building up an American Army, preference will be given to infantry and machine-gun units for training and service with French and British Armies; with the understanding that such infantry and machine-gun units are to be withdrawn and united with its own artillery and auxiliary troops into divisions and corps at the direction of the American Commander-in-Chief after consultation with the Commander-in-Chief of the Allied Armies in France.

"Subparagraph A. It is also agreed that during the month of May preference should be given to the transportation of infantry and machine-gun units of six divisions, and that any excess tonnage shall be devoted to bringing over such other troops as may be determined by the American Commander-in-Chief.

"Subparagraph B. It is further agreed that this program shall be continued during the month of June upon condition that the British Government shall furnish transportation for a minimum of 130,000 men in May and 150,000 men in June, with the understanding that the first six divisions of infantry shall go to the British for training and service, and that troops sent over in June shall be allocated for training and service as the American Commander-in-Chief may determine.

"Subparagraph C. It is also further agreed that if the British Government shall transport an excess of 150,000 men in June that such excess shall be infantry and machine-gun units, and that early in June there shall be a new review of the situation to determine further action."

The gravity of the situation had brought the Allies to a full realization of the necessity of providing all possible tonnage for the transportation of American troops. Although their views were accepted to the extent of giving a considerable priority to infantry and machine gunners, the priority agreed upon as to this class of troops was not as extensive as some of them deemed necessary, and the Abbeville conference was adjourned with the understanding that the question of further priority would be discussed at a conference to be held about the end of May.

The next offensive of the enemy was made between the Oise and Berry-au-Bac against the French instead of against the British, as was generally expected, and it came as a complete surprise. The initial Aisne attack, covering a front of 35 kilometers, met with remarkable success, as the German armies advanced no less than 50 kilometers in four days. On reaching the Marne that river was used as a defensive flank and the German advance was directed toward Paris. During the first days of June something akin to a panic seized the city and it was estimated that 1,000,000 people left during the spring of 1918.

The further conference which had been agreed upon at Abbeville was held at Versailles on June 1st and 2nd. The opinion of our Allies as to the existing situation and the urgency of their insistence upon further priority for infantry and machine gunners are shown by the following message prepared by the Prime Ministers of Great Britain, France, and Italy, and agreed to by General Foch.

BY CLEMENCEAU, ORLANDO AND LLOYD GEORGE

The Prime Ministers of France, Italy, and Great Britain, now meeting at Versailles, desire to send the following message to the President of the United States:

"We desire to express our warmest thanks to President Wilson for the remarkable promptness with which American aid, in excess of what at one time seemed practicable, has been rendered to the Allies during the past month to meet a great emergency. The crisis, however, still continues. General Foch has presented to us a statement of the utmost gravity, which points out that the numerical superiority of the enemy in France, where 162 Allied divisions now oppose 200 German divisions, is very heavy, and that, as there is no possibility of the British and French increasing the number of their divisions (on the contrary, they are put to extreme straits to keep them up) *there is a great danger of the war being lost* unless the numerical inferiority of the Allies can be remedied as rapidly as possible by the advent of American troops. He, therefore, urges with the utmost insistence that the maximum possible number of infantry and machine gunners, in which respect the shortage of men on the side of the Allies is most marked, should continue to be shipped from America in the months of June and July *to avert the immediate danger of an Allied defeat in the present campaign* owing to the Allied reserves being exhausted before those of the enemy. In addition to this, and looking to the future, he represents that *it is impossible to foresee ultimate victory in the war unless America is able to provide such an Army* as will enable the Allies ultimately to establish numerical superiority. He places the total American force required for this at no less than 100 divisions, and urges the continuous raising of fresh American levies, which, in his opinion, should not be less than 300,000 a month, with a view to establishing a total American force of 100 divisions at as early a date as this can possibly be done.

"We are satisfied that General Foch, who is conducting the present campaign with consummate ability, and on whose military judgment we continue to place the most absolute reliance, is not overestimating the needs of the case, and we feel confident that the Government of the United States will do everything that can be done, both to meet the needs of the immediate situation and to proceed with the continuous raising of fresh levies, calculated to provide, as soon as possible, the numerical superiority which the Commander-in-Chief of the Allied Armies regards as essential to ultimate victory."

A separate telegram contains the arrangements which General Foch, General Pershing, and Lord Milner have agreed to recommend to the United States Government with regard to the dispatch of American troops for the months of June and July.

BY GENERAL PERSHING

Such extensive priority had already been given to the transport of American infantry and machine gunners that the troops of those categories which had received even partial training in the United States were practically exhausted. Moreover, the strain on our Services of Supply made it essential that early relief be afforded by increasing its personnel. At the same time, the corresponding services of our Allies had in certain departments been equally overtaxed and their responsible heads were urgent in their representations that their needs must be relieved by bringing over American specialists. The final agreement was cabled to the War Department on June 5th, as follows:

The following agreement has been concluded between General Foch, Lord Milner, and myself with reference to the transportation of American troops in the months of June and July:

"The following recommendations are made on the assumption that at least 250,000 men can be transported in each of the months of June and July by the employment of combined British and American tonnage. We recommend:

"(a) For the month of June: (1) Absolute priority shall be given to the transportation of 170,000 combatant troops (viz., six divisions without artillery, ammunition trains, or supply trains, amounting to 126,000 men and 44,000 replacements for combat troops); (2) 25,400 men for the service of the railways, of which 13,400 have been asked for by the French Minister of Transportation; (3) the balance to be troops of categories to be determined by the Commander-in-Chief, American Expeditionary Forces.

"(b) For the month of July: (1) Absolute priority for the shipment of 140,000 combatant troops of the nature defined above (four divisions minus artillery 'et cetera' amounting to 84,000 men, plus 56,000 replacement); (2) the balance of the 250,000 to consist of troops to be designated by the Commander-in-Chief, American Expeditionary Forces.

"(c) It is agreed that if the available tonnage in either month allows of the transportation of a larger number of men than 250,000, the excess tonnage will be employed in the transportation of combat troops as defined above.

"(d) We recognize that the combatant troops to be dispatched in July may have to include troops which have had insufficient training, but we consider the present emergency is such as to justify a temporary and exceptional departure by the United States from sound principles of training, especially as a similar course is being followed by France and Great Britain.

"FOCH.
"MILNER.
"PERSHING."

The various proposals during these conferences regarding priority of shipment, often very insistent, raised questions that were not only most difficult but most delicate. On the one hand, there was a critical situation which must be met by immediate action, while, on the other hand, any priority accorded a particular arm necessarily postponed the formation of a distinctive American fighting force and the means to supply it. Such a force was, in my opinion, absolutely necessary to win the war. A few of the Allied representatives became convinced that the American Services of Supply should not be neglected but should be developed in the common interest. The success of our divisions during May and June demonstrated fully that it was not necessary to draft Americans under foreign flags in order to utilize American manhood most effectively.

On March 21st, approximately 300,000 American troops had reached France. Four combat divisions, equivalent in strength to eight French or British divisions, were available —the First and Second then in line, and the Twenty-sixth and Forty-second just withdrawn from line after one month's trench warfare training. The last two divisions at once began taking over quiet sectors to release divisions for the battle; the Twenty-sixth relieved the First Division, which was sent to northwest of Paris in reserve; the Forty-second relieved two French divisions from quiet sectors. In addition to these troops, one regiment of the Ninety-third Division was with the French in the Argonne, the Forty-first Depot Division was in the Service of Supply, and three divisions (Third, Thirty-second, and Fifth) were arriving.

Following the agreements as to British shipping, our troops came so rapidly that by the end of May we had a force of 600,000 in France.

Cantigny

On April 25th the First Division relieved two French divisions on the front near Montdidier and on May 28th captured the important observation stations on the heights of Cantigny with splendid dash. French artillery, aviation, tanks, and flame throwers aided in the attack, but most of this French assistance was withdrawn before the completion of the operation in order to meet the enemy's new offensive launched May 27th toward Château-Thierry. The enemy reaction against our troops at Cantigny was extremely violent, and apparently he was determined at all costs to counteract the most excellent effect the American success had produced. For three days his guns of all calibers were concentrated on our new position and counter-attack succeeded counter-attack. The desperate efforts of the Germans gave the fighting at Cantigny a seeming tactical importance entirely out of proportion to the numbers involved.

BY MAJOR FREDERICK PALMER

For days before the attack the heavy guns had avoided drawing attention to it by shelling Cantigny. At 4.45 on the morning of the attack the artillery began an adjustment fire in which each battery had a fifteen-minute interval; and at 5.45 all the guns began the real preparation. Now the heavies gave Cantigny all they could send and the little town was revealed to the eye of the waiting infantry in lurid flashes. The crashes and the screams and the bursts at the end of the screams in their unorchestrated, monstrous roar were like hundreds of other artillery preparations while the minutes ticked off to zero hour, and the enemy, aroused now to the fact that an attack was coming, began to respond.

At 6.45 in the early dawn of May 28th, as has happened many times before, the line of figures started up from the earth and began their advance. The formations were the same as those of the practice maneuvers, and the movement was equally precise as it kept to the time-table of the barrage. Each unit was doing its part, the tanks as they nosed their way forward doing theirs. Our shelling of the lower end of the town suddenly ceased; and then our men were seen entering the town exactly on time. Headquarters waited on reports, and they came of prisoners taken, of the further progress of units—all according to the charts. We had passed through the town; we were mopping it up; and we had reached our objective in front of the town. Our losses to that point were less than a hundred men, with three hundred and fifty prisoners. A small offensive as offensives go, but our own, and our first.

Going over the top in a frontal attack had been almost tame, it was so like practice exercises. The fact that our practice exercises had been so systematically applied, that, indeed, we had done everything in the book, accounted for the perfect success of Cantigny. There was a glad, proud light in the eyes of our wounded. They had been hit in a "real party." Nobody could deny that they were graduate soldiers now. But there was to be the reaction which always comes with limited objectives when you do not advance far

enough to draw the enemy's fangs—his guns. Upon the
roads along which men must pass to bring up supplies, upon
every point where men must work or men or wagons pass,
upon the command posts, he turns the wrath of his resent-
ment over the loss of men and ground, and in his rage con-
centrates most wickedly, most persistently and powerfully
upon the infantry which is trying to organize the new front.

The German artillery would show this upstart American
division its mistake in thinking that it could hold what it
had gained. Eight-inch shells were the favorites in the bombardment of our men, who now had Cantigny at their backs
as they dug in, while showers of shrapnel and gas added to
the variety of that merciless pounding that kept up for three
days. We suffered serious casualties now; but we did not go
back, and we took revenge for our casualties in grim use of
rifle and machine gun which, with the aid of prompt barrages,
repulsed all counter-attacks, until the Germans were convinced of the futility of further efforts.

Later, when I did the usual thing of rising at three in
the morning in order to go over our positions at Cantigny,
the sector had become settled in its habits though still active.
Part of the walls of the château which had had a single hit
when I first saw it were still standing; all the surrounding
village was in ruins almost as complete as if it had been in
the Ypres salient.

From the front line I watched the early morning "strafe"
of the German guns; the selected points of "hate," here and
there along the front receiving a quarter of an hour's attention, while the crushed remains of Cantigny were being subjected to additional pulverization. We held the line, but with
cunning men hidden in the earth. You hardly knew of their
presence unless you stumbled on them.

Everybody you met at the front had a certain air of pro-
prietorship in the sector; and back at headquarters the thor-
oughbred veteⅰan chief of staff and all the other officers of
that much-schooled First received you with their habitual
attitude, which seemed to say, "Any suggestions or criticism? We are always listening—but, understand, please,
we are the First Division."

CHATEAU-THIERRY AND BELLEAU WOOD

HOW AMERICA MET THE GERMANS AT THE MARNE

MAY 31ST-JULY 1ST

AMERICAN, FRENCH AND BRITISH OFFICIAL REPORTS
JOSEPHUS DANIELS MAJOR EVANS OTTO KAHN
LIEUTENANT VON BERG   JEAN PIERREFEU

No sooner had the Americans proved themselves at Cantigny than their troops were thrown into the front line to help in stopping the great German thrust of May 27th. By May 31st that drive had reached the Marne, and its spearhead had turned westward down the Marne valley and was aimed towards Paris, only forty miles away. Here it was, at the Marne town of Château-Thierry, that the Americans, a "motorized" machine-gun battalion, first met the German advance; and here it was that General Bundy refused to tell them to retreat.

Château-Thierry lies on both banks of the Marne, and the Americans were driven back with their French comrades from the section north of the river, but they held the southern bank with desperate tenacity, and blocked every effort of the vastly more numerous Germans to cross the river. That was the first glorious fight of Château-Thierry, extending from the evening of May 31st to June 3rd.

Meanwhile, just to the north of Château-Thierry, the entire American "Second Division," which included a brigade of marines, was lined up to block the German westward advance down the valley toward Paris. Active fighting with the Germans began here on June 2nd. On June 4th the Marine Brigade was ordered to make a counter-attack, to check the Germans by taking from them their foremost line in the now famous Belleau Wood. The fight for Belleau Wood and for the neighboring village of Bouresches saw some of the fiercest fighting of the War—Germany's best against America's best! Before that fight was over all Europe knew of the "marines," the American "devil-dogs," and how they could fight. The German advance on Paris was definitely checked by larger victories elsewhere by June 9th; but the fighting around Belleau Wood continued all through June. Other Americans came to the aid of the marines. The best German troops were sent there, too. The German generals were determined to make this a test battle; and they found it so. Not until July 1st did they definitely admit defeat. On that day American troops swept beyond the woods and captured the village of Vaux which lay further to the north and east; and the Germans drew back their line and left the Westerners in possession. A private letter by Major Evans tells the story. He was there.

Secretary Daniels also writes with pride of the success of his navy soldiers. Otto Kahn, the well-known American publicist, who was in Paris at the time, tells of the general fight and what Paris felt about it. Jean Pierrefeu, whose book on French "Headquarters" has be-

193

come the classic of French thought during the War, tells also of the inspiration of the Americans. But better reading still is contained in the official reports, which do not usually include heroics. Most interesting of all is the German summary of the American fighters given by Lieutenant von Berg, who gravely ranks their "Second Division" as almost equal to Germany's best, and who as gravely accepts as stupidity the adroit refusal of his few prisoners to give him any military information. "Most of them have never seen a map!" and "Their superiors keep them purposely without knowledge of military subjects!" That German had still something to learn about Americans.

"We kill or get killed!" said one captured marine to Lieutenant von Berg. And that speech also was officially reported. It must have sent a single tiny shiver of chilliest warning through official Germandom. "Reckless?" Yes; but of a recklessness that, if backed by a strong government and directed by an able general, must always lead to overwhelming victory.

C. F. H.

BY GENERAL PERSHING

THE third German offensive on May 27th, against the French on the Aisne, soon developed a desperate situation for the Allies. Our Second Division, then in reserve northwest of Paris and preparing to relieve the First Division,[1] was hastily diverted to the vicinity of Meaux on May 31st, and, early on the morning of June 1st, was deployed across the Château-Thierry-Paris road near Montreuil-aux-Lions in a gap in the French line, *where it stopped the German advance on Paris.* At the same time the partially trained Third Division was placed at French disposal to hold the crossings of the Marne, and its motorized machine-gun battalion succeeded in reaching Château-Thierry *in time to assist in successfully defending that river crossing.*

The enemy having been halted, the Second Division commenced a series of vigorous attacks on June 4th, which resulted in the capture of Belleau Wood after very severe fighting. The village of Bouresches was taken soon after, and on July 1st Vaux was captured. *In these operations the Second Division met with most desperate resistance by Germany's best troops.*

To meet the March offensive, the French had extended their front from the Oise to Amiens, about 60 kilometers, and during the German drive along the Lys had also sent re-

[1] The First Division was on the Montdidier front around Cantigny. See previous article.

enforcements to assist the British. The French lines had been further lengthened about 45 kilometers as a result of the Marne pocket made by the Aisne offensive. This increased frontage and the heavy fighting had reduced French reserves to an extremely low point.

Our Second Corps, under Maj. Gen. George W. Read, had been organized for the command of the 10 divisions with the British, which were held back in training areas or assigned to second-line defenses. After consultation with Field Marshal Haig on June 3rd, 5 American divisions were relieved from the British area to support the French. The Seventy-seventh and Eighty-second Divisions were moved south to release the Forty-second and Twenty-sixth for employment on a more active portion of the front; the Thirty-fifth Division entered the line in the Vosges, and the Fourth and Twenty-eighth Divisions were moved to the region of Meaux and Château-Thierry as reserves.

On June 9th the Germans attacked the Montdidier-Noyon front in an effort to widen the Marne pocket and bring their lines nearer to Paris, but were stubbornly held by the French with comparatively little loss of ground. In view of the unexpected results of the three preceding attacks by the enemy, this successful defense proved beneficial to the Allied morale, particularly as it was believed that the German losses were unusually heavy.

FRENCH OFFICIAL REPORT

Military Bulletin of June 1st

American troops checked German advanced forces which were seeking to penetrate Neuilly Wood, and by a magnificent counter-attack hurled back the Germans north of this wood.

Further south the Germans were not able to make any gains. On the Marne front an enemy battalion which had crept across to the left bank of the river above Jaulgonne was counter-attacked by French and American troops and hurled back to the other bank, after having suffered heavy losses. A footbridge which the enemy used was destroyed and 100 prisoners remained in our hands.

On May 31st, when the Germans were already in the outskirts of Château-Thierry, an American machine-gun unit was hurried thither in motor lorries. Château-Thierry lies on both banks of the Marne, which is spanned by a big bridge. A little to the northward a canal runs parallel to the river and is crossed by a smaller bridge.

The Americans had scarcely reached their quarters when news was received that the Germans had broken into the northern part of Château-Thierry, having made their way through the gap they had driven in our lines to the left of the town and then pouring along the streets to the bridge, intending to establish themselves firmly on the south bank and capture the town.

The American machine gunners and French colonials were thrown into Château-Thierry together. The Americans immediately took over the defense of the river bank, especially the approaches to the bridge. Fighting with their habitual courage and using their guns with an accuracy which won the highest encomiums from the French, they brought the enemy to a standstill.

Already wavering under the American fire, the Germans were counter-attacked by the French colonials and driven from the town. They returned to the attack the next night and under cover of darkness crept into the town along the river bank and began to work their way through the streets toward the main bridge. At the same moment a tremendous artillery bombardment was opened upon the southern half of the town.

When within range of the machine guns the Germans advanced under the cover of clouds of thick white smoke from smoke bombs, in order to baffle the aim of the American gunners. A surprise, however, was in store for them. They were already crossing the bridge, evidently believing themselves masters of both banks, when a thunderous explosion blew the center of the bridge and a number of Germans with it into the river. Those who reached the southern bank were immediately captured.

In this battle in the streets, and again at night, the young American soldiers showed a courage and determination which aroused the admiration of their French colonial comrades. With their machine guns they covered the withdrawal of troops across the bridge before its destruction, and although under severe fire themselves, kept all the approaches to the bank under a rain of bullets which nullified all the subsequent efforts of the enemy to cross the river. Every attempt of the Germans to elude the vigilance of the Americans resulted in disaster.

During the last two days the enemy has renounced the occupation of the northern part of Château-Thierry, which the American machine guns have made untenable. It now belongs to No Man's Land, as since the destruction of the bridges, it is not worth while for the French to garrison it.

Against their casualties the Americans can set a much greater loss inflicted by their bullets on the enemy. They have borne their full part in what a French staff officer well qualified to judge described as one of the finest feats of the war.

FRENCH GOVERNMENT CITATION

Issued December 8, 1918, in honor of the 4th American Brigade, fighting at Belleau Wood. This brigade consisted of two regiments of Marines, and a Machine-Gun battalion from the "Regulars" of the U. S. A.

During these operations [of early June], thanks to the brilliant courage, vigor, dash, and tenacity of its men, who refused to be disheartened by fatigue or losses; thanks to the activity and energy of the officers, and thanks to the personal action of Brig. Gen. Harbord, the efforts of the brigade were crowned with success, realizing after twelve days of incessant struggle an important advance over the most difficult of terrain and the capture of two support points of the highest importance, Bouresches village and the fortified wood of Belleau.

BY JOSEPHUS DANIELS

United States Secretary of Navy

It was June 6th that the attack of the American troops began against Belleau Wood and its adjacent surroundings, with the wood itself and the towns of Torcy and Bouresches forming the objectives. At 5 o'clock the attack came, and there began the tremendous sacrifices which the Marine Corps gladly suffered that the German fighters might be thrown back.

The marines fought strictly according to American methods—a rush, a halt, a rush again, in four-wave formation, the rear waves taking over the work of those who had fallen before them, passing over the bodies of their dead comrades and plunging ahead, until they, too, should be torn to bits. But behind those waves were more waves, and the attack went on.

"Men fell like flies," the expression is that of an officer writing from the field. Companies that had entered the battle 250 strong dwindled to 50 and 60, with a Sergeant in command; but the attack did not falter. At 9.45 o'clock that night Bouresches was taken by Lieutenant James F. Robertson and twenty-odd men of his platoon; these soon were joined by two reënforcing platoons. Then came the enemy counter-attacks, but the marines held.

In Belleau Wood the fighting had been literally from tree to tree, stronghold to stronghold; and it was a fight which must last for weeks before its accomplishment in victory. Belleau Wood was a jungle, its every rocky formation containing a German machine-gun nest, almost impossible to reach by artillery or grenade fire. There was only one way to wipe out these nests—by the bayonet. And by this method were they wiped out, for United States marines, bare chested, shouting their battle cry of "E-e-e-e-e y-a-a-h-h-h yip!" charged straight into the murderous fire from those guns, and won!

Out of the number that charged, in more than one instance, only one would reach the stronghold. There, with his bayonet as his only weapon, he would either kill or capture the defenders of the nest, and then swinging the gun about in its position, turn it against the remaining German positions in the forest. Such was the character of the fighting in Belleau Wood; fighting which continued until July 6th, when after a short relief the invincible Americans finally were taken back to the rest billet for recuperation.

In all the history of the Marine Corps there is no such battle as that one in Belleau Wood. Fighting day and night without relief, without sleep, often without water, and for days without hot rations, the marines met and defeated the best divisions that Germany could throw into the line.

The heroism and doggedness of that battle are unparalleled. Time after time officers seeing their lines cut to pieces, seeing their men so dog tired that they even fell asleep under shellfire, hearing their wounded calling for the water they were unable to supply, seeing men fight on after they had been wounded and until they dropped unconscious; time after time officers seeing these things, believing that the very limit of human endurance had been reached, would send back messages to their post command that their men were exhausted. But in answer to this would come the word that the line must hold, and, if possible, those lines must attack. And the lines obeyed. Without water, without food, without rest, they went forward—and forward every time to victory. Companies had been so torn and lacerated by losses that they were hardly platoons, but they held their lines and advanced them. In more than one case companies lost every officer, leaving a Sergeant and sometimes a Corporal to command, and the advance continued.

After thirteen days in this inferno of fire a captured German officer told with his dying breath of a fresh division of Germans that was about to be thrown into the battle to attempt to wrest from the marines that part of the wood they had gained. The marines, who for days had been fighting only on their sheer nerve, who had been worn out from nights of sleeplessness, from lack of rations, from terrific shell and machine-gun fire, straightened their lines and prepared for the attack. It came—as the dying German officer had predicted.

At 2 o'clock on the morning of June 13th it was launched

by the Germans along the whole front. Without regard for men, the enemy hurled his forces against Bouresches and the *Bois de Belleau,* and sought to win back what had been taken from Germany by the Americans. The orders were that these positions must be taken at all costs; that the utmost losses in men must be endured that the *Bois de Belleau* and Bouresches might fall again into German hands. But the depleted lines of the marines held; the men who had fought on their nerve alone for days once more showed the mettle of which they were made. With their backs to the trees and bowlders of the Bois de Belleau, with their sole shelter the scattered ruins of Bouresches, the thinning lines of the marines repelled the attack and crashed back the new division which had sought to wrest the position from them.

And so it went. Day after day, night after night, while time after time messages like the following traveled to the post command:

"Losses heavy. Difficult to get runners through. Some have never returned. Morale excellent, but troops about all in. Men exhausted."

Exhausted, but holding on. And they continued to hold on in spite of every difficulty. Advancing their lines slowly day by day, the marines finally prepared their positions to such an extent that the last rush for the possession of the wood could be made. Then, on June 24th, following a tremendous barrage, the struggle began.

The barrage literally tore the woods to pieces, but even its immensity could not wipe out all the nests that remained, the emplacements that were behind almost every clump of bushes, every jagged, rough group of bowlders. But those that remained were wiped out by the American method of the rush and the bayonet, and in the days that followed every foot of Belleau Wood was cleared of the enemy and held by the frayed lines of the Americans.

It was, therefore, with the feeling of work well done that the depleted lines of the marines were relieved in July, that they might be filled with replacements and made ready for a grand offensive in the vicinity of Soissons, July 18th.

And in recognition of their sacrifice and bravery this praise was forthcoming from the French:

Army Headquarters, June 30, 1918.

In view of the brilliant conduct of the Fourth Brigade of the Second United States Division, which in a spirited fight took Bouresches and the important strong point of Bois de Belleau, stubbornly defended by a large enemy force, the General commanding the Sixth Army orders that henceforth, in all official papers, the *Bois de Belleau* shall be named *"Bois de la Brigade de Marine."*

DIVISION GENERAL DÉGOUTTE,
Commanding Sixth Army.

BY MAJOR FRANK EVANS

The real fireworks broke on June 6th, when a general advance on the Brigade front to straighten out the line and recover territory was decided on. In the meantime the 23rd had been brought in from the left and put on our right, Holcomb's flank. Our Division sector had been shortened to about the front that the 6th had held, and we had two Battalions of the 5th and two of the 6th in line. At 5 p. m. we started out for our new objectives, on a wonderful day, and the twilight is so long here that it was practically broad daylight. The eastern edge of the Bois de Belleau and Bouresche were our main objectives, with Torcy and other parts of the Belleau, the 5th's, Sibley's battalion had the advance with Holcomb's in support. The Colonel and Capt. Laspiere, our French military adviser, went out to Lucy, the central point behind the advance. Sibley moved out in perfect order, and poor Cole told me the night before they got him that when Holcomb's 96th Company moved out later and came thru the woods and into the wheat fields in four waves, that it was the most beautiful sight he had ever seen. The artillery preparation was short, and one of the platoons of our machine gun company laid down a barrage. But out in the thick Bois de Belleau liaison was extremely difficult. The woods were alive with machine guns and at times where our lines and those of the 5th had passed thru they soon found Boche and M. G. S. in their rear.

In the meantime, because of the extreme difficulty of liaison and with a dark night closing in, orders came to consolidate. This came just before we had word from Sibley. It was just 9.45 when word came in that Bouresche had been taken by Robertson's platoon of the 96th, or rather, the 20-odd men of his platoon who had managed to break through a heavy machine gun barrage and enter the town.

Duncan hearing that Sibley's company was 200 yards in advance (an error) raced ahead with his 96th Company and was met by a terrific machine gun barrage from two sides of and from Bouresche. As Robertson told me, he had managed to get part of his platoon through the barrage, and looking back saw Duncan and the rest of the company charging down through the barrage "go down in files."

Just after Robertson gained the town and cleaned out the Boche after street fighting in which his orderly, Private Dunlavy, killed later in the defense of the town, captured and turned on them one of their machine guns, others filtered thru, and the 79th Company under Zane. Holcomb was very enthusiastic about Zane's handling of the town.

In the meantime, altho the capture of Bouresche was the most spectacular of the first fighting, Sibley was having heavier work in the Bois de Belleau. He reported early that there were many machine guns in the woods. At first prisoners came in easily, and the men who brought them back reported that the companies were cleaning up fast with few casualties. Young Timmerman charged one machine gun nest at the point of the bayonet and sent in 17 prisoners at a clip.

After the first batches of prisoners came into the courtyard of our P. C. and stood with hands up the orthodox Kamerad style, and the runners were full of the easy manner in which Sibley was going thru the woods, came a message that the woods ahead were full of machine guns and that one, on a rock plateau in the N. E. edge was especially troublesome, a nest estimated to hold between 10 and 12 guns. Then came word that he had reached the limit of his objective at the edge of the woods, and that he had surrounded the machine gun nest, and was awaiting orders. Then came word from the Brigade to dig in and consolidate the positions won.

We knew we could hold Bouresche; and the counter attack at 2.30 in the morning, altho they got within 30 feet of the town, was smothered by our fire. The 7th was spent in getting rations, water and ammunition out to both Battalions and the little Ford we have hung on to altho it was twice on the verge of salvage, ran thru a period of 36 hours over the road to Bouresche in daytime and at night, or to a point from which the stuff could be carried off to the left to the ravine running along the right of Sibley's position. All that day and the next Sibley's men rushed machine gun nests in hand to hand fighting. The guns were emplaced on crests in the thick woods, on rocks ridges, with fire to all points. Their light guns could easily be moved around to our flanks or rear and the Boche certainly knew the art of working thru, infiltrating, and opening fire from unexpected quarters. Many times the groups got a footing on those crests, only to have to fall back in the face of a deadly machine gun and thick grenade fire. It was work of the most reckless courage against heavy odds and they took their toll of us for every gun captured or disabled.

On the 9th Sibley was withdrawn to a point from which the artillery could hammer away at the machine gun nests which had been thoroughly located. For an hour fifty American and French batteries of 75s and 155s threw everything they had into these woods on the right. Hughes went in on the 10th and his first message was that the artillery had hammered the Bois de Belleau into mincemeat. Overton, who had taken over the 76th Company that day charged the old rock plateau position in brilliant fashion, killing or capturing every gunner and capturing all the guns, and with few casualties. He got his later when the Boches shelled him in his hastily dug-in position for 48 hours. Hughes captured six Minnenwerfers, about 30 guns, light and heavy.

Since the 10th, while the fighting has not been of that savage hand to hand fighting, we've been in there, the two regiments, always advancing, never giving an inch, attacking and smashing counter attacks by the literal score. They've had five and part of a sixth division versus our brigade and half the time three divisions at once. One of them, the 28th, is one of their finest.

They've had the fight knocked out of them and admit it. The last big draft of prisoners had been cut off from supplies for three days by our fire. They vary a lot, some fine, big chaps, and many old, undersized or very young. At first they thought we were Canadians, but the last lot say all the Germans know we have about 700,000 and they say they don't want to fight us, that we give them no rest, and that the artillery punishes them terribly. We've found lots of letters and diaries and the diaries are interesting. They start off with the Gott-mit-uns lines and boasts of what they will do to the Big Americans. They tell of lying in the woods under a terrific fire and about the big Americans who seem to know no fear. Then they .end—a complete story of disillusionment.

OFFICIAL GERMAN REPORT

Captured July 7, 1918

Intelligence officer of the Supreme Command at Army Headquarters, No. 7, J. No. 3,528, Army Headquarters, June 17, 1917.

Second American Infantry Division.

Examination of prisoners from the 5th, 6th, 9th, and 23rd Regiments captured from June 5th to 14th in the Bouresches sector.

Purpose of the Attacks

The prisoners were not informed of the purpose of the attacks. The orders for the attacks on Belleau Wood were made known only a few hours before the attacks took place.

Arrival in Line and Relief

The marine brigades went into sector from June 2nd to June 4th, and elements of the other two regiments from June 5th to 6th in the area Torcy-Vaux (4 KM. W. of Château-Thierry), one battalion from each unit being in the front line. There they relieved French troops of various divisions whose identity they did not know. They had no information concerning their relief. Only the prisoners from the marine brigade considered that on account of heavy losses their relief was imminent.

The 3rd Marine Brigade belongs to the Marine Corps, which was already in existence in the United States during peace time. The 1st and 2nd Marine Brigades are said to be still at home.

Section Two

Regarding the distribution of machine guns, the prisoners made contradictory statements. They claim that in the 3rd Marine Brigade, for instance, each regiment, in addition to the infantry battalion, has one machine-gun battalion of four platoons, each platoon having twelve machine guns. Furthermore, each brigade is said to have one brigade machine-gun battalion.

According to a captured order of battle of the 26th American Division (Intelligence Officer 7, No. 3,228, June 8, 1918), that division has only one machine-gun company to a battalion in each regiment. In case the vague statements of the prisoners are correct, the discrepancy can be perhaps explained by the fact that the Marine Corps was part of the United States peace army and was therefore equipped according to principles other than in the case of the 26th American Division, which has been formed from National Guard troops since the war began.

Elements of the 2nd American Division were put into the Moulanville (Verdun) sector from the middle of March to the middle of May for training, and were relieved by unknown French troops.

The division was then moved by rail to the vicinity of Vitry-le-François, where it remained about five days. From there the division was transferred by rail, via Coulommiers-Denis-Pont-Oise, into the regions west of Beauvais. The 5th Regiment of marines was in the vicinity of Gisors, thirty kilometers southwest of Beauvais. The 6th Regiment of marines was at Chars, seven kilometers northwest.

The division rested eight days in this region. Maneuvers on a large scale or with large units were not held; only exercises in minor tactics, hand grenade throwing, and target practice were carried out. A few long practice marches were made.

On May 31st the 3rd Marine Brigade was ordered to move and put into French motor trucks (twenty men or ten officers in each truck). The 5th Regiment of the marines was the first to leave and traveled via Beaumont, Lucarches, Ermenonville (west of Nateuilles), Plessis, Belleville, and Meaux to Lisy-sur-Ourcq, where they were unloaded after a journey of eighteen hours.

The next regiment to leave was the 6th Regiment of marines, which followed the same route, while the 9th and 23rd Regiments apparently moved via Beaumont, Ecoven Genesse, Aulnay (environs of Paris), Clave, Meaux, and were unloaded in the neighborhood of La Ferté-sous-Jouarre. The 5th Regiment of marines was put into line during the night of June 2nd-3rd as the first regiment of the division, the other elements taking up their positions in the sector in échelon.

Summary

The 2nd American Division may be classified as a very good division, perhaps even as assault troops. The various attacks of both regiments on Belleau Wood were carried out with dash and recklessness. The moral effect of our firearms did not materially check the advance of the infantry. The nerves of the Americans are still unshaken.

Value of the Individual

The individual soldiers are very good. They are healthy, vigorous, and physically well developed men of ages ranging from 18 to 28, who at present lack only necessary training to make them redoubtable opponents. The troops are fresh and full of straightforward confidence. A remark of one of the prisoners is indicative of their spirit: "We kill or get killed."

Method of Attack

In both attacks on Belleau Wood, which were carried out by one or two battalions, the following method of attack was adopted: Three or four lines of skirmishers at about thirty to fifty paces distance; rather close behind these isolated assault parties in platoon column; abundant equipment of automatic rifles and hand grenades. The assault parties carried forward machine guns and were ordered to penetrate the German position at a weak point, to swing laterally, and to attack the strong points from the rear.

Particulars on the American Position

No details are available. The prisoners are hardly able to state where they were in position. According to their statements, it may be assumed that the front line consists only of rifle pits one meter deep, up to the present not provided with wire entanglements. The organization of the positions in rear is unknown.

Morale

The prisoners in general make an alert and pleasing impression. Regarding military matters, however, they do not show the slightest interest. Their superiors keep them purposely without knowledge of military subjects. For example, most of them have never seen a map. They are no longer able to describe the villages and roads through which they marched. Their ideas on the organization of their unit is entirely confused. For example, one of them claimed that his brigade has six regiments, his division twenty-four. They still regard the war from the point of view of the "big brother" who comes to help his hard-pressed brethren and is, therefore, welcomed everywhere. A certain moral background is not lacking. The majority of the prisoners simply took as a matter of course that they have come to Europe in order to defend their country.

Only a few of the troops are of pure American origin; the majority is of German, Dutch, and Italian parentage, but these semi-Americans, almost all of whom were born in

America and never have been in Europe, fully feel themselves to be true-born sons of their country.

Von Berg,
Lieutenant and Intelligence Officer.

BY OTTO H. KAHN

It is the general impression that the tide of victory set in with Marshal Foch's splendid movement against the German flank on July 18th. That movement, it is true, started the irresistible sweep of the wave which was destined to engulf and destroy the hideous power of Prussianism. But the tide which gathered and drove forward the waters out of which that wave arose, had turned before. It turned with and through the supreme valor of our marines and other American troops in the *first* battle at Château-Thierry and at Belleau Wood, *in the first week of June.*

The American force engaged was small, measured by the standard of numbers to which we have become accustomed in this war, but the story of their fighting will remain immortal and in its psychological and strategic consequences the action will take rank, I believe, among the decisive battles of the war.

I am not speaking from hearsay. I was in France during the week preceding that battle, the most anxious and gloomy period, probably, of the entire war. What I am about to relate is based either on authoritative information gathered on the spot, or on my own observations. In telling it, nothing is farther from my thoughts than to wish to take away one tittle from the immortal glory which belongs to the Allied armies, nor from the undying gratitude which we owe to the nations who for four heart-breaking years, with superb heroism, fought the battle of civilization—our battle from the very beginning, no less than theirs—and bore untold sacrifices with never faltering spirit.

Just Before the Tide Turned

On the 27th of last May the Germans broke through the French position at the *Chemin des Dames,* a position which had been considered by the Allies as almost impregnable.

The First Attack

American Machine Gunners
making their first advance upon the enemy

They overthrew the French as they had overthrown the British two months earlier. Day by day they came nearer to Paris, until only thirty-nine miles separated them from their goal. A few days more at the same rate of advance, and Paris was within range of the German guns of terrific destructive power. Paris, the nerve center of the French railroad system and the seat of many French war industries, not only, but the very heart of France, far more to the French people in its meaning and traditions than merely the capital of the country; Paris in imminent danger of ruthless bombardment like Rheims, in possible danger even of conquest by the brutal invader, drunk with lust and with victory! As one Frenchman expressed it to me: "We felt in our faces the very breath of the approaching beast."

And whilst the Hunnish hordes came nearer and nearer, and the very roar of the battle could be dimly and ominously heard from time to time in Paris, there were air raids over the city practically every night, and the shells from the long-range monster guns installed some sixty or seventy miles distant, fell on its houses, places and streets almost every day.

They were not afraid, these superb men and women of France. They do not know the meaning of fear in defense of their beloved soil and their sacred ideals. There was no outward manifestation even of excitement or apprehension. Calmly and resolutely they faced what destiny might bring. But there was deep gloom in their hearts and dire forebodings.

They had fought and dared and suffered and sacrificed for well nigh four years. They had buried a million of their sons, brothers and fathers. They were bleeding from a million wounds and more. They said: "We will fight on to our last drop of blood, but alas! our physical strength is ebbing. The enemy is more numerous by far than we. Where can we look for aid? The British have just suffered grave defeat. The Italians have their own soil to defend after the disaster of last autumn. Our troops are in retreat. The Americans are not ready and they are untried as yet in the fierce ordeal of modern warfare. The Germans know well that in three months or six months the

Americans will be ready and strong in numbers. That is why they are throwing every ounce of their formidable power against us *now*. The Hun is at the gate *now*. Immeasurable consequences are at stake *now*. It is a question of days, not of weeks or months. Where can we look for aid *now?*"

And out of their nooks and corners and hiding places crawled forth the slimy brood of the Bolshevik-Socialists, of the Boloists, Caillouxists and pacifists, and they hissed into the ears of the people, "Make peace! Victory has become impossible. Why go on shedding rivers of blood uselessly? The Germans will give you an honorable, even a generous peace. Save Paris! Make peace!"

The holy wrath of France crushed those serpents whenever their heads became visible. Clemenceau, the embodiment of the dauntless spirit of France, stood forth the very soul of patriotic ardor and indomitable courage. But the serpents were there, crawling hidden in the grass, ever hissing, "Make peace!"

And then, suddenly out of the gloom flashed the lightning of a new sword, sharp and mighty, a sword which had never been drawn except for freedom, a sword which had never known defeat—the sword of America!

The Turning of the Tide

A division of marines and other American troops were rushed to the front as a desperate measure to try and stop a gap where flesh and blood, even when animated by French heroism, seemed incapable of further resistance. They came in trucks, in cattle cars, by any conceivable kind of conveyance, crowded together like sardines. They had had little food, and less sleep, for days.

When they arrived, the situation had become such that the French command advised, indeed ordered, them to retire. But they and their brave General would not hear of it. They disembarked almost upon the field of battle and rushed forward, with little care for orthodox battle order, without awaiting the arrival of their artillery, which had been unable to keep up with their rapid passage to that front.

They stormed ahead, right through the midst of a retreating French division, yelling like wild Indians, ardent, young, irresistible in their fury of battle. Some of the Frenchmen called out a well-meant warning: "Don't go in this direction. There are the boches with machine guns." They shouted back: "That's where we want to go. That's where we have come three thousand miles to go." And they did go, into the very teeth of the deadly machine guns. In defiance of all precedent they stormed, with rifle and bayonet in frontal attack, against massed machine guns.

They threw themselves upon the victory-flushed Huns to whom this unconventional kind of fierce onset came as a complete and disconcerting surprise. They fought like demons, with utterly reckless bravery. They paid the price, alas! in heavy losses, but for what they paid they took compensation in over-full measure.

They formed of themselves a spearhead at the point nearest Paris, against which the enemy's onslaught shattered itself and broke. They stopped the Hun, they beat him back, they broke the spell of his advance. They started victory on its march.

A new and unspent and mighty force had come into the fray. And the Hun knew it to his cost and the French knew it to their unbounded joy. The French turned. Side by side the Americans and the French stood, and on that part of the front the Germans never advanced another inch from that day. They held for a while, and then set in the beginning of the great defeat.

I was in Paris when the news of the American achievement reached the population. They knew full well what it meant. The danger was still present, but the crisis was over. The Boche could not break through. He could and would be stopped and ultimately thrown back, out of France, out of Belgium, across the Rhine and beyond!

The French, so calm in their trials, so restrained in their own victories, gave full vent to their joy and enthusiasm at the splendid fighting and success of the Americans. The talk of them was everywhere in Paris. Hundreds of thousands of American soldiers already in France, thousands coming upon every steamer, millions more to come if needed—and they had shown the great stuff they were made of! All gloom vanished overnight. The full magnificence of the French fighting morale shone out again—both behind the lines and at the front. *"Ils ne passeront pas!" "On les aura."*

BY JEAN DE PIERREFEU

Just at this instant, a perfect cloud of Americans swept over the country; endless columns of them packed every road, hastening in the direction of Coulommiers and Meaux. They were crowded as close as possible on immense auto trucks, perched in all sorts of grotesque positions, bareheaded, with their shirts open at the throat. They roared out the songs of their country at the top of their voices, while the people along the way greeted them with indescribable enthusiasm. The sight of these splendid youths from across the ocean, these smooth shaven twenty-year old youngsters with their spickspan new equipment, their vigor, and their health wrought a miraculous change in our feelings.

They formed a remarkable contrast to our regiments, clad in their tattered, faded uniforms, weathered by long campaigns, and to our hollow eyed, emaciated soldiers, reduced to mere bundles of nerves and kept going only by the fire which burned within them. We felt as if we were witnessing the magic effect of a transfusion of blood. It was as though life and vigor were flowing in warm waves through the exhausted body of France, weakened by its countless wounds; and in those days of heaviest trial, when the enemy stood again on the banks of the Marne and fancied that we had lost all hope, the hearts of the French were filled with a confidence which it is impossible for me to describe.

ITALY'S GREATEST VICTORY

AUSTRIA'S CATASTROPHE ON THE PIAVE

JUNE 15TH-23RD

HENRI KERVAREC   GENERAL VON HOETZENDORFF
MAX OSBORN   G. M. TREVELYAN
        LORD ROBERT CAVAN

The "Italian Marne" is the name by which Italian patriots have triumphantly designated their victory on the Piave River in June of 1918. Of the great series of successes by which the strength of the Central Powers was so completely broken, that of the Piave was the first. While in France the second struggle of the Marne was still in doubtful progress, Italy met the full force of Austria's last great blow—a blow intended to be as decisive as that of Ludendorff in France —and the Austrian attack was hurled back with enormous losses, at least two hundred thousand men.

The other Allies, Britain, France and even America, had their share in aiding the Italians in this tremendously important battle. The Britons especially did an important work, which is here described by Lord Cavan, their commander on the field. But the battle as a whole was fought and won by the Italians themselves. Their Allies' aid was but a small fraction of the whole. This is frankly recognized by the French official observer, M. Kervarec, in his account of the battle here given, and also by Mr. Trevelyan. The latter, as head of Britain's Red Cross service in Italy, has given us what is perhaps the clearest as well as the most sympathetic picture of all the stages of the Italian struggle which, like the Piave battle, came under his own eye.

The Teuton view of this battle naturally differs markedly from that of the Allies. That it was meant for a great forward movement is plainly shown by the preliminary address of General von Hoetzendorff, or "Marshal Conrad," as his soldiers called him. Its failure is then, by the German observer, Max Osborn, attributed entirely to the Heavens, that is to the flooding of the Piave River. This was the official view adopted by the Teutons—an assured victory interrupted by "an act of God," and thereby turned into a drawn battle. The Italians will tell you that the Austrians had been checked before the Piave rose, and that its flood did but increase the number of their prisoners.

BY HENRI KERVAREC

IN the series of great offensives that the Central Powers were to launch against the troops of the Entente, the Austrian offensive against the Italian front was meant, in the mind of the German General Staff, to hold fast the Franco-British troops which had been sent into Italy after Caporetto (October, 1917), and only a part of which had been withdrawn by Marshal Foch after the offensive against the English army of March 21, 1918. The German Staff hoped also in this way to prevent the sending of Italian troops to reënforce the French front. It is what was declared by the Pan-German *Taeglische Rundschau* at the very beginning of the attack. "The Austrian attack, carried out over a wide front, will make this exchange of troops impossible henceforward; the Italians will now be unable to allow men to be sent into France." In the excitement caused by the first shots, the Austrians on their side asked ironically if the French and English would be able, this time again, to send reënforcements across the Alps. "The Entente will no longer be able to repeat its theatrical gesture," wrote the *Pester Lloyd* on June 16th. "The English and the French have enough on their own hands."

Other reasons had motived this offensive; reasons of general strategy: it was intended to crush Italy for good and all by conquering Venetia; reasons of home policy: the double monarchy was torn by technical dissensions; and the people was suffering from lack of food. The prestige of the Hapsburgs could be saved only by a victory.

Austria thus launched a politico-military offensive, hoping for success and profit. This double character appears very clearly in the proclamation that General Conrad von Hoetzendorff had read to the troops on the morning of the attack.

BY GENERAL CONRAD VON HOETZENDORFF

The Official Address of June 14th, referred to by M. Kervarec

Soldiers! For months and months, resisting victoriously amidst the glaciers and the snows, accomplishing faithfully your duty in the tempests of winter, you have looked down upon the sunny plain of Italy. The time to go down into it has come. Like a whirlwind, you will overthrow the false and perjured ally of the past, as well as the friends she has called to her help. You will prove to the world that nobody can resist your heroism.

Your fathers, your grandfathers, and your ancestors, have fought and conquered the same enemy with the same spirit.

I am sure you will not fall below them, and even that you will rise above them. Heart and soul with you, I shall follow your movements, which will be an irresistible rush towards victory. Confiding firmly in you, I cry to you: "Overthrow everything before you."

FIELD-MARSHAL CONRAD.

BY HENRI KERVAREC

It is certain that the preparations had been carried out with particular care. The troops set free by the cessation of hostilities on the eastern front had been brought back to Italy, and trained for the coming offensive. In May, 1918, too, the heavy artillery that the Austrians had lent the Germans for their offensive of March 21st had been brought back. Carefully chosen attacking troops had been trained according to German methods. The doubtful regiments (composed of Czechs, Rumanians, and Slavs) had been withdrawn. In short, everything was ready for the accomplishment of the decisive event of the war, during which, according to the *Germania* of June 12th, "the flags of the Hapsburg were to fly out again."

What was the situation of the opposing armies in the beginning of June? From the Swiss frontier to the Adriatic, the front occupied a line that may be compared with the general line held for so long by the French front. It ran, first of all from North to South, from the Stelvio Pass to the mountain-mass of the Adamello. Then from the Adamello to the Monte Grappa, crossing the Val Guidicaria, passing to the north of the lago di Garda, cutting the Val Lagarina (upper Adige) by the Monte Pasubio, the north of Asiero, the south of Asiago, the front stretched from west to east. Finally, the third part, from the Grappa to the mouth of the Piave, to Cavazuccherina, by the Montello, and all along the river, the front ran roughly from the northwest to the southeast. In all 180 kilometers, held by sixty Austrian divisions, forming two armies, that of Conrad von Hoetzendorf, from the Swiss frontier, to the Monte Tomba, and that of Boroevic, from the Tomba to the sea.

The Italian forces, under the command of General Diaz, were at least equal in number.

The railways and roads were not much in favor of the Austrians: one line only in the district of Trent, that from Trent to Verona; three in Cadore and Friuli, that from Feltre to Treviso, that from Udine to Treviso, and that from Trieste to Mestre and Padua. Very little, in reality, for the handling of large numbers.

The Italians, on the other hand, had the advantage of the inner line, and a more highly developed railway system. They had at their disposal stations like Verona, Vicenza, Padua, Treviso, splendidly prepared for heavy traffic.

They were threatened, however, on their front and their flanks, from the lago di Garda to the sea. And they had to resist converging attacks directed towards Padua.

On June 14th an order promising them *glory, honor, good food, abundant booty, and especially, peace,* was read to the Austrian troops.

On the 15th, at three in the morning, began the preliminary cannonade with poisoned gas shells. At four o'clock the general attack was launched from the Val Lagarina to the sea. The efforts of the assailant were directed against some special points; on the plateau of Setti Communi, on both sides of the Brenta; on the Montello plateau, after which there is nothing to hinder a march towards the plains of Venetia; on the lower Piave, above San Dona.

It was very clear, towards the evening of the 15th, that the results hoped for had not been attained. The Italian High Command, as a matter of fact, had foreseen the attack: it would even seem that it had been informed of the time and the choice of the points specially aimed at. At any rate the Austrian command has accused the Slav troops of having betrayed the cause of the monarchy in this supreme battle. Whatever the truth may be, immediately the preliminary bombardment was started, a very active counter-bombardment was ordered on the Italian side so that when the Austrian infantry attacked it could only gain very little ground.

On the Setti Communi the advance was not worth speaking about, as the Austrian *communiqué* was obliged to admit on the 16th. The French, English, and Italian counterattacks soon set things to rights again. Further to the east, the Austrian succeeded in getting a footing on the slopes of the Montello, but could not reach its summit. To the south, they crossed the Piave. They even got a footing in the delta of the river, and thence threatened Mestre directly.

To sum up, at the end of the day, the mountain front was almost intact. Only the Piave had been crossed, and a dangerous breach been made in front.

The battle began again on the morning of the 16th. The Austrians, roughly handled on the Setti Communi plateau, and before the Monte Tomba, launched but few attacks, which went on dwindling away till the end of the battle in this sector (June 20th-21st).

The struggle on the Montello and the Piave was fiercer. The very energetic Italian counter-attacks recovered on the 16th and 19th the ground which had been momentarily lost. To the south of the Montello, the Austrians, who had taken Montebelluna, on the line from Feltre to Treviso, were thrown back, and lost 1,200 prisoners and some dozens of machine guns.

In the center, around Zenson, on the Piave, there was very hard fighting. But the enemy made no progress worth speaking of. In the south the Austrians advanced. For some time the situation became dangerous. San Dona was passed, as well as Capo Sile. The Fossetta Canal, to the east of Mestre, was crossed in several points. But on the 19th the advance was brought to a standstill. The Italians even recovered ground to the west of Zenson.

In the morning of the 20th, the enemy had been driven back to his starting point all along the line. He still held only a little ground on the lower course of the Piave.

In the evening of the 20th, the Italians could announce the failure of the offensive, and give out at the same time that they had made more than 12,000 prisoners and taken a great amount of war-material. The German press too began to lower its tone.

General Diaz, safe now in the north, had to resist only the threat coming from the East. The situation of Wurms's army, in the meanders of the Piave, was by no means enviable. It was holding marshes, with its back to a river that the slightest rain might swell. It could neither move nor dig trenches. It was an easy target for the Italian batteries and the Allied planes, and for the fleet of monitors moored at the mouth of the Piave. It was also extremely difficult to revictual it.

Consequently on June 23rd, the Austrian command began preparing the public for the disagreeable news of a retreat referring at great length to the difficulties caused by the rain and the rising of the river.

The *communiqué* of the 24th (Monday) admitted the defeat in these terms: "The situation created by the rising of the waters and the bad weather have obliged us to abandon the Montello and some sectors of the other positions conquered on the right bank of the Piave. The order given with this purpose, four days ago, already, has been carried out, in spite of the difficulties of the crossing from one bank to the other, in such a way that our movements were completely hidden from the enemy."

This movement had not escaped the notice of the Italians, as the Austrian High Command would have it believed, since General Diaz's *communiqué,* dated June 23rd, says: "From the Montello to the sea, the enemy, defeated and hard pressed by our brave troops, is recrossing the Piave in disorder."

At the same time, the capture of numerous prisoners was announced.

Thus came to an end that offensive of the Piave which was to be so stunning a blow that Treviso was marked as the first day's objective!

When the news of this incontestable victory was confirmed there was among the Allies, and especially in Italy an explosion of joy. Instinctively the peoples felt that a great event in the conduct of the war had taken place, and the

Italian people were particularly proud that this victory had been won by the soldiers of General Diaz.

The battle of the Piave was, in the first place, a battle fought in order to check the enemy, from the countering of the artillery, and the resistance offered by the advance posts. Then it was a counter-offensive, when it became necessary to wrest from the enemy the advantages he had won on the Montello and the Piave. If the battle of June 15th-23rd on the Piave cannot be compared with the battle of the Marne, as was done immediately after the victory, yet it must be declared that this victory, won when it was won, had very important consequences, which must be briefly pointed out in ending.

Firstly, it proved the superiority of the Italian army over the Austrian army—command and soldiers. The Allied troops which held the mountain sectors certainly played an important part in this battle—and King Victor Emmanuel has done them full justice. But the greatest effort was made by the Italian troops recruited in every part of Italy— Venetia, Piedmont, Lombardy, Calabria, Sicily, etc. The Italian soldier showed in this battle the traditional qualities of the race, tenacity and dash, thorough Roman obstinacy in defense, and patriotic enthusiasm in the attack. The high command proved its mastery by the way in which it used its railways and roads, and distributed its reserves and brought them at the right time up to the points threatened. In a word, the prestige of the Italian army, which had fallen after Caporetto, was completely restored.

The repercussion in Italy even was considerable. The support of the nation was at once insured to the government. As regards the general conduct of the war, it became almost immediately evident that the Austrian army would henceforward be incapable of taking the offensive. There there was a noteworthy decrease in the military power of the Central Empires.

But it was within the Austrian monarchy that the consequences of the defeat were the most immediate and far-reaching. It had been hoped that a victory would be won, and consequently the difficult and diverse problems which the

Austro-Hungarian Government had to face would be solved. Instead of a victory it was a defeat. Instead of the union which had been looked forward to, the divisions, the internal struggles on the contrary were going to spring up even more fiercely than before. As early as the end of June peculiarly grave words were pronounced in the Hungarian parliament. M. Wekerlé was obliged to recognize that the Austro-Hungarian losses reached 100,000 men. He was interrupted by deputies who shouted to him: "How many Hungarians?" The *Az Ujsag* of June 28th relates the speech of the deputy Ladislas Fenyes in the Hungarian parliament: "Whatever the Minister of National Defense may say, it has been proved that in the battle of the Piave, many Hungarian regiments suffered tremendous losses, or were completely annihilated. Even if the reports which are circulating in the country are untrue, it is nevertheless necessary that the voice of Hungary should come to the ears of the Austrian command, so that the Hungarian blood, sacrificed so often in vain may no longer be shed in torrents."

The *Az Est* of June 30th utters the same complaints and enables us more and more to measure the greatness of the Austro-Hungarian disillusionment: "The greater part of the 100,000 men we have lost on the Piave was composed of Hungarians. We have no exact information as to the proportion of nationalities, but the descriptions of the battle show us that the Hungarians were in the center of the mêlée. The Hungarian regiments have been sacrificed. It matters little to us that the enemy losses have been superior to ours. Our grief is sore indeed when we think that we have suffered the loss of hundreds of thousands of men, at the end of the fourth year of the war."

To attenuate the effect produced by the disaster on the Piave, and to attempt to disculpate itself, the Austrian Staff threw the responsibility of the check upon the Czechs. "We have unfortunately found that some Czech soldiers have gone over to the enemy, and that a certain number of their comrades are in contact with the Italians, whilst carrying on within our lines a dangerous propaganda." Another issued by Headquarters accuses the Jugo-Slavs of having betrayed, of having revealed to the Italians not only the date of the offensive but even the principal points of this offensive. "The exact moment," says this note, "must have been revealed by South Slav deserters. The enemy made arrangements to meet the expected bombardment with gas."

The government of King Charles I. perhaps hoped to reconcile the Austrian and the Hungarians by throwing them on the Jugo-Slavs and Czechs. These tactics, which were so long those of the Hapsburgs, were not to succeed this time. The Hungarians were not satisfied; the Jugo-Slavs were not any more so. The building was crumbling away on every side. The victory might have bolstered it up. The defeat suffered on the Piave on June 20, 1918, dealt Austria-Hungary the *coup de grâce*. The decomposition of the double monarchy was hastened by this military disaster.

BY MAX OSBORN

In the plain near San Dona and Capo Sile, General Wurms's storm battalions were sent over the Piave River and the canal. From Treviso General Diaz sent against them the 30th and 27th Corps, and General Croce's corps, newly formed from 18-year-old youths. The Austrians thus gallantly won a most important objective—the summit of the Italian hinge position was thrust through by the storming of the Montello. The rolling up of the whole of the Piave front from there appeared possible—indeed, certain.

Nature then pronounces an inexorable and cruel veto. Heaven opens and the deluge descends. The mountains foam, the crevasses made in them by time overflow as if weeping, and all the waters empty themselves into the Piave, which rises rapidly. The upper bridge is torn away by the irresistible pressure of the water, and the pontoons, loosened by the force of the waters, are driven against the lower bridge and pushed through it. The Italian artillery has in the bridges targets which cannot be missed for long. Fountains like the spouting of whales ascend from the river in ever quicker succession.

Suddenly airmen also appear. They come down silently from a great height in far-reaching volplanes. Now their

motors hum again and their machine guns rattle. A hail of
steel pelts down on the pontoons, which sink riddled. The
guns of the defense bark from the bank and the fragments
of their shrapnel endanger the lives of their own men, men
whom they wish to protect. One, two, three of the great
Caproni bombarding planes descend, shot down on the mud
of the Montello. A Nieuport comes down like a torch hurled
from heaven—the famous airman, Major Barracca, is a heap
of ashes. His list of victories is the same as that of his most
victorious Austrian adversary, Captain Brumowsky, who
conquered thirty-four opponents. Lieutenant von Hoffmann, in peace time a Ministerial official in Vienna, and his
band dash against the biplanes. Like raging bulldogs the
English now advance on their furiously swift Sopwiths
against our airmen, engineers, artillery, and infantry. Nothing, absolutely nothing, avails. The enemy airmen are too
numerous, the enemy's shells too many. Like Sisyphus mul-
tiplied a hundredfold the bridge builders work incessantly;
they fall and disappear in the flood without a cry; they
launch new pontoons; they think out new methods of transport from bank to bank—nothing helps; absolutely nothing
avails. Six times are the bridges and footways completed,
six times are they destroyed.

The divisions yonder on the green summit of the Montello, which resembles so completely in situation and importance the Podgera heights on the other side of the Isonzo,
fight with an uncovered rear, without heavy artillery, without reënforcements in men, munitions, or provisions. Only
one thing could now alter everything—namely, to carry the
attack so far forward that the Piave crossings fall out of the
range of the hostile artillery. Brave Hungarians and Lower
Austrians burst out of conquered caverns, officers going first.
Both Brigadiers of one division of Chasseurs fall. The attacking wedge presses deep into the mountain fastnesses;
close to the summit the troops settle themselves firmly in the
Italian trenches and caverns and wait not for dismissal or for
their places to be taken by reënforcements, nor for munitions and food. Cartridges have been used up, hand grenades
hurled away, the reserve ration eaten. What was found of

the Italians' provisions was also consumed. Reënforcements, however, only come by driblets. Chains of bearers bring boxes of ammunition from the river to the mountain, airmen throw bags of preserved food over the first line, but always in insufficient quantities. The one footbridge is repaired at last. The weather clears up; but renewed tempests of rain tear the bridge away again. Then the army command took the resolution, a hard but necessary one, to withdraw behind the Piave again.

BY G. M. TREVELYAN

Between the middle of April and the middle of June the Italian army began to be affected by a new idea—namely, that the enemy's morale was worse than their own, and that Austria-Hungary was politically in process of dissolution. The Pact of Rome, concluded early in April between the Italian and Jugo-Slav leaders, was the prelude to a systematic propaganda among the enemy forces, ably organized by Italian Intelligence officers, and zealously carried out by ex-prisoners belonging to the oppressed races of Austria-Hungary. In No Man's Land, musical Czechs serenaded their compatriots with Bohemian songs, and set gramophones going instead of machine guns. The Czecho-Slovaks, in Italian uniform, with the Bohemian national colors of white and red in their Alpino hats, became a common and favorite sight upon the roads.

This new way of envisaging the war went well with the ever-increasing importance of America in the mind's eye of the Italian soldier. The new National Internationalism of Mr. Wilson and his Fourteen Points vaguely adumbrated a broader outlook and a brighter age ahead, beginning with a better chance of winning the war. There seemed a new tide in the world's affairs, and Giuseppe vaguely felt that he was a part of it, while the enemy was fighting against the future. By the time that the Austrians tardily launched their great offensive, the Italian soldiers had an idea that their own morale was at least as good as the enemy's. And in military morale there is nothing good or bad but thinking makes it so.

When the Austrian blow fell at last there was no half measure about it. Although the internal condition of the Empire, political and economic, was even worse than we knew, the authorities believed that they could win such a victory as would relieve their almost desperate situation. But for this purpose the victory must this time be decisive. Their generals planned and their army confidently expected to go straight through at the first rush to Treviso, where they had allotted houses for the different regiments and officers. After that they believed that Italy's resistance would collapse.

The offensive was launched with equal fury along an unbroken line of attack stretching from the Asiago front opposite the British, right round by Grappa, the Montello, and the course of the Piave down to the sea. At dawn on June 15th it began along this great stretch of ground with a bombardment of terrible efficiency. Some of the British officers told me they had never seen better shooting or a hotter barrage in France. The result was that early that morning the Austrians carried with little resistance almost the whole front line of the Allies from Asiago to the marshes at the Piave mouth.

But their success on the mountains was short lived. The British, furious at losing any ground to the Austrians, drove them out again with fearful slaughter, and pursued them into their own lines, where all resistance ceased. The reaction of the French and Italians on the mountain front was also very rapid. Between Piave and Brenta, on the Grappa massif, the Austrians had begun by storming positions which commanded Bassano and threatened the whole line. But Diaz now knew that the proper reply to the new Ludendorff tactics of "infiltration" was instant counter-attacks, and these were carried out with magnificent vigor and success.

By the end of the second day all was well over in the mountain area. But on the low, long "mound" of the Montello and in the plain of the Piave the battle continued for another week of desperate and uncertain fighting. On the morning of the 15th the Austrians had crossed the Piave. In the north they had taken and held nearly half the Montello, and again farther down the course of the river, on both sides of Ponte di Piave and Santa Dona, they had securely lodged themselves on the further shore, and had pushed on from two to four miles, threatening to break through to Treviso.

It was an anxious affair, because the enemy's tactics of "infiltration" had the immense advantage that no one could see clearly more than twenty yards in front of him in that garden-like plain, where rows of vines and fruit trees in full leaf, all running from north to south, parallel with the fighting line, formed a series of low screens, ten or twenty yards apart. Except down the roads and the railway there were no avenues of vision. Neither were the Italians fighting in prepared lines of defense, as they had lost their first line on the river bank when the battle began, and were never driven back as far as their second. Both sides had equally little advantage of ground, and fought behind dyke banks, in ditches and drains, or in improvised trenches scratched in the soft soil.

Naturally under these conditions the battle was always swaying to and fro in rushes and rallies. The cry was perpetually being raised of an enemy "infiltration" in such and such a part of the blind garden battle; and on these occasions the danger was of panic. After the Caporetto experience the divisional, brigade, and regimental officers were all keenly on the lookout to stop the slightest sign of it, and I saw more than one incipient panic, due to an enemy "infiltration," very promptly and ably dealt with. Above all, the reserves were well handled, here locally as well as by Diaz on the grand scale. The Bersaglieri *ciclisti* were hurried up on their "push bikes" along the lanes to the threatened spot time after time, and never in vain.

The Austrians had brought a few light cannon across the Piave, but generally speaking their excellent artillery had had to stay on the farther shore. And since they had lost the mastery of the air, thanks not a little to the British airmen in the spring,[1] they could not get sufficient information as to how to direct their fire in accordance with the changing phases of the battle on the Italian side of the river. They adopted the policy of plumping big shells on the country lanes, of which they had the accurate range, thereby often blocking them for a time. But the Italians, always careful of their road communications, were quick to fill up the holes. As compared with San Gabriele or Vodice, it was a battle of machine gun and rifle wounds, at least for the Italians.

Thus, though the river had been crossed by the Austrian infantry, it was still the Italians' great defense. The mid-summer rain fell, the river rose, and the footbridges, always under the fire of the Italian artillery and of aëroplanes, Italian and British, became each day a more precarious means of sending over men, food, and rifle ammunition. Towards the end of the week the enemy prisoners complained of hunger and eagerly ate the loaves shared with them by their kindly captors. As the Italians held their ground more firmly than ever, the Austrians, eight days after they had crossed the river, slipped back across it under cover of night.

Then we all knew that Italy had been saved, and we rejoiced together. But we did not know that Austro-Hungary had no less surely been doomed, and must now disappear from the category of States. Diaz's defensive victory of June, 1918, may be added to the long list of "decisive battles of the world."

BY LORD CAVAN

Official Report of September, 1918

It had for some time been decided that the British troops should, during the summer months, occupy some portion of the mountain sector. The exact front selected was that lying between Asiago and Canove. By March 29th the relief of the Italian troops in this sector was concluded.

[1] In twelve months in Italy, the British claimed that they had destroyed 386 enemy aëroplanes and twenty-seven balloons, besides thirty-three machines driven down out of control. This is a large proportion of the not very great Austrian total of aircraft. The British official loss for the year was forty-seven machines missing and three balloons destroyed.

During April signs continued to accumulate that the enemy contemplated an offensive astride the Brenta, but it was not until the middle of May that it appeared probable that this operation would be combined with an attack across the Piave. By the end of May the general plan of the enemy for their forthcoming attack could be clearly foreseen. Subsequent events proved that the Italian High Command had made a forecast correct in nearly every detail.

Early on the morning of June 15th, after a short but violent bombardment, in which smoke and gas were freely employed, the Austrian attack was launched. The fronts of attack extended from S. Dona di Piave to the Montello on the plains, and from Grappa to Canove in the mountains, fronts of twenty-five and eighteen miles respectively. The whole of the British sector was involved.

The British front was attacked by four Austrian divisions. It was held by the 23rd Division on the right and the 48th Division on the left. On the front of the 23rd Division the attack was completely repulsed. On the front of the 48th Division the enemy succeeded in occupying our front trench for a length of some 3,000 yards, and subsequently penetrated to a depth of about 1,000 yards. Here he was contained by a series of switches which had been constructed to meet this eventuality. On the morning of June 16th the 48th Division launched a counter-attack to clear the enemy from the pocket he had gained; this attack was completely successful, and the entire line was reëstablished by 9 a. m.

Acting with great vigor during the 16th, both divisions took advantage of the disorder in the enemy's ranks, and temporarily occupied certain posts in the Asiago Plateau without much opposition. Several hundred prisoners and many machine guns and two mountain howitzers were brought back in broad daylight without interference. As soon as "No Man's Land" had been fully cleared of the enemy we withdrew to our original line.

The enemy suffered very heavy losses in their unsuccessful attack. In addition we captured 1,060 prisoners, 7 mountain guns, 72 machine guns, 20 flammenwerfer, and one trench mortar.

I wish here to place on record the prompt and generous assistance in both artillery and infantry given to me by General Monesi, Commanding the 12th Italian Division. As soon as it was discovered that the enemy had penetrated the front of the 48th Division, General Monesi placed all his available reserves at my disposal, and thus appreciably improved the situation.

Elsewhere the enemy had made progress at a number of points, but in no single instance up to his expectations. Everywhere he found himself faced with the most determined resistance. The Italian High Command had ample reserves available, and handled the situation with coolness and decision. Steps were at once taken to deprive the enemy of the gains which he had made.

Torrential rains brought the Piave down in flood, and added to the embarrassments of the enemy. Many of his bridges were washed away, and those which remained were constantly bombed by British and Italian aviators. By means of a succession of vigorous counter-attacks the enemy was gradually pressed back again both on the Piave and the mountain fronts. As a result, not only was the original front line entirely reëstablished, but that portion of the right bank of the Piave, between the Piave and the Sile Rivers, which had been in Austrian hands since November, 1917, was cleared of the enemy.

Captured orders and documents proved beyond doubt that the enemy's plans were extremely ambitious, and aimed, in fact, at the final defeat of the Allied forces in Italy. The result was a complete and disastrous defeat for Austria.

The work of the Royal Air Force, under Colonel P. B. Joubert, D.S.O., has been consistently brilliant, and the results obtained have, I believe, in proportion to the strength employed, exceeded those obtained in any other theater of war. Between March 10th and the present date 294 enemy aëroplanes and nine hostile balloons have been destroyed, and this with a loss of twenty-four machines. Much useful work in coöperation with the artillery has been carried out, and frequent and successful long-distance reconnoissances accomplished.

The action of the artillery, both British and the Italian, which had been temporarily placed under my command, deserves special mention. Constant and effective counter-battery work has been carried out. The damage done has been fully confirmed both by visual observation, photography, and prisoners' statements.

His Excellency General Montuori, under whose command I have had the honor to serve, has always been ready to assist me by his wise counsel. The interest he has taken in the British troops has been intense, and he has met all our demands in a spirit of the most loyal comradeship. I owe him the deepest debt of gratitude.

In questions of policy as regards the British Forces, His Excellency General Diaz has most kindly given me several interviews and allowed me to state my views freely. Both he and General Badoglio, the Sub-Chief of the Staff, could not have been more considerate.

The delicate and difficult task of fully interpreting orders and wishes of two Staffs speaking a different language has been tactfully and well carried out. My special thanks are due to Colonel Ragioni and Lieutenant-Colonel Sarfatti of the Italian Mission attached to my headquarters.

General Graziani, Commanding the 12th French Corps, has ever been ready to assist us on our right flank, and the same happy cordiality has existed between us as I have always found in France. I am most happy to report that the relations between ourselves and the Italian and French troops on either flank are most cordial, and have never given me one moment of uneasiness.

The inhabitants of this beautiful region have shown the most hospitable spirit to our men, and no serious complaint has reached me of damage to property, or incivility on either side. It is clearly the wish of the Italian nation to make their Allies happy and comfortable, and in this they have most royally succeeded.

SIBERIAN INDEPENDENCE PROCLAIMED

RUSSIAN DEMOCRACY RECEIVES ALLY AID AGAINST BOLSHEVISM

JULY 4TH

CARL W. ACKERMAN   BORIS BAKHMETEFF
SIBERIAN DECLARATION OF INDEPENDENCE
AMERICAN and JAPANESE GOVERNMENT STATEMENTS
NICOLAI TCHAIKOVSKY

In the maddened pool of massacre and self-destruction which Russia had become in 1918, the Allies could scarce decide which way to turn. That they must help their accepted allies, the Czecho-Slovak army, was obvious. But what help did they owe to Russian Democracy? What amount of assistance, if any, should they lend to each of the many leaders who arose everywhere, claiming to be the champions of real freedom, of equality and justice for all classes in Russia as against the narrow and brutish tyranny of the Bolshevists?

The problem was further complicated by the fact that the German Government did practically what it would in Russia. It marched troops here and there, and seemed likely not only to capture vast quantities of Ally munitions, but also to make for itself new bases for attack; both from the Black and Caspian Seas in the south, and, more especially, from new submarine harbors along the Arctic coast.

Ultimately the Allied governments decided to assist two, or perhaps we should call them three movements opposed to the Bolshevist rule and to Germany. The first of these actively engaged in was along the Arctic coast. Here Allied forces, chiefly British and American, took possession of the extreme northern or Murmansk coast in July, thus forestalling an army of Germans and Finns who were advancing toward it. In August the Allies extended their field by occupying the port of Archangel. To this they were invited by a peasant government of "Northern Russia." This government was upheld by members of the Democratic "Assembly" which the Bolshevists had overthrown, and it seemed about the nearest to a truly representative government to be found in European Russia. The elected head of this government was Nicolai Tchaikovsky, a former leader of Democracy in Russia. He, upheld by Ally forces, issued the manifesto of North Russia's purposes which is given herewith. In defense of Tchaikovsky's government the Allies, and especially the Americans, fought all through the fall and winter of 1918-19 in Arctic Russia.

In addition to supporting this North Russian government, the Allies also landed troops on the Pacific coast of Siberia, at Vladivostok. Their purpose here was primarily to aid the Czecho-Slovaks; but, when they found what seemed a fairly representative Democratic government being built up in Siberia, they supported this also. They were thus established in the east of Siberia with a double purpose. The Ally troops here were mainly Japanese and American; and we present the statements of both the United States Government and that of Japan, as to the landing and its objects. These troops did little fighting, but by their support of the Czecho-Slovak army they enabled the latter to build a strong organization which temporarily crushed the Bolshevist movement in Siberia.

Meanwhile the Russians of Siberia were building up a government of their own, which is here described by Mr. Ackerman, an American eye-witness of much of the Siberian tumult. His book is our best source of knowledge for that confused and tragic period. "The United Siberian Government" declared its independence of Bolshevist Russia on July 4th, selecting the date of its proclamation out of compliment to the United States. Indeed, all the feeble Democracies seeking to establish themselves upon the exhausted ruins of Eastern Europe and Siberia have turned with passionate hopefulness and eager longing to America. They have counted on, and prayed for, the aid of the great Democracy.

C. F. H.

BY CARL W. ACKERMAN [1]

THROUGHOUT the summer [of 1918], from June to September, the armies of the Czecho-Slovaks fought their way back and forth over Siberia, and by fall all of the local Soviets in Siberia had been overthrown: the Bolshevik power had been destroyed, and from Samara and Perm to Vladivostok the ghost of Bolshevism had disappeared. This the brave armies of the Czecho-Slovaks had accomplished, depending entirely upon their own physical strength and upon the supplies which they found in Russia and which they captured from the Red army. There is no territorial advance in the annals of the war as dramatic and rapid as was that of the Czecho-Slovak revolutionary army in that vast ex-empire of Siberia. These 50,000 Czecho-Slovak soldiers had established an organization in every important city along the great Trans-Siberian Railway. They maintained order; assumed direction of the railroads without interfering with any local government except those avowedly Bolshevists.

Thus, at the beginning of September, Siberia was free from the Red rule, and we find the people of that country getting together with the object of electing an All-Russian

[1] Reprinted by permission from "Trailing the Bolsheviki." Copyright, 1919, by Charles Scribner's Sons.

Government. Various governments had been in process of formation in the neighborhood of Samara and the Ural Mountains, Tomsk and Vladivostok, but these obviously did not trust each other, and the demand for a central representative government was so great that delegates from all of the governments in Siberia, including the Siberian Government itself, met in the city of Ufa and elected an All-Russian directorate with five ministers and five assistants. The prime minister was Afkzentieff and his assistants were Bolderoff, Astroff, Chiakovski, and Vologodsky. The directorate took over full power of the various governments and decided to make Omsk the new capital of Russia until they could move to either Moscow or Petrograd, because the object of the conference at Ufa was to found a new Russian Government, which, with the support of the Czecho-Slovaks and the Allies, might ultimately succeed the Bolsheviki Government which was at that time coöperating with the German organization in the East. The backbone of this new government was the Siberian Government which had been organized the latter part of June and which had selected July 4th, the American Independence Day, as the date for their declaration of the temporary independence of Siberia. This document is important because of its historical interest, because the formation of this All-Russian Government was the only one in Russia since the March, 1917, revolution, which could have been considered as having a mandate direct from the people. It is also important because it shows the beginning of a new government, the development of which was prevented entirely through the lack of interest and support from the Allied governments.

Considerable opposition to the All-Russian Government, especially from the Monarchist party, developed. The peasant class as a whole were indifferent and knew little about political affairs. They could be swung by the party offering the best promises to their personal welfare, and there was the additional danger that the church, which sympathized with the extreme Monarchist group, could swing the peasants their way, for the peasants were superstitious and could be influenced by the church, as has been the case for centuries in the past. The Monarchist party believed the future of Russia lay with General Denekin and the army fighting in Southern Russia. It believed that, when those forces and the Siberian forces joined, Denekin would become dictator or a monarchy would be declared.

The All-Russian Government struggled along through the summer and fall. Envoys were sent to the Allied countries in an effort to obtain their sympathy and support. Prince Lvoff, who had been premier in the provisional government in 1917, was sent to the United States as a special representative of the All-Russian Government. Russians throughout the Allied countries gave this government their moral support. Alexander Kerensky, who had been minister of justice and premier of the provisional government, telegraphed his support to Omsk, and it looked as if Siberia was to witness the birth of a real Russian representative democracy. The new government, however, was confronted by difficult conditions:

1. While it had the support of the Czecho-Slovak National Council and the military backing of that revolutionary army, it could not obtain the whole-hearted support of the Allied representatives in Siberia, and

2. The government had to struggle immediately with the problem of reconstruction in the industry and social life of the nation.

Although the Allies, the French, British, and American representatives, had promised to support the Czecho-Slovaks, several months passed before troops were landed at Vladivostok and Archangel, and after they were landed, instead of their coöperating with the Czecho-Slovak forces, they remained in eastern Siberia as an army of occupation in fact, if not in principle. After the Czechs had been fighting four months they began to ask why the Allies did not hurry their armies across Siberia, and they began to doubt whether they could rely upon Allied assistance.

Meanwhile the living conditions of the people grew worse. Millions of refugees rushed to Siberia from central Europe and from Asia and other parts of the world. Siberia became densely overcrowded, food increased in price as it became more and more impossible for Siberia to feed the influx of citizens. The factories had been closed because of a lack of raw materials and capital to operate them. The railroads were badly demoralized. The Allies could not agree upon a method of operation or control and the new government, with hundreds of questions of administration to decide every day, soon found it could not keep up with the public demands. It was faced by a certain collapse unless the Allies assisted whole-heartedly in the reorganization and reconstruction of Russia.

How this was to be accomplished was the issue which again divided the Allies. England, France, and Japan maintained that the only hope for the reorganization of Russia lay in a strong military organization, and urged the creation and development of an All-Russian army. Admiral Kolchak had been brought to Siberia by representatives of Great Britain because of his great ability as an organizer and executive, which he had displayed as commander of the Russian Black Sea fleet, and because of his loyalty to the Allies, which had been tested both before and during the revolution. Admiral Kolchak had been made the minister of war of the All-Russian Government, and had begun the reorganization of a Russian army with the coöperation and assistance of General Knox, the British commander, who had been for seven years military attaché of the British embassy in Petrograd.

Representatives of the United States, under instructions from their government and also because of their own ideas, had been contending that Russia could never be assisted in her reconstruction period unless the economic organization was first given new life. This is where the policies differed. One group of Allies maintained that Russia's hope lay in military intervention. Another group of Powers insisted that economic rehabilitation should be the beginning, and that the question of a large army should be left entirely to the Russian people and the Russian Government.

The All-Russian Government was in a quandary. With the Allies apparently hopelessly divided and with conditions growing worse and the public demands for order and bread multiplying every hour there developed a struggle among the Russians themselves as to the best means of bringing about the rebirth of Russia.

DECLARATION OF THE TEMPORARY INDEPENDENCE OF SIBERIA

July 4, 1918.

The Siberian Provisional Government, assuming plenary power in the land after the expulsion of the Bolshevik usurpers, in line with other important tasks, considers it imperative to bring Siberia out of that undefined situation in which it was in consequence of the dispersal by the Bolsheviks of the Siberian Provincial Duma and the continuation of the Bolshevik domination of European Russia.

The Siberian Provisional Government is clearly conscious that every delay in deciding the question of defining the state nature of Siberia is very pernicious in its consequences in connection with the present international situation; but, notwithstanding this, it would not take upon itself the responsibility of defining the future fate of its fatherland, if it did not have in this respect an authoritative indication on the part of the Siberian Provincial Duma, as expressed in the latter's declaration of January 27, 1918.

Supported solely by this declaration, in which the Siberian Provincial Duma definitely shows itself in favor of granting Siberia the full attributes of a state, the Provincial Government now holds it possible, in view of the acuteness of the moment, to take upon itself the task of settling this question without waiting for a new convocation of the Duma.

Upon this basis, and in view of the fact that the attributes of the Russian state do not exist as such, a considerable portion of the Russian territory being in the actual possession of the Central Powers, and another portion seized by the Bolshevik usurpers of the people's rule, the Siberian Provisional Government solemnly declares to all the world that henceforth it alone, together with the Siberian Provincial Duma, is responsible for the destiny of Siberia, and announces full freedom of independent relations with foreign Powers, and also declares that henceforth no other authority than the Siberian Provincial Government can act on the territory of Siberia or undertake obligations in the name of same.

At the same time the Siberian Provincial Government considers it is its sacred duty to state that the convocation of the All-Siberian Constituent Assembly, to which it will hand over its authority as is its unswerving intention, and to the earliest accomplishment of this will devote all its strength.

Nevertheless, the Siberian Provincial Government holds it absolutely necessary to declare not less solemnly, that it does not consider Siberia to be forever torn from those territories which as a whole composed the state of Russia, and believes that all efforts must be directed to the reconstruction of Russia as a state. The Provisional Government considers that, when this high aim is happily achieved, the character of the future relations between Siberia and European Russia will be determined by the All-Siberian and All-Russian Constituent Assemblies. Bearing this in mind the Siberian Provincial Government enters upon its responsible work with the firm assurance that it will be supported therein by all the patriotic and thinking elements of the country.

The President of the Council of Ministers and
Minister for Foreign Affairs, VOLOGODSKY.

UNITED STATES GOVERNMENT STATEMENT
Issued on August 3, 1918, at Washington, D. C.

In the judgment of the Government of the United States —a judgment arrived at after repeated and very searching consideration of the whole situation—military intervention in Russia would be more likely to add to the present sad confusion there than to cure it, and would injure Russia, rather than help her out of her distresses. Such military intervention as has been most frequently proposed, even supposing it to be efficacious in its immediate object of delivering an attack upon Germany from the east, would, in its judgment, be more likely to turn out to be merely a method of making use of Russia than to be a method of serving her. Her people, if they profited by it at all, could not profit by it in time to deliver them from their present desperate difficulties, and their substance would meantime be used to maintain foreign armies, not to reconstitute their own or to feed their own men, women, and children. We are bending all our energies now to the purpose, the resolute and confident purpose, of winning on the western front, and it would, in the judgment of the Government of the United States, be most unwise to divide or dissipate our forces.

As the Government of the United States sees the present circumstances, therefore, military action is admissible in Russia now only to render such protection and help as is possible to the Czecho-Slovaks against the armed Austrian and German prisoners who are attacking them, and to steady any efforts at self-government or self-defense in which the Russians themselves may be willing to accept assistance. Whether from Vladivostok or from Murmansk and Archangel, the only present object for which American troops will be employed will be to guard military stores which may subsequently be needed by Russian forces and to render such aid as may be acceptable to the Russians in the organization of their own self-defense.

With such objects in view, the Government of the United States is now coöperating with the Governments of France and Great Britain in the neighborhood of Murmansk and Archangel. The United States and Japan are the only powers which are just now in a position to act in Siberia in sufficient force to accomplish even such modest objects as those that have been outlined. The Government of the United States has, therefore, proposed to the Government of Japan that each of the two Governments send a force of a few thousand men to Vladivostok, with the purpose of coöperating as a single force in the occupation of Vladivostok and in safeguarding, as far as it may be, the country to the rear of the westward-moving Czecho-Slovaks, and the Japanese Government has consented.

In taking this action the Government of the United States wishes to announce to the people of Russia in the most public and solemn manner that it contemplates no interference with the political sovereignty of Russia, no intervention in her internal affairs—not even in the local affairs of the limited areas which her military force may be obliged to occupy—and no impairment of her territorial integrity, either now or hereafter, but that what we are about to do has as its single and only object the rendering of such aid as shall be acceptable to the Russian people themselves in their endeavors to regain control of their own affairs, their own territory, and their own destiny. The Japanese Government, it is understood, will issue a similar assurance.

These plans and purposes of the Government of the United States have been communicated to the Governments of Great Britain, France, and Italy, and those Governments have advised the Department of State that they assent to them in principle. No conclusion that the Government of the United States has arrived at in this important matter is intended, however, as an effort to restrict the actions or interfere with the independent judgment of the Governments with which we are now associated in the war.

It is also the hope and purpose of the Government of the United States to take advantage of the earliest opportunity to send to Siberia a commission of merchants, agricultural experts, labor advisers, Red Cross representatives, and agents of the Young Men's Christian Association accustomed to organizing the best methods of spreading useful information and rendering educational help of a modest kind in order in some systematic way to relieve the immediate economic necessities of the people there in every way for which an opportunity may open. The execution of this plan will follow and will not be permitted to embarrass the military assistance rendered to the Czecho-Slovaks.

JAPANESE GOVERNMENT STATEMENT
Also issued at Washington, August 3, 1918

The Japanese Government, actuated by sentiments of sincere friendship toward the Russian people, have always entertained most sanguine hopes of the speedy reëstablishment of order in Russia and of the healthy, untrammeled development of her national life.

Abundant proof, however, is now afforded that the Cen-

tral European Empires, taking advantage of the defenseless
and chaotic condition in which Russia has momentarily been
placed, are consolidating their hold on that country and are
steadily extending their activities to Russia's eastern possessions.   They have persistently interfered with the passage of Czecho-Slovak troops through Siberia.   In the forces
now opposing these valiant troops German and Austro-Hungarian prisoners are freely enlisted, and they practically assume a position of command.

The Czecho-Slovak troops, aspiring to secure a free and
independent existence for their race and loyally espousing
the common cause of the Allies, justly command every sympathy and consideration from the co-belligerents, to whom
their destiny is a matter of deep and abiding concern.

In the presence of the danger to which the Czecho-Slovak
troops actually are exposed in Siberia at the hands of the
Germans and Austro-Hungarians, the Allies have naturally
felt themselves unable to view with indifference the un-
toward course of events, and a certain number of their troops
already have been ordered to proceed to Vladivostok.

The Government of the United States, equally sensible
of the gravity of the situation, recently approached the Japanese Government with proposals for the early dispatch of
troops to relieve the pressure weighing upon the Czecho-
Slovak forces.   The Japanese Government, being anxious
to fall in with the desire of the American Government, have
decided to proceed at once to make disposition of suitable
forces for the proposed mission, and a certain number of
these troops will be sent forthwith to Vladivostok.

In adopting this course, the Japanese Government remain constant in their desire to promote relations of enduring
friendship, and they reaffirm their avowed policy of respecting the territorial integrity of Russia, and of abstaining
from all interference in her internal politics.   They further
declare that upon the realization of the objects above indicated they will immediately withdraw all Japanese troops
from Russian territory, and will leave wholly unimpaired
the sovereignty of Russia in all its phases, whether political
or military.

BY BORIS BAKHMETEFF

Announcement by the Ambassador from Democratic Russia

Direct and authoritative information has been received by the Russian Embassy concerning the program and intentions of the groups which have newly revealed themselves in Siberia, and which without bloodshed or violence have succeeded the Soviets, the latter having disappeared naturally by the very fact of the valiant Czecho-Slovak troops liberating different cities and regions of Russia. It appears at present that the group in Vladivostok, known under the title of "The Siberian Temporary Government," is closely united and, in fact, does not differ in any way from the authorities established in Omsk, which seem to be but a part of the same Government.

The United Siberian Government states that it was elected on the 26th of January, 1918, by the members of a regional Siberian Duma—representative assembly. The point where this Government has temporarily transferred its center is Vladivostok, the other members of it remaining at Omsk. A message from those at Omsk has just been received, stating that owing to combined efforts of the Czechoslavs and the military organizations of the Siberian Government itself, the following cities have been liberated from the Bolsheviki: Marlinsk, Novo Nicolaievsk, Tomsk, Narime, Tobolsk, Barnaoul, Carcaralinsk, Atchinski, and Crasnoiarsk.

Everywhere the people belonging to different classes and political groups have manifested vivid interest and sympathy with the organization of their army, which is intended to reestablish, together with the Allies, a battlefront against Germany, and the formation of which is proceeding very successfully. Their relations with the Czecho-Slovak are brotherly.

To that most valuable information the "Temporary Government of Siberia" adds a public statement of its political aims, which are: The creation of a Russian Army, well disciplined, in order to reëstablish, in coöperation with the Allies, a battlefront against Germany. Siberia being an inseparable part of United Russia, the Temporary Government of Siberia believes it to be its first duty to safeguard, in the territory of Siberia, the interests of the whole of Russia, to recognize all the international treaties and agreements of Russia with friendly nations which were in force until October 25, 1917, the moment of the Bolshevist uprising.

The Siberian Government is tending to reëstablish government and order in Siberia and to start the reconstruction of a unified Russia and the creation of a central All-Russian authority which would be generally recognized.

BY NICOLAI TCHAIKOVSKY

Temporary President of Northern Russia, his manifesto of August 31, 1918

Archangel, August 31st.—In the region of Northern Russia the yoke of the Bolsheviki is thrown off. In accord with the Allies, the Government of the region of Northern Russia, not recognizing the peace treaty of Brest, has set as its aim the expulsion of the Germans out of the boundaries of Russia and the creation anew of a great and indivisible Russia.

Owing to the initiative of the League of Regeneration of Russia, composed of representatives of all political parties, except the extreme ones, the Government of the region of Northern Russia was formed by delegates of the Northern Provinces to the Constituent Assembly and by representatives of the Zemstvos and towns of the region.

The municipalities and judicial bodies are reconstituted. The Russian Army is again created and on the basis of discipline. The Allies are aiding us. Mobilization has been declared in the northern region.

Desiring to secure real liberty and a democratic régime, the Government of Northern Russia, joining hands with other regional Governments, has as final aim the formation of a single Government for the whole of Russia based on universal suffrage.

The Government of Northern Russia appeals to all Russian citizens to rally around the banner of salvation of their native country, of the liberties gained, and the rebirth of Russia.

GERMANY'S LAST EFFORT AT ATTACK

THE "PEACE ASSAULT" AND THE GRIM AMERICAN RE-SISTANCE ALONG THE MARNE

JULY 15TH

GENERAL GOURAUD   JOHN BUCHAN
GENERAL PERSHING   LIEUTENANT KURT HESSE
GENERAL BARON VON ARDENNE

The failure of repeated German attacks against the French line in June, the great disaster to Austria on the Piave, and, more than all, the successful fighting of the Americans around Château-Thierry and the swift rush of their thousands of eager soldiers to the front, all this must have been clear warning to the German commanders that the end was near. Ludendorff determined on one more desperate throw for victory. All through June and early July he had been gathering his munitions and his men. He issued a bulletin assuring them that this was to be the last great effort demanded of them. It was to be the *Friedensturm,* the "Peace Assault," which was to conquer the Allies' last resistance.

This great Peace Assault struck southward against the Ally line on July 15th. Centering against the long beleaguered fortress city of Rheims, the assault extended almost thirty miles on either side, spreading along the Marne from Château-Thierry on the west almost to the Argonne forest on the east.

At its western extreme the assault was met and turned back disastrously by the Americans, one regiment in particular, the Thirty-eighth of the Third Division, covered itself with glory by holding back the larger part of two whole German divisions, though its neighbors in the Ally line had retreated, leaving it to meet attack from the front and from both flanks. "We kill or get killed" had not been an empty boast of those earlier American prisoners.

Between the "stone wall" American defense and Rheims itself the Germans were more successful. They won the crossings of the Marne and by July 17th had penetrated almost to Epernay, the capture of which would have encircled Rheims and might have compelled its surrender. But again their bolt was shot; their strength was exhausted; Epernay was never reached. Southward the foe penetrated on July 16th to the hamlet of St. Aignan before they were checked by a counter-attack. That was Germany's "high-water mark" in her final push for victory.

East of Rheims the Peace Assault had been checked even more decisively on its opening day. Here French troops under General Gouraud, with some American aid, broke the German attacks by a powerful artillery and machine-gun fire, causing the Germans enormous losses without gain. Such was the *Friedensturm.*

242

Read the account of it by the standard British historian, Buchan; or better still, read the story of the American resistance by Lieutenant Hesse, a gallant German who took part in the battle. His narrative could not secure publication in Germany until after the War. It was too frank for German readers. But it reveals the truth; for generations hereafter Americans will be traditionally regarded in Germany as the most desperate fighters of the War. To them belongs the credit of having broken the German *morale*. You could get that standpoint from any one of the German prisoners in France in 1918: "We had them beaten, if you Americans had stayed out," or "You go back home, and we'll beat them again."

Such a statement does not mean that America's share in the War or the effort put forth by Americans was anything like so tremendous and so exhaustive as were the efforts of France and Britain. It means, however, that the United States troops were still fresh and youthful, while Europe's were outworn; that Europe had lost a large majority of its ablest fighters; and that the American "boys" were inspired by a high and holy faith in the justice of their cause, which made death seem a little thing. It means, too, that General Pershing's insistence on the American theory of rifle training had borne rich fruit. American soldiers used their rifles as a hunter would, not blazing away all their ammunition in blind volleys at a distant foe, but waiting, grimly enduring the chance-directed firing of the enemy until the opportunity came to retaliate with well-placed and deadly shots. That was the "bestial brutality" of the American fighting which amazed Lieutenant Hesse. The old Bunker Hill battle-cry of General Putnam, "Hold your fire until you can see the whites of their eyes," was almost literally reproduced in the American fighting along the Marne. It smashed the German's confidence in his own attack; and it smashed the German Empire. C. F. H.

BY GENERAL GOURAUD
Official Appeal to his Army on July 16th

To the French and American Soldiers of the Army:

WE may be attacked from one moment to another. You all feel that a defensive battle was never engaged in under more favorable conditions. We are warned, and we are on our guard. We have received strong reënforcements of infantry and artillery. You will fight on ground which by your assiduous labor you have transformed into a formidable fortress, into a fortress which is invincible if the passages are well guarded.

The bombardment will be terrible. You will endure it without weakness. The attack in a cloud of dust and gas will be fierce, but your positions and your armament are formidable.

The strong and brave hearts of free men beat in your

breasts. None will look behind, none will give way. Every man will have but one thought—"Kill them, kill them in abundance, until they have had enough." And therefore your General tells you it will be a glorious day.

BY JOHN BUCHAN

Ludendorff, seeking a final decision, did not unduly limit his objectives. He wanted no less than the line of the Marne between Epernay and Châlons as the fruit of the first day's advance. The attack was arranged in two sections—on a front of twenty-seven miles, between Fossoy, southeast of Château-Thierry, and Vrigny; and on a front of twenty-six miles east of Rheims, between Prunay and the Main de Massiges. In each area he used fifteen divisions for the first wave, twenty-three of them fresh divisions from his general reserve, and seven of them borrowed from Prince Rupprecht's group. He had a large number of tanks, which he allotted to the area east of Rheims, where the low downs of Champagne made the going easier for machines which had not the skill of the Allied type in covering rough country.

At midnight on Sunday, July 14th, Paris was awakened by the sound of great guns. At first she thought it an air raid, but the blaze in the eastern sky showed that business was afoot on the battlefield. She waited for news with a solemn mind, for she knew that the last phase had begun of the struggle for her possession. The "preparation" lasted till four o'clock; but before the dawn broke the Germans were aware of a new feature in the bombardment. The French guns were replying, and with amazing skill were searching out their batteries and assembly trenches, so that when zero hour came the attacking infantry in many parts of the line were already disorganized. Foch's intelligence service had done its work; he had profited by the enemy's bravado, and he read their plans like an open book.

About 4 a. m., just at dawn, the German infantry crossed the parapets. Von Boehn was instantly successful, for it was no part of Foch's plan to resist too doggedly at the apex of the salient. The Germans passed the Marne at various points between Château-Thierry and Dormans, reached the crest of the hills on the south shore, and extended to the valley where lay the villages of St. Agnan and La Chapelle. It was an advance of from one to three miles on a front of twenty-two. That evening von Boehn's line lay from Fos soy, south of the Marne and three miles east of Château-Thierry, by Mezy, St. Agnan, La Chapelle, Comblizy, north of Mareuil le Port, through Chatillon, north of Belval, through Cuitron and Clairizet to the Bois de Vrigny. It was a substantial advance; but one thing it had utterly failed to achieve. It had not widened the salient. No impression had been made upon the French front in the Montagne de Rheims region, and the gatepost on the west at Château-Thierry stood like a strong tower. In the former area the Italian 2nd Corps, fighting among thick woods in the upper glen of the Ardre, barred the way to Epernay by the Nanteuil-Hautvillers road. In the latter area the Americans formed the right wing of Dégoutte's army, and at Vaux and Fossoy they first checked and then rolled back the German wave, clearing that part of the south bank of the river, and taking 600 prisoners.

These were the troops who, according to the German belief, would not land in Europe unless they could swim like fishes or fly like birds. Like the doubting noble of Samaria, the Germans had declared, "If the Lord would make windows in heaven, might this thing be." But the inconceivable had been brought to pass. Birnam Wood had come to Dunsinane.

East of Rheims von Mudra and von Einem made no headway at all. They were opposed by one who was not only a paladin of chivalry, but a great and wily tactician. Gouraud's counter-bombardment dislocated the German attack before it began; his deep outpost zone caused it to spend itself idly with heavy losses; his swift counter-attacks checked the "infiltration" before it could be set going. Ground was, indeed, given up north of Souain and Prosnes, and between Tahure and Massiges on the old Champagne battle-ground, and the Germans entered Prunay. But not a French gun was lost, and Gouraud's battle zone was untouched. The German tanks were all stopped by anti-tank guns or land mines. The French losses were trifling: only 3,000 men passed that day through Gouraud's casualty stations. It was indeed such a situation as had faced Nivelle at the end of the first day of the Second Battle of the Aisne. But the failure was far graver for Ludendorff, for he was staking all on an immediate victory.

Nevertheless the end was not yet. The Germans had still at least sixty divisions in reserve, and they were battling for dear life. The unsuccess of the first day must be redeemed, and at any cost Epernay must be reached and the Montagne isolated. Could this be done, there was still time to form á new front on the western flank and push down the Marne to Paris. The French south of the river in the St. Agnan valley had lost their power of direct observation, and so could not use their guns effectively against the German bridges. The danger point was the road to Epernay up the Marne valley, and all day on the 16th Berthelot was hotly engaged. He fell back 4,000 yards, but in the evening his center was still holding on the line Festigny-Neuilly-Belval. Further west the French had better fortune, for in the afternoon they counter-attacked between Comblizy and St. Agnan, won the ridge overlooking the Marne, and proceeded to make havoc among the German pontoons. In Champagne that day there was no advance. Von Mudra and von Einem were utterly exhausted. On the fringes of the Montagne the French and Italian troops on Berthelot's right maintained their positions. The day closed with ill omens for the enemy. Since the French on the St. Agnan ridge could sweep the river crossings, it would be hard for von Boehn to maintain his eight divisions beyond the river.

Yet on Wednesday, the 17th, he still persisted. There was hard fighting on Berthelot's right wing, where the Italian 2nd Corps was engaged on the Upper Ardre, and the Germans made progress at the Bois de Courton and towards Nanteuil. The Italians, however, by a brilliant counter-attack retook the village of Clairizet. South of the Marne the French center was pressed further up the river; but by the evening it had retaken Montvoisin and the high ground to the west between that place and Festigny. Von Boehn made a great effort to win back the ridge just south of the Marne, but failed; and all day the battle swung backwards and forwards without material result. But by the evening the eight German divisions were very weary, and their communications across the river were in serious jeopardy. They had shot their bolt, and at the farthest point had advanced some six miles from their old battle-ground.

BY GENERAL PERSHING
From his official report

The enemy had encouraged his soldiers to believe that the July 15th attack would conclude the war with a German peace. Although he made elaborate plans for the operation, he failed to conceal fully his intentions, and the front of attack was suspected at least one week ahead. On the Champagne front the actual hour for the assault was known and the enemy was checked with heavy losses. The 42nd Division entered the line near Somme Py immediately, and five of its infantry battalions and all its artillery became engaged.

Southwest of Rheims and along the Marne to the east of Château-Thierry the Germans were at first somewhat successful, a penetration of eight kilometers beyond the river being effected against the French immediately to the right of our 3rd Division.

The following quotation from the report of the Commanding General 3rd Division gives the result of the fighting on his front: "Although the rush of the German troops overwhelmed some of the front-line positions, causing the infantry and machine-gun companies to suffer, in some cases a 50 per cent. loss, no German soldier crossed the road from Fossoy to Crezancy, except as a prisoner of war, and by noon of the following day (July 16th) there were no Germans in the foreground of the 3rd Division sector except the dead."

On this occasion *a single regiment of the 3rd Division wrote one of the most brilliant pages in our military annals.* It prevented the crossing at certain points on its front, while on either flank the Germans who had gained a footing pressed forward. Our men, firing in three sections, met the Ger-

man attacks with counter-attacks at critical points and succeeded in throwing two German divisions into complete confusion, capturing 600 prisoners.

BY KURT HESSE

The Marne-Drama of July 15, 1918, *seen from the angle
of the fighting grenadier regiment No.* 5,
36th *Infantry Division*

"To-morrow we shall march on Paris!" Thus we expressed ourselves to the commander of the Third Battalion
of the French line Infantry Regiment No. 2, which, driven
to the Marne by our briskly attacking grenadiers, was forced
to surrender, 800 men strong, on the evening of May 30th.
"*Non, Monsieur, à Paris! Jamais! Pensez à* 1914! *La
Marne!*" [1] Seriously and with dignity the French Lieutenant-Colonel thus replied, and we honored his pride—and
grew pensive ourselves for a moment.   But then our joy in
the glorious success of the day had the upper hand: the Marne
was reached, in four days from the *Chemin des Dames* across
the Aisne and Vesle to the mythical stream.   Hardly any
casualties.   The enemy, on the other hand, was most severely
damaged.   Only—on to Paris!

In the night between the 30th and the 31st of May, however, the 36th Infantry Division received the command: "The
position won must be held!" No advance? Here was disappointment! But one could not see far to the right or the
left; and when the water-carriers early in the morning went
down to the Marne, they encountered fire aimed at them from
the other shore.   We had a new enemy opposite us—one
who no longer thought of retreat.

Between this enemy and us was the Marne, a river with a
swift current, over 60 meters broad at Château-Thierry, very
deep and canalized.   The valley resembles that of the Weser,
except that it is usually somewhat broader.   Slopes to the
right and left are luxuriously covered with woods, orchards
and vineyards; there are numerous villages, pastures full of
cattle.   When on the morning of May 31st I stood with my
commander on the heights to the east of Château-Thierry

[1] "Not, Monsieur, to Paris! Never! Remember 1914! The Marne!"

—truly, a paradise lay before me, the sun smiled over it, a brisk wind blew across the valley. Here one breathed a different air; no war—peace.

Of the enemy nothing could be seen. Scarcely a man was visible in the next five weeks. Only now and then a sharp report when some one carelessly showed himself. We took great pains to point out targets for the artillery, but usually without success.

Men on leave, who came from Charleville in the first days of July, told us, when we had at that time withdrawn quietly to Fère-en-Tardenois, 20 kilometers north of the river: "On July 15th we shall cross the Marne!"

We knew for ourselves that we would attack. As in the days of March, we practiced that kind of attack in which we advanced where the enemy offered the least resistance; we did not storm the strong front, the "forehead," as it were, but attacked it from the flanks and the rear; we followed the firing body and cleared the way, coöperating effectively with the artillery and mine throwers. But at night we heard first a very muffled shot, then for a while there was calm. Suddenly there rose a rustling and whizzing which grew sharper and sharper, then a blow which started a roaring in one's ears and made the heart of the bravest tremble. The infantry rushed out of the houses into the fields, for it had no protection against the grenades of the heavy French railway guns, and then returned to its quarters at dusk and quiet descended. The infantrymen were supposed to find recreation, but they could not enjoy life, and many a man had to be buried before command was given for the new attack.

A few days before the assault—on July 12th—we learned details of the operation about to be performed. We were ordered to keep our inquiries within the narrowest limit. Thus only commanders of regiments and battalions and very few leaders of companies were able to view the first and second places for preparation, the roads for marching, the positions for action, the places for vehicles and all the many points about which one wanted to find out. My troop, the Grenadier Regiment No. 5, was to cross at the right flank of

the 36th Infantry Division near Jaulgonne at two places:
to the right, together with the 10th Infantry Division, our
proved fighting companion of the 21st and 27th of May, the
first days of storm of the offensive of Quentin and of the
Chemin des Dames; to the left with the brave Infantry Regiment 175.   Infantry and machine-gun troops were to cross
on pontoons, and later on ferries; artillery and vehicles were
to be drawn after them over bridges.

At Fismes we practiced in advance with some pontoons
on the Ourcq: embarking and disembarking and crossing
over.   In order to carry out this peace-time maneuver, the
infantry had to march 18 km. twice, in scorching heat and
dust which lay piled up high like a wall upon the road that
led through the woods from Fère-en-Tardenois.   Tired to
death, they returned to their quarters, whence they were
driven again in the night by firing.   And this a few days
before the attack!

The actual command for the operation came very late.   I
was just sitting and working over it, when a perfectly strange
grenadier was announced.   With excitement but modestly he
asked if it were true that Americans were stationed over
there and that our attack was betrayed.   I quieted him, but
inquired carefully here and there what the general opinions
on the attack might be.   There was thorough confidence in
the leaders; but there was an indefinite feeling that the
affair would not succeed.   "The infantry has the right instinct," veterans of the front used to say.

Whoever saw clearly had to think seriously of failure.
The enemy had taken several prisoners from us, among
others an officer of photometry who, contrary to orders, had
carried important maps with him.   From here and there
we heard of deserters.   In defiance of all war experiences
little had been done to keep our purpose secret; thus at nine
o'clock in the morning, while enemy aviators had been circling above for over four hours, our munition columns still
stood crowded together on the streets.

The enemy fire increased each day.   When on July 13th
we moved to the places of preparation, thick clouds of gas
lay on the wood of Jaulgonne.   "It will turn out all right,"

was the general consolation. The last offensive had given us courage, less to the troops than to the commanders. Were the men at the front mistaken at the time when they felt that their warning had not been heeded enough? To be sure, it would have made a strange impression if, a few days before the attack, timid voices should have been heard from a division. And it was quite comprehensibly human that an officer of the general staff, who had exerted his whole strength and intelligence for the hard work of preparing the attack and was looking forward to success, should be shy of saying: "It can't be carried through!" Two forces were exerting their pressure—the hope roused by ambition: "Perhaps we will succeed after all; the enemy's fighting is so poor"; and then the man at the top who was accustomed to an inconsiderate process of removal whenever he noticed that positions were filled by the wrong men.

The two days which we spent 5 km. away from the Marne under cover of the woods passed favorably. We had to suffer little from shooting. The weather was tolerable; it rained somewhat, but the infantry which, to be sure, was quite without cover, had already endured worse things.

"On July 15, 1.10 o'clock in the morning, our own artillery fire is to begin, at 3.40 in the morning the artillery fire will be advanced 300 m.

"Infantry is to cross over.

"At 4.50 in the morning the volley is to start and the infantry storm is to begin."

Thank heaven, now there was clearness! Except for trifles, the entire apparatus was in good shape; to be sure, some bearers of carrier pigeons were missing; the wireless station had lost its way. But the main point was that all posts had their orders in time.

On July 14th in the evening, soon after dark, the infantry troops were led to the front positions. They lay 600-800 m. away from the river on the slopes, in the midst of the forest, which faced the enemy and descended to the Marne. Covers (trenches or shelters) had not been prepared; the only things which marked the positions were tablets which one could not see in the night.

Scarcely ever have I experienced such a dark night as the one from July 14th to 15th. In the woods one could not see one's own hand in front of one's eyes, and ran against trees. The ground was smooth and slippery, the air filled with gas; now and then there was a roaring—for the enemy sent across some heavy grenades.

This lasted hour after hour. The infantry for whose march two hours had been calculated (for a march of 4 km.) had not arrived at its positions. The leaders required infinitely much longer time than they had planned, to find the way which they had seen once by daylight.

The hardships for our men were enormous. And when they had arrived at last, the announcements did not sound very edifying: casualties already during the march; great exhaustion of the troops, some ill from marching, some lost. But—they stood where they were supposed to stand.

When is it going to start? We were in a torpor. At last! A mad artillery fire started. I looked at my watch: 1 o'clock in the morning! Had our artillery made a mistake? It wasn't supposed to begin till 1.10 in the morning! Out of the holes in which we sat—and back into them fast! Before and behind us the missiles struck. The enemy had begun! Ten minutes later we began, not like one blow, as we had been ordered, but starting out here and there; our fire swelled to a mighty strength for ten minutes, so that we had the hope: now everything will turn out all right! Then it grew weaker again and weaker. Frequently the enemy fire was much stronger than ours.

Soon telephone lines forward and backward were destroyed. If only the program is carried out right! At 3.50 in the morning no report. From the rear you are pressed: "Report how things are! Has the infantry crossed the river?" Answer: "There is no report yet. The enemy fire is terrible. But we suppose that everything is going on as planned." At 4.30 in the morning at last a report from the front: the fusileer battalion, the left front attacking battalion, reports that the prepared positions were subjected to the strongest enemy fire, that two companies were fully broken up and that there were grave doubts about the success of the attack. This report is immediately passed on verbatim. No word has come as yet, if the crossing has succeeded. The regiment's staff sends out patrols, to make sure of the situation. At last, after hours, a more accurate report arrives.

The first battalion, which was to attack to the right, has been caught terribly in the narrow path that leads down to the river, by enemy fire. Only parts have reached the river. The pioneers have given up. The pontoons have been left 100 meters before the Marne; it is impossible to cross here, as strong enemy infantry is defending the other shore stubbornly with numerous machine guns. To the left things look a little better. The fusileer battalion has reached the river with two companies and is crossing. Strong parts of the IInd battalion, which were to follow as reserves and which have been led forward very skillfully by Cavalry Captain von Plehwe, the victor of May 30th, have already arrived at the other shore of the river and are holding the railroad embankment which lies about 600 m. to the south of the river. The casualties of F 5 are very severe, those of II 5 a little lighter. The attack has halted. A strong enemy prevents farther advance.

This is the first picture. The infantry without protection lying in the midst of the great forest of Jaulgonne, which has such dense thickets that it is impossible to pass through, and on the other hand, has scarcely a tree strong enough to serve as cover against an infantry bullet. Now the massed fire of the enemy artillery bursts into them: not a spot is saved. Here fire from a heavy battery keeps on continually. The striking in the forest is terrible, nerve-racking. The clearing over there is caught every five minutes by a light battery and in a short time is a black crater. And the small path to the right is spread over with shrapnels, which glow fiery in their courses, like comets. Our men run aimlessly hither and thither; no cover! And again roaring, dull reports: gas grenades! Put on the gas masks! One could not see anything before—now still less! Many are seized with a dull despair. They feel helpless: if it would only be day! The wounded scream. At last a hoarsely gasped command from the leader of the company, even now seriously conscious of his duty: "Begin! Has every man a gun?" Now forward on the narrow paths which are struck so fiercely, which, nevertheless, are the only ways that lead down to the river. The pioneers stand somewhat lower down. Their leader does not know what to do. He has only a few men. The infantry take hold themselves and carry the pontoons the several hundred meters to the river.

A new situation for the artillery. Everything is out of joint. Several dead and a shattered machine gun stay lying beside the pontoons. Only let us go on, away from here! There are other pontoons below.

The accompanying artillery arrives—for each infantry regiment has one to two batteries, in our case a field-gun battery and a mountain battery. One gun has been ruined by good shots, a second has broken a shaft. The leaders ask: "Is it wise to advance farther?" They were commanded to halt and seek a place where they might be stationed if possible outside the firing range. But the mountain battery has already driven into the narrow path through the wood, upon which the 1st battalion marched ahead, and is now caught, for it cannot budge either to the right or the left nor forward. And one shot after the other hits those fine, proud troops. The horses writhe on the ground, and the munitions explode.

Down by the river, the pioneers of the fusileer regiment have worked better. Two pontoons are ready, six should be there. Overladen the first man crosses. A machine gun shoots from over there, but too high. All duck, throw themselves down. Has our artillery had no effect? The bank is steep. The first infantrymen pull themselves up by the willows and hang there—a wire obstacle! No one had ever seen that, and no telescope had been able to discover it. Was a trench behind it? Our men feel their way. It is still quite dark. One of them steps on something soft, which suddenly gives way, and now the hand-to-hand fight has come. The enemy is entrenched here and has till now taken cover against our artillery fire. One moment— and then we have the upper hand. That is always the way with all "bitter hand-to-hand fights"—that fear of the cold steel seizes the one or the other and he runs away.

The crossing is comparatively quick. We look at the time. "For heaven's sake, the firing body is already marching!"—"Form positions!" The companies are assigned new aims, as everything has turned out differently than as it was planned.

The railroad tracks are crossed, the railroad station Varennes taken after a short fight, we go on past the road Moulins-Varennes—already 1,000 m. south of the Marne! —and up the southern slopes of the valley. Suddenly from the right there are sounds of sharp firing and screams. In the morning mist, in the high grain field, one can see storm columns advance, dressed in brown—Americans!

Now and then they stand still and shoot. Our men come running back. The situation is extremely critical. Where are our neighbors, the 6th grenadiers? The attack must have been given up. The grenadiers are blindly shooting their volleys "according to program." This is to last until 11 o'clock in the morning, then they will be free for other tasks. But these they could hardly have carried out anyway, for observation of the battle is very hard; low mists veil the landscape, the grain is high, and movements are covered by the many little woods and orchards. The commanders of the IInd battalion of the fusileers, Cavalry Captain von Plehwe and Captain Eben who are far at the front of their companies, realize that there is extreme danger in delay. All able to shoot, aim against the enemy on the right flank.

One must admit he is courageous unto death. Not till the machine-gun fire and the desperate shooting of our infantry had reaped a bloody harvest in his lines, did he halt and run back. But we take breaths of relief. Yet it is clear to each one of us: our own attack has failed! We must see to it that we can hold the position we have won with our weak forces, numerically much smaller than the enemy's.

The railroad line seems adequate for the defense. It is situated somewhat high and offers protection against fire, although on the other hand it is naturally a good target for the enemy artillery. Methodically the parts which are farther front are drawn back to this point. The right endangered flank is strongly reënforced. Toward 11 o'clock in the morning there is communication with our neighbor to the left. He has fared a little better, but is now fighting hard too. The Grenadier Regiment No. 6 at first came across with strong forces, but encountered a superior foe and was annihilated. One of our companies which strangely broke through the enemy line—the 6th, under Lieutenant Oberg—believes that there are German troops ahead and advances 4 km. deep, along the eastern slope of the Surmelin valley, right into the enemy. Below to the right, American infantry columns are marching; above, to the left, the enemy batteries are firing continually, till at last the little band is discovered. Now it is in a difficult position, but holds its own bravely till evening. Its death-defying leader and a few men make their way through the enemy lines backwards to another part of the German troops, and rejoin us. This was a ray of light, but it was the only one in this operation, and therefore I mention it.

On the afternoon of July 15th it was possible to improve the line somewhat, as the enemy on the Marne, probably from fear of a double flanking movement, drew back its position somewhat; but this did not change anything in the final result of the day. *It was the severest defeat of the war!*

One only had to descend the northern slopes of the Marne: *never have I seen so many dead, nor such frightful sights in battle. The Americans on the other shore had completely shot to pieces in a close combat two of our companies. They had lain in the grain, in semicircular formation, had let us approach, and then from 30 to 50 feet had shot almost all of us down.* This foe had nerves, one must allow him this boast; but he also showed a bestial brutality. "The Americans kill everything!" That was the cry of horror of July 15th, which long took hold of our men. At home meanwhile they were sarcastic about the imperfect training of this enemy, about the American "bluff" and the like. The fact that on July 15th more than 60 per cent. of our troops led to battle were left dead or wounded upon the battlefield may substantially be charged to his credit.

Our hopes that perhaps on the rest of the attacking front we might achieve better results unfortunately proved vain. To be sure, the usual reports arose: "Rheims has fallen!" "To our left the Bavarian division has advanced 15 km.!" But there was unhappily no truth in them, as happened so often. Everywhere the same sight: courageous, death-defying attack, the severest casualties and no success in any way worth mentioning. At the Marne front a long, narrow bridgehead had been made. It was naturally expected that the strongest attacks would be aimed against this in a short while. We prepared for this situation, but had small hope of being able to keep our position: 1 to 2 km. behind us was the river—this did not help our prospects. On July 17th the first attacks were started. They were repulsed. On the 18th the enemy went at it with more energy and brought armored tanks into the fight. But without success.

Like salvation we welcomed the command: "Front to be withdrawn behind the Marne!" In the night between the 18th and 19th of July we withdrew. The Marne bridges were afire. One bridge was already destroyed. Yet we crossed in tolerable condition. The enemy, at any rate, noticed nothing, so that our patrols left behind on the southern shore could remain over there several hours and could return unmolested.

We hoped for rest. A day like the 15th of July affects body and nerves for weeks. Our lines were thinned. Low spirits took hold of most of the men. So infinitely many dear comrades we had left over there. Many of them we had not been able to lay in the earth. It had all been like a warning: your turn too is coming! Thus thought the man at the front. Then the report reached us: trouble to the right. The enemy, enormously strong, has attacked from the woods of Villers-Cotterets, has advanced 15 km. on the first day. We must go back." We gnashed our teeth, but believed it, even before we received details officially. And these troops, which had just endured such hardships, had the task of giving their last, of hurling themselves as an obstacle against the overwhelming storm wave. They did this calmly and patiently, sacrificed the remainder of the veterans of 1914, and did not lose their honor.

BY GENERAL BARON V(ARDENNE

Semi-official Statement issued to the (nan public in August

Our three great battles of assau from March 21st to July 15th caused the enemy losses amounting to 1,225,000 men. On July 15th our attempted surprise failed, and, despite his losses, the enemy's numerical superiority had increased. Then the German command, swift as lightning and without the least hesitation, knew how to find the transition to the now necessary, although momentary, defensive.

That was a strategic masterpiece which merits admiration. Moltke once said that the defensive could, under certain conditions, be the stronger form of combat, especially in sections of ground which are particularly favorable for defense and inaccessible to hostile enemy flanking attacks. There a numerically inferior force may compel superior enemy forces to costly frontal attacks. The German command adopted this principle in its battles after July 15th.

THE BEGINNING OF THE END

FOCH LAUNCHES THE GREAT ALLIED ADVANCE

JULY 18TH

FERDINAND FOCH, MARSHAL OF FRANCE
JOHN BUCHAN   GENERAL PERSHING
GEORG WEGENER   GENERAL VON LUDENDORFF
GENERAL MANGIN   GENERAL DEGOUTTE
KARL ROSNER

France had made Joffre a Marshal in 1914 after the First Battle of the Marne; in 1918, after the Second Battle of the Marne, she conferred the same honor upon General Foch, the actual presentation of his Marshal's "baton" taking place on August 21st.

Thus did France mark her belief that these were the two main and decisive actions of the War. This second Marne battle may well be reckoned as beginning on May 31st at Château-Thierry, and extending to August 6th, when the American divisions drove the still retreating foe back across the Vesle River. Thus from start to finish the Americans held a foremost place in the tremendous fighting which broke the German advance and turned it into a despairing retreat.

The day on which the long series of defensive battles turned definitely to aggression was July 18th. On that morning General Foch, sure now of the superior strength of his armies, hurled the "Tenth Army" of General Mangin against the foe just south of Soissons. In the Tenth Army were the First and Second American Divisions. Suddenly, without the usual warning of a heavy artillery preparation, these troops swept over the German line, burying it under the unexpected attack.

As swiftly as they could, the Germans brought up reënforcements, more and more thousands of their best troops, to stay the advance. In vain! When the resistance to General Mangin's army became too heavy, it paused; and another army struck instead.

This second phase of the advance was taken up by General Dégoutte's "Sixth Army," which lay just south of Mangin's forces, around Château-Thierry. In this so-called "French" army, the weight of the advance was again taken by the American troops whom Pershing had loaned to France's necessity. Fighting all through later July and early August, these were the Americans who kept the Germans still retiring. In September they struck again along the same lines and drove the Germans from the Vesle River back to the Aisne, from which they had started in their great drive of May. Not until then was the "Marne salient" wholly wiped out. But through all those weeks the Germans were compelled to keep many of their best divisions on this front, thus weakening elsewhere their ever weakening line.

Of this tremendously important battle we give many estimates, that

259

of Buchan the best and clearest British writer on this theme, the official American estimate of Pershing, the German views, official and critical, of Ludendorff, the commander, and Wegener, the established patriotic critical authority. France speaks through both the commanding generals, Mangin and Dégoutte, as well as through the trumpet call to the Americans issued by General Foch before the battle.

C. F. H.

BY MARSHAL FOCH
Official Address issued July 4, 1918

AFTER four years of struggle the plans of the enemy for domination are stopped. He sees the number of his adversaries increase each day, and the young American Army bring into the battle a valor and a faith without equal. Is not this a sure pledge of the definitive triumph of the just cause?

BY JOHN BUCHAN

A defensive need not be stagnant and supine. It may be as vigilant and aggressive as any attack. From March 21st to the middle of July the mind of Foch was working intensely on the problem before him. He had to repel from day to day Ludendorff's hordes, and conserve and nurse his own mass of maneuver; but he had also to discover the answer to the new German tactics, and frame his own tactical plan against the day of *revanche*. Hints of his solution appeared in the June fighting on the Matz and in the Italian resistance on the Piave, and by midsummer his scheme was complete. The gist of his tactical reply lay in three points: first, the organization of his outpost line in great depth, not unlike von Armin's device at Third Ypres, so that the first enemy shock might spend itself in the void; second, a highly-complex use of artillery to break up a concentration once it was located; and, third, a system of rapid counter-attacks to check "infiltration" at the start. That was for the defense. For his own advance, when the time for it came, he had recast Ludendorff's tactics in a better form, and had subordinated them to a strategical plan of far greater boldness and ingenuity than anything as yet originated by the German General Staff. For these tactics he had a weapon of supreme value in his new light tanks, which, modeled on the British "whippet," were now appearing in large quantities on the French front. Already, in local counter-attacks on the Aisne, they had proved their merit; they were soon to paralyze the enemy's defense in a decisive battle.

But no plan is effective without numbers to execute it, and for the first time Foch had numbers at his command. The achievements of America in war finance, in ship construction, and in production of *matériel* were adequate to the seriousness of her purpose, and there could be no higher praise. Already her levies of men had passed the two million point, and their preliminary training had been expedited to such a degree that soon after midsummer she was landing in France every five weeks as many troops as the sum of Germany's annual recruitment. The retreat from St. Quentin had been for the Allies a blessing in disguise, for it had induced America to perform one of the most miraculous exploits in history. In April 117,212 American soldiers had landed in Europe; in May, 224,345; in June, 276,372; and of the total of 617,929 more than half had been carried in British ships. The rate was increasing, too, with every week. Moreover, America had shown the most admirable generosity and good sense in the use made of her forces. She naturally looked forward to great American armies in France commanded, like the French and the British, by her own generals. But in order to facilitate training it was desirable to postpone the realization of this ideal, and she consented to brigade her men with French and British troops. The American divisional unit [1] was maintained, but it served for the present under French or British army and corps commanders. For a month or two it was inevitable that the number of American troops capable of being used in the first line would be only a small proportion of the total in France.[2] But the presence of these great potential reserves had the inestimable advantage that it enabled Foch to use his seasoned troops boldly, since material for replacing them was mounting up daily.

It is hard to tell how far Germany was aware of the

[1] An American division numbered 30,000 men.
[2] There were at the moment twelve American divisions in the line in France.

full danger awaiting her in this addition to the Allied strength. Whatever her General Staff may have thought, her politicians and her press gave no sign that they realized its gravity. Sneers at America were the stock-in-trade of every German newspaper and most German orators. The great American army could not swim or fly, therefore it would never arrive; the Americans only shouted to keep warm, and would bring everything to market except their own skins; the bravos of the West were no better than Falstaff's men in buckram; only the wastrel and the degenerate ever enlisted in the American ranks—such are a few phrases culled from writers of established reputation. The financiers told the people that it was fortunate that America had entered the war, since she was the only country from which a big indemnity could be extracted. Even in July, 1918, the boasting continued. One German journal during that month declared that the American millions would be found to be only "soldiers of a child's game, mostly made of paper cuttings"; and on July 4th the *Deutsche Tageszeitung* wrote: "To-day, on the anniversary of the American Day of Independence, the Entente will fill the world with sounding praises of this help. America herself will produce a world of bluff in the shape of phrases, threats, and assertions—all bluff, pure bluff, celebrated in Paris by a review." A blindness from the gods had fallen upon the people, and their pride was to be followed hot-foot by Nemesis, the avenger.

Ludendorff was an experienced soldier, and less easily deceived. But he considered that he had still a chance of winning the victory which he had promised his people. He had waited six weeks—the same time as elapsed between the Battle of the Lys and the Third Battle of the Aisne—and he had collected every reserve from every front on which there were German troops. He had brought a new army, the IXth, under von Eben,[3] from the East, to act as an "army of pursuit" when the Allied front was broken. His plan was to strike out from the awkward salient in which von Boehn had been entrapped, and to press beyond the Marne and cut the great lateral railway from Paris to

[3] He was succeeded on the 9th of August by von Carlowitz.

Nancy. At the same time von Mudra (who had succeeded Fritz von Below) with the Ist Army, and von Einem with the IIIrd Army, were to strike east of Rheims between Prunay and the Argonne. If these operations succeeded, Rheims and the Montagne de Rheims would fall, and the French front would be divided into two parts which would never again be joined. Then, sweeping westward, with the help of von Eben, von Boehn would march on Paris down the valley of the Marne. Foch would hurry up his scanty reserves—Ludendorff believed that they were all but exhausted, and that the Americans were too untrained to be dangerous—to the threatened point, and at that moment von Hutier and von der Marwitz would break through the Amiens-Montdidier front and descend on the capital from the north. Then would Haig be finally cut off from Pétain, and Pétain would be broken in two, and victory, complete and cataclysmic, would follow. The Germans christened the coming battle the *Friedensturm,* the action which would bring about a "German peace."

The enemy was so confident that he made little secret of his plans. From deserters and prisoners Foch gathered the main details long before the assault was launched. His problem was not an easy one, for he had vital objectives, like Paris and the Nancy railway, far too near his front. It was not likely that von Boehn could advance far unless he broadened his salient; but the attack of von Mudra and von Einem east of Rheims was a grave matter, for, if they succeeded, all the difficulties of the salient would vanish, and the disadvantage of position would lie wholly with the French. He resolved to meet the shock as best he could, and at the right moment to use every atom of reserve strength to strike at the enemy's nerve center, as a wary boxer, when his antagonist has overreached himself, aims at the "mark." It was a bold decision, for the Allied Generalissimo had followed Montrose's maxim, and "put it to the touch to win or lose it all." If he failed it would be hard to save Paris. But if he succeeded— To a watcher of the auspices the German front on the map wore a look of happy omen, for it had that shape of a sickle, with the handle in

Champagne and the center of the blade on the Ourcq, which it had borne on the crucial day of September 9, 1914. That day Foch had struck and shattered the first German dream; now, after four years, he played for the same tremendous stake among the same hills and forests.

Foch had planned on a majestic scale a battle of the Napoleonic type. All the cherished stages of the great Emperor were provided for. The advance guard should take the first shock, make clear the enemy's intention, and pin him down to a definite field of action. Next, at the right moment, a blow should be delivered at the enemy's weakest flank. Last should come the thrust against the now embarrassed center, and whatever the gods might send thereafter in the way of fortune. To carry out this scheme it was essential that the Germans should not repeat their performance at the Third Battle of the Aisne, and drive back the French too far. Some retirement was inevitable, but it must be calculated and defined. In von Boehn's area it would be all to the good that the apex of the German salient should extend well south of the Marne till it became as deep as it was broad; it would only make the conditions better for the next stage. But the gateposts must stand, and at all costs the salient must not be widened. The critical area was east of Rheims. There the enemy must be held in the battle positions, for if he pressed too far he would render Rheims and the Montagne untenable, and instead of an ugly salient would create a broad arc curving securely into Champagne.

Between Dormans, on the Marne, and Rheims Foch had the Ninth Army, under Berthelot, who had for nearly two years been chief of the Allied Mission in Rumania. With Berthelot at the Montagne de Rheims was the Italian 2nd Corps, containing picked Alpini battalions. On his left, from Dormans to Faverolles, lay the Sixth Army, under Dégoutte, who, in April, 1917, had commanded the Moroccan Division at Moronvilliers. With Dégoutte was the 1st American Corps, under General Liggett, numbering six divisions—the 1st, 2nd, 3rd, and 4th of the Regular Army, and the 26th and 28th National Guard. Between Faverolles and Soissons lay the Tenth Army, under Mangin. Mangin, it will be remembered, had been the hero of the winter battles at Verdun in 1916, and had commanded the Sixth Army at the Second Battle of the Aisne. After that for many months he had been lost in obscure commands; but now he was to vindicate his claim to rank among the greatest Allied generals. East of Rheims, holding the gate of Champagne, was the Fourth Army, under Gouraud. With him was the 42nd American Division, known as the "Rainbow," since it was drawn from every State.

The time had now come for Foch's counter-stroke. He had resolved to thrust with all his available reserves against the weak enemy flank between Soissons and Château-Thierry. It offered a superb mark. In the first place, von Boehn was fighting with his head turned the wrong way, and in case of a flank attack must make hasty and difficult adjustments. In the second place, the German communications were parallel to their front. The great road from Soissons by Fère-en-Tardenois to Rheims, with its branches running south to the Marne, was the main feeder of the whole German line in the salient. If that were cut anywhere north of Rozoy supply would be gravely hampered. Moreover, all the railway communications between the salient and the north depended upon the junction of Soissons. If that junction were captured or rendered unusable, the Marne front would suddenly find itself some thirty miles from a railhead. It is inconceivable that the German Staff should not have been alive to such a risk, and the only explanation is that they believed that Foch had no serious reënforcements. At the moment, between Soissons and Château-Thierry, von Boehn had only eight divisions in line and six in support; but he had large reserves inside the salient, and the new IXth Army, under von Eben, was forming in the rear for its advance on Paris.

When Foch decided to stake everything on his attack, he took one of those risks without which no great victory was ever won. Prince Rupprecht had still his twenty-two fresh divisions threatening the Amiens gate, and more than one French commander viewed the hazard with grave perturbation. There were anxious consultations between Foch, Pétain, and Fayolle, who commanded the group of armies. But the general most intimately concerned, Sir Douglas Haig, had no doubts. He was prepared to weaken his own line rather than cripple Foch's great bid for a decision. He gladly consented to the withdrawal of the eight French divisions from Flanders, and he sent a British corps to fight under Mangin and Berthelot.

Ever since the Third Battle of the Aisne had died away Mangin had been engaged in preparing a jumping-off ground for his assault. By many local attacks he had worked his way out of the gully between Ambleny and St. Pierre Aigle, and, farther south, had reached the east bank of the Savières. He wanted to be clear of the forest and the ravines, and to have a starting-point on the edge of the plateau. From Longpont there runs eastward from the forest for twenty miles a high and narrow ridge, culminating in the heights north of Grand Rozoy. This gave him an avenue for his advance, for if he could win its eastern end he would command not only the vale of the Ourcq, but the whole plateau eastward towards the Vesle. By the morning of Thursday, the 18th, there had been a readjustment of the French forces. Mangin's Tenth Army, which was to conduct the main operations, was in its old place between the Aisne and Faverolles, on the Savières; but Dégoutte's Sixth Army, which had been holding the line from Faverolles to St. Agnan, drew in its right to Vaux, a mile west of Château-Thierry, and the gap between it and Berthelot was filled by the French reserve army, the Fifth, under de Mitry.

Mangin's reënforcements were assembled during the 17th in the shade of the Villers-Cotterets forest. The morning of the 18th dawned, after a night of thunderstorms and furious winds. There was no gun fired on the northern section, but at 4.30 out from the shelter of the woods came a great fleet of French "mosquito" tanks; and behind them, on a front of thirty-five miles, Mangin's army and Dégoutte's left wing crossed the parapets.[4] The tactics of Cambrai

---

[4] Dégoutte had begun an artillery "preparation" at 3.30 which lasted for an hour and a half. During that time his pickets were working forward into the German outpost zone.

had been faithfully followed. From Fontenoy, on the Aisne, to Belleau, six miles northwest of Château-Thierry, was the front of action, and before the puzzled enemy could realize his danger the French and Americans were through his first defenses. At the First Battle of the Marne Foch's generals had told him that they could no longer hold on. "You cannot hold on!" he replied. "Then I will attack." He was the incarnate spirit of the offensive, and that spirit, kept in leash for four arduous months, had grown with its confinement till, transmitted to every soldier of his command, it had become a devouring fire.

The advance of the 18th was like a great bound forward. The chief work was done by Mangin's left wing, which swept through the villages of Pernant and Mercin, and by half-past ten in the morning held the crown of the Montagne de Paris, half a league from the streets of Soissons, and within two miles of the vital railway junction. Farther south, his center reached Berzy-le-Sec, on the edge of the great Soissons-Fère-en-Tardenois road, which was now cut.[5]

His right wing took Léchelle, Vierzy, and the Bois de Mauloy. Dégoutte by the evening held the front Chouy-Neuilly St. Front, and thence by Priez and Courchamps to Belleau, though an enemy salient remained about Noroy-sur-Ourcq. His American troops took Courchamps, Torcy, and Belleau. Sixteen thousand prisoners fell to the French, and some fifty guns; and at one point Mangin had advanced as much as eight miles—the longest advance as yet made in one day by the Allies in the West. Foch had narrowed the German salient, crumpled its western flank, and destroyed its communications. He had wrested the initiative from the enemy, and brought the *Friedensturm* to a dismal close.

He had done more, though at the time no eye could pierce the future and read the full implications of his victory. Moments of high crisis slip past unnoticed; it is only the historian in later years who can point to a half-hour in a crowded day and say that then was decided the fate of a cause or a people. As the wounded trickled back through

[5] The advance described in this paragraph was made chiefly of the American First and Second Divisions acting under General Mangin.

the tossing woods of Villers-Cotterets, spectators noted a strange exaltation in their faces. When the news reached Paris the city breathed a relief which was scarcely justified with the enemy still so strongly posted at her gates. But the instinct was right. The decisive blow had been struck. Foch was still far from his Appomattox, but he had won his Gettysburg. He had paralyzed the nerve-center of the enemy, and driven him down the first stage of the road to defeat.

When the Allies breasted the Montagne de Paris on that July morning, they had, without knowing it, won the Second Battle of the Marne, and, with it, the war. Four months earlier Ludendorff had stood as the apparent dictator of Europe; four months later he and his master were fleeing to a dishonored exile.

BY GENERAL PERSHING

"Order of the Day" issued to United States forces on August 27, 1918

It fills me with pride to record in general orders a tribute to the service achievements of the 1st and 3rd Corps, comprising the 1st, 2nd, 3rd, 4th, 26th, 28th, 32nd, and 42nd Divisions of the American Expeditionary Forces.

You came to the battlefield at a crucial hour for the Allied cause. For almost four years the most formidable army the world has yet seen had pressed its invasion of France and stood threatening its capital. At no time has that army been more powerful and menacing than when, on July 15th, it struck again to destroy in one great battle the brave men opposed to it and to enforce its brutal will upon the world and civilization.

Three days later, in conjunction with our allies, you counter-attacked. The Allied armies gained a brilliant victory that marks the turning point of the war. You did more than to give the Allies the support to which, as a nation, our faith was pledged. You proved that our altruism, our pacific spirit, and our sense of justice have not blunted our virility or our courage.

You have shown that American initiative and energy are as fit for the tasks of war as for the pursuits of peace.

You have justly won unstinted praise from our allies and the eternal gratitude of our countrymen.

We have paid for our success with the lives of many of our brave comrades. We shall cherish their memory always and claim for our history and literature their bravery, achievement, and sacrifice.

This order will be read to all organizations at the first assembly formations following its receipt.

PERSHING.

From General Pershing's final official report of September, 1919

The Marne salient was inherently weak and offered an opportunity for a counter-offensive that was obvious. If successful, such an operation would afford immediate relief to the Allied defense, would remove the threat against Paris and free the Paris-Nancy railroad. But, more important than all else, it would restore the morale of the Allies and remove the profound depression and fear then existing.

Up to this time our units had been put in here and there at critical points, as emergency troops to stop the terrific German advance. *In every trial, whether on the defensive or offensive, they had proved themselves equal to any troops in Europe.* As early as June 23rd and again on July 10th at Bombon, I had very strongly urged that our best divisions be concentrated under American command, if possible, for use as a striking force against the Marne salient. Although the prevailing view among the Allies was that American units were suitable only for the defensive, and that at all events they could be used to better advantage under Allied command, the suggestion was accepted in principle, and my estimate of their offensive fighting qualities was soon put to the test.

The selection by the Germans of the Champagne sector and the eastern and southern faces of the Marne pocket on which to make their offensive was fortunate for the Allies, as it favored the launching of the counter-attack already planned. There were now over 1,200,000 American troops in France, which provided a considerable force of reserves.

Every American division with any sort of training was made available for use in a counter-offensive.

General Pétain's initial plan for the counter-attack involved the entire western face of the Marne salient. *The First and Second American Divisions, with the First French Moroccan Division between them, were employed as the spearhead of the main attack,* driving directly eastward, through the most sensitive portion of the German lines, to the heights south of Soissons. The advance began on July 18th, without the usual brief warning of a preliminary bombardment, and these three divisions at a single bound broke through the enemy's infantry defenses and overran his artillery, cutting or interrupting the German communications leading into the salient. A general withdrawal from the Marne was immediately begun by the enemy, who still fought stubbornly to prevent disaster.

The First Division, throughout four days of constant fighting, advanced 11 kilometers, capturing Berzy-le-Sec and the heights above Soissons and taking some 3,500 prisoners and 68 field guns from the 7 German divisions employed against it. It was relieved by a British division. The Second Division advanced 8 kilometers in the first 26 hours, and by the end of the second day was facing Tigny, having captured 3,000 prisoners and 66 field guns. It was relieved the night of the 19th by a French division. The result of this counter-offensive was of decisive importance. *Due to the magnificent dash and power displayed on the field of Soissons by our First and Second Divisions the tide of war was definitely turned in favor of the Allies.*

Other American divisions participated in the Marne counter-offensive. A little to the south of the Second Division, the Fourth was in line with the French and was engaged until July 22nd. The First American Corps, Maj. Gen. Hunter Liggett commanding, with the Twenty-sixth Division and a French division, acted as a pivot of the movement toward Soissons, capturing Torcy on the 18th and reaching the Château-Thierry-Soissons road on the 21st. At the same time the Third Division crossed the Marne and took the heights of Mont St. Père and the villages of Charteves and Jaulgonne.

In the First Corps, the Forty-second Division relieved the Twenty-sixth on July 25th and extended its front, on the 26th relieving the French division. From this time until August 2nd it fought its way through the Forest de Fère and across the Ourcq, advancing toward the Vesle until relieved by the Fourth Division on August 3rd. Early in this period elements of the Twenty-eighth Division participated in the advance.

Farther to the east the Third Division forced the enemy back to Roncheres Wood, where it was relieved on July 30th by the Thirty-second Division from the Vosges front. The Thirty-second, after relieving the Third and some elements of the Twenty-eighth on the line of the Ourcq River, advanced abreast of the Forty-second toward the Vesle. On August 3rd it passed under control of our Third Corps, Maj. Gen. Robert L. Bullard commanding, which made its first appearance in battle at this time, while the Fourth Division took up the task of the Forty-second Division and advanced with the Thirty-second to the Vesle River, where, on August 6th, the operation for the reduction of the Marne salient terminated.

In the hard fighting from July 18th to August 6th the Germans were not only halted in their advance but were driven back from the Marne to the Vesle and committed wholly to the defensive. The force of American arms had been brought to bear in time to enable the last offensive of the enemy to be crushed.

The First and Third Corps now held a continuous front of 11 kilometers along the Vesle. On August 12th the Seventy-seventh Division relieved the Fourth Division on the First Corps front, and the following day the Twenty-eighth relieved the Thirty-second Division in the Third Corps, while from August 6th to August 10th the Sixth Infantry Brigade of the Third Division held a sector on the river line. The transfer of the First Corps to the Woevre was ordered at this time, and the control of its front was turned over to the Third Corps.

On August 18th General Pétain began an offensive between Rheims and the Oise. Our Third Corps participated in this operation, crossing the Vesle on September 4th with the Twenty-eighth and Seventy-seventh Divisions, and overcoming stubborn opposition on the plateau south of the Aisne, which was reached by the Seventy-seventh on September 6th. The Twenty-eighth was withdrawn from the line on September 7th. Two days later the Third Corps was transferred to the region of Verdun, the Seventy-seventh Division remaining in line on the Aisne River until September 17th.

The Thirty-second Division, upon its relief from the battle on the Vesle, joined a French corps north of Soissons and attacked from August 29th to 31st, capturing Juvigny after some particularly desperate fighting and reaching the Chauny-Soissons road.

On the British front two regiments of the Thirty-third Division participated in an attack on Hamel July 4th, and again on August 9th as an incident of the Allied offensive against the Amiens salient. One of these regiments took Gressaire Wood and Chipilly Ridge, capturing 700 prisoners and considerable *matériel*.

BY GEORG WEGENER

Semi-official press statement issued in Berlin on July 31, 1918

The wooded country on the front of attack gave our enemies the best opportunities to assemble masses of artillery and other necessaries of attack, together with their storm troops, and to keep them concealed.

These preparations were hidden even from the most careful aërial observation. The enemy has brought the art of camouflage to the very highest development. In that he was materially helped by the fact that he possessed greater supplies of necessary materials and of labor. In this respect, as in so many others, matters are much more difficult for us.

In order to deceive us, too, he worked arduously at making defensive positions and carried out visible movements which looked like a withdrawing of troops. Despite that, we were not deceived regarding his intentions. We knew he was preparing to attack and that every wood and gully was full of troops and materials. Only regarding the exact time of the attack we had no knowledge. We could accept the belief, however, that as our offensive was to take place further to the east its effect would be to make the enemy renounce the execution of his plans for an offensive.

That hope, however, on account of the fact that our offensive did not reach our expectations, was not realized, and the enemy could, therefore, carry out his plans at a favorable moment. The moment of attack at dawn on July 18th was psychologically a good choice. It is only human that, with the coming of daylight, the tension which darkness produces should have been relaxed, a feeling of greater security should have taken its place, and the strained attention demanded during the night should have been involuntarily decreased. Fatigue comes over the watching troops.

The enemy had in secret built a large number of tanks of a surprisingly small type, which had the advantage of greater mobility and were easily maneuvered. These tanks led the way, and between and behind them, morally strengthened by their presence and protection, came storm troops.

To low visibility in the early morning was added the difficulty of a complete view of the territory on which the attack took place, on account of the broken nature of the ground; the high standing corn concealed the advancing infantry masses and hid the low-built tanks. Thus our artillery could not be effective. Such were the circumstances and the nature of the French attack.

BY GENERAL VON LUDENDORFF
Official Statement of August 4th

Foch's plan was undoubtedly to cut off the entire arc of our front south of the Aisne by a break-through on the flank. But with the proved leadership of our Seventh and Ninth Armies that was quite impossible.

We figured with an attack on July 18th and were prepared for it. The enemy experienced very heavy losses, and the Americans and African auxiliary troops, which we do not underestimate, suffered severely.

By the afternoon of the 19th we already were fully masters of the situation and shall remain so. We left the abandoned ground to the enemy according to our regular plan. "Gain of ground" and "Marne" are only catchwords without importance for the issue of the war. We are now, as before, confident.

A later statement, made by General Ludendorff in 1919

On July 18th the enemy attacked after a short, sharp artillery preparation and under shelter of a screen of smoke. He employed masses of infantry and a greater force of tanks than had ever before been concentrated in one drive. The tanks, however, were unimportant except as they were used to carry men through our lines. These men then attacked us from the rear or formed machine-gun nests which were very effective.

South of Soissons our infantry did not resist this attack as firmly as I had hoped, although we had a division in line there which had been considered particularly reliable. A gap was made in our line, and this soon widened. This situation north of the Ourcq River made it necessary to withdraw our troops further south. The success of the enemy came to me as a shock, and I sent immediate reënforcements, which, however, owing to the difficulties of transport, were slow in arriving.

On July 19th our situation was much more satisfactory. Even the troops who had been surprised on the preceding day now rallied and fought well. The reason they gave for their former failure was *the wholly unexpected nature of the attack.* One General of a division told me he had personally visited our foremost line on July 17th, and there had been not the slightest sign of the enemy's activity.

BY GENERAL MANGIN [6]
Official Address issued August 7, 1918

Officers, Noncommissioned Officers, and Soldiers of the American Army:

Shoulder to shoulder with your French comrades, you

[6] General Joseph Mangin commanded the French Tenth Army in which the First and Second American Divisions made their attack of July 18th.

threw yourselves into the counter-offensive begun on July 18th. You ran to it as if going to a feast. Your magnificent dash upset and surprised the enemy, and your indomitable tenacity stopped counter-attacks by his fresh divisions. You have shown yourselves to be worthy sons of your great country and have gained the admiration of your brothers in arms.

Ninety-one cannon, 7,200 prisoners, immense booty, and ten kilometers of reconquered territory are your share of the trophies of this victory. Besides this, you have acquired a feeling of your superiority over the barbarian enemy against whom the children of liberty are fighting. To attack him is to vanquish him.

American comrades, I am grateful to you for the blood you generously spilled on the soil of my country. I am proud of having commanded you during such splendid days and to have fought with you for the deliverance of the world.

Personal statement by General Mangin as to the assault begun July 18th

This constituted a regular classic battle of maneuver. The battle opened with the driving back of the enemy line ten kilometers in the first two days under the shock of a sudden attack. Then he brought up reserves and rallied.

After that the objective was clear and definite. It was the eastern end of the long ledge that runs unbroken save by the Savière Valley from west of Villers-Cotterets Forest to the region of Grand Rozoy and Arcy. That was the key position of the struggle, as it dominated the northwestern plateau toward Soissons, which was the bastion of the enemy's resistance. Once we were masters of that on August 2nd, the enemy's retreat was inevitable. He knew it, too, and the battle was won.

BY GENERAL DÉGOUTTE

Address issued August 9, 1918, to the French and American Army under his command. The United States Congress ordered that this address be entered in full upon the Congressional record.

Before the great offensive of July 18th, the American

troops, forming part of the Sixth French Army, distinguished themselves by clearing the "Brigade de Marine" Woods and the village of Vaux from the enemy and arresting his offensive on the Marne and at Fossoy.

Since then they have taken the most glorious part in the second battle of the Marne, rivaling the French troops in ardor and valor.

During twenty days of constant fighting they have freed numerous French villages and made, across a difficult country, an advance of forty kilometers, which has brought them to the Vesle.

Their glorious marches are marked by names which will shine in future in the military history of the United States: Torcy, Belleau, Plateau d'Etrepilly, Epieds, Le Charmel, l'Ourcq, Seringes-et-Nesles, Sergy, La Vesle, and Fismes.

These young divisions, who saw fire for the first time, have shown themselves worthy of the old war traditions of the regular army. They have had the same burning desire to fight the boche, the same discipline which sees that the order given by their commander is always executed, whatever the difficulties to be overcome and the sacrifices to be suffered.

The magnificent results obtained are due to the energy and the skill of the commanders; to the bravery of the soldiers.

I am proud to have commanded such troops.

DÉGOUTTE,
The Commanding General of the Sixth Army.

BY KARL ROSNER

[In his book of reminiscences, Rosner, the personal news reporter of the Kaiser, thus describes the latter's hurried visit to his generals on hearing of the disaster of July 18th.]

As the King mounts the steps before the entrance, Marshal Von Hindenburg comes to meet him—dignified, stately, without haste, without hesitation. Only one cavalry officer, his adjutant and son-in-law, follows him at a considerable distance.

The King stretches out a hand to the General and nods his head vigorously. His lips move but his voice fails him. A thousand conflicting thoughts seize his mind. All the bitterness of the past few tortured days he has stored up till now, brooded over it, carried it with him until he might unfold it all here to Hindenburg. He wants to unburden everything.

"Your Majesty has seen much in these hard days," says Hindenburg; "the war has shown a hard face. I am happy to welcome Your Majesty here again, and if Your Majesty commands——?" He glances through the open door.

The King nods. He wants only one thing—to hear, to be alone with Hindenburg and know the truth, to learn how they think matters will develop. He hastens into the villa.

General Ludendorff is seated at a desk poring over papers. He glances up, let's the monocle fall from his eye, rises quickly, and advances toward the King.

The King says, to start conversation: "You have had a strenuous tour, Excellency."

The General notices the nuance. "Excellency!" Ordinarily he is addressed as "General"—"my dear General." Does this mean anger, disgrace? That matters as little to him as a fly buzzing in the distance.

Hindenburg interrupts: "I believe that Your Majesty may desire first of all our opinion as to how we got into the critical situation in which we are at present."

The King nods. His eyes close. The Marshal's words are much too slow for his burning impatience. Hindenburg briefly explains the army's plight. The King exclaims: "The men went back on us?"

Hindenburg meets his gaze quietly and continues: "We thought that the drafts sent to the divisions which were fighting southwest of Soissons, would have put up a stronger resistance than they did. The troops gave way and we have lost many prisoners."

He pauses to ponder for a moment, and resumes his account of the fighting: "Your Majesty knows that they attacked us with several hundred whiffet tanks. These are apparently a newly perfected type of small, speedy tank which rush behind our lines and convert themselves into machine gun nests. The result was that almost immediately our front lines were broken at several points. The men ahead were fighting and defending themselves as best they could, when suddenly they were taken unawares by the rattle of hostile machine guns in their rear. During the ensuing confusion the men did not know just what had happened, except that they were surrounded; and they lost their heads. It was not until we brought up supports from the rear and got our second line into action that we could check the enemy, after heavy sacrifices, and organize a new line. That is the course of events as we now understand them——"

The King nods, remains silent, tugs at his coat, then asks abruptly, dryly: "Will the new line hold?"

The Marshal stands four-square, huge, unmoved. "That really cannot be foretold, Your Majesty. Our line is between the Aisne and the Marne, and a big enemy offensive is before us. It may go on for days. We have certainly got to count on new attacks on a grand scale, and have, as we are discovering more plainly every day, to reckon with at least a dozen fresh assaulting divisions in the enemy's first line. They must have reserves behind those."

Perturbed and excited, yet eager to appear firm and deliberate, the King asks again: "So we shall retire still farther—give up more ground?" But his voice fails him, and the words escape him ungraciously, almost rudely.

He checks himself carefully and continues: "I merely beg you to bear in mind, in dealing with this situation, the effect upon the very restive sentiment back home in Germany as well as upon the Allies and the rest of the world. We have to meet increasing criticism and antagonism at home with every day that passes. The significance of this opposition cannot be overestimated—in the interest of the throne."

Marshal Hindenburg observes with professional calm: "Certainly, Your Majesty, these things weigh heavily enough upon our hearts. Naturally I am occupied first and foremost with the purely military responsibilities confided to our care and loyalty, with the safety of the army, with accomplishing our military object——"

A pause ensues.

Turning deliberately to General Ludendorff and then back again to the King, Hindenburg continues: "Perhaps my comrade——?"

"Certainly," replies the King curtly, suddenly recalling his thoughts. What Hindenburg had told him had not soothed his nerves. He has something more in his mind. He regards Ludendorff alertly, with a defiant light in his eye. Ludendorff clears his throat and stiffens slightly.

"I beg to impress upon Your Majesty that I received news that the enemy had broken our line only this morning, while discussing our new Flanders' offensive. This painful surprise——"

The King suddenly raises his head and interrupts. "Then we were all thoroughly taken by surprise?" This short, bitter question flashes out like a challenging thrust. The King is angry and threatening.

But the General continues his first line of thought as if nothing had happened: "The surprise was not in there being an attack. We expected that from the moment our advance East of Rheims was halted, and Marshal Foch had his reserves at his disposal. The surprise was in the failure of our front line, and the extent of the enemy's initial success."

The General steps over to the chart table, adjusts his monocle, and glancing at the map before him, continues: "The danger in which we are placed by the depth of the enemy's penetration makes it our first task to strengthen the lines at this point—at any cost—against further assault. It is a pivotal position defending the whole Seventh Army, fighting in the Marne elbow. Unless we can feel certain of our Western flank, we cannot undertake further operations around Rheims, or withdraw in an orderly way from the South bank of the Marne. So long as we are not in safety at that point, or until we can erect a new front which is safe from the assaults of the enemy, we are not complete masters of the situation and cannot resume the initiative.

Here is where we have got to settle things. Here we must decide our further plan of campaign."

The King listens with distrust and suspicion. One sees the cloven hoof thrust out again. His blood rises. So! Fortify the line, but if that does not succeed, surrender more territory—establish a new front—eventually withdraw from the Marne! The blood rushes to his face! He taps with his foot! Tumultuous passions master him!

A second retreat from the Marne! An unexampled humiliation! And what of the world, which he sees as a circle of evil, spiteful spectators, surrounding the stage on which he has fought and wrestled for his kingdom for four years? A second and unrecallable check! A new front! But where? The old line on the Aisne? Or the Meuse? And then the Rhine? He sees the end yawning before him—the black spectre from which he had averted his face and shut his eyes in horror so many times that day. A fearful vision floats before him—the disorganized, embittered armies streaming homewards—the shock of disappointment to the nation already shattered and crushed by its sacrifices and privations—the rising of unchained agitators—the breaking forth of the millions who have avidly awaited this moment for years!

Summoning all his resolution, in order not to lose his composure, he blurts out at last: "No! I trust we shall not give up a single foot of the soil we have won!"

As they leave the room, a young officer is waiting with a paper in his hand to be approved by Ludendorff. It is the text of the evening telegram of the Wolff Bureau. The King takes it from Hindenburg's hands and reads:

BERLIN, OFFICIAL, July 18, 1918.

The French attacked with heavy forces and tanks between the Aisne and the Marne and made some gains. Our reserves have been brought into action.

He handed the sheet back without a word. How harmless it sounded. And yet, unless God works a miracle, this is the turning of the tide!

BREAKING THE HINDENBURG LINE

CANADA AND THE UNITED STATES AID THE BRITISH DRIVE

AUGUST 8TH-SEPTEMBER 30TH

MARSHAL VON HINDENBURG   FREDERICK McKENZIE
PHILIP GIBBS   GENERAL SIR F. MAURICE
UNITED STATES OFFICIAL STATEMENTS

General von Ludendorff in his narrative of the War, so often misleading, reaches to a moment of what seems frankness when he declares that to him the "blackest day of the War" was August 8, 1918. It was on that day that the British began what they have called the "Battle of Amiens," that is the beginning of their great drive to recover what they had lost in the first German thrust of the mighty Kaiser-battle. This British drive was meant to supplement the great Franco-American drive begun on July 18th, and was thus the second forward stride in the Ally march to victory. Its peculiar tragedy to Ludendorff lay in the fact that he now realized that he could no longer rely upon his troops; they yielded easily before the British. They believed no longer in his reckless promises of victory. Their thoughts had turned toward defeat and peace and home; they sought life rather than death.

This was the natural consequence of the Ludendorff system of "shock troops" by which he had carried through his spring offensive. Now that his shock troops were almost all annihilated, the remaining forces of his army were naturally of lower morale. Not from Ludendorff but from other sources we learn that the German regiments retreating from the front on August 8th shouted to the fresh troops who took their places: "Don't fight!" and "You are only prolonging the War!" These people had waked at last to the desperate madness of their leaders; they realized that America had decided the War against them.

Again and again the British advance swept the Germans back; they were confessedly retreating now to their old and strongly fortified Hindenburg Line. Toward the close of August they were definitely back upon that line along almost the whole British front; and then without giving them time to rally, the British struck at that celebrated line and successfully carried it in several places.

The first triumphant breaking of the Hindenburg Line was achieved by Canadian forces on August 26th. The final smash which drove the Germans from the entire line in complete retreat was accomplished on September 29th. In this great attack two United States Divisions, the Twenty-seventh and the Thirtieth, took a leading part.

It was during these months of August and September that the German leaders began to realize that their own game of "propaganda" had been turned against them. To the American "leaflets" scattered by aviators over the German camps, Marshal Hindenburg attributes the breaking of the German morale.

BY MARSHAL HINDENBURG
Address issued September 6, 1918

SOLDIERS:
We are in the midst of a heavy battle with the foe. If numerical superiority alone were to guarantee victory, then Germany would long since have been crushed to the ground. The enemy knows, however, that Germany and her allies can never be vanquished by arms alone.

What are the facts? In the east we have forced peace, and in the west we are also strong enough to do the same despite the Americans. But we must be strong and united.

Why does the enemy incite the colored races against the German soldiers? Because he wants to annihilate us.

The enemy also endeavors to sow dissension in our ranks by means of leaflets dropped from aëroplanes above our lines. Ten thousand of these are sometimes gathered up in a day. The enemy knows what strength resides in our State and Empire; hence he seeks by his leaflets and false rumors to arouse distrust among us. There have always been some traitors to the Fatherland, a few deliberately false, others unintentionally so. Most of these now reside in neutral countries, having deserted us to escape sharing in our battles and privations, and to escape being executed as traitors.

Be on your guard, German soldiers.

From Hindenburg's Memoirs

On the morning of August 8th our comparative peace was abruptly interrupted. In the southwest the noise of battle could clearly be heard. The first reports, which came from Army Headquarters in the neighborhood of Péronne, were serious. The enemy, employing large squadrons of tanks, had broken into our lines on both sides of the

Amiens—St. Quentin road.   Further details could not be given.

The veil of uncertainty was lifted during the next few hours, though our telephone lines had been broken in many places.   There was no doubt that the enemy had penetrated deeply into our positions and that batteries had been lost.   We issued an order that they were to be recovered and that the situation must everywhere be restored by an immediate counter-attack.   We sent officers to ascertain precisely how matters stood, to secure perfect harmony between our plans and the dispositions of the various staffs on the shaken front.   What had happened?

In a very thick haze a strong English tank attack had met with immediate success.   In their career the tanks had met no special obstacles, natural or—unfortunately—artificial.   The troops on this front had certainly been thinking too much about continuing the offensive and not enough of defense.

In any case, it would have cost us heavy losses to dig trenches and construct obstacles when we were in direct contact with the enemy, for as soon as the hostile observers noticed any movement, even if it were a matter of a few individuals, their artillery immediately opened fire.   It seemed our best plan to lie quietly in the high corn, without cover against enemy shells it is true, but at the same time safe from enemy telescopes.   In this way we were spared losses for the time being, but ran the risk of suffering even greater losses if the enemy attacked.   It was not only that little work had been done on the first line; even less had been done on the support and rear lines.   There was nothing available but isolated sections of trenches and scattered strong points.   On these so-called quiet fronts the troops were not numerous enough for trench-digging on any large scale.

On this August 8th we had to act as we had so often acted in equally menacing situations.   Initial successes of the enemy were no new experience for us.   We had seen them in 1916 and 1917, at Verdun, Arras, Wytschaete and Cambrai.   We had only quite recently experienced and mastered another at Soissons. But in the present case the situation was particularly serious. The great tank attack of the enemy had penetrated to a surprising depth. The tanks, which were faster than hitherto, had surprised Divisional Staffs in their headquarters and torn up the telephone lines which communicated with the battle front. The Higher Command-posts were thus isolated, and orders could not reach the front line. That was peculiarly unfortunate on this occasion, because the thick mist made supervision and control very difficult. Of course our anti-tank guns fired in the direction from which the sound of motors and the rattle of chains seemed to come, but they were frequently surprised by the sight of these steel colossi suddenly emerging from some totally different quarter. The wildest rumors began to spread in our lines. It was said that masses of English cavalry were already far in rear of the foremost German infantry lines. Some of the men lost their nerve, left positions from which they had only just beaten off strong enemy attacks and tried to get in touch with the rear again. Imagination conjured up all kinds of phantoms and translated them into real dangers.

Everything that occurred, and was destined to prove our first great disaster, is comprehensible enough from the human point of view. In situations such as these the old war-hardened soldier does not lose his self-possession. He does not imagine; he thinks! Unfortunately these old soldiers were in a fast vanishing minority and, moreover, their influence did not always and everywhere prevail. Other influences made themselves felt. Ill humor and disappointment that the war seemed to have no end, in spite of all our victories, had ruined the character of many of our brave men. Dangers and hardships in the field, battle and turmoil, on top of which came the complaints from home about many real and some imaginary privations! All this gradually had a demoralizing effect, especially as no end seemed to be in sight. In the shower of pamphlets which was scattered by enemy airmen our adversaries said and wrote that they did not think so badly of us; that we

must only be reasonable and perhaps here and there renounce something we had conquered. Then everything
would soon be right again and we could live together in
peace, in perpetual international peace. As regards peace
within our own borders, new men and new governments
would see to that. What a blessing peace would be after
all the fighting! There was, therefore, no point in continuing the struggle.

Such was the purport of what our men read and said.
The soldier thought it could not be all enemy lies, allowed
it to poison his mind and proceeded to poison the minds of
others.

On this August 8th our order to counter-attack could
no longer be carried out. We had not the men, and more
particularly the guns, to prepare such an attack, for most
of the batteries had been lost on the part of the front
which was broken through. Fresh infantry and new artillery units must first be brought up—by rail and motor
transport. The enemy realized the outstanding importance
which our railways had in this situation. His heavy and
heaviest guns fired far into our back areas. Various railway junctions, such as Péronne, received a perfect hail of
bombs from enemy aircraft, which swarmed over the town
and station in numbers never seen before. But if our foe
exploited the difficulties of the situation in our rear, as luck
would have it, he did not realize the scale of his initial
tactical success. He did not thrust forward to the Somme
this day, although we should not have been able to put
any troops worth mentioning in his way.

A relatively quiet afternoon and an even more quiet
night followed the fateful morning of August 8th. During these hours our first reënforcements were hurried to the
front.

The position was already too unfavorable for us to be
able to expect that the counter-attack we had originally
ordered would enable us to regain the old battle front. Our
counter-thrust would have involved longer preparation and
required stronger reserves than we had at our disposal on
August 9th. In any case we must not act precipitately.

On the battle front itself impatience made men reluctant to wait. They thought that favorable opportunities were being allowed to slip, and proceeded to rush at unsurmountable difficulties. Thus some of the precious fresh infantry units we had brought up were wasted on local successes without advantaging the general situation.

The attack on August 8th had been carried out by the right wing of the English armies. The French troops in touch with them on the south had only taken a small part in the battle. We had to expect, however, that the great British success would now set the French lines also in motion. If the French pushed forward rapidly in the direction of Nesle, our position in the great salient projecting far out to the southwest would become critical. We therefore ordered the evacuation of our first lines southwest of Roye and retired to the neighborhood of that town.

I had no illusions about the political effects of our defeat on August 8th. Our battles from July 15th to August 4th could be regarded, both abroad and at home, as the consequence of an unsuccessful but bold stroke, such as may happen in any war. On the other hand, the failure of August 8th was revealed to all eyes as the consequences of an open weakness. To fail in an attack was a very different matter from being vanquished on the defense. The amount of booty which our enemy could publish to the world spoke a clear language. Both the public at home and our Allies could only listen in great anxiety. All the more urgent was it that we should keep our presence of mind and face the situation without illusions, but also without exaggerated pessimism.

BY F. A. MCKENZIE

A Canadian participant

The battle of Amiens ranks among the most successful, satisfactory and splendid achievements of the Canadian Corps. Some victories, splendid and successful, are yet so costly that the victor at the end is inclined to question if the gain has been worth while. Other victories are attained piecemeal, bit by bit. But in this battle the triumph was won at one great sweep and with the minimum of cost. The enemy were completely outwitted. Their lines were broken and the Canadians penetrated through them to a depth of twelve miles on a single day, a greater advance than made by the Allies in that time on any previous occasion. In less than a fortnight the enemy were driven out of thirty villages, and the German menace to Amiens and the coast was broken. Over 10,000 prisoners were taken and several hundred guns captured. It was a clean-cut, straight bit of work, which ranks among the great performances of the war.

The corps was accompanied by the Third Cavalry Division, which included both British and Canadian cavalry, and a tank brigade. The Canadians formed part of a triple force that was to undertake the attack, each section working as an independent unit. To the right of it were the French. The Canadians had never had an opportunity of studying the French in battle at so close a range, but they soon learned their great qualities. "They've the greatest 'come back' you ever knew," said one Canadian, summing up the general impression. "They don't look much at first, but they cannot be downed. When they have been knocked over once, they spring back at the enemy like tiger cats. They are the boys!"

To the left of the Canadians were the Australians. Both had shared great fights together before this day. Each had learned something of the other's qualities. Between the two existed the most cordial coöperation and the friendliest rivalry possible. It was to be a race now between Canadians and Australians to see which should go farthest forward in the shortest possible time.

On the night of August 7th the Canadians took up their position on a line of 7,500 yards between the front of Villers-Bretonneux and Domart. Their guns were all in position, hundreds of them, many of the guns with several hundred rounds of shell to hand. Behind the infantry were armored cars, motor machine-gun batteries, cyclists, and cavalry, all ready to strike. At half-past four in the morning the artillery opened, and almost simultaneously the infantry went over. The enemy for an hour or two previously had been showing some signs of uneasiness, maintaining a considerable artillery fire on some sections of the line. They had no idea what was awaiting them. The Canadians forced their way through the German positions almost as though they had been dummy defenses. They went through trench after trench, through line after line, from village to village. They broke in on the enemy's artillery lines before the gunners had time to attempt to get away, capturing the guns by the many score. These guns were promptly turned round and used against the Germans themselves. The motor machine-gun troops swept in their armored cars down the main roads. Cavalry, following up the infantry, charged through point after point where the Germans were attempting to hold, and showed what cavalry can still do even in these days of machine guns. Inniskillings and Fort Garrys fought saddle to saddle that day.

Then came the tanks, "whippets" that could do their thirty miles an hour, and big mother tanks moving at more steady gait, but still fast enough to outpace enemy infantry. These cleared up machine-gun nests and hunted the enemy out of their sheltered strong points, like hounds harrying a fox. Where the infantry were held up, the tanks cleared the way. When the tanks made an opening, the foot men followed. Where the retreating enemy were attempting to re-form, the cavalry were on them. Here and there the Germans fought desperately, but the surprise was too complete for them to put up any tremendous resistance. Robbed of their artillery, which the Canadians had captured, deprived of their strong points, they could do little.

The scene on this day was more like old-time war than many men who had been four years fighting had ever seen before. The troops were moving out in the open, cavalry riding gayly across fields, infantry charging enemy posts, artillery pouring up along the roads. One feature markedly different from old days was the airmen who swept over the German lines, bombing, coming down low and machine-gunning, discovering and signaling back news of every place where the Germans were preparing a fresh stand.

I am not going to attempt to tell the tales of personal gallantry. To do so would require a book in itself. The troops entered into the fight in the spirit of a great adventure. The piper of a Highland battalion rode on the top of a tank, playing it into action. Men of Quebec and men of Winnipeg, troops from Vancouver and Edmonton, Toronto and Nova Scotia, Saskatchewan and New Brunswick, all had their splendid tales of brave doings, tales which their Provinces will treasure for generations to come.

At the end of the first day the Canadians counted up their spoils. They had advanced 14,000 yards, had captured 6,000 prisoners, and taken over 100 guns. The Germans, pouring up fresh troops, attempted to stop their advance. Within a few days no less than sixteen German divisions were identified against them. Five days afterwards, at the conclusion of the first stage of the battle, they counted up their gains again. They had now penetrated 22,000 yards into the enemy lines. Four of the German divisions facing them had been completely routed, nearly 150 guns and over 1,000 machine guns had fallen into their hands. Twenty-five towns and villages had been rescued and 10,000 prisoners taken. Before the battle was over these figures were made yet greater.

Outside Amiens the Canadians gathered a great park of guns, over 200 of all sizes, captured in the battle. When they came to compare records with the Australians, it was found that there was so much credit due to both that they refused to attempt to divide the glory.

The position along the Arras front on the morning of August 26th, before the next attack started, demands description. Following the great advance of March and April, the German armies were planted within a few miles of Arras itself. Their line ran around Fampoux, a suburb of Arras; further south they had created a salient which reached to within a little over 3,000 yards of the eastern boundaries of the city. Our troops and theirs fought for the wastes of Neuville Vitasse. The Germans were holding most of the ruined village, and our men were constantly fighting amidst the heaps of chalk and rubble which marked where the place once had been. The Canadian front extended from just below the sugar factory south of Neuville Vitasse in the south to the suburb of Bailleul on the north. The Canadians themselves, however, actually held only the line from Fampoux to the sugar factory. The extreme north of the line was occupied by a famous British division, acting in cooperation with them.

Arras itself had months before been deserted by the great mass of people who had clung to it through its earlier bombardment. It was open to enemy fire from the heights of Monchy to the east and from strong German positions to the northeast. It lay in a valley. Its enemies held a semicircle of great hills around, and could hurl death into it at their pleasure. A few hundred people still lived among the ruins, refusing to leave their homes. One old lady in particular, living outside the wreck of what once had been the Cathedral, touched us all by her simple faith and quiet optimism. She was a refugee. She had come from a district now in German hands, and she made her home in the most dangerous corner of Arras, protecting her window with a mattress, keeping her own little room neat and tidy, looking smilingly, quietly, shrewdly at all chance visitors. I had seen her before this day, as had most visitors to Arras. "Are you not afraid?" a friend of mine once asked her. I wondered how he dared to question her. "I trust in Providence," she replied.

The object of the Canadian Corps was to capture on the first day the village of Monchy, standing on the hilltop some eight thousand yards away. Below it they aimed to clear up the entire country from Neuville Vitasse to Wancourt and Guémappe. All these places—Neuville Vitasse, Wancourt, Guémappe, and Monchy—were nothing but ruins intermingled with pill-boxes, concrete gun-positions, dugouts, and houses reënforced with thick concrete walls. It seemed to me when I visited Neuville Vitasse a few hours later that it presented the most dreadful picture of ruin I had ever seen. The trees were mere broken stumps of blackness.

The village itself was so destroyed that there was not sufficient wall left whole to form one side of a decent chicken-house. A few piles marked what Neuville Vitasse once had been. The biggest pile told where the church stood. Shells had so pounded this that the pile consisted not so much of stones as of chalk and rubble, with here and there a ghastly sign that there had once been a graveyard around the church.

The Germans had expected an attack, although they had certainly not expected that the attack would be made by the Canadians. The troops immediately facing this front had been sent from Amiens to rest after the Canadians had given them their drubbing there. Their surprise can be imagined when they saw that the men from the Dominion were attacking here too. The Germans had withdrawn their heavy guns behind the River Scarpe, directly facing Monchy. They were concentrating their defense not so much on their front lines as upon the first ridge in the rising ground between Arras and Monchy. Here they had placed a strong force, with numerous machine guns and an abundant supply of trench mortars.

Various light field-pieces were scattered behind, and Monchy itself was fortified with some massive concrete emplacements. The Germans reckoned that they would break the force of our attack on the line of the first ridge, where our troops would be bound to suffer heavily from the machine-gun fire. If we got through it, they thought that they could then sweep off our infantry when advancing over the gradually rising country towards the town itself. They had another line of trenches outside Monchy in the direction of Arras.

This simple plan of defense ought to have been effective. The German positions were so placed that they commanded a great sweep of country in front of them, where there was little shelter, and where troops must suffer heavily if they attempted to advance. Unfortunately for the Germans, the Canadians had no idea of advancing that way. In place of making a frontal attack, they swept round to the side of the German trenches, enfiladed them, stormed them, and then swept to the northern side of Monchy itself.

The first German lines were captured with great ease. The morale of the troops in the trenches had been shaken by our overwhelming bombardment. The faces of the soldiers were ghastly even in the semi-darkness. The terror of the appalling death which was being hurled around seemed written in their eyes. Most of them put up no fight at all. Their counter-barrage at this point was very poor. Having swept through the first lines, our troops went on and round, and on again. The German artillery, which had been saved up for this moment, opened up a heavy fire, according to orders, on the place where they thought our men would be. But the shells exploded mainly among empty fields or among the enemy's own men.

Our real trouble came from machine guns. The place was thick with them, light portable weapons which could be moved from point to point and which could rain death. Once our men got among the guns with bayonets the gunners had little chance. After these were overcome Germans surrendered in groups. A German officer came up to a padre who was among the front lines of his troops: "Are you an officer?" asked he. "I am," answered the padre. "Then I surrender to an officer with my men," the German declared. And he ordered up forty soldiers, who seemed only too delighted to yield.

By 7.30 in the morning Monchy was ours. Shortly afterwards, while the troops which had won the crest of the hill held the trenches and prepared to meet counter-attacks, another regiment, one of the most historic in the Canadian Corps, went over the other side of the ridge. Here it met with fierce opposition. The Germans were holding a very strong trench in front of the village of Boiry, and the ridges between the two places gave them the advantage of position. They also held in force several woods on the high land northwards, woods crammed with machine guns and snipers. They had their guns well placed still further behind. And so when the Canadians tried to advance they were met by terrific sniping and machine-gun fire. It was impossible to push forward far without considerable artillery preparation Our men forced themselves a few hundred yards beyond

Monchy, dug themselves in, and held on. Meanwhile the Germans, gathering strength and operating particularly from one wood, Jig-saw Wood, repeatedly counter-attacked. Their counter-attacks were repulsed, but the Canadians were unable for the time to make further progress. And so on the afternoon of that day the lines to the north rested a little eastwards of Monchy.

Further south another Canadian force had attacked early in the day, jumping off from Neuville Vitasse. The troops in front of Neuville were a Western division that had fought over this ground at an earlier date and were familiar with every bit of the ruins. On the previous evening they had raided Neuville Vitasse itself and had sent their outposts to the very edge of the wrecked mound that was once the church. They advanced over the top in two sections, pushing through the country so as to hem in the village of Wancourt itself. The Germans held on to Wancourt for some time, but by the early afternoon the Canadians had got so far around it that the Germans retired over the ridge behind. There was a still fiercer fight for the next village, Guémappe, but before the day was over it too was taken.

By late in the afternoon it was possible to estimate our gains. The Canadian Corps had advanced considerably over 6,000 yards and had attained all its objectives. We had taken a considerable number of prisoners, in all close on 2,000. The Germans had, however, very successfully covered their retreat and withdrawn the major part of their forces, and, while some guns were captured, the amount of artillery taken was not considerable.

The battle during the latter part of the week was really a preparation for a coming greater blow. We were clearing up ugly corners and securing good "jumping-off" places. The Canadians were working in the closest coöperation with the British. The famous British division on our left flank, under the direction of the Canadian command, was pushing forward. British artillery coöperated. One never knew, moving behind our lines, whether one were coming on a Canadian or an Imperial battery. A degree of unity was attained between Imperials and Canadians such as had never been reached in any previous operation of the war.

Every one knew at the week-end that a fresh blow was coming. Battalions which had been taken out of the line after the very heavy fighting on Monday and Tuesday were brought up again, sometimes with only a few hours' rest and sometimes with none at all. The artillery duel grew greater day by day. The Germans met our concentration of guns by a big concentration of their own. The air war became still more virulent, and the honors of the fighting in the air were shared by both sides.

The cavalry moved up towards the week-end, ready to take the first opportunity of striking a blow such as they had struck in front of Amiens. Tanks, big and small, were to be seen grouped at various places. Even the big tanks moved briskly now, very differently from the old, lumbering machines of the days of the Somme. The "whippets" could run like hounds after their prey. One famous Western general employed a "whippet" tank to get about from one part of the line to the other. When the "whippet" could take him no further forward, he pushed ahead on foot. He was wounded during the fighting.

We had already penetrated the old Hindenburg Line, the "pill-boxes" and trenches. Fronting us now were a series of support sections of the line. First came the Drocourt-Queant line, which ran almost straight along our front, passing through the Arras-Cambrai road between Vis-en-Artois and Villers lez Cagnicourt. Several switch lines radiated from it, of which the most formidable was the Buissy, named after a village through which it ran.

The new battle began on the morning of September 2nd with an appalling barrage, which made the artillery firing of the previous day seem as nothing. Then our troops struck. The Germans had clearly made preparations at the last moment for a withdrawal and had taken most of their artillery behind the lines of the Canal du Nord. They held various villages in strength, and put up a stout resistance in them.

There was quite a fight around Villers. The first troops that attempted to advance here were unable to get forward.

A fresh battalion of Toronto men coming up found itself faced by a strong enemy position, on ground which it thought we had already occupied. There was a double German line, a sunken road at the bottom of a slope and a trench on the high ground above it. Fourteen machine guns swept the Canadian ranks. It was impossible to obtain any shelter. Men flung themselves down, but the Germans were so placed that they could shoot them as easily lying down as standing up. Here discipline and training told. Companies moved quickly to either side, while others maintained the fight on the front. One soldier, single-handed, charged and captured a machine gun and six men. Others moved along, bombing, storming, charging, until they had captured 65 men and 14 machine guns, killing or wounding the remainder of the defenders. The battalion losses in this fight were cruelly heavy.

It was evident that the Germans dreaded our tanks. While they had little time to prepare "booby traps," they made time to prepare certain bridges as tank traps.

Buissy switch, the real end of the Hindenburg Line here, was a surprise, but not in the way we had expected. Reports had come of the great strength of this section of the line. The Germans had clearly prepared to offer strong resistance at this point. The countryside beyond Villers rose steadily to a crest. The double lines of the Buissy switch were placed to the side of this rising ground so that they could sweep the front with machine-gun fire.

The land here was like a great moor, with no shelter. The switch trenches were very broad, to make it impossible for tanks to cross over them. But the enemy had neglected to dig these trenches deeply enough or to wire them. Large sections were quite shallow. The explanation given to us afterwards was that they had considered it so impossible for us ever to reach this point that they had not thought it worth while undertaking the work.

They paid dearly for their carelessness. The troops in this section of the line fought hard and long. Days afterwards the heaps of dead still left showed their courage. But against the tactics and determination of the Canadians the

German resistance was useless. The Canadians had learned in this advance never to attack a place in front if it could be taken in the flank, and they knew better than to attempt to storm positions until the artillery had done its work.

Pushing on beyond the Drocourt-Queant line and the Buissy switch, we came on villages that had not been ruined. Villers itself had only been partly damaged by shell fire, but beyond it Ecourt St. Quentin and the adjacent villages of Romecourt and Saudemont were undamaged. In one of these places our troops came on fifty French villagers who had been living there under German rule since 1914. They were almost incoherent with happiness, laughing, cheering, and talking wildly. They told how they had been kept, year after year, how many of their relatives had been taken away, themselves forced to work hard and long for the enemy. Before the battle opened, said they, the Germans were confident that they could keep us back. Then, when the great blow was struck, confusion seemed to fall on them. These civilians looked as though they had had a bad time.

No one who has not lived for weeks or months in a ruined countryside can realize the delight it was to us coming on a place like Ecourt. I wanted to stand and gaze at it. The church bore no scratch and the houses were undamaged by shells. Ecourt had clearly been a German railhead. A big main line ran into it, and an enormous dump was left by the Germans when they fell back. They had had no time either to remove or to destroy it. The very railway here was uninjured.

The place had been Germanized as much as possible. The streets had German names. I found great satisfaction—schoolboy satisfaction, if you like—in climbing up some iron-work and prizing off the walls with a German bayonet wooden signs naming two streets "Kaiserstrasse" and "Hindenburgstrasse." The houses were full of pictures from German papers. Cartoons decorated the walls. Official declarations were to be seen everywhere.

BY PHILIP GIBBS

An eye-witness statement issued August 27th

In July it was Rupprecht's army that was the chief threat against us, and it was an army of perhaps 250,000 fresh troops, apart from those in line waiting to be hurled against us if the German Crown Prince could do without them. We knew then that some of Rupprecht's divisions had been sent down hurriedly to his relief, but the question still remained whether the armies holding our part of the battlefront would still be strong enough to attack us or strong enough to check any attempt of ours to advance against them.

After that the tide turned in an astonishing way. It is now the enemy who is on the defensive, dreading the hammer blows that fall upon him day after day, and the initiative of attack is so completely in our hands that we are able to strike him at many different places.

Since August 8th we must have taken nearly 50,000 prisoners and nearly 500 guns, and the tale is not yet told because our men are going on, taking new strides, new batches of Germans, and more batteries.

The change has been greater in the minds of men than in the taking of territory. On our side the army seems to be buoyed up with the enormous hope of getting on with this business quickly. They are fighting for a quick victory and a quick peace so they may get back to normal life and wipe this thing clean from the map of Europe and restore the world to sane purposes. That is, I am sure, their hope, and for almost the first time in very truth they see something of its reality in sight.

But there is a change also in the enemy's mind. Those German soldiers and their officers are changed men since March 21st, when they launched their offensive. They no longer have even a dim hope of victory on this western front. All they hope for now is to defend themselves long enough to gain peace by negotiation. Many of them go even further than this and admit they do not care how peace comes so long as there is peace. They are sullen with their own officers, and some of those whom I saw to-day were more than sullen.

The arrival of the Canadians on August 26th was an immense surprise to the Germans. The last heard of them was outside of Roye after their glorious advance on the left of the French, and the last thing in the world which the enemy expected was to find them right in the north beyond Arras. That was a brilliant piece of secret maneuver. Before the Germans had any inkling of their presence the Canadians were advancing upon them with a sweep of shell-fire in front of them. Without encountering much resistance, they swung around by Guémappe and Wancourt over the high ground on each side of the Cojeul.

Germans of the 214th Division, made up of men from Rhineland, Stettin, Lower Schleswig, and Hessians, were aghast at this sudden assault, and either retired or gave themselves up in the early stages of the Canadian advance.

Their resistance stiffened on the crest of Monchy Hill, and there was fierce fighting all night in the trench on the top of Wancourt Spur. But the Canadians were determined to get this place, and with great individual gallantry and good leadership and most dogged spirit, they worked around the machine guns which were holding them off and rushed them in the darkness. By morning they held the spur, and this body of Canadians, who had taken over 820 prisoners yesterday morning, added another 150, with many machine guns, most of which were captured in the valley below the ridge. All told, the Canadians and Scots attacking with them had taken about 1,800 prisoners.

The highest point most desired by the Canadians was the old Wancourt tower on the tip of the crest, and this they gained in time for a new departure this morning, having to change their direction three times, owing to the lie of the ground, and face south instead of east after the beginning of the battle, which is always a difficult operation.

A little further north other Canadian troops, who had crossed Orange Hill and Monchy, that hill which dominates many miles of country, so that the loss of it a few months ago was serious to us, advanced again this morning to two woods on equally high ground beyond for which our men strove many times in vain in May of last year. Those are the Bois du Sart and the Bois de Vert, which we used to see like green eyes staring down on our lines around Wancourt and Henin, and from which always there used to come wicked machine-gun fire when any of our troops moved in the open valley below.

The success of our infantry is the more remarkable because in this battle very few tanks have been used, and machine-gun nests had to be taken in many cases without their help.

This advance gives a sense of the enormous movement behind the British lines, and there is not a man who is not stirred by the motion of it. They are feeling that they indeed are getting on with the war. It is like a vast tide of life moving very slowly but steadily.

BY GENERAL SIR F. MAURICE [1]

The British part in the great general attack upon the whole German front was timed to begin in the early morning of September 27th. On the evening before a great bombardment opened on a thirty-mile front, from a point about two miles northwest of St. Quentin, as far as the Sensée River northwest of Cambrai. Then in the gray light of early dawn the 4th, 6th, 17th and Canadian Corps, thirteen divisions in all, of Byng's Third Army and Horne's First Army advanced on the Cambrai front, stormed the immensely strong Canal du Nord, swept beyond Bourlon Wood and Fontaine-Notre-Dame, the extreme limits of our advance in the first battle of Cambrai of November, 1917, and captured Sailly, more than six miles from their starting point, taking over 10,000 prisoners and 200 guns. By this blow Cambrai was threatened from the north, whereas in the previous battle we had attempted to approach the town from the southeast, where the St. Quentin Canal was a formidable obstacle to our troops, and we had in one bound

[1] Reproduced from "The Last Four Months," by the kind permission of the American publishers, Messrs. Little, Brown and Co. Copyright, 1919.

got sufficiently near to the railway lines (which converged on Cambrai and made of it one of the most important junctions in the hands of the Germans) to be able to deny their use to the enemy.

Ludendorff, in his anxiety to protect Cambrai, had been withdrawing troops from Flanders. Doubtless he remembered our experiences in the third battle of Ypres, and recalled the fact that the Flanders mud had there done more to check our progress than had the German troops. The season was already far advanced and there had been a good deal of rain. The state of his reserves was such that in order to meet the American advance west of the Meuse, and the British advance on Cambrai, both of them blows aimed at his vitals, he had to take chances somewhere, and he decided to take them on the Flanders front. He left less than five divisions to hold the seventeen miles of front, from near Vormezeele, four and a half miles south of Ypres, to Dixmude, and on September 28th this thin line was attacked and overwhelmed by the Belgian army, supported by some French divisions, and by six divisions of Plumer's Second Army, the whole under the command of King Albert.

The success won by the gallant Belgian king, who had seen his army cooped in for four years behind the floods of the Yser, and had only left it at rare intervals, living with his Queen in a little villa within range of the German guns and in a district incessantly attacked by the enemy's bombing aëroplanes, was startlingly complete and exceeded the wildest expectations. The Flanders ridges, up which we had hewn our way at heavy cost in three and a half months of fighting in the autumn of 1917, were won in less than forty-eight hours. The French and Belgians, following up this success vigorously on the left of the battle, swept forward beyond Passchendaele, and by the evening of October 1st had penetrated almost to the outskirts of Roulers, while Plumer, throwing in three more divisions, drove across the Messines Ridge, cleared the Lys valley from Armentières to Comines, and advanced to within two miles of Menin. Thus Lille, like Cambrai, was menaced from the north.

While King Albert was putting the finishing touches to his victory the crisis of the great battle had been reached and passed. The bombardment which had begun on the evening of September 26th on the front of the British Fourth, Third and First Armies, had been continued on the front of the Fourth Army throughout the twenty-seventh and twenty-eighth, while the other two armies were fighting their way towards Cambrai. During the final stage of that bombardment nearly one million shells, weighing some twenty five thousand tons, were poured into the German lines. This wholesale expenditure of ammunition took place during about one-tenth of the period of the whole battle, and on considerably less than one-tenth of the fronts attacked.

During the war of 1870-1871 the total number of rounds fired by the German artillery in the field amounted to 360,000, as compared with 4,362,500 *tons* of shells fired by the British artillery alone on the Western Front, and yet, so tremendous had the effect of the German guns appeared to be in those days, that Napoleon III. told his enemies after his surrender at Sedan that he felt himself beaten by their artillery. Science and industry have in less than fifty years developed man's power of destruction to an extent which makes comparison with the past futile.

With this artillery attack we reverted to former methods, and the reason for doing so was that immediately behind that part of the German front to be attacked by the Fourth Army ran the St. Quentin Canal, which merges near Cambrai in the navigable Scheldt, is capable of taking the largest barges and is unfordable. With such an obstacle in their path tanks could not be used to prepare the way for the infantry, except against such portions of the German line as lay west of the canal, and against the two stretches where the canal ran underground, one of about four and a half miles between Bellicourt and Vendhuile, the other of about a thousand yards long just north of St. Quentin known as the Le Tronquoy Tunnel. So the guns came into their own. It was long since the Germans had been subjected to such a dose of shelling, and many of their troops having come from the Eastern Front, or being fresh drafts from

Germany, had never experienced a really intense and prolonged bombardment. The moral effect of this cannonade was therefore very great. It drove the enemy into his deep dug-outs and tunnels, and prevented his carrying parties from bringing up food and ammunition to them.

At 5.30 a. m. on September 29th Rawlinson's Fourth Army attacked the heart of the Hindenburg Line on a front of twelve miles with the 9th and 3rd British Corps and the 2nd American Corps, with the Australian Corps in support behind it. Debeney's First French Army extended the battle front to the south and attacked St. Quentin, while two corps of the Third British Army prolonged it to the north as far as the loop in the St. Quentin Canal at Marcoing. This was the decisive day of the great battle and was marked by many glorious feats of arms. The 9th Corps attacked the St. Quentin Canal at and north of Bellenglise, the 46th Division, North Midland Territorials, leading, the men advancing equipped with life-belts, requisitioned from the Channel steamboats, and carrying mats and rafts. Here and there they managed to cross by foot bridges, which the enemy had been unable to destroy, but the majority dropped down the sheer sides of the canal, swam across, clambered out and stormed the German trenches on the top of the eastern bank. Then swinging southward they surprised the enemy before he had realized the new direction of the attack, and on this one day the division captured over 4,000 prisoners and 70 guns.

The 2nd American Corps attacked the Bellicourt Tunnel front, which the Germans, knowing that it was exposed to tank attack, had fortified with especial care. The 30th American Division stormed through the intricate web of barbed wire and the network of trenches which surrounded Bellicourt, and breaking clean through this section of the main Hindenburg Line, carried the village, only to be attacked in the rear by the German machine gunners who had come out of their subterranean shelters in the tunnel. The Australians coming up in support had to tackle these pests without the aid of artillery or tanks, for both the barrage and the tanks had gone forward with the Americans, but they overcame them, and another breach in the Hindenburg Line was effected.

The 27th American Division, attacking on the left of the Thirtieth, had an especially difficult task, for the westerly bend in the canal at Vendhuile made it impossible for the British troops farther north to keep pace with the advance of the Twenty-seventh, and its left flank was exposed to cross-fire of artillery and machine guns from the ridge northeast of Vendhuile on the eastern bank of the canal. Two regiments of the division, the 106th and 107th, had therefore to fight desperately hard to safeguard the left of the division, while the right and center pushed on to the village of Bony. Later the British 12th and 18th Divisions forced their way across the canal to the north of the tunnel, and relieved the pressure on the left flank of the 27th American Division which had beaten off repeated and fierce German counter-attacks.

On September 30th and on the following days the yielding enemy was driven back on the whole front of the Fourth, Third and First Armies. On the right of the Fourth Army the 1st British Division had, by the thirtieth, gained possession of the Le Tronquoy Tunnel, and crossed the canal to the north of St. Quentin, a feat as splendid as that of the 46th Division on the previous day. Its immediate consequence was that the Germans retired from St. Quentin, which fell into the hands of the French on October 1st. The Australians, passing through the Americans, sent the right center of our battle-front forward to within touch of the last line of the Hindenburg system, which ran through Beaurevoir. The New Zealanders and the 3rd British Division crossed the canal to the south of Cambrai, while the Canadians all but encircled the town to the north. By October 3rd the Fourth Army had broken through the Beaurevoir line, and by the fifth the whole line of the canal, and the Hindenburg defenses along it, were in our hands.

The victory was complete and decisive, and in winning it the three British armies had captured 36,500 prisoners and 380 guns. Thirty British and two American divisions with a British cavalry division had defeated thirty-nine German divisions, holding the strongest defenses ever devised by the wit of man. At last after four years of dogged effort the great trench barriers had been pierced, for between the British army and its objective, Maubeuge, there lay but one German line, which the enemy, believing the Hindenburg system to be proof against all assaults, had not troubled to complete. This line lay some fourteen miles back, and its artificial defenses consisted of nothing more formidable than a thin fence of barbed wire, with the sites of the trenches to be dug behind it marked out upon the ground. The victors of Cambrai looked out over rolling, wooded, and well-watered country with something of the joy and wonder which filled the soldiers of Xenophon when at the end of their great march they first saw the sea. The leafy trees, the harvested fields, the green meadow lands and the valleys were to an army which had lived and fought for four years surrounded by hideous devastation, with the stink of the blood-soaked, battle-torn ground ever in their nostrils, more convincing evidence of achievement than tens of thousands of prisoners and hundreds of guns.

The effect of the three great blows on the Meuse-Champagne front, on the St. Quentin-Cambrai front, and in Flanders was, as Foch had hoped it would be, to cause the Germans to yield in the intervals between those attacks. By the end of September the enemy had begun to withdraw between Lens and Armentières before the left of our First Army and our Fifth Army, and there were signs of retirement from the St. Gobain bulge. He was at once pressed by the French and British forces on these fronts, and the battle thereupon enveloped the whole 250 miles from Dixmude to the Meuse. Foch's great conception had been realized; he had delivered his big kick and the whole German front was crumbling under it. For a time, on the British front at least, the German *morale* broke down, prisoners were taken from the German infantry in great numbers and without much resistance, and there were signs of confusion and disorder in the enemy ranks, though the German artillery retained much of its efficiency and the machine gunners continued to fight with their old devotion and skill.

St. Mihiel

American Troops pressing the
German retreat. The hill of
Mont Sec, the center of the de-
fense, rises in the background

More important still, the resolution of the German High Command was badly shaken. There were no men in Germany to replace the tremendous losses in the field, and many of Ludendorff's divisions were reduced to mere skeletons. He had piled up behind his front, for his great offensive, enormous stocks of shell, and of military stores, and had had neither the time nor the transport to remove them. The Allies had captured thousands of guns. The output of the German munitions factories was quite incapable of making good these losses, and he had ample evidence that the Allied factories had not yet reached the zenith of their production. In September Haig had more guns, more machine guns, more ammunition and more aëroplanes than he had ever possessed, while the growth of the American army was daily bringing more and more guns into line.

With dwindling resources, Ludendorff saw himself faced by three great dangers: in the east the Americans, more numerous and efficient than he had believed they could possibly be, were threatening his communications between Metz and Mézières; in the center the British army had beaten the best of his troops in their strongest defenses, and he had no more Hindenburg lines to stay its progress; in Flanders the Belgians, whom he had classed as capable only of defense, had won their way into the open and were fighting with unexpected dash. Lastly, Bulgaria had collapsed, Mackensen was in dire straits and was clamoring for reenforcements to enable him to escape from the Balkans. Under the pressure of these calamities Ludendorff threw up the sponge on the evening of September 28th. The next day he and Hindenburg met the Kaiser and the Foreign Secretary, who had come to Headquarters, and insisted on an immediate request for an armistice.

BY GENERAL PERSHING
From his report of December 5, 1918

Other divisions attached to the Allied armies were doing their part. It was the fortune of our Second Corps, composed of the Twenty-seventh and Thirtieth Divisions, which had remained with the British, to have a place of honor in cooperation with the Australian Corps on September 29th and October 1st in the assault on the Hindenburg Line where the St. Quentin Canal passes through a tunnel under a ridge. The Thirtieth Division speedily broke through the main line of defense for all its objectives, while the Twenty-seventh pushed on impetuously through the main line until some of its elements reached Gouy. In the midst of the maze of trenches and shell craters and under crossfire from machine guns the other elements fought desperately against odds. In this and in later actions, from October 6th to October 19th, our Second Corps captured over 6,000 prisoners and advanced over thirteen miles. The spirit and aggressiveness of these divisions have been highly praised by the British Army commander under whom they served.

U. S. GOVERNMENT STATEMENT

Operations of the Second American Corps Against the Hindenburg Line, September 27-October 1, 1918

In September, 1918, the Second American Corps (Twenty-seventh and Thirtieth Divisions) was placed at the disposal of the Fourth British Army for operations against the Hindenburg Line east of Péronne.

On the night of September 23rd-24th the Thirtieth Division took over what was known as the Nauroy sector, with a front of 3,750 yards, about 1,000 yards west of the main Hindenburg Line, and approximately on the old Hindenburg Outpost Line. On the next night the Twenty-seventh Division took over the Gouy sector, on the left of the Thirtieth Division and connecting with it; its front was 4,500 yards, approximately along the old British front line trenches, very close to the Hindenburg Outpost Line.

On September 27th, a preliminary operation was undertaken to straighten the line of the Thirtieth Division and to bring the Twenty-seventh up to the start line for the main attack. The Thirtieth Division succeeded, but by the afternoon of September 28th the Twenty-seventh Division was back nearly in its original position.

At 5.50 a. m., September 29th, the corps attacked, supported by the Australian Corps. The Second British Corps attacked simultaneously on its right, and the Third British Corps on its left. The attack was to be led by tanks, behind a rolling barrage. The start line was slightly to the east of the Hindenburg Outpost Line, and the objective east of Nauroy and Gouy. The plan provided that after the Americans had reached their objectives the Australians were to pass through them and continue in the advance.

The Thirtieth Division was already on the start line, close behind the initial line of the barrage. The Twenty-seventh, however, had not yet been able to take the three strong points—the Knoll, Guillemont Farm and Quennemont Farm—and was consequently about 1,000 yards behind the barrage line, which was east of them. The question of changing the barrage lines for this division was raised, but decided in the negative, the brigade designated to make the attack having reported at 6 p. m. on the 28th that it expected to be within 400 yards of the barrage lines, or possibly even on the intended starting line, before the hour for attack.

The barrage fell as planned at 5.50 a. m., September 29th, stood for four minutes on the initial line, and then advanced at the rate of 100 yards in four minutes. The Thirtieth Division advanced behind it, Sixtieth Brigade in first line. The One Hundred and Seventeenth Infantry was to follow across the tunnel, then deploy, facing south and cover the right of the Australians after the relief. Arrangements were made to seize the southern exit of the tunnel which lay in the division sector.

The German barrage was not heavy, but nevertheless there were many casualties, especially in the support battalions. Smoke and fog rendered it difficult to keep direction and contact. The One Hundred and Twentieth Infantry on the right crossed the Hindenburg line and occupied Nauroy, the One Hundred and Seventeenth reached its proper position, facing southeast and connecting the One Hundred and Twentieth with the Forty-sixth British Division. The One Hundred and Nineteenth, however, on the left, was enfiladed by machine guns from its own left, and had to form a defensive flank in that direction, reaching back to the tunnel and then connecting with the Twenty-seventh Division. A battalion of the One Hundred and Seventeenth and one of the One Hundred and Eighteenth were sent to support this flank. In this position the Australians passed through the lines and relieved the Thirtieth Division on the afternoon of September 29th.

In the Twenty-seventh Division, the Fifty-fourth Infantry Brigade made the attack under the same difficulties on account of fog and smoke. It also received machine-gun fire in enfilade from the direction of Vendhuile, outside its sector to the left. Part of the right regiment, the One Hundred and Eighth, by a detour to the south avoided Quennemont Farm and reached the Hindenburg Line south of Bony. Groups from all attacking battalions succeeded in penetrating between the strong points and reaching the Hindenburg Line; but by dusk only the extreme right retained its footing in that line. Here the division was relieved by the Australians, and remained in support; numerous groups, however, aggregating 1,000 men remained with the Australians and assisted them in cleaning up the Hindenburg Line on the right, taking it throughout the rest of the sector, and occupying part of the village of Bony.

The following is a quotation from the dispatch of Marshal Sir Douglas Haig, dated January 7, 1919: "North of Bellenglise the Thirtieth American Division (Major Gen. E. M. Lewis), having broken through the deep defenses of the Hindenburg Line, stormed Bellicourt and seized Nauroy.

"On their left the Twenty-seventh American Division (Major Gen. J. F. O'Ryan) met with very heavy enfilade machine-gun fire, but pressed on with great gallantry as far as Bony, where a bitter struggle took place for the possession of the village."

ST. MIHIEL

GERMANY LOSES HER FOUR-YEAR SALIENT AGAINST VERDUN

SEPTEMBER 12TH

CROWN PRINCE FREDERICK WILLIAM
GENERAL VON GALLWITZ   GENERAL PERSHING

No contest of the War was more definitely complete, more fully successful, or more expeditious than this first wholly American battle of St. Mihiel. Ludendorff had established a persistent policy of belittling everything American in the hope of persuading the German people that no great new factor had changed the nature of the War, that it was still the same old struggle in which they had so often won victories. Hence since he could not deny that the Americans had suddenly captured the entire St. Mihiel region, he announced that he had intended withdrawing from it anyway, and the Americans had only slightly hurried his retreat.

As a matter of plain fact, however, though no one but the German head-strategist himself can say what purposes he had in mind, the German and Austrian soldiers who actually held the St. Mihiel region had no knowledge of any prospective retreat. Their numbers were as large, and their intention of holding their position was as strong, as on any other section of the German front. Indeed, they were far more self-assured than the Germans farther north who were already, as we have seen, losing all they had won in the Kaiserbattle. The St. Mihiel troops, on the contrary, were in a sector where the Germans had established themselves in 1914 and for four years had never been driven back. Their shelters behind the trench line were of marvelous elaborateness of strength and comfort, and were fully stocked for another winter of such comfort as trench warfare could afford. The Crown Prince, who commanded in this section, had apparently but the feeblest understanding of the character of the American forces opposed to him. His statement about them, issued at the very moment before this battle, is peculiarly illuminative in its total misunderstanding.

What this first American Army did in General Pershing's first wholly independent operation was to take from the Germans the famous St. Mihiel salient, covering about two hundred square miles of ground. This salient, thrusting its apex in behind Verdun on the Meuse River, had always been a point of dangerous threat against France and especially against Verdun and Paris. The Americans, two hundred thousand strong, struck the salient upon both its sides at once, attacking eastward from around Verdun and northward from the region of Nancy and Lunéville. Both attacks succeeded, and the entire salient was caught within a pincer-like clutch. The Germans, about a hundred thousand strong, made a hurried retreat. The two attacking forces pressed forward until they met at Vigneulles, a town in the center of the base of the salient. At this meeting, they had pinched off and enclosed within the captured salient some twenty thousand enemy troops, some few of whom escaped, but most of whom surrendered.

The general impression made by the attack was expressed by one American newspaper correspondent, who wrote: "The enemy did not offer the opposition expected of him, but that was partly due to the perfection in the conception and execution of the attack by which he was stopped. Prisoners tell how division called to division in vain for aid, little knowing that the source from which it sought help was in even more desperate straits."

BY CROWN PRINCE FREDERICK WILLIAM

Statement given to the newspapers September 4, 1918

Regarding the American forces in France, I've found that the majority don't know what they are fighting for, but we feel, of course, the effect of the entry of the Americans. They have sent over very much material, and are now sending very much human material.

The French fight brilliantly and are bleeding to death. They do not hesitate at any sacrifice. With the English, the individual man is very good and tenacious, but the leadership is deficient. Among the Americans I have found that the majority do not know what they are fighting for. I asked an American prisoner what they are fighting for and he answered, "For Alsace." Then to the question, "Where is Alsace," he replied, "It's a big lake."

Statement from his Memoirs

The American attacks were in themselves badly planned; they showed ignorance of warfare; the men advanced in columns and were mowed down by our remaining machine guns. No great danger lay there, but their tanks pierced our thin lines—one man every twenty meters—and fired on us from behind. Withal the Americans had at their disposal an incredible quantity of heavy and very heavy artillery. Their preliminary firing greatly exceeded in intensity and heaviness anything we had known at Verdun and on the Somme.

BY GENERAL BARON VON GALLWITZ
Who was in personal command of the German forces at St. Mihiel

Before the attack on the St. Mihiel triangle the American troops had been greatly strengthened. Their divisions had been welded together into army corps. By the beginning of September we learned of the formation of an independent Pershing American army, which was lying between the second and eighth French armies.

American divisions had fought honorably in the big battles which ended with the failure of our offensive at the Marne in July and August. It was an obvious suggestion to follow up this gradual development with some big feat, accomplished exclusively or largely by American troops under their own supreme command. An opportunity offered itself at St. Mihiel which had long been known.

Our position between the Meuse and the well-known height of Combre, southeast of Verdun, looked like an outstanding nose. It had taken this formation after the first battle in the Summer of 1914, and had been retained, fortified and honored as the field of many single combats. We had seven divisions that occupied this line, but they were reduced in number and among them were three of the militia and one Austrian division. The peril of this faulty triangle had always been patent to us. It lent itself to attack on all sides. We had repeatedly discussed the question of giving up this triangle. The chief in command agreed with me that no big battle in this territory was permissible.

But while we waited, the crisis came on apace. We never had time to carry off the materials we had gathered during an occupation of several years. On the other side lay the consideration that the yielding of a position held for years would be interpreted as a sign of weakness. Naturally we disregarded such considerations when the situation in other parts of the theatre of war was difficult.

There had been indications that something was brewing on the other side, but we were not certain as to which direction the attack might take. We were informed that the objective of the Americans was Metz and the territory east of that fortress, which would threaten our communication with the rear. The centre of the enemy rear guard and communications was located on the southern side of the triangle, while on the northwest side everything was quiet, indicating that danger in the latter quarter was remote.

Then from foreign sources came the news that the American attack had been postponed—that the army was not yet ready for a big offensive movement.

We were surprised, therefore, when, on September 12, a concentrated attack was launched against the triangle. It was soon demonstrated that this was not a partial attack, but the execution of a great concentrated drive. The order to retire, which I gave on my own responsibility, but too late, could not prevent the loss of many troops and much material which had to be left behind.

The first deep advance took place on the southern side and was directed against two of our divisions, extending some twenty-three kilometers. Against the front covered by this attack nine or ten American divisions were led into battle, six being held in reserve.

The two divisions which I had in reserve behind the southern front could not succeed in turning the tide. The artillery and infantry collaborated better than ever, but there was little skill in profiting by the advance. The American fliers made themselves very disagreeable. We learned that 800 of them were active at the front. Our units retired from the Mihiel position in order, although with losses. All of the retiring divisions, except one that was scattered (one which held Alsace-Lorraine men), were still employed in the front lines. Although our retirement had been effected in good order, the enemy naturally considered it as forced.

I have experienced a good many things in the five years of war and have not been poor in successes, but I must count the 12th of September among my few black days.

BY GENERAL PERSHING
From his final report of November, 1919

In conference with General Pétain at Chantilly on May 19th it had been agreed that the American army would soon take complete charge of the sector of the Woevre.

The counter-offensives against the Marne salient in July, and against the Amiens salient in August had gained such an advantage that it was apparent that the emergency, which justified the dispersion of our divisions, had passed. The moment was propitious for assembling our divisions. Scattered as they were along the Allied front, their supply had become very difficult. From every point of view the immediate organization of an independent American force was indicated. The formation of the army in the Château-Thierry region and its early transfer to the sector of the Woevre, which was to extend from Nomeny, east of the Moselle, to north of St. Mihiel, was therefore decided upon by Marshal Foch and myself on August 9th, and the details were arranged with General Pétain later on the same day.

At Bombon on July 24th there was a conference of all the commanders-in-chief for the purpose of considering allied operations. Each presented proposals for the employment of the armies under his command, and these formed the basis of future coöperation of the Allies. It was emphatically determined that the allied attitude should be to maintain the offensive. At the first operation of the American army the reduction of the salient of St. Mihiel was to be undertaken as soon as the necessary troops and material could be made available. On account of the swampy nature of the country it was especially important that the movement be undertaken and finished before the fall rains should begin, which was usually about the middle of September.

Arrangements were concluded for successive relief of American divisions, and the organization of the First American Army under my personal command was announced on August 10th, with La Fertesous-Jouarre as headquarters. This army nominally assumed control of a portion of the Vesle front, although at the same time directions were given for its secret concentration in the St. Mihiel sector.

The force of American soldiers in France at that moment was sufficient to carry out this offensive, but they were dispersed along the front from Switzerland to the Channel.

The three Army Corps headquarters to participate in the St. Mihiel attack were the First, Fourth, and Fifth. The First was on the Vesle, the Fourth at Toul, and the Fifth not yet completely organized. To assemble combat divisions and service troops and undertake a major operation, within the short period available and with staffs so recently organized, was an extremely difficult task. Our deficiencies in artillery, aviation, and special troops, caused by the shipment of an undue proportion of infantry and machine guns during the summer, were largely met by the French.

The reduction of the St. Mihiel salient was important, as it would prevent the enemy from interrupting traffic on the Paris-Nancy Railroad by artillery fire and would free the railroad leading north through St. Mihiel to Verdun. It would also provide us with an advantageous base of departure for an attack against the Metz-Sedan Railroad system which was vital to the German armies west of Verdun, and against the Briey Iron Basin which was necessary for the production of German armament and munitions.

The general plan was to make simultaneous attacks against the flanks of the salient. The ultimate objective was tentatively fixed as the general line Marieulles (east of the Moselle)—heights south of Gorze-Mars la Tour-Etain. The operation contemplated the use on the western face of 3 or 4 American divisions, supported by the attack of 6 divisions of the Second French Army on their left, while 7 American divisions would attack on the southern face, and 3 French divisions would press the enemy at the tip of the salient. As the part to be taken by the Second French Army would be closely related to the attack of the First American Army, Gen. Pétain placed all the French troops involved under my personal command.

By August 30th, the concentration of the scattered divisions, corps, and army troops, of the quantities of supplies and munitions required, and the necessary construction of light railways and roads, were well under way.

In accordance with the previous general consideration of operations at Bombon on July 24th, an Allied offensive extending practically along the entire active front was eventually to be carried out. After the reduction of the St. Mihiel sector the Americans were to coöperate in the concerted effort of the Allied armies. It was the sense of the conference of July 24th, that the extent to which the different operations already planned might carry us could not be then foreseen, especially if the results expected were achieved before the season was far advanced. It seemed reasonable at that time to look forward to a combined offensive for the autumn, which would give no respite to the enemy and would increase our advantage for the inauguration of succeeding operations extending into 1919.

On August 30th, a further discussion with Marshal Foch was held at my headquarters at Ligny-en-Barrois. In view of the new successes of the French and British near Amiens and the continued favorable results toward the *Chemin des Dames* on the French front, it was now believed that the limited Allied offensive, which was to prepare for the campaign of 1919, might be carried further before the end of the year. At this meeting it was proposed by Marshal Foch that the general operations as far as the American Army was concerned should be carried out in detail by:

(*a*) An attack between the Meuse and the Argonne by the Second French Army, reënforced by from four to six American divisions.

(*b*) A French-American attack, extending from the Argonne west to the Souain Road, to be executed on the right by an American Army astride the Aisne and on the left by the Fourth French Army.

To carry out these attacks the 10 to 11 American divisions suggested for the St. Mihiel operation and the 4 to 6 for the Second French Army, would leave 8 to 10 divisions for an American Army on the Aisne. It was proposed that the St. Mihiel operation should be initiated on September 10th and the other two on September 15th and 20th, respectively.

The plan suggested for the American participation in these operations was not acceptable to me because it would require the immediate separation of the recently formed First American Army into several groups, mainly to assist

French armies. This was directly contrary to the principle of forming a distinct American Army, for which my contention had been insistent. An enormous amount of preparation had already been made in construction of roads, railroads, regulating stations, and other installations looking to the use and supply of our armies on a particular front. The inherent disinclination of our troops to serve under Allied commanders would have grown and American morale would have suffered. My position was stated quite clearly that the strategical employment of the First Army as a unit would be undertaken where desired, but its disruption to carry out these proposals would not be entertained.

A further conference at Marshal Foch's headquarters was held on September 2nd, at which Gen. Pétain was present. After discussion the question of employing the American Army as a unit was conceded. The essentials of the strategical decision previously arrived at provided that the advantageous situation of the Allies should be exploited to the utmost by vigorously continuing the general battle and extending it eastward to the Meuse. All the Allied armies were to be employed in a converging action. The British armies, supported by the left of the French armies, were to pursue the attack in the direction of Cambrai; the center of the French armies, west of Rheims, would continue the actions, already begun, to drive the enemy beyond the Aisne; and the American Army, supported by the right of the French armies, would direct its attack on Sedan and Mézières.

It should be recorded that although this general offensive was fully outlined at the conference no one present expressed the opinion that the final victory could be won in 1918. In fact, it was believed by the French high command that the Meuse-Argonne attack could not be pushed much beyond Montfaucon before the arrival of winter would force a cessation of operations.

The choice between the two sectors, that east of the Aisne including the Argonne Forest, or the Champagne sector, was left to me. In my opinion, no other Allied troops had the morale or the offensive spirit to overcome successfully the difficulties to be met in the Meuse-Argonne sector and our

plans and installations had been prepared for an expansion
of operations in that direction. So the Meuse-Argonne front
was chosen. The entire sector of 150 kilometers of front,
extending from Port-sur-Seille, east of the Moselle, west to
include the Argonne Forest, was accordingly placed under
my command, including all French divisions then in that zone.
The First American Army was to proceed with the St. Mihiel
operation, after which the operation between the Meuse and
the western edge of the Argonne Forest was to be prepared
and launched not later than September 25th.

As a result of these decisions, the depth of the St. Mihiel
operation was limited to the line Vigneulles-Thiaucourt-
Regnieville. The number of divisions to be used was reduced
and the time shortened. Eighteen to 19 divisions were to be
in the front line. There were 4 French and 15 American
divisions available, 6 of which would be in reserve, while
the two flank divisions of the front line were not to advance.
Furthermore, 2 Army Corps headquarters, with their corps
troops, practically all the Army Artillery and Aviation, and
the First, Second, and Fourth Divisions, the first two destined to take a leading part in the St. Mihiel attack, were
all due to be withdrawn and started for the Meuse-Argonne
by the fourth day of the battle.

The salient had been held by the Germans since September, 1914. It covered the most sensitive section of the enemy's position on the Western Front; namely, the Mézières-
Sedan-Metz Railroad and the Briey Iron Basin; it threatened the entire region between Verdun and Nancy, and interrupted the main rail line from Paris to the east. Its primary
strength lay in the natural defensive features of the terrain
itself. The western face of the salient extended along the
rugged, heavily wooded eastern heights of the Meuse; the
southern face followed the heights of the Meuse for 8 kilometers to the east and then crossed the plain of the Woevre,
including within the German lines the detached heights of
Loupmont and Montsec which dominated the plain and afforded the enemy unusual facilities for observation. The
enemy had reënforced the positions by every artificial means
during a period of four years.

On the night of September 11th, the troops of the First Army were deployed in position. On the southern face of the salient was the First Corps, Maj. Gen. Liggett, commanding, with the Eighty-second, Ninetieth, Fifth, and Second Divisions in line, extending from the Moselle westward. On its left was the Fourth Corps, Maj. Gen. Joseph T. Dickman, commanding, with the Eighty-ninth, Forty-second, and First Divisions, the left of this corps being opposite Montsec. These two Army Corps were to deliver the principal attack, the line pivoting on the center division of the First Corps. The First Division on the left of the Fourth Corps was charged with the double mission of covering its own flank while advancing some 20 kilometers due north toward the heart of the salient, where it was to make contact with the troops of the Fifth Corps. On the western face of the salient lay the Fifth Corps, Maj. Gen. George H. Cameron, commanding, with the Twenty-sixth Division, Fifteenth French Colonial Division, and the Fourth Division in line, from Mouilly west to Les Eparges and north to Watronville. Of these three divisions, the Twenty-sixth alone was to make a deep advance directed southeast toward Vigneulles. The French Division was to make a short progression to the edge of the heights in order to cover the left of the Twenty-sixth. The Fourth Division was not to advance. In the center, between our Fourth and Fifth Army Corps, was the Second French Colonial Corps, Maj. Gen. E. J. Blondlat, commanding, covering a front of 40 kilometers with 3 small French divisions. These troops were to follow up the retirement of the enemy from the tip of the salient.

The French independent air force was at my disposal which, together with the British bombing squadrons and our own air forces, gave us the largest assembly of aviation that had ever been engaged in one operation. Our heavy guns were able to reach Metz and to interfere seriously with German rail movements.

At dawn on September 12th, after four hours of violent artillery fire of preparation, and accompanied by small tanks, the Infantry of the First and Fourth Corps advanced. The infantry of the Fifth Corps commenced its advance at 8

a. m. The operation was carried out with entire precision. Just after daylight on September 13th, elements of the First and Twenty-sixth Divisions made a junction near Hatton-chatel and Vigneulles, 18 kilometers northeast of St. Mihiel. The rapidity with which our divisions advanced overwhelmed the enemy, and all objectives were reached by the afternoon of September 13th. The enemy had apparently started to withdraw some of his troops from the tip of the salient on the eve of our attack, but had been unable to carry it through. We captured nearly 16,000 prisoners, 443 guns, and large stores of material and supplies. The energy and swiftness with which the operation was carried out enabled us to smother opposition to such an extent that we suffered less than 7,000 casualties during the actual period of the advance.

During the next two days the right of our line west of the Moselle River was advanced beyond the objectives laid down in the original orders. This completed the operation for the time being and the line was stabilized to be held by the smallest practicable force.

The material results of the victory achieved were very important. An American army was an accomplished fact, and the enemy had felt its power. No form of propaganda could overcome the depressing effect on the morale of the enemy of this demonstration of our ability to organize a large American force and drive it successfully through his defenses. It gave our troops implicit confidence in their superiority and raised their morale to the highest pitch. For the first time wire entanglements ceased to be regarded as impassable barriers and open-warfare training, which had been so urgently insisted upon, proved to be the correct doctrine. Our divisions concluded the attack with such small losses and in such high spirits that without the usual rest they were immediately available for employment in heavy fighting in a new theater of operations. The strength of the First Army in this battle totaled approximately 500,000 men, of whom about 70,000 were French.

From General Pershing's Report at the Time of the Attack

The French were generous in giving us assistance in corps and army artillery, with its personnel, and we were confident from the start of our superiority over the enemy in guns of all calibers. Our heavy guns were able to reach Metz and to interfere seriously with German rail movements. The French independent air force was placed under my command, which, together with the British bombing squadrons and our air forces, gave us the largest assembly of aviators that had ever been engaged in one operation on the western front.

From Les Eparges around the nose of the salient at St. Mihiel to the Moselle River the line was, roughly, forty miles long and situated on commanding ground greatly strengthened by artificial defenses.

After four hours' artillery preparation, the seven American divisions in the front line advanced at 5 a. m. on September 12th, assisted by a limited number of tanks, manned partly by Americans and partly by French. These divisions, accompanied by groups of wire cutters and others armed with bangalore torpedoes, went through the successive bands of barbed wire that protected the enemy's front line and support trenches in irresistible waves on schedule time, breaking down all defense of an enemy demoralized by the great volume of our artillery fire and our sudden approach out of the fog.

Our First Corps advanced to Thiaucourt, while our Fourth Corps curved back to the southwest through Nonsard. The Second Colonial French Corps made the slight advance required of it on very difficult ground, and the Fifth Corps took its three ridges and repulsed a counter-attack. A rapid march brought reserve regiments of a division of the Fifth Corps into Vigneulles and beyond Fresnes-en-Woevre. At the cost of only 7,000 casualties, mostly light, we had taken 16,000 prisoners and released the inhabitants of many villages from enemy domination, and established our lines in a position to threaten Metz.

BULGARIA'S DOWNFALL

THE ALLIES ADVANCE FROM SALONIKA

SEPTEMBER 15TH-29TH

GENERAL D'ESPEREY   GENERAL MILNE
ELEUTHERIOS VENIZELOS   KING FERDINAND

Bulgaria was the first of the Central Powers to break down. For a year past she had been supported only by the strength of her allies. Her people, never eager for the War, came more and more to lay the whole blame for it upon their scheming king, Ferdinand.

Then came the American aid upon the western front; and the Ally army under General D'Esperey, which had been unable in previous years to make any advance from Salonika, found itself suddenly free to strike. There was no longer any danger of the Salonika troops being called away to the west front, and there was no longer any fear of their being needed to repress a royalist revolt in Greece. Greece was now confident in the Allies' cause, and under her Prime Minister Venizelos was eager to prove her devotion to her friends—and perhaps to profit largely in the reconstruction of the Balkans.

Hence D'Esperey, instead of heading a forlorn hope fighting with backs to the wall in Salonika, found himself commanding an eager army of Greeks and Serbians as well as Britons, French and even a few Italians from Albania. Moreover, the Bulgarian forces opposed to him had suddenly lost heart. They understood the meaning of the American invasion of Europe; and all their German regiments and officers were hastily leaving them for the west front. Bulgaria was beaten before the attack began; and when, on September 15th, D'Esperey's drive did come, there was a momentary resistance, then a complete break in the Bulgar ranks, and a general flight.

As early as September 24th the Bulgarian Government sent commissioners to seek peace at any price, and on September 29th the armistice was signed, the first of the series which terminated the War. That armistice included a frank and unconditional surrender; and the Bulgar king, fearing dire punishment from his own subjects promptly abdicated his throne and fled from his country. He had always been a German, not a Bulgar; and he became a German once more.

Following the Bulgarian surrender, the Austrian and German troops still remaining in Serbia, began a hurried evacuation of the country. The Serbian troops pressing eagerly forward reached the outskirts of their ancient capital of Nish on October 12th. Here the Germans tried to hold them back, for the loss of Nish would include the loss of that uninterrupted railroad line from Berlin to Constantinople, which had been their chief commercial triumph and advantage won in the earlier

321

years of the War. But the eager Serbian troops were not to be denied. Everywhere the remaining peasants of the land were joining them as they advanced. They carried Nish with a rush on October 13th. On November 3rd they reëntered Belgrade, their chief city. Then, crossing the Danube, they advanced against the everywhere fleeing Austrians and occupied the ancient Serb territory of Bosnia. On November 10th they marched in triumph into Serajevo, the city wherein the slaying of Duke Franz Ferdinand had roused the Austrians against them.

BY GENERAL FRANCHET D'ESPEREY
Official Report of September 30, 1918

ON September 15th, in the forenoon, two French divisions and one Serbian division, making an attack on the formidable mountain barrier formed by the Vetrenik, the Dobropolje, and the so-called Sokol, made a breach in the enemy front which was to bring about the falling-in of the front. By this breach, which was gradually widened, the Serbian armies and the French and Greek troops supporting them went forward with untiring energy, in spite of the exceptional difficulties of the ground and of the desperate resistance of the enemy, towards their main objective—the region of Kavadar-Demir Kapoo. They reached this region on September 22nd, cutting at one stroke the communications of the First Bulgarian army operating on the Vardar, and those of the 11th Bulgar-German army fighting to the north of Monastir. The French and Serbian troops rivaled each other in endurance, courage and self-sacrifice.

All the Allied forces gradually took part in the attack. On September 18th the British-Greek divisions, after stubborn fighting, captured the enemy positions of Doiran, retaining in this region very important forces. From September 21st the Italian, Greek and French troops of the Allied army of Monastir moved up. On September 22nd the general pursuit commenced, and was carried out with splendid ardor and energy.

On September 23rd the Serbians crossed the Vardar towards Krivelak. On the 24th the French cavalry entered Prilep. On the 25th Ishtip was captured, as well as the formidable barrier of the Beles. The British opened up the road to Strumitza, which they entered on the 26th. On the same day the Serbians reached Kotchana and Veles, and the Italian, French and Greek troops were marching on Kicovo.

By the evening of the 26th the Bulgarians asked for a suspension of hostilities, and announced the dispatch of plenipotentiaries.

In the course of these glorious operations, which the hasty throwing in of German reënforcements was unable to prevent, the Allied armies captured a great number of prisoners and immense booty. Allied air squadrons took a most active and efficient part in the battle, continually reporting to headquarters, bombarding and ceaselessly machine-gunning the enemy troops and convoys, sowing disorder among them and preventing them eluding our grasp.

BY LORD MILNE
Official Report of the British General in command

In connection with the offensive by the Serbians and French in the mountain country between the Vardar and Cerna Rivers, which began on September 15th, operations were carried out by the Anglo-Greek force with the object of keeping hostile reserves in the Vardar Valley. On September 1st the 27th Division had captured a portion of the enemy's line west of the Vardar. On the 18th the British and Greeks attacked, and after severe fighting Doiran town and a considerable extent of the enemy's first and second lines were captured. The attack was renewed on the 19th, and further progress was made, while the enemy had to use his reserves to restore his front, and no troops were able to leave the line in front of the British to oppose the Serbians. The principal part of the fighting was borne by the 22nd Division, the 77th Infantry Brigade and the Greek Seres Division. All troops, both British and Greek, fought with great determination. The Greek soldiers showed remarkable valor and tenacity.

Owing to the cutting of his communications by the Serbians, the enemy started a retirement in the Vardar Valley on the night of September 21st.

British Semi-official Press Report of October 2nd

It may not be uninteresting to describe the nature of the enemy positions on this formidable sector. On the western side his lines, which had been properly compared in previous offensives to a medieval stronghold consisting of a bastion and flanking bastion, rise in successive strength to the famous Dub at the summit of the Pip Ridge and on to the Grand Couronné, which might be called the "keep" of the fortress. These are of enormous natural strength, reënforced by all the ingenuity of modern warfare, and are held by an enemy who never fights so stubbornly and courageously as when on the defensive. The ground on the left looking north is dominated by the Pip Ridge, each projection of which seems intended by Nature for defense. In the center and on the horizon is the Grand Couronné, over two thousand feet above sea level and a thousand feet above our starting-point. On the right broken hills rise above Lake Doiran, and to win these hills and reach the eastern support of the Grand Couronné one must first pass Jumeaux Ravine and Petit Couronné, the Bulgars' strong allies in our previous offensives. On the northeast of the lake the ground over which we had to attack is a flat plain, broadest at the foot of the Kursa Balkans and tapering and curving round the lake. It is menaced from the north by the vast *massif* of the Belashitza, on the lowest slopes of which are defenses which must be overcome if progress is to be made in the narrow plain, which, to the north of Lake Doiran, is less than two miles broad.

Our bombardment commenced at dawn on September 16th over the whole front between the Vardar and Lake Doiran. On the northeast of the lake was silence. The bombardment continued for forty-eight hours, cutting wires, smashing trenches and dugouts, neutralizing the enemy's batteries, and making the Bulgarians wonder what was coming next and when it was coming. Ravines and valleys filled with smoke made a picture like a photograph printed from a fogged negative, and nothing but the ridges was visible.

On this side of the lake the attack began at five on the

morning of the 18th, and fighting continued all day with tremendous intensity. Along the eastern slope of Pip Ridge
our infantry advanced and drove back the Bulgar, forcing
him to commit his reserves to this sector, and having thus
gallantly engaged and preoccupied him, took up a position
in conformity with that held by the Greek and British troops
who were operating in the center. Here the enemy's front
line trenches and Sugar Loaf Hill were taken after bitter
fighting. On the right the Greeks signalized their first extensive operation in conjunction with British troops by conspicuous dash and tenacity. They passed by Jumeaux ravine,
enveloped Petit Couronné, and stormed Hill 340, from which
the enemy temporarily dislodged them, only to be driven out
again by our Allies, who now hold the hill and the line from
it to Doiran town to the north of Teton Hill. In the course
of these operations, in which the heaviest but not the least
glorious fighting fell to British troops on the left, whose
dogged occupation of the enemy facilitated the advance on
the right, over eight hundred prisoners were taken, a very
definite foothold of some three square kilometers won, the
enemy troops pinned down, and our movements on the northeast of the lake and those of the Serbians advancing rapidly
on the lateral line of communication of the Bulgars to the
west were saved from interference.

Far to the east of the lake the British and Greeks, shortly
after midnight, advancing from the foot of the Kursa
Balkans across the plain, under cover of darkness, formed
up in the wooded ground behind the railway embankment below the village of Popovo. From Popovo the Allied troops
went forward very early in the morning, and by half-past
seven they had taken the village of Akindjali and its strongly
fortified outpost position by assault. They then fought their
way in a northwest direction across the plain to the enemy
trenches at Nikolitch, which they entered at five in the afternoon. It was a difficult operation carried out in its early
stages in darkness and later under a blazing sun, across open
country to a line six miles from their starting-point, without artillery preparation, against an enemy who knew every

yard of the ground and had perfect observation from the steep slopes to the north.

If the fighting on the west of Lake Doiran was heavy on September 18th it was equally severe on the following day, when the main purpose of the British and Greek troops was decisively attained. This purpose was not merely territorial gain, but the retention of enemy troops, which would otherwise have been used against the Allied advance in the vast area between the Vardar, the Negotin-Prilep road, and the Cerna. Here the Serbs, Jugo-Slavs, French and Greeks were pushing forward with amazing rapidity, and the Bulgar could send no help from the Doiran front to stem the onset. Just as the movement northeast of the lake to the positions below Nikolitch, where the British troops on September 18th consolidated the line which had been won by the Greeks, assisted the attack to the west of the lake, so the latter played its part in the main scheme of the Allied command. At the end of the first day's fighting the British and Greeks could claim nearly a thousand prisoners and valuable ground, the Petit Couronné and Hill 340. On the second day they attacked again. There was a chance of winning Pip Ridge and the Grand Couronné, and there was the certainty of pre-occupying the Bulgar when he would rather have been using his strength elsewhere. The certainty was made good.

On the left the British attacked with the utmost determination, but on the Pip Ridge they were stopped by nests of machine guns which had been cleverly moved from their prepared positions to avoid our shell fire. They went back and re-formed, and went forward again. They fought with supreme courage, not knowing the value of their sacrifice, but making it in trust, and thus, though they had to go back to their original positions, they carried out to the full their task of detaining the enemy.

The two days' fighting on the rocky hillsides under a blazing sun, with a temperature well over ninety degrees in the shade, was followed by apparent quiet. The Bulgars were not merely unable to counter-attack, but were preparing to go. On the night of September 19th they put up a heavy barrage in fear of a further attack from us. On September 20th there was desultory shelling. On September 21st behind the Doiran front the enemy began to blow up his ammunition dumps, burn his rail-head and supply depots, send up trains to save what he could not destroy, and crowd the roads to the north with all the preliminaries of retirement. So the Bulgar must go, and he has realized it. A spirit of victory is in the air.

BY COLONEL FRANTZIS

Statements issued by the Greek Military Attaché in London

The Greek army, actually superior in number to the Allied contingents, taking each one separately, participated in the operations on different points. Our cavalry, passing beyond Veles in the direction of Uskub, cut definitely the retreat of the Bulgarian army by the main route Monastir-Kalkandelen-Uskub. Our contingents, after having crossed Mount Veles, descended into the Strumnitza Valley, to cut the main road over the Kresna Pass, so that the Bulgarian army of the Struma was compelled hurriedly to abandon Eastern Macedonia by different routes. The greatest part of the Bulgarian army of the Struma will be annihilated, leaving thousands of prisoners and enormous booty.

Salonika, September 29th.

The Italian, Greek and French troops operating on the left wing of the Allied Armies continued the pursuit of the retreating enemy rearguards towards Kichevo, and advanced to the north of Ochrida and to the west of the lake of the same name, where they reached the Elbassan road.

In the center French cavalry entered Uskub, while the Serbian armies, supported by French and Greek forces, continued their advance on Kumanovo, Egripalanka and Djumaia.

Farther to the east some British and Greek divisions advanced in the direction of Pechevo and Petric.

Our troops are winning new successes. In the region west of Prilep our troops, in coöperation with French troops, captured Barbarec pass and made good progress in the Treska valley. In the region north of Strumnitza, our

troops occupied the crest of Plaskavitza Planina to the east
of Ichtib and continue to press back the enemy. Three heavy
batteries fell into our hands. To the east of Strumnitza,
our troops, coöperating with the English, progressed along
the valley of the Strumnitza in the direction of Petritch.
On the Struma front several Greek patrols made a thrust
into the enemy lines, keeping him constantly out of breath.
The Commander-in-Chief of the Allied Army of the Orient
says, in a *communiqué,* the following about our troops : "The
Greek troops are once more displaying their brilliant apti-
tude for mountain warfare by conquering high-handedly the
roads issuing in the valley of high Treska and rapidly pro-
gressing in a northerly direction. To the right, crossing in
a few hours the Plaskavitza summits, the Greek divisions
have incessantly repulsed the Bulgarian divisions that were
vainly trying to stem their advance and captured in a single
point three heavy batteries and plenty of war material. In
the Strumnitza region, in liaison with British troops, they
continued to press back the enemy, who are hastily destroying great quantities of provisions accumulated in the valley."

BY GENERAL D'ESPEREY

Official Telegram to the Greek Prime Minister, M. Venizelos

At the moment when the success of the offensive operations which have been begun on the Macedonian front is
being affirmed, I desire to express to you my entire satisfaction at the brilliant conduct of the Greek units which are
taking part in the battle.

In particular, the Seres division, attacking west of Lake
Doiran in very difficult country, has just covered itself with
fresh glory, taking possession of extremely strong positions,
which were bitterly defended, and capturing a large number
of prisoners. Certain of these units have still further added
to the renown which they had already won in the attack on
the Skra di Legen.

Among the units which have recently arrived the 35th
infantry regiment has just asserted its worth by storming,
in coöperation with French units, the important Preslap
massif and the village of Zborsko. All the Greek units more-

over are competing with one another in endurance and dash, and I am persuaded that they will soon win fresh laurels.

BY ELEUTHERIOS VENIZELOS

Athens, September 30, 1918.

To the Commander of the Army, and Generals commanding army corps and divisions:

The signing of the military convention with the enemy crowns the battles of the National Army with complete triumph. The Government desires to congratulate the National Army and to express the gratitude of the nation for the work which it has completed. Reconstituted in the midst of so many difficulties, the National Army both from old and from new Greece has succeeded, in fighting by the side of the Allied Armies, in establishing not only the military prestige but the honor of the country as well.

The collapse of our nearest enemy heralds to us a favorable ending for our struggle and for that of our Allies. We do not of course know when this end will arrive. But with such an Army, fighting by the side of such Allies, the nation looks forward to the future with full confidence. Glory and honor to the National Army.

VENIZELOS.

BY LORD MILNE

Order of the Day of September 20th, addressed to the Greek forces aiding his command

On this the first occasion on which the Greek troops have fought by the side of the English, I wish to express to you my admiration for the way in which you have fulfilled the mission entrusted to you. You have attacked with incomparable dash naturally strong positions rendered almost impregnable by a stubborn Army.

The result of your efforts is already visible in the retreat of the Bulgarian Army. I thank you for your gallantry and tenacity, which are above all praise. I am proud to have had you under my command.

Address by Lord Milne to the Greek Forces on October 3rd

On behalf of all the ranks of the British Forces in Macedonia I beg to convey to you and to the gallant Hellenic Army our appreciation of the fine spirit of comradeship which you display in your message of thanks to us. Without the aid of the Hellenic Forces the present victory would not have been won.

BULGARIAN GOVERNMENT STATEMENT

Sofia, September 24, 1918.

In view of the conjunction of circumstances which have recently arisen, and after the position had been jointly discussed with all competent authorities, the Bulgarian Government, desiring to put an end to the bloodshed, authorized the Commander-in-Chief of the army to propose to the Generalissimo of the armies of the Entente at Salonika a cessation of hostilities and the entering into of negotiations for obtaining an armistice and peace. The members of the Bulgarian delegation left yesterday evening in order to get into touch with the plenipotentiaries of the Entente belligerents.

THE ARMISTICE

Signed on the evening of September 29th by General D'Esperey and by a Bulgarian Commission appointed by the Bulgarian Government and consisting of General Lonkhoff, M. Liapcheff, Minister of Finance, and M. Radeff, a former Cabinet leader.

Bulgaria agrees to evacuate all the territory she now occupies in Greece and Serbia, to demobilize her army immediately, and surrender all means of transport to the Allies.

Bulgaria also will surrender her boats and control of navigation on the Danube and concede to the Allies free passage through Bulgaria for the development of military operations.

All Bulgarian arms and ammunition are to be stored under the control of the Allies, to whom is conceded the right to occupy all important strategic points.

The military occupation of Bulgaria will be entrusted to British, French, and Italian forces, and the evacuated portions of Greece and Serbia, respectively, to Greek and Serbian troops.

The armistice means a complete military surrender, and Bulgaria ceases to be a belligerent.

The armistice will remain in operation until a final general peace is concluded.

BY KING FERDINAND OF BULGARIA

The first of the series of abdications by which the defeated monarchs abandoned their schemes of conquest

Sofia, October 4, 1918.

By reason of a succession of events which have occurred in my kingdom and which demand a sacrifice from each citizen, even to the surrendering of one's self for the well-being of all, I desire to give as the first example the sacrifice of myself.

Despite the sacred ties which for thirty-two years have bound me so firmly to this country, for whose prosperity and greatness I have given all my powers, I have decided to renounce the royal Bulgarian crown in favor of my eldest son, his Highness the Prince Royal Boris of Tirnovo.

I call upon all faithful subjects and true patriots to unite as one man about the throne of King Boris, to lift the country from its difficult situation and to elevate new Bulgaria to the height to which it is predestined.

THE FALL OF TURKEY

THE CAPTURE OF DAMASCUS AND CONSTANTINOPLE

SEPTEMBER 18TH-OCTOBER 30TH

GASTON BODART   W. T. MASSEY   H. C. OWEN
SIR EDMUND ALLENBY   SULTAN MOHAMMED VI.

The Scriptural name of Armageddon, the great final battle between right and wrong, has been applied to so many different battles of the Great War that confusion may easily result. But the one battle which geographically deserves the name is that fought by General Allenby and his British troops against the Turks from September 18th to 22nd. This final struggle between West and East, Europe and Asia, took place across the actual plains of Armageddon or Megiddo in central Palestine, and it broke the last remnant of the Turkish power.

The British under General Allenby had captured Jerusalem in December of 1917; but Turkish forces, directed by German officers and strengthened by German troops, still maintained an unbroken front north of Jerusalem and blocked the further British advance for almost a year. In February of 1918 the Britons attacked from Jerusalem and seized Jericho, the ancient stronghold of the Jordan valley. But after that many of General Allenby's best troops were taken hurriedly away from him and rushed to France to aid in blocking the great German advance there. So that not until September were the British able again to concentrate in Palestine a force sufficient for attack.

On September 18th General Allenby struck the foe suddenly at Rafat, broke their line and set them to retreating north through Palestine. With Arab aid he kept constantly attacking them until by the end of September their army was completely destroyed. Its members had died, surrendered, or vanished in utter flight.

On October 1st, Damascus, the ancient metropolis of the East, the symbol of sovereignty was occupied by the British. On October 8th a French fleet seized the Turkish port of Beirut. By this time the British forces in Mesopotamia were also advancing from Bagdad, and scattering the remnants of Turkish force from that region. By the end of October all the Turkish bases of supply were in Ally hands.

Turkish commissioners from Constantinople now sought the Allied naval commander in the East, the British admiral, Calthorp, and placed Turkey unreservedly in his hands. On October 30th, on the island of Lemnos in the Ægean Sea, Admiral Calthorp and the Turkish commissioners signed an armistice of complete surrender. On No-

vember 9th, British troops took possession of those fortifications of
the Dardanelles which had so long held their ships at bay. And on
November 10th the vanguard of the British fleet took possession of
Constantinople.

Talaat Bey, the nominal leader of the Turkish Government, resigned. Enver Bey, its military leader, disappeared in secret flight;
and the newly appointed Sultan, Mohammed VI., issued a formal
address approving the change. He announced his faith in Ally justice,
his regret for the crimes committed by his people, especially against
the Armenians, and his intent to have these crimes investigated and
punished. Fortunately, however, neither the investigation nor the control of Armenia was any longer left in Turkish hands.

The Teuton view of the Turkish breakdown is here given by their
official investigator, Dr. Bodart. Mr. Massey was with the Britons
in Palestine and Mr. Owen in Constantinople.

BY GASTON BODART

THE long and at times obstinate conflicts in the valley
of the Jordan gave Allenby time to complete the railway connections between Cairo and Jerusalem. In order
to have a word to say regarding the prospective conquest
of Syria, France sent a fresh division to coöperate with
Allenby's forces.

On September 18th, 1918, the great English-French
attack on the Turkish lines between the Jordan and the sea
began. It was flanked on the west by the artillery fire of
the numerous warships, and to the east of the Hedjaz
Railroad by the rebellious Arab tribes under their new King
Hussein. The powerful and well-directed offensive, with
its preponderance of numbers particularly as to cavalry,
which was here of great service, met with complete success. On the first day the Turkish lines were already penetrated to a depth of eight kilometers.

The principal battle took place on the 19th between
Rafat and the coast and led to the complete penetration of
the Turkish lines. The Seventh and Eighth Turkish Corps
were almost annihilated. On September 22nd the passage
of the Jordan was forced, and on the 26th Nablus was
occupied, the British cavalry relentlessly pursuing the
enemy.

The ruins of the Turkish army retreated in part toward
Tiberias, and in part over Aman toward Damascus, which
was occupied on September 30th by an Australian cavalry

division. The French forces turned toward Beirut, which they occupied on October 6th. The Turkish reserves under Liman von Sanders, which had been hurriedly brought up, did not succeed in changing the turn of affairs, but succumbed to the general demoralization now pervading the Turkish army.

This was beyond a doubt the most complete victory of the Entente in the war, for it had resulted in the complete annihilation of the enemy who not only lost 70,000 men as prisoners, but his entire artillery as well, including the brave Austro-Hungarian batteries which held out to the last. After the British had occupied Aleppo on October 26th, the Porte asked for an armistice, which was concluded at Mudros on October 30th, 1918.

BY W. T. MASSEY

Our progress during September was rapid, and the extent of our advance, on a very wide front, is so great that it may be the impression at home that we were weakly opposed. That would be wholly wrong. A document which has been captured shows that the ration strength of the Turkish Eighth Army was 39,783 men, of the Seventh Army 28,575, of the Jordan Group 5,223, and of the Fourth Army 21,899. On the lines of communication were 4,958 men, and of animals there were 39,234.

These figures may be exaggerated. But it is clear that General Allenby was opposed by an army of over 100,000, who, at any rate in places, fought strongly, and at times got to grips both with bomb and bayonet. The prisoners exceed 70,000. The dead, I believe, are not more than 10,000. Many got away home by other roads.

We have learned much from captured documents illustrating the strength of the enemy opposed to us. In the equipment of the Turkish army large support was given by the Germans. In the Yilderim army group there were 509 guns, including thirty in the repair shops. Of the balance we have captured over 350 of various calibers. There has not been time to search the hundreds of square miles of mountainous country, but doubtless others are hidden in the hills with many hundreds of machine guns and an enormous amount of gun ammunition.

With the Turks were 15,635 Germans, including several battalions of infantry, machine-gun companies, artillery, and the remainder technical troops running the railways, transport, signal service, etc. There was thus a large stiffening of Germans, with many technicians, and they were generally found wherever the enemy put up a strong resistance. The prisoners include a large number of Germans and Austrians.

The sheiks of the Ruwalla tribe, one of the most powerful in Arabia, brought 3,000 horsemen and the Haurani peasantry others, so that when near Deraa there was a force of 11,000 camelry, horsemen, and Arab irregulars with the column, which on September 16th got to the Hedjaz Railway, south of Deraa, and blew up the line.

Next day the north town was destroyed, with six kilometers of railway and an important bridge. On the night of the 18th they cut the line between Deraa and Nabulus, in the Yarmuk Valley, burning the station of Mezerib and the rolling stock, with six German lorries. The following day they moved south of Deraa, having made a complete circle round the town, and blew up the bridge. An armored car saw two airplanes and riddled them with bullets.

As the line was repaired it was again destroyed, so that the enemy's railway communication between Damascus and the main Turkish Army was broken for five days. The Amman garrison was cut off for eight days. Wherever the Arabs camped enemy planes bombed them, flying low and using machine guns. At one period near Deraa the enemy planes made frequent bombing raids, but were ineffectual to prevent the complete disorganization of the railway service. When General Allenby's attack began the Arabs fought their way up the railway line. One section, under Shereef Nasser, marched seventy miles in twenty-four hours, fighting part of the way, and reached the outskirts of Damascus on September 30th.

The work of the Air Service has been most praiseworthy. The difficulty of the cavalry keeping contact with the vast front has been overcome by the untiring energies of the airmen. One pilot for four days had an average of eight hours each flying day, and on occasions had to fly low, subjected to heavy machine-gun fire. His machine returned from one expedition with seventy-four bullet holes, but was unhit in any vital part. Our planes south of Amman secured the surrender of 2,000 Turks. The pilot, seeing a long-drawn-out column, dropped a message to say that if they did not surrender they would be bombed. He returned to the aërodrome and six machines shortly afterward were sent out with bombs, and while circling the ground the signal was laid out recalling them; the Turks had hoisted the white flag.

September 30th.

The operations of the last few days afford an illustration that the rôle of cavalry in present-day warfare over a front so wide as this makes it almost impossible to keep touch with the daily movements. General Allenby's mounted troops are being supremely successful, never missing an opportunity of hitting hard and swiftly, following up one big movement immediately by another equally vigorous, until the three cavalry divisions have to-day converged on Damascus. Troops from the Northern and Southern Hemispheres are now looking on the most ancient of living cities. Masses of British Yeomanry and Australian and Indian Horse, a force larger probably than was ever before assembled under one command, have outmaneuvered the Turkish forces, dealing the death blow to the Seventh and Eighth Armies before attacking the Fourth Army over the Jordan. Only those who have seen the superb cavalry of General Allenby's army could appreciate the possibilities, and not many of those in Palestine dreamed it was possible that Damascus was within reach of the wide stretch of the cavalry arm.

In ten days the mounted troops have covered fully 150 miles, in a country that yielded no food for man or beast, and are now practically surrounding the white city, set in a most beautiful green frame. The glorious gardens, rendered more refreshing to eyes used to the glare of the Eastern sun by comparison with the desolate, stony hills overlooking the verdant scene from all sides, are momentarily put to military uses by the enemy. In the mud-walled garden inclosures are nests of machine guns which at present we have not attempted to disturb. There are obvious signs that the Turk's days of possession of the city are numbered. Since the morning the enemy has been burning vast stores, and there have been numerous explosions of ammunition and petrol. Military establishments are ablaze, and the enormous wireless installation for communication with Constantinople and Berlin has been blown up. From the position of the fires it is believed that the two railway stations have been destroyed.

So far the city seems to have escaped, though with the high wind the huge fires are dangerous, the city being built mainly of wood. Every soldier looking on the city hopes it will be preserved, but it would be in keeping with the blighting influence of the Turk on everything he touches if by his action Damascus, which has changed hands many times in the 4,000 years of its life, should be destroyed for the first time by the Turks. Happily, that fate appears to be unlikely.

As a preliminary to jumping off for this jeweled goal, a portion of the cavalry moved to Deraa with orders to advance up the eastern road. A larger column took Tiberias and secured the bridge over the Jordan south of Lake Hule. The blowing up of the central arch of the ancient structure did not prevent the crossing, owing to the swimming of the river by an entire Australian regiment. Yesterday the cavalry halted at Kuneitra while supplies were brought over the steep, winding road from the Jordan Valley, many miles of which are absolutely the worst surface in the world for highways. It is a mass of unrolled lava bowlders strewn in the roadway. Progress was extremely difficult for wheels, but the cavalry's spirit surmounted all obstacles.

As the sun was setting last night the move forward from Kuneitra began with the weird and impressive spectacle of thousands of horsemen passing in the darkness. There was no sound save the horses' hoofbeats and the rumble of wheels. The Australian Mounted Division led, the Yeomanry and Indian cavalry following. Hardly any part of the country was visible in the gloom, except where the irregular crest of Mount Hermon blotted out the stars. Less than a dozen miles on the journey a brisk action delayed the advance for three hours. They were precious hours, for we knew that what remained of the Fourth Army was trekking north to Deraa, partially disorganized and with scanty transport, and we were anxious to bag the whole lot.

On the steep, rough hills overlooking the road, with a wadi in front, several hundred Turks and Germans waited with machine guns, with a couple of field guns well placed to cover the road. They had the advantage of the light of the waning moon. We got them in flank with a few casualties, and took prisoners. Those escaping up the hill were captured early in the morning. The German machine gunners were greatly surprised by the rapidity of our advance. At 8 o'clock our troops on the western road reached the southwestern edge of the hills holding Damascus in their hollow. There was one small but effective charge on the plateau, and strong opposition athwart the road at Kaukeb, ten miles from Damascus, the enemy striving hard to delay our advance until the destruction of the stores in the city's environs was complete.

At noon there was a spirited mounted attack at Kaukeb by the Australian Light Horse, who overrode the enemy in a brilliant charge, and enabled the brigade's cavalry to ride forward along the road west of the city and pursue the enemy attempting to get away on the Rayak road. This advance, within visual range of the Damascus minarets, has already yielded many prisoners. The regiment of Light Horse and one of French cavalry are just sending in 3,500 between them, while the Australian brigade brought machine guns into action on two hills dominating the road and killed all the transport animals and many men who blocked the road. Another force went across country to intercept parties of Turks retiring on Damascus in front of Deraa and heavily shelled the enemy before they reached the villages on the southern outskirts of the city.

October 1st.

General Allenby's triumphant march northward into Syria early this morning drove the Turks completely out of possession of Damascus, and there is now not a Turkish soldier in the city nor a Turkish official doing duty. The ap-

pearance of the Australian Mounted Division northwestward
of the city at noon yesterday set the seal on the doom of the
Turkish Government in the place on which Arabs center
their eyes. To-day the city was enveloped by British, Australian, and Indian troops, and the King of the Hedjaz's
Arab army has marched in. The few Turks who got away
are scattered and demoralized. Fully 12,000 Germans and
Turks are prisoners. In and about the city a number of
guns have been captured. The roads are a shambles where
the enemy resisted. Transport has been smashed and most
of the material left behind has been destroyed by the Germans, though some valuable transport, including a complete
park of cavalry limbers, was untouched. The prisoners captured since September 19th are probably more than 60,000.

I was under the impression that Damascus would display
the usual Arab calmness of demeanor and accept our appearance as Kismet, while appreciating the prospect of a
change from bad to good government, and would receive us
with their customary immobile features, giving no outward
and visible sign of their inward feelings.

I rode into the town with an armored-car officer when
the road was deemed unsafe owing to snipers in those luscious
gardens surrounding this fascinating and truly Oriental city.
I was amazed at the heartiness of the welcome accorded the
British uniform. The people were far from taking our
victory as an ordinary incident of life. They threw off
their stolid exterior, and received us with ecstatic joy. They
closed their shops and made a holiday, put on festival dress,
and acclaimed the day as the greatest in the 4,000 years of
the history of Damascus. Only a few British officers have
as yet entered the city, but each has been received with the
same whole-hearted fervor. Here, at least, they have seen
what the British name stands for. At Jerusalem the British
Army was welcomed by all sects and creeds with deep feelings of thankfulness, but their condition, rendered pitiable
through starvation, prevented their welcome from being so
demonstrative, though equally sincere, as to-day's. When a
soldier appeared in the streets of Damascus he was surrounded by the excited and delighted throng. Crowds gath-

ered to hear the news. When I told some English-speaking people, of whom there are many, of the latest victory on the western front and of the Bulgarian armistice their enthusiasm was remarkable.

But they were more keenly interested in General Allenby's army's tremendous stride through Palestine and Syria. The enormous captures of prisoners and war material, of which they had no conception, more than anything else, meant to them the finish of the Turk. They said: "You are settling our long accounts with them." The thoroughness with which it has been done gave them the impression that our army was composed of supermen. With eyes unused to complete and orderly equipment, they admired the soldierly turnout of the men who have fought and ridden a hard 150 miles, and acclaimed them their deliverers. They looked upon this army as the saviors of the downtrodden peoples of this part of the East. This amazing tribute to Britain and British freedom lasted all day; at nightfall the population gave a fireworks exhibition of captured Verey lights. Even the street of St. Paul called "Straight" was illuminated from end to end.

The opportunities for rejoicing were increased by the arrival of the Arab Army, which operated on our right flank. Our cavalry during the march from Deraa arrived at Damascus at 6 this morning, the northwestern outskirts being occupied by the Australian Mounted Division last night. Soon after daybreak the Arab Army entered the city, and the streets became alive with picturesquely clothed Arabs on light steeds, almost overburdened with elaborately appointed saddlery. Arab horsemen and camelry dashed about the streets, proclaiming the victory and making much noise and continually firing their rifles. This lasted till midnight, and the inhabitants, tired out and happy, allowed the city to become normally calm.

BY GENERAL ALLENBY

His official report of the fighting on September 20th at Armageddon

Our left wing, having swung around to the east, had reached the line of Bidieh, Baka, and Messudiyeh Junction, and was astride the rail and roads converging at Nabulus.

Our right wing, advancing through difficult country against considerable resistance, had reached the line of Khan-Jibeit, one and one-fourth miles northeast of El-Mugheir and Es-Sawieh, and was facing north astride the Jerusalem-Nabulus road.

On the north our cavalry, traversing the Field of Armageddon, had occupied Nazareth, Afule, and Beisan, and were collecting the disorganized masses of enemy troops and transport as they arrived from the south. All avenues of escape open to the enemy, except the fords across the Jordan between Beisan and Jisr-ed-Dameer were thus closed.

East of the Jordan Arab forces of the King of the Hedjaz had effected numerous demolitions on the railways radiating from Deraa, several important bridges, including one in the Yurmak Valley, having been destroyed. Very severe losses have been inflicted on the masses of Turkish troops retreating over the difficult roads by our air services.

A German airplane, later ascertained to have been carrying mails, landed in the midst of our troops at Afule. The pilot, who believed the place still to be in Turkish hands, destroyed the machine and its contents before he could be secured.

BY H. COLLINSON OWEN
British Eye-witness

Lemnos, November 10, 1918.

The final act to one of the greatest dramas of the war was enacted yesterday when, in accordance with the terms of the armistice with Turkey, British troops landed unopposed to occupy the Gallipoli Peninsula.

We left Mudros in a destroyer at 4 in the morning to see the landing, and arrived off Cape Helles about 9. The first outward sign that we were in such historic waters was the sight of a mast sticking up off the rocky coast of Imbros. This marked the spot where the big monitor *Raglan* and the smaller one, *M-28*, went down when standing up hopelessly against the *Goeben* and the *Breslau* at the time of their ill-starred sortie last year.

Later in the day, up toward the Narrows, we saw the

remains of submarine *E*-15, which ran ashore when trying to ascend the strait and was torpedoed from a launch by our own men under heavy fire, and a little further up, the rusty bottom of the Turkish battleship *Messudiyeh,* looking like an immense turtle, marked one of our submarine successes. We passed over deep waters that concealed the remains of sunken British and French battleships, the *Ocean, Irresistible, Majestic, Goliath, Triumph,* and *Bouvet.* We anchored just off V beach, where the *River Clyde* was run ashore.

The Turkish troops occupying the peninsula had been removed some days before, and for the time being not a single Turk was to be seen. V Beach along to Cape Helles and so to W Beach is as unlovely and barren a strip of coastline as can be imagined. Above us to our right were the remains of the old fort of Sedd el Bahr, which the fleet knocked to pieces in the first bombardment. We walked up steep ground, passed over old trenches, both our own and the enemy's, and saw new ones constructed in case of the further attack which for months past the Turks had been expecting. Everywhere, too, were elaborate telephone connections. Here, on the ground which we had won and given up again, the Turks were expecting to fight us once more. The two heavy guns which we captured and blew up were still lying there, not far from a modern heavy battery with deep ammunition dugouts cut in rocky soil and a plentiful supply of six-inch shells neatly arranged in galleries.

We embarked again near the *River Clyde* in a patrol launch, and proceeded up the strait. Intelligence officers on board, maps in hand, were marking down various points of information and verifying the positions of batteries. Altogether, on both sides of the strait, there are about fifty batteries containing guns ranging from 6-inch to 14-inch, a considerable portion of which are modern. We passed within five yards of an ugly Turkish mine floating on the surface. We went ashore at Chanak and walked to Hamidieh battery, a mile and a half away, which is the strongest on the strait. At Chanak were Turks in plenty, both soldiers and otherwise, and everybody appeared quite well fed. The population appeared pleased to see a group of British officers walking about, glad that the war for them was over.

Hamidieh fort was quite deserted. It has played a big part in the operations against the Dardanelles. It has three 14-inch guns, dating back to the eighties, and six 9.2-inch guns. Looking from one of the emplacements one could see right down to the mouth of the strait and beyond. A small party of Turkish soldiers will be temporarily left to put the guns clean and in order, and we shall hold the forts until such time as the Allies shall have decided what is exactly to happen to the Dardanelles in the future.

By the time we returned to Cape Helles a big transport and an old type cruiser, both loaded with British troops, were lying there. The unwieldy craft nosed slowly ashore and put her nose to the pier just alongside the bow of the *River Clyde*. Our men—troops who have seen much hard service in Macedonia—stepped ashore with their kits, and that was all the incident there was to the second landing in Gallipoli.

BY G. WARD PRICE
British Official Observer

Constantinople, November 10th.

At Chanak lay a gray transport steamer with British troops on board. She had arrived a little before us, and the khaki figures that lined her rail, staring curiously at the low-lying little town, with its old stone castle and its throng of equally interested inhabitants, were on their way to garrison the forts of the Narrows further up. With a Turkish pilot on board to guide us through the rest of the minefields, the destroyer made her way on into the Sea of Marmora, and increased her speed to thirty knots. So that at 3 o'clock this afternoon, under a cloudy sky, but one filled with the diffused lights of the East, we rounded the point of the old Seraglio and entered the Golden Horn.

There was no demonstration of any kind. It seemed as if no one had even noticed the arrival of this herald of the British fleet. But as we drew near to the quay one saw that the houses and windows were thronged with people. The crowd had an unusual tone of red about it, derived from all the crimson fezzes bobbing to and fro as their wearers strained for a glimpse. And a few waved handkerchiefs. A German officer stood on the quay close to where the destroyer gradually came alongside. He was more interested than any one, but affected indifference and yawned with care from time to time. A little group of German soldiers and sailors gradually formed behind him as if for mutual moral support. For years they had been the self-ordained military gods of this place, but now their altars are overthrown and they see Turkish naval officers of high rank hurrying past them to pay respects to the representative of a nation they once thought they could despise. We are, indeed, much surrounded by an unwelcome neighborhood of Germans. Germans look down on us from their office windows opposite the quay. Here in my bedroom at the Pera Palace Hotel there are Germans talking in the rooms on either side of me as I write. I gather from fragments overheard that they are packing up. One is pleased to think that their compatriots throughout Turkey are doing the same. As we drove up from the quay, too, there seemed a considerable number of Germans, and also Austrians, in the streets. The Austrians saluted the party of British officers. The Germans swaggered by with a stare, the noncommissioned officers and men smoking cigars, which give them to English eyes a peculiar appearance of pretentiousness.

BY SULTAN MOHAMMED VI.

Proclamation of December 6, 1918

My sorrow is profound at the mistreatment of my Armenian subjects by certain political committees acting under my government.

Such misdeeds and the mutual slaughter of sons of the same fatherland have broken my heart. I ordered an inquiry as soon as I came to the throne so that the fomenters might be severely punished, but various factors prevented my orders from being promptly carried out.

The matter is now being thoroughly investigated. Justice will soon be done and we will never have a repetition of these ugly events.

STORMING THE ARGONNE

AMERICA'S BIGGEST BATTLE

SEPTEMBER 26TH-OCTOBER 16TH

GENERAL PERSHING   GENERAL LUDENDORFF

To Americans the Argonne struggle will ever remain the chief battle of the War. Their chieftain, General Pershing, presents with careful restraint the fully established facts, that here lay the strongest German defenses, because here, as the Germans well knew, their lines of supply were most dangerously near their front, and hence defeat would be most disastrous. The French and British generals had readily conceded to the fresh and powerful American troops the duty and honor of attacking this most impregnable section of the German defense. They have said frankly that none but the Americans could have stormed the Argonne.

When that attack began on September 26th, the Ally Governments were still planning for another winter of endurance, and for a "Spring drive" in 1919 which should force the Germans out of France. When on October 16th the victorious Americans entered Grand-Pré, north of the Argonne, all men knew that Germany was beaten, that not 1919 but the few remaining weeks of 1918 were to behold her expulsion from France.

Both in the number of men engaged and in the number slain, this was by far the biggest battle in American history. In the deadly desperation of its fighting, it was second to none. A million soldiers made the attack; and the Germans, fighting behind their almost impenetrable defenses, had perhaps half as many. In mere size, therefore, this battle ranks among the great ones of the War; and in decisive importance it ranks among the half dozen of the greatest.

We should not, however, think of this tremendous smashing of the German front as being wholly an American affair. U. S. troops had indeed to bear the main brunt of the battle; but west of the Argonne the French army under General Gouraud undertook an advance simultaneous with theirs, and kept close pace with them. The French took more prisoners than the Americans, 20,000 as against 18,000. But then the fighting in the Argonne was not such as leaves many living men to be made prisoners. General Ludendorff himself here states that the German withdrawal from before Gouraud was only such as was made necessary by the American advance, which was cutting in behind his other armies and encircling them.

Britons regard their breaking of the Hindenburg Line in the north as an equal exploit with this breaking it in the south. But no one has

questioned, or ever seriously will question, the splendid character of
the American fighting which won the Argonne.

C. F. H.

BY GENERAL PERSHING

From his final report

THE definite decision for the Meuse-Argonne phase of
the great Allied convergent attack was agreed to in my
conference with Marshal Foch and General Pétain on September 2nd. It was planned to use all available forces of the
First Army, including such divisions and troops as we
might be able to withdraw from the St. Mihiel front. The
Army was to break through the enemy's successive fortified
zones to include the Kriemhilde-Stellung, or Hindenburg
Line, on the front Brieulles-Romagne sous Montfaucon-
Grandpré, and thereafter, by developing pressure toward
Mézières, was to insure the fall of the Hindenburg Line along
the Aisne River in front of the Fourth French Army, which
was to attack to the west of the Argonne Forest. A penetration of some 12 to 15 kilometers was required to reach the
Hindenburg Line on our front, and the enemy's defenses
were virtually continuous throughout that depth.

The Meuse-Argonne front had been practically stabilized
in September, 1914, and, except for minor fluctuations during the German attacks on Verdun in 1916 and the French
counter-offensive in August, 1917, remained unchanged until the American advance in 1918. The net result of the four
years' struggle on this ground was a German defensive system of unusual depth and strength and a wide zone of utter
devastation, itself a serious obstacle to offensive operations.

The strategical importance of this portion of the line was
second to none on the western front. All supplies and evac-
uations of the German armies in northern France were
dependent upon two great railway systems—one in the north,
passing through Liège, while the other in the south, with
lines coming from Luxemburg, Thionville, and Metz, had
as its vital section the line Carignan-Sedan-Mézières. No
other important lines were available to the enemy, as the
mountainous masses of the Ardennes made the construction
of east and west lines through that region impracticable.

The Carignan-Sedan-Mézières line was essential to the Germans for the rapid strategical movement of troops. *Should this southern system be cut by the Allies before the enemy could withdraw* his forces through the narrow neck between Mézières and the Dutch frontier, *the ruin of his armies in France and Belgium would be complete.*

From the Meuse-Argonne front the perpendicular distance to the Carignan-Mézières railroad was 50 kilometers. This region formed the pivot of German operations in northern France, and the vital necessity of covering the great railroad line into Sedan resulted in the convergence on the Meuse-Argonne front of the successive German defensive positions. The distance between "No man's land" and the third German withdrawal position in the vicinity of the Meuse River was approximately 18 kilometers; the distance between the corresponding points near the tip of the great salient of the western front was about 65 kilometers, and in the vicinity of Cambrai was over 30 kilometers. The effect of a penetration of 18 kilometers by the American Army would be equivalent to an advance of 65 kilometers farther west; furthermore, such an advance on our front was far more dangerous to the enemy than an advance elsewhere. The vital importance of this portion of his position was fully appreciated by the enemy, who had suffered tremendous losses in 1916 in attempting to improve it by the reduction of Verdun. As a consequence it had been elaborately fortified, and consisted of practically a continuous series of positions 20 kilometers or more in depth.

In addition to the artificial defenses, the enemy was greatly aided by the natural features of the terrain. East of the Meuse the dominating heights not only protected his left but gave him positions from which powerful artillery could deliver an oblique fire on the western bank. Batteries located in the elaborately fortified Argonne forest covered his right flank, and could cross their fire with that of the guns on the east bank of the Meuse. Midway between the Meuse and the forest the heights of Montfaucon offered perfect observation and formed a strong natural position which had been heavily fortified. The east and west ridges abutting on the Meuse and Aire River valleys afforded the enemy excellent machine-gun positions for the desperate defense which the importance of the position would require him to make. North of Montfaucon densely wooded and rugged heights constituted natural features favorable to defensive fighting.

When the First Army became engaged in the simultaneous preparation for two major operations, an interval of 14 days separated the initiation of the two attacks. During this short period the movement of the immense number of troops and the amount of supplies involved in the Meuse-Argonne battle, over the few roads available, and confined entirely to the hours of darkness, was one of the most delicate and difficult problems of the war. The concentration included 15 divisions, of which 7 were involved in the pending St. Mihiel drive, 3 were in sector in the Vosges, 3 in the neighborhood of Soissons, 1 in a training area, and 1 near Bar-le-Duc. Practically all the Artillery, Aviation, and other auxiliaries to be employed in the new operations were committed to the St. Mihiel attack and therefore could not be moved until its success was assured. The concentration of all units not to be used at St. Mihiel was commenced immediately, and on September 13th, the second day of St. Mihiel, reserve divisions and Army Artillery units were withdrawn and placed in motion toward the Argonne front.

That part of the American sector from Fresnes-en-Woevre, southeast of Verdun, to the western edge of the Argonne Forest, while nominally under my control, did not actively become a part of my command until September 22nd, on which date my headquarters were established at Souilly, southwest of Verdun. Of French troops, in addition to the Second French Colonial Corps, composed of 3 divisions, there was also the Seventeenth French Corps of 3 divisions holding the front north and east of Verdun.

At the moment of the opening of the Meuse-Argonne battle, the enemy had 10 divisions in line and 10 in reserve on the front between Fresnes-en-Woevre and the Argonne Forest, inclusive. He had undoubtedly expected a continuation of our advance toward Metz. Successful ruses were carried out between the Meuse River and Luneville to deceive him as to our intentions, and French troops were maintained as a screen along our front until the night before the battle, *so that the actual attack was a tactical surprise.*

The operations in the Meuse-Argonne battle really form a continuous whole, but they extended over such a long period of continuous fighting that they will here be considered in three phases, the first from September 26th to October 3rd, the second from October 4th to 31st, and the third from November 1st to 11th.

Meuse-Argonne, First Phase

On the night of September 25th, the 9 divisions to lead in the attack were deployed between the Meuse River and the western edge of the Argonne Forest. On the right was the Third Corps, Maj. Gen. Bullard commanding, with the Thirty-third, Eightieth, and Fourth Divisions in line; next came the Fifth Corps, Maj. Gen. Cameron commanding, with the Seventy-Ninth, Thirty-seventh, and Ninety-first Divisions; on the left was the First Corps, Maj. Gen. Liggett commanding, with the Thirty-fifth, Twenty-eighth, and Seventy-seventh Divisions. Each corps had 1 division in reserve and the Army held 3 divisions as a general reserve. About 2,700 guns, 189 small tanks, 142 manned by Americans, and 821 airplanes, 604 manned by Americans, were concentrated to support the attack of the infantry. We thus had a superiority in guns and aviation, and the enemy had no tanks.

The axis of the attack was the line Montfaucon-Romagne-Buzancy, the purpose being to make the deepest penetration in the center, which, with the Fourth French Army advancing west of the Argonne, would force the enemy to evacuate that forest without our having to deliver a heavy attack in that difficult region.

Following three hours of violent artillery fire of preparation, the Infantry advanced at 5.30 a. m. on September 26th, accompanied by tanks. *During the first two days of the attack, before the enemy was able to bring up his reserves, our troops made steady progress through the network of defenses.* Montfaucon was held tenaciously by the enemy and was not captured until noon of the second day.

By the evening of the 28th a maximum advance of 11 kilometers had been achieved and we had captured Baulny, Epinonville, Septsarges, and Dannevoux. The right had made a splendid advance into the woods south of Brieulles-sur-Meuse, but *the extreme left was meeting strong resistance in the Argonne.* The attack continued without interruption, meeting six new divisions which the enemy threw into first line before September 29th. He developed a powerful machine-gun defense supported by heavy artillery fire, and made frequent counter-attacks with fresh troops, particularly on the front of the Twenty-eighth and Thirty-fifth Divisions. These divisions had taken Varennes, Cheppy, Baulny, and Charpentry, and the line was within 2 kilometers of Apremont. We were no longer engaged in a maneuver for the pinching out of a salient, but were necessarily committed, generally speaking, to *a direct frontal attack against strong, hostile positions fully manned by a determined enemy.*

By nightfall of the 29th the First Army line was approximately Bois de la Cote Lemont-Nantillois-Apremont —southwest across the Argonne. Many divisions, especially those in the center that were subjected to cross-fire of artillery, had suffered heavily. The severe fighting, the nature of the terrain over which they attacked, and the fog and darkness sorely tried even our best divisions. On the night of the 29th the Thirty-seventh and Seventy-ninth Divisions were relieved by the Thirty-second and Third Divisions, respectively, and on the following night the First Division relieved the Thirty-fifth Division.

The critical problem during the first few days of the battle was the restoration of communications over "No man's land." There were but four roads available across this deep zone, and the violent artillery fire of the previous period of the war had virtually destroyed them. The spongy soil and the lack of material increased the difficulty. But the splendid work of our engineers and pioneers soon made possible the movement of the troops, artillery, and supplies

most needed. By the afternoon of the 27th all the divisional
artillery, except a few batteries of heavy guns, had effected
a passage and was supporting the infantry action.

Meuse-Argonne, Second Phase

At 5.30 a. m. on October 4th the general attack was renewed. The enemy divisions on the front from Fresnes-
en-Woevre to the Argonne had increased from 10 in first
line to 16, and included some of his best divisions. The
fighting was desperate, and only small advances were realized, except by the First Division on the right of the First
Corps. By evening of October 5th the line was approximately Bois de la Cote Lemont-Bois du Fays-Gesnes-Hill
240-Fleville-Chehery, southwest through the Argonne.

It was especially desirable to drive the enemy from his
commanding positions on the heights east of the Meuse, but
it was even more important that we should force him to
use his troops there and weaken his tenacious hold on positions in our immediate front. The further stabilization
of the new St. Mihiel line permitted the withdrawal of certain divisions for the extension of the Meuse-Argonne operation to the east bank of the Meuse River.

On the 7th the First Corps, with the Eighty-second Division added, launched a strong attack northwest toward Cor-
nay, to draw attention from the movement east of the
Meuse and at the same time outflank the German position
in the Argonne. The following day the Seventeenth French
Corps, General Claudel commanding, initiated its attack
east of the Meuse against the exact point on which the German armies must pivot in order to withdraw from northern
France. The troops encountered elaborate fortifications and
stubborn resistance, but by nightfall had realized an advance
of 6 kilometers to a line well within the Bois de Consenvoye,
and including the villages of Beaumont and Haumont. Continuous fighting was maintained along our entire battle front,
with especial success on the extreme left, where the capture
of the greater part of the Argonne Forest was completed.
The enemy contested every foot of ground on our front in
order to make more rapid retirements farther west and with-

draw his forces from northern France before the interruption of his railroad communications through Sedan.

We were confronted at this time by an insufficiency of replacements to build up exhausted divisions. Early in October combat units required some 90,000 replacements, and not more than 45,000 would be available before November 1st to fill the existing and prospective vacancies. We still had two divisions with the British and two with the French. A review of the situation, American and Allied, especially as to our own resources in men for the next two months, convinced me that the attack of the First Army and of the Allied Armies further west should be pushed to the limit. But if the First Army was to continue its aggressive tactics our divisions then with the French must be recalled, and replacements must be obtained by breaking up newly arrived divisions.

In discussing the withdrawal of our divisions from the French Marshal Foch and General Pétain, on October 10th, the former *expressed his appreciation of the fact that the First Army was striking the pivot of the German withdrawal,* and also held the view that the Allied attack should continue. Gen. Pétain agreed that the American divisions with the French were essential to us if we were to maintain our battle against the German pivot. The French were, however, straining every nerve to keep up their attacks and, before those divisions with the French had been released, it became necessary for us to send the Thirty-seventh and Ninety-first Divisions from the First Army to assist the Sixth French Army in Flanders.

At this time the First Army was holding a front of more than 120 kilometers; its strength exceeded 1,000,000 men; *it was engaged in the most desperate battle of our history,* and the burden of command was too heavy for a single commander and staff. Therefore, on October 12th, that portion of our front extending from Port-sur-Seille, east of the Moselle, to Fresnes-en-Woevre, southeast of Verdun, was transferred to the newly constituted Second Army with Lieut. Gen. Robert L. Bullard in command, under whom it began preparations for the extension of operations to the east in the direction of Briey and Metz. On October 16th the command of the First Army was transferred to Lieut. Gen. Hunter Liggett, and my advance headquarters was established at Ligny-en-Barrois, from which the command of the group of American Armies was exercised.

Local attacks of the First Army were continued in order particularly to adjust positions preparatory to a renewed general assault. The First and Fifth Divisions were relieved by the Forty-second and Eightieth Divisions, which were now fresh. An attack along the whole front was made on October 14th. The resistance encountered was stubborn, but the stronghold on Cote Dame Marie was captured and *the Hindenburg Line was broken.* Cunel and Romagne-sous-Montfaucon were taken and the line advanced 2 kilometers north of Sommerance. A maximum advance of 17 kilometers had been made since September 26th and the enemy had been forced to throw into the fight a total of 15 reserve divisions.

During the remainder of the month important local operations were carried out, which involved desperate fighting. The First Corps, Maj. Gen. Dickman commanding, advanced through Grandpré; the Fifth Corps, Maj. Gen. Charles P. Summerall commanding, captured the Bois de Bantheville; the Third Corps, Maj. Gen. John L. Hines commanding, completed the occupation of Cunel Heights; and the Seventeenth French Corps drove the enemy from the main ridge south of La Grande Montagne. Particularly heavy fighting occurred east of the Meuse on October 18th, and in the further penetration of the Kriemhilde-Stellung on October 23rd the Twenty-sixth Division entering the battle at this time relieved the Eighteenth French Division.

Summarizing the material results which had been attained by the First Army by the end of October, we had met an increasing number of Germany's best divisions, rising from 20 in line and reserve on September 26th, to 31 on October 31st; *the enemy's elaborately prepared positions, including the Hindenburg Line, in our front had been broken; the almost impassable Argonne Forest was in our hands;* an advance of 21 kilometers had been effected; 18,600 prisoners, 370 cannon, 1,000 machine guns, and a mass of material captured; and the great railway artery through Carignan to Sedan was now seriously threatened.

The demands of incessant battle which had been maintained day by day for more than a month had compelled our divisions to fight to the limit of their capacity. Combat troops were held in line and pushed to the attack until deemed incapable of further effort because of casualties or exhaustion; artillery once engaged was seldom withdrawn and many batteries fought until practically all the animals were casualties and the guns were towed out of line by motor trucks. *The American soldier had shown unrivaled fortitude in this continuous fighting during most inclement weather and under many disadvantages of position.* Through experience, the Army had developed into a powerful and smooth-running machine, and there was a supreme confidence in our ability to carry through the task successfully.

While the high pressure of these dogged attacks was a great strain on our troops, it was calamitous to the enemy. His divisions had been thrown into confusion by our furious assaults, and his morale had been reduced until his will to resist had well-nigh reached the breaking point. Once a German division was engaged in the fight, it became practically impossible to effect its relief. The enemy was forced to meet the constantly recurring crises by breaking up tactical organizations and sending hurried detachments to widely separated portions of the field.

Every member of the American Expeditionary Forces, from the front line to the base ports, was straining every nerve. Magnificent efforts were exerted by the entire Services of Supply to meet the enormous demands made on it. Obstacles which seemed insurmountable were overcome daily in expediting the movements of replacements, ammunition and supplies to the front, and of sick and wounded to the rear. *It was this spirit of determination animating every American soldier that made it impossible for the enemy to maintain the struggle until* 1919.

BY GENERAL VON DER MARWITZ
The Commander's Address to the German Fifth Army, opposing the
Americans in the Argonne

It is on the unconquerable resistance of the Verdun front
that depends the fate of a great part of the western front,
perhaps even of our nation. The Fatherland must rest assured that every commander and every man realizes the
greatness of his mission and that he will do his duty to the
very end. If they do this, the enemy's attack will, as here-
tofore, break against our firm will to hold.

BY GENERAL LUDENDORFF[1]

In the final operations, aiming at a definite decision of
the war, General Pershing acted an important part. In
the big offensive toward Sedan on both sides of the Argonne
forest, which French and Americans made together, the
American troops had their main forces between the Meuse
and the Argonne. If, in autumn, 1918, it was General
Foch's scheme to encircle the German main forces at the
Meuse, near the Belgian-French frontier, or in the inner
part of Belgium, it was General Pershing's task to lead, on
the right wing, the decisive attack against the rear communications of the German army in the north of France.

In the Champagne the Germans noticed in time the imminent big attack and organized their defense, between the
Meuse and the Argonne. After the battle at the St. Mihiel
front had come to an end, the headquarter of the Fifth
German Army thought that the American attacks would
be carried on to the north of Verdun, on the eastern bank
of the Meuse, not on the western. Full justice must be
done to the skillful and far-sighted way—very much like
the way the Germans acted before the beginning of their
offensive in spring—in which the Americans hid the extensive preparations for their intended attack between the
Meuse and the Argonne, though they were obliged to put
off the time of the beginning by several days. They were

[1] From Ludendorff's "The American Effort." Copyright by the
Atlantic Monthly Co., May, 1922.

helped very much by the conformation of the ground, the network of railways and roads, and the weather, which allowed them to replace and reënforce the defensive divisions by offensive troops, which were carried up by motor vans in the very night before the beginning of the attack, unnoticed by the enemy. Thus, during the night between the 25th and 26th of September, the French defensive divisions were replaced by seven fresh American divisions. Thus a wholly American sector was built—one of nine divivions, which were divided up in three groups, and formed the First American Army under General Pershing's command. During these weeks the trench-war had been fought intensively, and the moral qualities of the troops were raised by orders pointed to what the Americans had done thus far, and tickling their ambition and pride.

More than the French, the Americans thought the success to be dependent on surprise. Their success, which was so much bigger than that of the French, justified their view. The preceding artillery fire during the night did not last more than three hours. At 5 A. M. the infantry sallied forth from the trenches, which had been dug out for the assault. The main forces advanced in the middle, in the direction of Malancourt-Montfaucon-Nautillois-Cunel. Favored by dense mist, and helped by numbers of tanks and an extraordinarily strong artillery, they succeeded in pressing back the German front by five miles, and in taking possession of the first area of entrenchments. But the line which in American maps was drawn as aim of the first day had not been reached. Already in the night, new attacks of wide extent began, and went on up to the evening of the 29th of September; but they did not get on considerably further than they had come the day before.

In the Argonne the German lines were withdrawn spontaneously. On September 30th the actions were stopped for several days, probably on account of the big losses and the strain of the troops, perhaps on account of difficulties of supply. On October 4th the Americans resumed their attacks, with fresh forces, after an hour and a half of most vehement fire of artillery. As the action was no longer a surprise, the enemy's advance at first, in the middle of the last day's battlefield, was small. But this time the weight of the attack lay more to the west at the Aire, the attack being extended up to the Argonne.

By October 10th the Americans had taken the whole part of the Argonne forest south of the lower part of the Aire, and advanced in the plain up to the line St. Fuvin-Brieulles, fighting hard and suffering great losses. In the meantime, beginning at October 8th, the attack spread to the eastern bank of the Meuse. But here the Americans, coöperating considerably with French divisions, did not gain much ground to the north. After October 12th the action did not seem to be directed methodically any longer. Shortly after, the heavy battles, which had been carried on with rare pertinacity, slackened for a time.

The Americans' success did not so much consist in the gain of ground as the line which was aimed at had not been attained, but in the effect which it exercised on the situation in the Champagne, where the French, during a fortnight, did not get on nearly as well in their hard battles against the German Third Army. Only in consequence of the American advance in the Argonne and to the east of it the Third German Army was obliged to withdraw behind the Aisne and the Aire during the nights between the 9th and 12th of October.

After a pause of more than two weeks the Americans, who, in the meantime, had augmented to a group comprising two armies, resumed their offensive from the line Grandpré-Aincreville, in concert with the operations of the Allies. The weight of the attack lay as before on the left bank of the Meuse and, pressing to the north, it was intended to seize the Meuse passages above Sedan. Here, too, the Americans most successfully influenced the general situation; by pressing back the opposite German lines in frontal attacks, they forced the German Headquarter to withdraw the German lines from the Aisne, where at the same time they had been assaulted by the French, mostly unsuccessfully. The German report of November 3rd displayed this fact.

THE AWAKENING OF THE GERMAN PEOPLE

THE SAILORS' MUTINY AT KIEL

OCTOBER 2ND-NOVEMBER 5TH

MAJOR VON DER BUSSCHE   MARSHAL HINDENBURG
EMPEROR WILLIAM II.   DR. KARL LIEBKNECHT
F. SEFTON DELMER

By the autumn of 1918 the German leaders saw probably quite clearly that they had lost the War; but they expected to have all winter in which to negotiate a peace, with plenty of time to parley and threaten and to confuse their people, and so make the future secure and comfortable for themselves. Then, quite suddenly, came Foch's great hammer-blows at the end of September, the breaking of the Hindenburg Line both in the Argonne and in Flanders. Generals Hindenburg and Ludendorff found themselves unexpectedly facing a desperate situation; and in swift haste they sent word to Berlin that peace must be made at once. Their official representative was Major Bussche, and his noted address of explanation, delivered to the Reichstag on October 2nd, is here given in full.

Even Major Bussche, however, was not quite sufficiently frank. He astounded the Reichstag by his demand for peace, but he coupled this with such boasts of continued military power that the German Government did not take his demand seriously. They thought there was still time to play their leisurely game of negotiation. Therefore Hindenburg himself, in the noted telegram from the front here given, reëmphasized the words of his messenger. Peace must be sought *at once.*

Yet the position of all the leaders remained characteristically German. They were beaten and so they would make an equal peace. That was their theory; and hence their first grandiloquent offers roused no peace response from the Allies. Dishonest even in defeat, the German leaders laid the blame of their breakdown upon Bulgaria, or upon Turkey, and refused for one moment to admit the truth, that it was they themselves, the Germans, who were being beaten to their knees in France, and that all other issues were subordinate to this. Hence they had still to fight on, although Ludendorff, the shrewdest among them, resigned his place and withdrew from the command during October.

Meanwhile, their confession of defeat had shaken Germany to its depths. Through all the years of War, the German people had been told that they were winning. Now the clouds of falsehood by which they had been surrounded began to clear—though, alas, only to a very small degree. A tumultuous murmur arose everywhere.

358

Emperor William rushed to what seemed to him extremest measures, so as to save himself. He got himself a new Chancellor, one
who was reputed to be a liberal and a pacifist, Prince Max of Baden;
and through Prince Max he proclaimed a new constitutional government. He even liberated prisoners who had been arrested for opposing
his arbitrary rule, among them being that Dr. Karl Liebknecht whose
appeal to the people is here given.

Liebknecht summoned the people to a Socialistic revolt and the
formation of a republic. Similar calls came from every side. The
old doglike submission to authority broke under the strain. There
were strikes everywhere, and soldiers' and sailors' mutinies. The most
notable of these was at Kiel. Here the "Grand Fleet" was ordered
out to sea; whereon the sailors blocked its departure by refusing to
sail forth to a useless death. The cry of the hour became, "Down
with the Hohenzollerns." Tyranny, strong in the hour of strength,
proved weak indeed in the hour of weakness.

Ludendorff, writing of those days of October in his memoirs, has
tried to say that the German cause was lost because of the weakness
of the German people, their refusal to fight further. The statement
is a contemptible evasion, a false branding of a people who had fought
with amazing strength and endurance. If they refused now to fight
further, it was because Ludendorff himself had shown them the uselessness of fighting. The German slogan of the time became, "Better a
miserable peace, than hopeless misery without peace."

C. F. H.

BY MAJOR FREIHERR VON DER BUSSCHE

Official Statement made by command of the army chiefs, Hindenburg
and Ludendorff, and delivered to the Reichstag on October 2nd

IN a few days the situation has fundamentally changed.
The collapse of the Bulgarian front has entirely upset
our disposition of troops. Our communications with Constantinople were threatened, as well as the shipping route indispensable for the transport of our supplies on the Danube.
We were compelled, if we were not to leave the Entente a
free hand in the Balkans, to send German and Austro-Hungarian divisions ear-marked for the Western front to those
regions, abandoning the Black Sea and Rumania. We were
obliged to make an immediate decision. The entrainment of
our troops had already begun. We have every justification
for hoping that the situation in the Balkans may be reëstablished, at all events sufficiently to guard our own interests.
Unfortunately, as I shall explain, this cannot be done without great detriment to the situation as a whole.

Almost simultaneously with the offensive in Macedonia,

violent enemy attacks have been made in the West. They have not found us unprepared. All possible measures have been taken to hold them up. Divisions from the East were on the way to relieve the sorely tried divisions in the West. Unfortunately a portion of these troops had to be diverted to the Balkans. The last men capable of bearing arms had been withdrawn from the East. We calmly awaited the decisive battle. The Entente knew how to conceal from us where the attacks would take place. From the sea to Switzerland preparations for the attack were in progress. The most extensive was against Lorraine and the Sundgau, and we were forced to distribute our reserves and to keep the whole front in a state of readiness for the attack. Considerable forces had to be stationed, especially in Lorraine and in the Sundgau, for the defense of German territory.

After carrying out the necessary movements, we were absolutely convinced that we should emerge victorious from the coming battles, and that we should be able to break the opposition of our enemies by the enormous losses which we anticipated they would suffer. Consequently, by putting in reserves at the right time, we have been able to hold up the enemy at all those places where, by means of tanks, by surprise attacks or superiority in numbers, he has penetrated our lines. The fighting of the last six days may be termed successful for us, in spite of the loss of prisoners and material.

In comparison with our successes in the spring offensive the enemy has made little progress. In the majority of cases his continuous onslaughts have been countered with unusual obstinacy on the part of our troops. According to our own reports the enemy has suffered the heaviest losses.

The majority of our troops have fought splendidly and made superhuman efforts. Their old brave spirit has not died out. The numerical superiority of the enemy has not been able to terrorize our men. Officers and men vie with each other in deeds of valor.

In spite of these facts, the High Command has been compelled to come to the enormously difficult decision that in all human probability there is no longer any prospect of forcing the enemy to sue for peace. Two factors have had a decisive influence on our decision, namely, tanks and our reserves.

The enemy has made use of tanks in unexpectedly large numbers. In cases where they have suddenly emerged in huge masses from smoke clouds, our men were completely unnerved. Tanks broke through our foremost lines, making a way for their infantry, reaching our rear, and causing local panics, which entirely upset our battle control. When we were able to locate them our anti-tank guns and our artillery speedily put an end to them. But the mischief had already been done, and solely owing to the success of the tanks we have suffered enormous losses in prisoners, and this had unexpectedly reduced our strength and caused a more speedy wastage of our reserves than we had anticipated. We were not in a position to make use of similar masses of German tanks. Our manufacturers, under the existing pressure, were absolutely unable to supply them in large numbers, without causing other more important things to be neglected.

The question of reserves has, however, been the decisive factor. The army entered the fray with depleted numbers. In spite of using every possible device, the strength of our battalions sank from about 800 in April, to 540 by the end of September. And these numbers were only secured by the disbanding of 22 infantry divisions (66 infantry regiments). The Bulgarian defeat has eaten up 7 more divisions. There is no prospect whatever of raising the strength. The current reserves, consisting of men who are convalescent, combed-out men, etc., will not even cover the losses of a quiet winter campaign. The inclusion of the 1900 class will only increase the strength of the battalions by 100, and that is the last of our reserves.

The losses of the battle which is now in progress are, as I have stated, unexpectedly large, especially as regards officers. That is a decisive factor. If the troops are to stem the onslaught or to attack they require more than ever the example of their officers. The latter must, and have, sacrificed themselves unreservedly. The regimental commanders and leaders fought in the front lines together with their men. I will give one example only. In two days of fighting one division lost all its officers, dead or wounded, three regimental commanders were killed. The small number of reserve officers has sunk to nothing. The same applies to the N.C.O.'s.

The enemy, owing to the help he has received from America, is in a position to make good his losses. The American troops, as such, are not of special value, or in any way superior to our men. In those cases in which, owing to numbers alone, they gained an initial success, they were finally held at bay by our troops. They were, however, able to take over large portions of the front, thereby permitting the English and French to liberate some of their experienced divisions and in this way form an almost inexhaustible supply of reserves.

Up till now our reserves have been adequate to fill the gaps and drafts have duly arrived. The hardest attacks were repulsed. The fighting was described to be of unparalleled severity. Then our reserves began to fail. If the enemy continues the attack, the situation may demand a withdrawal from extensive sectors of the front. We can continue this kind of warfare for a measurable space of time, we can cause the enemy heavy losses, devastating the country in our retreat, but we cannot win the war.

This decision and these events caused the idea to ripen in the minds of the Field Marshal and Ludendorff to propose to the Kaiser the breaking-off of hostilities, so as to spare the German people and their Allies further sacrifice. Just as our great offensive of July 15th was abandoned, when the sacrifice entailed no longer warranted its continuation, so the decision now had to be taken that *it was hopeless to proceed with the war*. There is still time. The German army is still strong enough to hold the enemy for months, to achieve local successes and to expose the enemy to fresh sacrifices. But every day brings the enemy nearer his goal, and will make him less inclined to conclude a peace with us which will be satisfactory on our side.

Therefore no time must be lost. Every day the situation may become worse, and give the enemy the opportunity of recognizing our momentary weakness, which might have the most evil consequences for peace prospects as well as for the military situation. Neither the army nor the Homeland should do anything which would make our weakness apparent; on the other hand, the army and the Homeland must stand together more closely than before.

Simultaneously with the peace offer a united front must be shown at home, so that the enemy recognize our unbending will to continue the war, if the enemy will not make peace with us, or only a humiliating one. If this should be, then the endurance of the army will depend on a firm attitude at home, and on the power of the Homeland to inspire the army.

BY MARSHAL VON HINDENBURG

Statement issued in confirmation of the preceding address

BERLIN, October 3rd.

TO THE IMPERIAL CHANCELLOR:

The High Command insists on the immediate issue of a peace offer to our enemies in accordance with the decision of Monday, September 29, 1918.

In consequence of the collapse of the Macedonian front, and the inevitable resultant weakening of our reserves in the West, and also the impossibility of making good the heavy losses which have occurred during the battles of the last few days, there is no prospect, humanly speaking, of forcing our enemies to sue for peace. The enemy, on the other hand, is continuing to throw fresh reserves into the battle.

The German army still stands firm and is defending itself against all attacks. *The situation, however, is growing more critical daily, and may force the High Command to momentous decisions.*

In these circumstances it is imperative to stop the fighting in order to spare the German people and their allies unnecessary sacrifices. Every day of delay costs thousands of brave soldiers their lives.

VON HINDENBURG.

BY EMPEROR WILLIAM II.
Proclamation issued to the Army on October 6th

For months past the enemy, with enormous exertions and almost without pause in the fighting, has stormed against your lines. In weeks of the struggle, often without repose, you have had to persevere and resist a numerically far superior enemy. Therein lies the greatness of the task which has been set for you and which you are fulfilling. Troops of all the German States are doing their part and are heroically defending the Fatherland on foreign soil. Hard is the task.

My navy is holding its own against the united enemy naval forces and is unwaveringly supporting the army in its difficult struggle.

The eyes of those at home rest with pride and admiration on the deeds of the army and navy. I express to you the thanks of myself and the Fatherland.

The collapse of the Macedonian front has occurred in the midst of the hardest struggle. In accord with our allies, I have resolved once more to offer peace to the enemy, but I will only extend my hand for an honorable peace. We owe that to the heroes who have laid down their lives for the Fatherland, and we make that our duty to our children.

Whether arms will be lowered still is a question. Until then we must not slacken. We must, as hitherto, exert all our strength tirelessly to hold our ground against the onslaught of our enemies.

The hour is grave, but, trusting in your strength and in God's gracious help, we feel ourselves to be strong enough to defend our beloved Fatherland.

WILHELM.

Supplementary Statement of October 10th

The hour is grave! We are fighting for the future of the Fatherland and for the protection of the soil of the Homeland. To that end we need the united action of the intellectual, moral, and economic powers of Germany. On the cooperation of those powers our invincibility rests. The will for defense must bind all separate views and separate wishes into one great unity of conception. God grant us something of the spirit of the war of liberation.

WILHELM.

Proclamation of October 28th, addressed to the new Imperial Chancellor, Prince Max, and announcing a Representative form of government

YOUR GRAND DUCAL HIGHNESS:

I return herewith for immediate publication the bill to amend the Imperial Constitution and the law of March 17, 1870, relative to the representation of the Imperial Chancellor, which has been laid before me for signature.

On the occasion of this step, which is so momentous for the future history of the German people, I have a desire to give expression to my feelings. Prepared for by a series of Government acts, a new order comes into force which transfers the fundamental rights of the Kaiser's person to the people.

Thus comes to a close a period which will stand in honor before the eyes of future generations. Despite all struggles between invested authority and aspiring forces, it has rendered possible to our people that tremendous development which imperishably revealed itself in the wonderful achievements of this war.

In the terrible storms of the four years of war, however, old forms have been broken up, not to leave their ruins behind but to make a place for new, vital forms.

After the achievements of these times, the German people can claim that no right which may guarantee a free and happy future shall be withheld from them.

The proposals of the Allied Governments which are now adopted and extended owe their origin to this conviction. I, however, with my exalted allies, indorse these decisions of Parliament in firm determination, so far as I am concerned, to coöperate in their full development, convinced that I am thereby promoting the weal of the German people.

The Kaiser's office is one of service to the people. May,

then, the new order release all the good powers which our people need in order to support the trials which are hanging over the empire and with a firm step win a bright future from the gloom of the present.

WILHELM, I. R.

(Countersigned.)
Max, Prince of Baden.

BY DR. KARL LIEBKNECHT
Published address of November 1st

DEAR COMRADES: For more than four years our rulers have been engaged in a robber war for the oppression of our neighbors. During the last ten or twelve years these same rulers have preached the bad doctrine of "Slavic danger." They sowed in our hearts fear of the Slavs. But this was merely camouflage for further imperialistic aggression. As if the way to St. Petersburg lay through Belgium and northern France, they gave orders to let the armies loose.

During these four years the peoples of the world have bled until they can bleed no more. And what have we won? Have we won one hundredth part of what we and our rulers started out to get? Instead of this, we have lost until we have nothing more to lose. One thing we have won—the hatred of mankind.

And now we have, through the President of America, asked our enemies for peace. Comrades, now comes for you a fitting opportunity. Unite. Hold together under the banner of the "International." You should not hold yourselves as discouraged. It was never your war. You were driven by your rulers into the world slaughter. You have got what you deserved. It now lies with you to dismiss your rulers.

Act at once. It is your only prospect. Stretch the tyrant at your feet with a mighty blow. He now wavers. A well-aimed blow will at this time win your freedom, and will to some extent recompense you for all the blood that has been shed during the last four sad years.

Lay down your weapons, you soldiers at the front. Lay

down your tools, you workers at home. Do not let yourselves be deceived any longer by your rulers, the lip patriots, and the munitions profiteers. Rise with power and seize the reins of government. Yours is the force. To you belongs the right to rule. Answer the call for freedom and win your own war for liberty.

For more than four years have your oppressors used' you as the tools with which to fill their pockets. More than four years have they offered your sons, fathers, brothers, as victims and have starved millions, so that they might coin profits out of your blood.

Had you won the war you would have remained helpless slaves; you are beaten. Victory is within your grasp. It lies with you to seize it.

Comrades! Soldiers! Sailors! And you workers! Arise by regiments and arise by factories. Disarm your officers, whose sympathies and ideas are those of the ruling classes. Conquer your foremen, who are on the side of the present order. Announce the fall of your masters and demonstrate your solidarity. Do not heed the advice of the Kaiser Social Democrats. Do not let yourselves be led any longer by unworthy politicians, who play you false and deliver you into the hands of the enemy.

Stand fast like many of the genuine Social Democrats in your companies and regiments. Seize the quarters of your officers; disarm them immediately. Make sure that your officers sympathize with you. In case they do so, let them lead you. Shoot them immediately in case they betray you after they have declared themselves supporters of your cause.

Soldiers and marines! Fraternize! Take possession of your ships. Overpower first your officers. Place yourselves in communication with your comrades on land and seize all harbors and open fire, if necessary, on loyal groups.

Workers in munition factories: You are the masters of the situation. Stop work immediately. From this moment on you are only making bullets which will be used against you and yours. The bullets which you now make will never reach the front.

Stop making bayonets which will be thrust into your

entrails by the knights of the Government. Arise, organize, seize weapons and use them against those who plan to make slaves of you after they have made their own peace. End the war yourselves and use your weapons against the rulers.

BY F. SEFTON DELMER

A British observer in Germany

The Kiel mutiny, as Kurt Eisner and others told me, exploded at a date before that fixed upon by the revolutionary headquarters in Berlin. The Kiel sailors' premature action was destined to have far-reaching political consequences. In a lecture delivered in Berlin in March, 1919, Captain Baron von Forstner spoke openly of the doings of the Fleet during the last days of October, 1918. According to von Forstner the mutiny was brought to a head by the belief that there was to be more fighting and by the story that the German Admiralty had ordered the High Sea Fleet to put to sea with the object of "lightening the task of the German Army in the evacuation of the Belgian coast and its hinterland." It was rumored among the sailors that officers in their letters home had divulged some such orders. The men were in no mood for a forlorn hope and flatly declared that they would not fight.

The mutiny spread like wildfire from ship to ship. Although the sailors were kept on board the vessels at anchor and no intercourse permitted with the shore, they managed to exchange Morse messages by means of lights shown from the signal deck and from the portholes, and thus to arrange a concerted plan of action. In some mysterious manner, too, "defeatist" pamphlets were distributed on board the ships, the officers being powerless to prevent their circulation.

When on the 30th of October orders were finally given to weigh anchor, it was found, said Captain von Forstner, that on each ship the mutineers had put the capstan apparatus out of gear, and the fleet could not budge. Nor could the crews be pacified except by the countermanding of the order to sail. When the Admiral attempted to go on board the *Thüringen* to expostulate with the men, the *Helgoland*, which was lying near the *Thüringen*, trained her guns on his torpedo boat. Nothing daunted, he threatened at the first shot to torpedo the ship, and the muzzles of the guns were turned away again. The men finally allowed themselves to be arrested and sent on shore. They went, well knowing from their arrangement with the marines in Kiel that they would, ere long, be liberated.

In vain did the Admiralty send the third squadron, the *Bayern, Kronprinz Wilhelm, Grösser Kurfürst, König* and *Markgraf* to Kiel. Their crews, too, soon showed themselves to be disaffected. By the 5th of November almost all the ships, both at Kiel and at Wilhelmshaven, were flying the red flag of the coming Socialist Republic. On the 9th of November, as a last appeal to the men's patriotism, orders were once more given to put to sea, on the ground that British ships were off the German coast. In response only two small cruisers, the *Königsberg* and the *Köln*, and half a torpedo boat flotilla under Captain Harder obeyed; needless to say they returned without having got into touch with the enemy. "From this moment the German Navy ceased to be." It only remained to await the amazing day when the German ships, like so many hounds in leash, nosed their way across the North Sea to Scapa Flow.

The military had kept these events in Kiel such a close secret that when, as a last resort, the Majority Socialist deputy, Herr Noske, and the Democrat Under-Secretary of State, Herr Haussmann, were suddenly, on the 4th of November, summoned by Prince Max's Government to proceed from Berlin to Kiel to try to deal with the mutineers, neither of these two statesmen had the faintest notion of the very grave condition of affairs prevailing at the naval bases on the North Sea. Even to-day few Germans have anything but the haziest knowledge of what took place on board the fleet in 1918. Noske found that the troops that had been sent against the Kiel naval garrison had, on their arrival, either been coolly disarmed or had voluntarily gone over to the mutineers. To his amazement he beheld the "red flag" flying from the battleships of the High Sea

Fleet, and on the night of November 4th heard its guns bombarding parts of the town that were thought to be loyal to the Kaiser.

Of the 80,000 sailors and marines that according to Noske's computation were then in Kiel, the majority were already in open rebellion while the remainder were at best passive. Not an officer dared show his nose in street or barrack. To try to quell the mutiny in such circumstances by force of arms would have been sheer folly. A whole army corps, at the very least, would have been needed for the task. Noske therefore determined to have recourse to soft words. He spoke to the sailors as a friend and fellow Socialist. He found them the more tractable as they had no special leaders, the Berlin Independents having been taken unawares. At a mass meeting held on the Wilhelm Platz at Kiel, in the streaming rain, on the 5th of November, it was agreed by the sailors that Noske should take over the command of the town. In the meantime Prince Henry of Prussia had fled from the Castle, and as a rumor had got abroad that he had shot down a sailor in his flight, the new governor had some trouble in preventing the rebels from going in pursuit of him. The whole countryside was in a ferment, and Noske found that he had to swim with the stream. It shows the administrative skill of the man that, as he afterwards boasted, not a shot was fired during the remainder of November and December, the two months he was in command at Kiel.

By his clever temporising, Noske entirely forestalled and outwitted the Independents who had been at such pains to prepare the movement. Socialist as he was, he would, had he been in a position to do so, gladly have used machine guns as his argument in restoring order; but, finding himself powerless, with considerable finesse he feigned sympathy with their ideals and thus succeeded in keeping a dangerous movement within bounds. His tactics at Kiel doubtless gave a hint to his colleagues in Berlin; for Ebert and Scheidemann, on the 9th of November and the following days, employed similar plans with a success that can be gauged by the chagrin of the Independents when they found themselves ousted from the leadership of the revolution. In this way the whole movement was skillfully sidetracked from the dangerous lines of Sovietism on to the safer lines of democracy.

Before Noske had got to Kiel, however, whole battalions of ardent proselytisers from among the Kiel sailors had shot like rockets east and south over Germany to flash their doctrines into Hamburg, Lübeck, Cologne, Gotha, Weimar, Gera, Municn and Berlin. At these towns they at once got into secret touch with the soldiery, preaching to them the gospel of the ideal Soviet world that was coming and appealing to them not to fire a shot when the moment came for the proletariat to storm the government citadels. These missionaries of revolution were all in mufti and moved about unsuspected among the civil population. Great was the amazement of the good citizens of Munich when on the first day of the revolution, November 7th, they found the streets suddenly full of bluejackets, armed with rifles, hand grenades and side arms. The sailors whom I saw in Munich were smart, good looking, well dressed young men, who had obviously been selected on account of their fitness for propaganda purposes. Most of them were, moreover, excellent platform speakers. The funds that supported the Independents' movement came to a large extent from M. Joffe, the Bolshevist Minister accredited by Lenine to the Court of Berlin. Joffe, on his enforced departure, on the 5th of November, 1918, entrusted further large sums of money to Dr. Oskar Cohn, and, as Dr. Cohn confessed in January, 1919, these funds were used by him for revolutionary purposes. The German Government had imagined that Germans were immune from *défaitisme*. The famous sealed train in which Germany sent Lenine and his comrades across the Vistula into Russia will stand in history as a modern parallel to the story of the Trojan Horse. With grim humor, after Brest-Litovsk, Russia answered with a similar device, sending the said Joffe to Berlin with millions of roubles in his purse with which in its turn to debauch the proletariat of the State that had debauched Russia. Germany's General Staff, blind till it was too late, permitted the trick. General Hoffmann, with that bitter boxer-like smile of his, complained to me in Berlin, in March, 1919, the rattle of Spartacist machine guns outside lending irony to his remarks, that he had in vain implored Ludendorff not to allow Joffe to come into Germany, but to have him perform his diplomatic functions, for caution's sake, from some town on the Russian side of the frontier.

The extreme left wing of the Independents, known as Spartacists, turned for their inspiration to Russian sources. The term Spartacist, first used in 1916, was specially applied to the disciples of Spartacus, the anonymous author of the typewritten and secretly distributed political letters, the first of which was issued on the Emperor's birthday in 1916. By the August of that year it was known that Spartacus was none other than Karl Liebknecht. The letters were afterwards surreptitiously published in pamphlet form, and used for propaganda purposes. They contained very sharp attacks on the Majority Socialists, whom they accused of being the willing tools of the Imperial Government. Similar letters called *The Deeds of Judas,* evidently from the same pen, were smuggled through in great numbers to the soldiers at the front, their leading doctrine being Internationalism. Their watchword was "The working classes have no country to defend."

AUSTRIA'S BREAKDOWN

ITALY SMASHES THE AUSTRIAN FRONT AT VITTORIO

OCTOBER 24TH-NOVEMBER 3RD

GENERAD ARMANDO DIAZ   G. M. TREVELYAN
CAPTAIN ALESSANDRO SAPELLI   EMPEROR CHARLES

The autumn of 1918 brought home to Austria and Hungary the tragic consequences of their savage and selfish policy of 1914. The arbitrary union of the two nations for dominion over others meant nothing to either under the pressure of disaster. The Hapsburg family had long despaired of any favorable issue of the War; so had their subjects. Every one in the Dual Kingdom was thinking only of saving himself as best he might. Austrians and Hungarians had been in constant dispute during 1918, each nationality accusing the other of trying to thrust upon it the main burdens of the War.

Then came the downfall of Bulgaria and Turkey. To Germany these tragedies had been distant and only important as an excuse for justifying her own surrender. To Austro-Hungary, however, the Eastern breakdown meant that the Allied army of D'Esperey was actually on her heels, was threatening to invade her from the east, headed by those terrible Serbians who had refused to perish in their mountains, and who had such grim cause to seek revenge. Austria had still a strong army opposing Italy on the west front. But of what use to defend the front door, with the whole back way lying open to the Serbians!

When Marshal Foch summoned the Italians to take their part in the great general offensive of the Allies, the Austrian army was beaten before it fought. The Italians under General Diaz struck eagerly all along the front on October 24th. The Austrians held firmly for two days, then they broke and scattered as completely as either the Turkish or Bulgarian forces had done. The battle was chiefly an Italian pursuit.

Instantly the Austrian Government seized the opportunity of the defeat to ask for peace on any terms. Only German compulsion had kept Austria so long in the War. Now the commissioners whom she hurried to meet General Diaz were as ready for complete surrender as were the Bulgarians and Turks. The armistice went into effect on November 3rd, just as the Italians marched triumphantly into Trieste, which had been the goal of all their fighting during the War.

Practically indeed there was no longer an Austro-Hungary. It had disintegrated into its natural elements. Hungary went through a revolution in the last days of October and declared itself an independent kingdom determined upon peace. The Slav provinces of the south welcomed the invading Serbians as liberators. The Czechs of the north had already proclaimed their independence. Emperor Charles announced his own abdication on November 12th, but it is a little difficult to see just what there was left for him to abdicate— except it were the immediate possession of a palace in Vienna, already menaced by an angry and despairing mob.

BY GENERAL ARMANDO DIAZ

The High Command, November 4th, 12 noon.

THE War against Austria-Hungary which, under the high guidance of His Majesty the King, supreme Chief, the Italian Army, inferior in number and means, commenced on May 24, 1915, and with unshaken faith and tenacious valor conducted uninterruptedly and most strenuously for 41 months, is won.

The gigantic battle engaged on the 24th of October ultimo, and in which there took part 51 Italian divisions, three British, two French, one Czecho-Slovak, and one American regiment, against 73 Austro-Hungarian divisions, is finished.

A fulminating and highly daring advance by the Twenty-ninth Army Corps on Trent, by blocking the way of retreat of the enemy's armies in the Trentino, overthrown on the West by troops of the Seventh Army and on the East by those of the First, Sixth and Fourth Armies, yesterday determined the complete collapse of the adversary's front.

From the Brenta to the Torre the irresistible dash of the Twelfth and Tenth Armies and of the Cavalry divisions, is driving back further and further the fleeing foe.

In the plain H. R. H. the Duke of Aosta is advancing rapidly at the head of his invincible Third Army eager to return to the positions they already victoriously conquered and had never lost.

The Austro-Hungarian Army is annihilated; it has suffered very heavy losses in the stubborn resistance on the first few days and during the pursuit; it has lost very considerable quantities of material of all sorts and almost entire its magazines and depots.

The remains of what was one of the most powerful armies in the world are going back, in disorder and hopeless, up the valleys they had descended with proud surety.

DIAZ.

BY G. M. TREVELYAN

During the autumn the old Austria-Hungary passed quietly away, and by a process more like that of nature's growth than of man's violence, was dissolved into the vigorous and turbulent races of which it had been composed.

But though the Austro-Hungarian State was dead, the Austro-Hungarian army was still alive. And it was the army alone that had ever given real unity to the Empire. Men remembered that in 1848, when there had been a similar crisis, the army under Radetzky, having triumphed in Italy, restored the fallen State for another seventy years. It might, indeed, be hoped that on this occasion the tide of time had set in more strongly against the Dynasts; and it was certain that the British had broken the Hindenburg Line, the enemy's backbone. But there still stood firm in its positions the Austro-Hungarian army, the epitome of the coercive union of the races who were politically flying asunder. Until the army was destroyed the old system was still in being.

The battle that was fought and won in the last week of October was to prove how an army will go on fighting just because it is an army; how it will fight well until it suffers a decided reverse, and will then, and only then, go completely to bits for political and moral reasons. If the Austrians had held the Piave line on October 27-29, 1918, their army would not have disintegrated; and conversely, if the Italians had defeated Radetzky at Custozza, the army might then have broken up for political reasons, and the Emperor Franz-Josef might have reigned a few months instead of seventy years. In time of revolution the winning or losing of battles counts not less but more than in times of stable government.

In the early days of October Diaz and Badoglio had already made their plan for the destruction of the Austrian forces. The main break-through was to be effected by the crossing of the Middle Piave on both sides of the Montello by the Twelfth, Eighth, and Tenth Italian Armies, the last-named being commanded by Lord Cavan, who brought down the greater part of his three British divisions from the Asiago plateau.

But before the break-through on the Piave was attempted, the Fourth Italian Army began, at dawn on October 24th, a furious assault on the enemy's mountain positions on the Grappa massif between the Piave and the Brenta. This operation, though not itself immediately successful, served as a containing action to help the subsequent attacks across the river. Similarly, in the Macedonian offensive, the British and Greeks had held the Bulgarians by their fiercely-contested onslaught at Doiran, which enabled the Serbians and French to carry through successfully their magnificent penetration of the line beyond Monastir. On the Grappa the Austrian army, so far from showing itself already in process of dissolution, resisted with the utmost tenacity. Some of the heights were captured and recaptured alternately eight times; the Arditi were thrown in again and again; and the Italians stood up day after day to losses as severe as those that their regiments had been accustomed to suffer in the great offensives on the Isonzo.

But the Fourth Army on Grappa was doing what was required of it, and meanwhile all three armies on the Piave succeeded in their objective. The Twelfth, where the Alpini and the French vied with each other in a fierce rivalry, fought its way up the Piave gorge and cut the communications of the Austrians, who were defending the Grappa massif, so that they too joined the general *débandade.*'

The Eighth Army, working from the Montello, succeeded on October 27th in throwing a division across the Piave on their left, but failed on their right flank next to the British on account of bridging difficulties. Things for a moment looked serious; but prompt coöperation between the Allies saved the situation. On the night of October 27th-28th two divisions from the Eighth Army, under General Basso, passed over the British bridges to the south, erected and previously used by Lord Cavan's Tenth Army. But these bridges also gave way before the requisite force had crossed. General Basso, however, once across, turned northwards, and without reckoning his numbers or his isolated position, "with soldierly instinct," as Lord Cavan writes, attacked the enemy, and cleared the front of the Eighth Army, from which he had been detached. That army was thus enabled to cross the river and race forward over hill and dale to Vittorio, thence to cut the Valmarino communications of the enemy.

Meanwhile the Tenth Army, under Lord Cavan, the right wing of the whole attack, had enjoyed an even more rapid success. Lord Cavan's forces consisted of the 14th British Army Corps on the north, and on the south the 11th Italian Army Corps, with which our Unit was serving. In the Tenth Army sector, as indeed in front of the whole line of attack, the bed of the Piave was a mile and a half broad, consisting of islands of shingle and brushwood, divided by half a dozen or more channels of the river flowing "ten miles an hour in time of flood," and "three and a half miles an hour at summer level." If, therefore, it rained heavily for many hours in the mountains above, the crossing would be impossible. And it was late in October! There was very little of "foregone conclusion" about the battle when it began.

On the night of October 23rd-24th, by a brilliant preliminary operation, the northern part of the largest island, the Grave di Papadopoli, was captured by the British infantry, who crossed the swirling flood in flat-bottomed boats, rowed by *pontieri* of the Italian *genio*. The way was thus prepared for the great attack by the English and the Italian corps of the Tenth Army on the night of October 26th-27th.

The preliminary bombardment began half an hour before midnight, and with it began the rain. It was an anxious business waiting by the river bank for the attack at dawn, knowing that if the rain did not stop—and why should it stop in November?—the whole scheme must miscarry. But stop it did, when the attack began, and it never rained again anywhere where I was till I had been a fortnight in Trieste, except for half an hour's drizzle on the morning of October 29th. The weather-god, like every one else, had begun to *Wilsoneggiare,* as the Italian papers called the prevailing political tendency in Europe.

At 6.45 a. m., October 27th, the British and the Italians, under Lord Cavan's orders, moved to the attack, to capture the remaining part of the system of islands and the farther shore. A fair number of Italian and Austrian wounded were carried back across the river to our ambulances in the first twenty-four hours. But we saw less of this battle than of others at which we had assisted, because the infantry went right over the islands, through the swift channels that took their toll of them, and away across country beyond the river, leaving miles behind them every wheeled vehicle—artillery, supplies, and ambulances—unable to cross the channels until the bridges were made. The British bridges, as already recorded, broke down on the night of October 27th-28th; and the Italian bridges for carrying wheeled traffic, which were our concern, were only completed to the farther shore after dusk on the evening of October 28th.

On the afternoon of the 27th I had walked over to the farther bank by footbridges, passing on the islands a few corpses and many piles of Boche helmets thrown away wherever the Austrians had fled from the Italian attack. The infantry were already far forward, out of sight even from the farther bank. On the morning of the 28th I walked into San Polo, a village two miles beyond the farther bank, and found all the Italians there in high spirits, though very hungry, captured Austrian cannon still facing down the street, and all the signs of recent fighting. But the line was somewhere far ahead.

In fact, the back of the business had been broken, as far as the Tenth Army was concerned, in the short, fierce struggle on the 27th, when the Austrians proved incapable of standing up to our men. They put up their last serious rearguard action on the evening of the 29th, after which, as Lord Cavan writes, "the defeat became a rout."

From this moment forward we had but few wounded to carry; but even so, the ambulances found it hard work merely to keep in touch with the Bersaglieri of the 23rd and the infantry of the 37th Divisions in their wild rush to the Tagliamento and beyond. Our difficulty was every one's difficulty, the fact that the retiring Austrians had blown up the bridges over the series of rivers, though happily, in their haste, not quite all of them. Both British and Italian troops suffered severely from want of food, especially in the early days of the crossing, because the wheeled traffic could not keep up with the infantry any faster than the pontoons could be slung over the rivers. One began, by hard experience, to understand many of the minor but all-important reasons why the enemy had followed up so slowly over the same ground a year before; and then it had been pouring and the rivers flooded, whereas now the weather at least was perfect.

The Austrian armies were now everywhere in flight and dissolution. The enemy's divisions in line had mostly fought well, but the Czechs and Poles in reserve scarcely fired a shot, and surrendered wholesale on being dispatched to relieve the broken divisions. Once the retreat set in, morale gave way throughout, except among some of the German-Austrians. Even the Magyars wished only to get back to defend their new independent State. The fairly won military success of the Twelfth, Eighth, and Tenth Armies, operating on the political situation, had cleared an almost unopposed field of advance in mountain and plain for all the other armies of Italy. The way to Trent and Trieste was open.

They were wonderful and happy days for every one, those days of the great deliverance, with the barbarian once more fleeing from the soil sacred through the centuries to the Latin race. But only we who had traversed the same roads in such bitterness of spirit twelve months before could feel it to the full. *"O giornate del nostro riscatto!"* The inhabitants of Veneto and Friuli, after their year of servitude, were going about in happy crowds, hundreds together, men, women, and children, unable to do anything but laugh and talk with their liberators, who, themselves radiant with delight, were many of them wearing evergreen branches in token of victory.

Every day, as we advanced, we met ever longer columns of weedy prisoners, their hands deep in their gray overcoat pockets, shepherded in thousands at a time by two or three cheerful Tommies, or two or three majestic mounted Carabinieri. Many, I think, had "bowed the head for bread" rather than remain with a starving army or return to a starving land. On the side of every road and in every market town stood the yellow cannon and lorries, and all the deserted gear of the disbanding hosts. And in the ditches along every high road and lane between the Piave islands and Trieste the soldiers had thrown away their "Dolly Varden" Boche helmets; sometimes sooner, sometimes later in the flight each man had divested himself of that heavy badge of servitude. So it was given us to see "proud Austria rammed to wreck."

On the night of November 2nd it chanced that I had a long way to walk back beyond the Piave, not wishing to take the car back over the bridge. I was walking under the stars through the scenes of our June battle, ghostly in the starlight. As I went, I became aware of a singing and cheering all around for miles away. I was quite alone, and could only guess its significance; but when at last I struck our old Treviso main road, I asked the first group of soldiers I met what was the meaning of the still-continued, universal shout. They told me that the Austrians had sent a general to the Comando Supremo to ask for an armistice. I shall never forget the distant and continuous noise of a whole army scattered over the plain, shouting all night in its joy under the glistening winter stars because their warfare was accomplished, and Europe at last was free.

During these days, for the first time since I had been in Italy, I heard that Austrian prisoners had been insulted, though never injured. This new feeling of personal anger against the Austrian soldiery as human beings did not last long among their good-natured captors. It was entirely due to the tales told by the liberated populations of robbery and ill-treatment. The stories of the inhabitants, of which I heard many, were all of the same tenor. All their cattle and all the food that they produced had been taken and never paid for, while they themselves had been kept on a very low ration. Again, as in Shelley's day, the peasant of the Venetian plain had

> "heaped his grain
> In the garner of his foe."

Everything movable of any value had been packed up and sent off into Austria-Hungary. The robbery of the whole countryside for the benefit of the conquerors had been organized and official; but there had not been a systematized destruction of what could not be taken off, such as the Germans had carried out in France.

As to personal treatment, they all spoke of their year's taskmasters as *brutte bestie*. They had no other word for them in any village between Piave and Isonzo. They all said the Magyars ("Ungaresi") were the worst brutes, which, from what I heard and saw in Serbia in 1914, did not surprise me. The Croats, Bohemians, and even German-Austrian privates had as a rule behaved tolerably. The worst tyranny had come from the officers, especially the higher officers, and, most of all, the allied officers of Germany proper, who had always urged harsh treatment. God grant that that type of "higher officer" may now disappear out of Austria and out of Europe. It has caused enough misery for one planet in one æon.

BY CAPTAIN ALESSANDRO SAPELLI [1]

Former Governor of Benadir, one of Italy's colonies in Africa

Of all the dangers undergone, of all the desperate struggles, the gigantic efforts, the heroic exploits of the titanic battle waged by Italy, the world took little notice until after the disaster of Caporetto. Then Italy began to be spoken of, but more in reference to the danger to which France would be exposed should the forces of the Central Empires, passing through the Po Valley, succeed in attacking her from Savoy and the Delphinate—a frontier which, since 1914, the declaration of Italian neutrality had permitted France to leave undefended, enabling her to take from thence the 500,-000 men that were the decisive factor in winning the first battle of the Marne.

Yet, even after Caporetto, the decisions of the Allies were painfully slow, perhaps because they considered Italy definitely out of the fight. The Austro-German invasion of Italy, however, the consequence of a moral deficiency and not of a military defeat, was stopped though Italy had failed to get the Allied support she looked for. The Allied re-enforcements, absolutely inadequate to the situation, had orders to entrench themselves on the Mincio, more than 100 kilometers behind the firing line.

After this heroic check of the invaders at the Piave, silence again enveloped all things pertaining to Italy. Then came the great Austrian offensive of June, 1918, that ended for the enemy so miserably, as every one will remember. This Austrian reverse again revealed the power of Italy to strike in self-defense, but was not a result of Italian initiative. Much was said about it, partly, perhaps, because it helped to draw public attention from a critical situation on the western front between Bapaume and Chauny, but surely more because it seemed that this Italian victory might be—as it proved to be—the first of a series of successes leading into the offensive that should bring the Allies to final victory. A signal success was just then needed to strengthen the morale of the Allies, and Italy produced it by her staggering blow that turned the Austrian attack into a crippling defeat.

Thus Germany lost the support of her powerful ally; and with the strengthening of the Allied armies by the arrival of the American troops, and the unification of the supreme command in Marshal Foch, the chances in favor of the Allied arms tremendously increased. Indeed from that moment, when Italian valor transformed the threatening host of Austria into an army of discouragement, Hindenburg, pressed on all sides along the whole front from the sea to the Argonne, abandoned all hopes of a victory in France and began hasty dispositions for a shortening of the front and a full retreat to the formidably defended lines of the Rhine, where prolonged resistance would have given his country at least a diplomatic victory.

Most people at this juncture regarded the Italians as played out, after their efforts in June, 1918, and as quite incapable of anything more than to hug the shores of the Piave. The peculiar thing to note is that Austria alone seemed aware of the menace against her represented by Italy; but that Austria herself apprehended the worst is clearly proved by her stubborn refusal to send help to Germany, and her policy of constantly increasing her armies opposite the Italians on the Piave and the Alpine front.

Then came the final Italian victory—so suddenly, and with consequences so enormous and so immediate, that there seemed hardly time to speak of the battle itself, which nevertheless was not only a masterpiece of military technique, but a marvelous example of human will and intrepidity.

With always the same fixed idea of descending through the valley of the Po, along the Brenta and Adige valleys, cutting out Venice and the Veneto, the Austrians had been concentrating their forces in the mountain region. Yet, not having recovered from the defeat suffered at the hands of the Italians in June, knowing that no help was forthcoming from Germany, and seriously affected by the Bulgarian defection, Austria did not dare to resume the offensive. This situation had not escaped the keen eye of General Diaz; and, even though he had failed to get the Allied support he looked for, he launched his offensive.

The Brenta and the Piave in their upper courses move, one from west to east and the other from east to west, as if they were about to meet. Separated about midway of their length by the massif of Monte Grappa and Monte Pertica, they reach the sea, almost parallel, in a southeasterly direction. The Italian Army formed a semicircle, its left wing touching Monte Baldo, the center on Monte Grappa and Montello, between the two rivers, Piave and Brenta, and the right on the west side of the Piave.

The plan of General Diaz, perfectly carried out by his army commanders, was to press hard at the center, thus calling all the Austrian forces toward the point where the valleys seem to meet; to maneuver the armies directly on the right of the Grappa in such a way that the line would extend itself towards the west, with the front facing north; take possession of Monte Cuero, on the left of the Piave; force the mountain passes leading to the high valley, and shut off the enemy's retreat towards Belluno. From the Altipisino dei Sette Communi, simultaneously, an army should descend to trap the foe in the valley between Quero and Fonzaso; while, lastly, the extreme left should at the same time have advanced through the Valle Arsa upon Rovereto and Trento, engaging the Austrian reserves in that quarter and reaching Trento ahead of any retreating Austrian columns.

The most dangerous of these actions was that assigned to the troops stationed to the east of Monte Grappa, who would have had the right flank and their shoulders unprotected. But, to guard against this danger, the Italian high command ordered an advance of the troops lined up along the lower Piave, who were to move towards the Livenza, the Tagliamento, and the old Isonzo line, thus forming a right angle with the remaining line of the front covering the action at the center, and could eventually constitute its reserve.

This plan, which was begun on October 24th (exactly one year from the Caporetto disaster), starting with a violent feint in the zone of Monte Grappa (that cost the sacrificing of 20,000 Italian lives, and 60,000 wounded), was developed without hesitation during the next few days. For some hours it looked as if the encircling movement would come to naught, on account of the sudden flooding of the Piave that carried away all the bridges, at a moment when only a part of the Eighth and Tenth Army had passed to the left shore. But, thanks to the activity of the Italian Army Engineers in reestablishing communications, and the uninterrupted forwarding of supplies and munitions, the latter carried out by our Capronis, and the tenacious resistance of our First Division against the attempts of the Austrian troops to push the Italians back to the Piave, the most powerful difficulties created by Nature were overcome by Man. However, even by the evening of the 27th, the plans of the command were slated to win. The enemy had reënforced its lines in front of the Grappa, and was wasting itself in desperate attacks, in attempting to reconquer the positions, leaving thus ample time for the converging and encircling movement of the Eighth, Tenth, and Twelfth Armies, that, by the 28th, had already reached the heights of Valdobbiadene.

From that moment, the fate of the Austrian Army was sure. In its retreat, it would be obliged to extend itself through the valleys, lose tactical contact and moral cohesion. The battle was lost so far as the Austrian Army was con-

cerned. It still resisted with the strength of desperation, but, on the 3rd of November, when the victorious Italians had already to their credit prisoners amounting to 416,116 soldiers, 10,658 officers, and 6,818 cannon, the Austrian General Weber von Webenau accepted the conditions of the Armistice dictated by the Council of Versailles. That which had been one of the most thoroughly organized armies in the world had nothing left to it but disorganized bands of soldiers, of its former seventy-three divisions, which had been completely routed by six Allied divisions and fifty-one Italian divisions. The Italians, on the 11th, had already reached the Brennero, ready to march on the southern frontiers of the German confederation. But, on that same day also, the Teutonic Empire, left alone in the field, threatened by enemies on all sides, obtained an armistice.

The results of the victory on the Piave were superior to all expectations, but worthy of the genius with which the plans of the battle had been laid and executed—and, above all, of the heroism and fighting qualities of the soldiers who "carried on."

BY EMPEROR CHARLES OF AUSTRIA-HUNGARY
His Abdication, proclaimed on November 11th

Since my accession I have incessantly tried to rescue my peoples from this tremendous war. I have not delayed the re-establishment of constitutional rights or the opening of a way for the people to substantial national development. Filled with an unalterable love for my peoples I will not, with my person, be a hindrance to their free development. I acknowledge the decision taken by German Austria to form a separate State. The people has by its deputies taken charge of the Government. I relinquish every participation in the administration of the State. Likewise I have released the members of the Austrian Government from their offices. May the German Austrian people realize harmony from the new adjustment. The happiness of my peoples was my aim from the beginning. My warmest wishes are that an internal peace will be able to heal the wounds of this war.

(Signed) CHARLES.

THE FINAL ALLY DRIVE TO VICTORY

THE AMERICANS CAPTURE THE SEDAN LINE

NOVEMBER IST-IITH

GENERAL SIR F. MAURICE   GENERAL PERSHING
                MARSHAL. FOCH

With Austria begging for an armistice, with the German people loudly demanding peace, and the German army hopeless and disorganized, there was no question now of delaying the final Ally attack until 1919. True, Marshal Foch had difficulties enough on his own side. The Ally supply system had almost completely broken down under the strain of the huge unexpected advances of the armies. When Foch consulted with his British and American colleagues, Haig and Pershing, they were frank in saying that a further advance was almost equal to starvation for the soldiers, but they both eagerly agreed that the effort was worth attempting. In the few bleak days that might remain before winter made advance absolutely impossible, they would drive home one more blow.

So on November 1st another general assault was begun all along the line of the stupendous battle from Alsace to the English Channel. As in the September drive, the main effort was to be exerted at the two extremes, by the Britons with French and Belgian and American aid in the north, and by the Americans with French aid in the south. The French armies of the center were merely to fight enough to keep the Germans busy in front of them. If the German center did not retreat when the two wings were driven back, the entire army might well be enclosed and captured.

Against this final drive the Germans made nothing like their previous defense. The shadow of defeat was on them, and they knew it. Ludendorff had resigned, Hindenburg was little more than a figurehead, Mackensen was beleaguered in Rumania; and royally titled generals could not for real service take up the parts of these lost fighting leaders. The American progress was twice as rapid as that of September. On November 6th their troops held the heights above Sedan, and had thus broken the main German supply line in the south. The Crown Prince was scurrying back onto German territory, abandoning the headquarters at Montmédy which he had held for four long years. Pershing made ready for another drive, this time across the border into Germany itself, or rather into the French land of Lorraine held prisoner by Germany for half a century.

Meanwhile the British advance in the north captured Valenciennes on November 2nd. It was the last French city held by the Germans in the north. The Ally line swept forward through Belgium. The line of the Scheldt River was carried, with American aid, on November 4th; and by the 11th, Ghent and Mons and a dozen lesser Belgian cities were restored to freedom.

The narrative of this glorious advance is here given by General Maurice, the British chief of staff, whose book, "The Last Four Months," is the clearest, broadest, most unprejudiced picture of the closing campaign which we may ever see. General Maurice takes up also, from an expert standpoint, the much disputed question of the wisdom of the Allies in consenting to the Armistice and abandoning their "victory drive." Marshal Foch's noted telegram of November 9th is also given. This was the last call to battle in the Great War.

BY GENERAL SIR F. MAURICE [1]

THERE was no chance now for the leisurely retreat to the Meuse which Ludendorff had planned. It was essential to withdraw to the river as quickly as possible, but to do this without incurring irremediable disaster it was still as necessary as it had been since the end of September to delay to the utmost the British advance on Namur and the American progress towards Sedan.

This was the position of which Foch proposed to take advantage by continuing the general plan of his great battle. Gouraud and the Americans were to strike for Mézières and Sedan and block the southern exits, while the British armies made for Maubeuge and Mons and threatened Namur before the Germans in western Belgium could get away. The advance on Namur would force the Germans to come out of the greater part of Belgium in a hurry or be cut off, and would save that sorely tried land from the destruction which was inevitable if it became the scene of pitched battles, while the advance on Mézières and Sedan would have the same effect on the German center. The French armies in the center were, therefore, to continue their rôle of harassing and delaying the German retreat, and the Belgian armies were to keep the Germans busy on the Scheldt. The French troops on King Albert's right, however, with the help of two American divisions sent up to reënforce them, were to assist the British advance by forcing the line of the Scheldt about Audenarde.

[1] Reprinted by permission from General Maurice's book, "The Last Four Months," Copyright, 1919, by Little, Brown and Co.

On November 1st the last drive began, as had that of September, with a Franco-American attack, and again there lay in front of the American left a stretch of mountain forest, the Forest of Bourgogne, a northern extension of the Argonne. Again the intention was to force the Germans out of the forest by a combined advance of the Americans to the east of it, and of Gouraud's army to the west. This time the plan was completely successful. On the right of the American battle front the Third American Corps attacked in the Meuse valley, while the Fifth American Corps broke clean through such parts of the Kriemhilde line as it had not previously captured, and made an advance of about five miles in the one day. Simultaneously Gouraud extended his hold on the heights on the eastern bank of the Aisne opposite Vouziers.

The Germans were in no mind for a repetition of the Argonne struggle. Before the battle started their morale had begun to give way under the steady pressure of the American advance, and now it gave way altogether, while the American divisions which had done most of the hard fighting in October had either been rested and their ranks refilled, or had been relieved by fresh divisions, with the result that the First American Army was as full of vigor and energy as it had been on September 26th, despite the continuously wet and cold weather on the bleak hills of the Meuse.

On November 2nd the First American Corps on the left of the First Army drove forward six miles, captured Buzancy, and lined the eastern edge of the Bourgogne Forest, Gouraud at the same time reaching its western edge throughout its length. The Germans immediately evacuated the forest and began a general retreat before the First American Army and Gouraud's right.

During the night of November 3rd the infantry of the Second American Division, giving the weary Germans no time to reorganize a defense, made a remarkable pursuit and advanced in the darkness straight through the German lines for a distance of five miles. This great progress enabled the Americans to bring forward long-range guns and to shell the railway stations of Longuyon and Montmédy, through which the Crown Prince was trying to get away as much as possible of his war material.

The clearing of the Bourgogne Forest had enabled Gouraud to join hands with the Americans on November 3rd to the north of the forest, and he thus obtained a straight front of some nine miles beyond the Aisne east of Attigny. He was now able to threaten the retreat of the German troops holding the formidable Brunehilde line further west between Attigny and Rethel, by pushing forward his right wing in conjunction with the American advance. On November 4th he drove the enemy back from the southern portion of the canal which connects the Aisne near Attigny with the Meuse near Sedan. This maneuver compelled the Germans to fall back from the Brunehilde line in order to avoid being cut off from Mézières, and the French entered Rethel on November 6th.

Meanwhile, by November 5th the American front had sprung forward another six miles, and on the evening of the 6th, despite the endeavors of the German machine gunners to delay the pursuit, a division of the First American Corps reached the Meuse opposite the southern outskirts of Sedan, twenty-one miles from its starting point of November 1st. Gouraud, with a longer distance to go and with the resistance of the German troops, who had fallen back from the Brunehilde line, to overcome, did not reach his objective, Mézières, until the evening of the tenth.

While the First and Fifth American Corps were advancing northwards towards Sedan the right of the Third Corps began to strike out eastwards, and it crossed the Meuse and occupied Dun on November 4th. Thence on the following days, the Third, Second Colonial and Seventeenth French Corps on the right of the First American Army gradually wore down the resistance of the Germans in the wooded Meuse hills, and on the morning of November 11th, when the armistice came into effect, the Franco-American front was within six miles of Montmédy, where the German Crown Prince had lived during the battle of Verdun, when he was not in his dugout on the Montfaucon Hill. Though Montmédy was not entered by the Allies until the Germans had withdrawn in accordance with the armistice terms, they found on arrival that defeat had not changed the German nature, for the little town was pillaged by the enemy's troops before they left. These operations on the east bank of the Meuse towards Montmédy were extended southwards by the Second American Army, which began the long threatened movement toward the Briey iron fields.

While the French and Americans on the southern battle front were completing the task set them by Foch, the British armies were again in motion. The Germans at the end of October, after their defeat on the Selle, occupied the line of the Scheldt from Ghent to a point about two miles south of Valenciennes, whence their front ran southwards to the River Sambre, which it reached a little above Landrecies. The distance between the Scheldt and the Sambre on this line was not more than eighteen miles, and the southern five of these eighteen miles were taken up by the Mormal Forest. Sir Douglas Haig's first care was, therefore, to get more room for his advance between the Sambre and the Scheldt, and particularly to force the enemy to fall back from the tangle of reclaimed land, cut up by innumerable dykes, which stretches north of Valenciennes as far as the Condé Canal. Accordingly, on November 1st, while the Americans and French were attacking on the Meuse-Argonne front, the Seventeenth Corps of the Third British Army, and Twenty-second and Canadian Corps of the First Army, attacked south of Valenciennes, and after two days' heavy fighting had by the evening of November 2nd turned the line of the Scheldt from the south, and the Canadian Corps had entered Valenciennes.

This at once gave Haig the elbow room he required, and as there was no time to spare, if the enemy were to be prevented from making good his retreat to the Meuse, the Fourth, Third and First Armies attacked on November 4th on a thirty-mile front, from the Sambre Canal eight miles south of the Mormal Forest to the north of Valenciennes. The British right had the difficult tasks of crossing the Sambre Canal, which is as wide as the Scheldt Canal stormed on September 29th, and contained more water, and of forcing a way through the Mormal Forest. This forest was not so serious an obstacle as it had been in August, 1914, when after the battle of Mons it caused the separation of the British army into two parts, one retreating on each side of it, for the Germans had obtained a great quantity of timber from it for their trenches, huts and dugouts, and they had also improved the roads through it. Nevertheless, it afforded a resolute enemy splendid opportunities for defense, and both it and the canal prevented the Fourth Army from making free use of its tanks.

The British army was now fighting on the very ground on which it had first assembled in France, before it advanced to Mons, and was about to take complete revenge for its early misfortunes. After an intense bombardment, a dense artillery barrage rolled forward, and behind it, with the help of tanks wherever they could be used, the infantry on the whole thirty miles broke into the German positions. On the right the First and Thirty-second Divisions fought their way across the canal, and by nightfall were more than three miles to the east of it. Farther north the Germans were driven far back into the Mormal Forest, and troops of the Twenty-fifth Division, crossing the Sambre on rafts, captured Landrecies at the southeast corner of the forest. Landrecies was defended by a battalion of the German 1st Guard Reserve Division; it was in Landrecies that British Guards first met the Germans, when on August 25, 1914, they repulsed a night attack in the streets of the town. North of the Mormal Forest the Thirty-seventh Division and the New Zealanders, after repulsing a heavy German counter-attack, drove the enemy back beyond the Valenciennes-Avesnes railway, which runs through the center of the forest from west to east, and the New Zealanders, surrounding the old fortified town of Le Quesnoy, compelled its garrison to surrender. By the evening the left of the Third Army, and the right of the First Army, were on a front five miles beyond Valenciennes. On the British right Debeney's First French Army had also forced a crossing over the Sambre Canal to the north of Guise and kept pace with the advance of our Fourth Army.

In this battle the resistance of the enemy was definitely broken and he never rallied again. The three British armies captured 19,000 prisoners and 450 guns, and Debeney gathered in 5,000 more prisoners. South of Ghent the two French corps on King Albert's right, each of which now had an American division with them, drove back the Germans along the Scheldt, and the Ninety-first American Division captured Audenarde.

From this time until the end the pursuit was delayed mainly by the very complete destruction of the roads and railways by the Germans as they fell back, and by the consequent difficulty of getting up supplies to the troops. The enemy's difficulties in retreat were, however, much greater. Far into Belgium the roads were blocked with masses of transport and the railways with thousands of trucks, for the removal of which the Germans had not sufficient engines. Our aëroplanes, swooping down from the sky, attacked the German convoys and railway lines with machine-gun fire and with bombs, causing great destruction and frequent panics. A single battalion of the Twenty-fifth Division on November 5th captured thirty guns, which the German artillerymen had abandoned when attacked from the air.

By November 5th our troops were well beyond the Mormal Forest. On the 7th the Guards entered Bavai, on the 8th the Fourth Army occupied Avesnes. On the 9th the Guards and Sixty-second Division occupied the fortress of Maubeuge, the French taking Hirson on the same day. On the 8th the Germans began to flee from the Scheldt, and the British Fifth and Second Armies, with the French and Americans on their left, who had been preparing to deliver a great attack on the river line on November 11th, finding that the enemy was slipping away, followed hard after him and made rapid progress.

Peruwelz, Tournai and Renaix were occupied in succession, while by a last dramatic stroke of fortune the 3rd Canadian Division entered Mons a few hours before the Armistice was signed.

There were many curious coincidences between our first and last contact with the Germans in arms. Officers of our

Cavalry who had fought at Mons in 1914 found themselves on November 11, 1918, on the scene of their original encounter with the German troopers, while most curious of all, the Second Battalion of the Royal Irish Regiment, which had fought in the Third Division in the loop of the canal northeast of Mons on August 23, 1914, was with the Sixty-third Division cutting that loop when hostilities ceased.

The opinion is widely held that the Armistice of November 11th was premature. It is argued that we had the German armies at our mercy, and that the foundations of peace would have been more sure if we had ended the war by forcing the surrender in the field of a great part of those armies, or, failing that, had driven our beaten enemy back across the Rhine and followed him into the heart of Germany. The reception of the German troops by the German people, their march into the German towns through triumphal arches and beflagged streets with their helmets crowned with laurels, and the insistent statements in Germany that the German armies had not been defeated, that the Armistice had been accepted to save bloodshed, and to put an end to the sufferings of the women and children aroused amazement and disgust in the victors. There was very real anxiety lest after all we had failed to convince Germany that war did not pay; it was felt that we ought to have brought the realization of what war means home to the German people in their own country, and that, had we done so, the long-drawn-out negotiations in Paris would have been concluded more speedily and more satisfactorily. It is worth while, therefore, examining the situation as it was at the time of the Armistice, and considering the case as it presented itself to the men who had to decide whether hostilities should cease or not.

There is no question but that the German armies were completely and decisively beaten in the field. The German plenipotentiaries admitted it when they met Marshal Foch, and von Brockdorff-Rantzau admitted it at Versailles, when he said after the Allied peace terms had been presented to him: "We are under no illusions as to the extent of our defeat and the degree of our want of power. . . . We know that the power of the German army is broken."

Even if these admissions had not been made, the condition of the German lines of retreat to the Rhine is conclusive evidence of the condition of their armies. Every road was littered with broken-down motor-trucks, guns, machine guns and trench mortars. Great stacks of supplies and of military stores of all kinds were abandoned. Every railway line was blocked with loaded trucks which the Germans had been unable to remove. The sixty miles of railway in the valley of the Meuse between Dinant and Mézières was filled from end to end with a continuous line of German freight trains carrying guns, ammunition, engineering equipment, and other paraphernalia. On the Belgian canals alone over eight hundred fully charged military barges were found.

It is beyond dispute that on November 11th the lines of communication immediately behind the German armies had been thrown into complete disorder by the streams of traffic which were converging on the Meuse bridges, disorder greatly intensified by the attacks of the Allied airmen. The German armies, unable to resist on the fighting front, could no longer retreat in good order, partly because of the congestion on the roads and railways behind them, which not only hampered the movements of the troops, but prevented the systematic supply to them of food and ammunition, partly owing to the fact that there were not horses left to draw the transport of the fighting troops.

If ever armies were in a state of hopeless rout, the German armies were in the second week of November, 1918. The morale of the troops was gone, the organization of the services on which they depended for their needs had collapsed. This being so, why did we allow the German armies to escape from a hopeless position? Why did we not at once follow up the military advantage which we had gained at such cost?

In order to get an answer to these questions I visited the fronts of the Allied armies shortly after the conclusion of the Armistice. I there found, after traveling down the line from north to south, that amongst the fighting troops of the

Belgian, British, French and American armies the opinion was unanimous that they had got the Germans on the run and could have kept them on the run indefinitely, or until they laid down their arms. On the American front in particular, where there were large numbers of troops ready and eager to go forward who had not yet taken part in a great battle, there was a very strong feeling that they had been robbed of the fruits of victory.

When, however, I inquired the opinion of those behind the fighting fronts who were responsible for feeding the troops and keeping them supplied with all that was necessary to enable them to march forward, I heard a different story. Everywhere I was told that the Allied armies, which were on or were marching towards the Meuse, had on November 11th reached, or very nearly reached, the farthest limit at which for the time being they could be kept regularly supplied. The reasons for this were twofold. In the first place the Allied lines of communication grew steadily longer as the Germans were driven back, and even before our victorious advance began the state of the railways and the amount of rolling stock in France had caused anxiety. For four and a half years the railway systems of Northeastern France had been strained to the limit of their capacity, and the effects of that strain were beginning to be serious in 1918. Both we and the Americans had made great efforts to improve and extend the railway systems in our respective zones. During 1918 the British military railway administration in France built or reconstructed 2,340 miles of broad-gauge and 1,348 miles of narrow-gauge railways, while to supplement the French rolling stock we sent to France 1,200 locomotives and 52,600 cars. The shipment across the Channel of such cumbrous and heavy objects as locomotives and trucks was a slow and difficult business, and the needs of the armies were always growing faster than were the resources of the railways.

If these were our difficulties, those of the American army were greater, owing to the rapid growth of the army during the latter half of the year 1918, the shortage of shipping capable of crossing the Atlantic, and the necessity of giving first place to the transportation of troops and of war material. Up to the end the railways under American control in France suffered from a deficiency in rolling stock, and had great difficulty in meeting the demands of the large forces engaged in the Meuse-Argonne battle at the end of an ever-lengthening line of communications.

The French armies, which in the middle of September had been extended along the outside of the great bow made by the German lines between St. Quentin and Verdun, had the longest distances to advance in following up the German retreat, and before the advance began the French Government had cut down the railway transportation in the interior of the country to the bare minimum necessary for the preservation of the industrial and social life of France, and even then was unable to meet the full demands of the French armies and to supplement the railway material which Great Britain and America had been able to produce. The Belgian armies had hardly any resources of their own and no means whatever of developing their means of transportation. The result of all this was that the mere lengthening of the Allied lines of communications by the German retreat, apart altogether from any other action by the enemy, threw a very great strain upon the Allied railway administrations.

The Germans were, however, very active and skillful in damaging the roads and railways before they retreated, and this damage was extended by the destructive power of the artillery of both sides. Every railway bridge, large or small, was blown up, the railway embankments were cut, long stretches of track were destroyed, the stations were burned down, and the telegraph lines were almost obliterated and the instruments removed. The Germans had left behind them mines buried under the railway lines, and these exploded often after the first damage had been repaired and the trains were running, with the result that there was constant interruption to the traffic. One of our Army Commanders told me that, owing to the constant explosion of mines behind his front, during the last stages of the advance of his army his railhead was retreating faster than his troops were advancing.

The consequence of this was that on November 11th, despite the most strenuous and devoted work by all concerned in the repair and working of the railways, the farthest points at which supplies could be delivered by rail were from thirty-five to fifty miles in a direct line behind the front, and often double this distance by road. This gap had to be bridged by the motor transport, which, of course, had to use the roads. But the destruction of the roads by the Germans was as thorough as their destruction of the railways. Not only were the bridges destroyed, but mines were sprung at every cross-road. I remember counting eleven mine craters on three miles of the main road between Le Quesnoy and Mons. This damage could only be very roughly repaired, while the wet weather and the heavy traffic of the German retreat and of our advance increased the work of destruction. The heavy motor lorries, loaded with supplies and ammunition, had to plow their way slowly through these broken roads from the railheads to the troops, and return to the railheads to fill up. At the time of the Armistice the motor lorries were working in double and treble shifts, and the strain upon them caused by the bad roads and the incessant work was such that in the Fourth Army on November 11th more than half of the lorries at the service of the army had broken down. *The troops were receiving no more than bare necessities, and at one time had with them nothing more than the day's food carried by the men.*

BY GENERAL PERSHING

The detailed plans for the operations of the Allied armies on the western front changed from time to time during the course of this great battle, but the mission of the First American army to cut the great Carrignan-Sedan-Mézières Railroad remained unchanged. Marshal Foch coördinated the operations along the entire front, continuing persistently and unceasingly the attacks by all Allied armies; the Belgian army, with a French army and two American divisions, advancing eastward; the British armies and two American divisions, with the First French army on their right, toward the region north of Givet; the First American army and Fourth French army toward Sedan and Mézières.

On October 21st my instructions were issued to the First army to prepare thoroughly for a general attack on October 28th that would be decisive, if possible. In order that the attack of the First army and that of the Fourth French army on its left should be simultaneous, our attack was delayed until November 1st.

The immediate purpose of the First army was to take Buzancy and the heights of Barricourt, to turn the forest north of Grandpré, and to establish contact with the Fourth French army near Boult-aux-Bois. The army was directed to carry the heights of Barricourt by nightfall of the first day and then to exploit this success by advancing its left to Boult-aux-Bois in preparation for the drive toward Sedan. By strenuous effort all available artillery had been moved well forward to the heights previously occupied by the enemy, from which it could fully cover and support the initial advance of the Infantry.

On this occasion and for the first time the Army prepared for its attack under normal conditions. We held the front of attack and were not under the necessity of taking over a new front, with its manifold installations and services. Our own personnel handled the communications, dumps, telegraph lines, and water service; our divisions were either on the line or close in rear; the French artillery, aviation, and technical troops which had previously made up our deficiencies had been largely replaced by our own organizations; and our army, corps, and divisional staffs were by actual experience second to none.

On the morning of November 1st, three Army corps were in line between the Meuse River and the Bois de Bourgogne. On the right the Third Corps had the Fifth and Ninetieth Divisions; the Fifth Corps occupied the center of the line, with the Eighty-ninth and Second Divisions, and was to be the wedge of the attack on the first day; and on the left the First Corps deployed the Eightieth, Seventy-seventh, and Seventy-eighth Divisions.

Preceded by two hours of violent artillery preparation,

the Infantry advanced, closely followed by "accompanying guns." The Artillery acquitted itself magnificently, the barrages being so well coördinated and so dense that the enemy was overwhelmed and quickly submerged by the rapid onslaught of the Infantry. By nightfall the Fifth Corps, in the center, had realized an advance of almost 9 kilometers, to the Bois de la Folie, and had completed the capture of the heights of Barricourt, while the Third Corps, on the right, had captured Aincreville and Andevanne. Our troops had broken through the enemy's last defense, captured his artillery positions, and had precipitated a retreat of the German forces about to be isolated in the forest north of Grandpré. On the 2nd and 3rd we advanced rapidly against heavy fighting on the fronts of the right and center corps; to the left the troops of the First Corps hurried forward in pursuit, some by motor trucks, while the Artillery pressed along the country roads close behind. Our heavy artillery was skillfully brought into position to fire upon the Carignan-Sedan Railroad and the junctions at Longuyon and Conflans. By the evening of the 4th, our troops had reached La Neuville, opposite Stenay, and had swept through the great Foret de Dieulet, reaching the outskirts of Beaumont, while on the left we were 8 kilometers north of Boult-aux-Bois.

The following day the advance continued toward Sedan with increasing swiftness. The Third Corps, turning eastward, crossed the Meuse in a brilliant operation by the Fifth Division, driving the enemy from the heights of Dun-sur-Meuse and forcing a general withdrawal from the strong positions he had so long held on the hills north of Verdun.

By the 7th the right of the Third Corps had exploited its river crossing to a distance of 10 kilometers east of the Meuse, completely ejecting the enemy from the wooded heights and driving him out into the swampy plain of the Woevre; the Fifth and First Corps had reached the line of the Meuse River along their respective fronts and the left of the latter corps held the heights dominating Sedan, the strategical goal of the Meuse-Argonne operation, 41 kilometers from our point of departure on November 1st. *We had cut the enemy's main line of communications. Recognizing that nothing but a cessation of hostilities could save his armies from complete disaster, he appealed for an immediate armistice* on November 6th.

Meanwhile general plans had been prepared for the further employment of American forces in an advance between the Meuse and the Moselle, to be directed toward Longwy by the First Army, while the Second Army was to assume the offensive toward the Briey Iron Basin. Orders directing the preparatory local operations involved in this enterprise were issued on November 5th.

Between the 7th and 10th of November the Third Corps continued its advance eastward to Remoiville, while the Seventeenth French Corps, on its right, with the Seventy-ninth, Twenty-sixth, and Eighty-first American Divisions and 2 French divisions, drove the enemy from his final foothold on the heights east of the Meuse. At 9 p. m. on November 9th appropriate orders were sent to the First and Second Armies in accordance with the following telegram from Marshal Foch to the Commander of each of the Allied armies.

BY MARSHAL FOCH

The enemy, disorganized by our repeated attacks, retreats along the entire front.

It is important to coördinate and expedite our movements.

I appeal to the energy and the initiative of the Commanders-in-Chief and of their armies to make decisive the results obtained.

Continuation of General Pershing's Report

In consequence of the foregoing instructions, our Second Army pressed the enemy along its entire front. On the night of the 10th-11th and the morning of the 11th the Fifth Corps, in the First Army, forced a crossing of the Meuse east of Beaumont and gained the commanding heights within the reëntrant of the river, *thus completing our control of the Meuse River line.* At 6 a. m. on the 11th notification was received from Marshal Foch's headquarters that the Armistice had been signed and that hostilities would cease at 11

GERMAN SUBMARINES

Of 441 submarines built and laid down by Germany, 28 were available at the beginning of the war, 343 were built during the war and 70 were being built at the signing of the armistice. The number available in 1917 during the period of greatest destruction of allied shipping was 212.

Source of information: Navy Department.

Summary of Situation, November 11, 1918

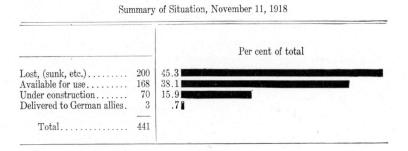

		Per cent of total
Lost, (sunk, etc.).........	200	45.3
Available for use.........	168	38.1
Under construction.......	70	15.9
Delivered to German allies.	3	.7
Total..............	441	

Disposition Since November 11, 1918

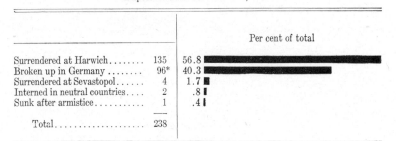

		Per cent of total
Surrendered at Harwich........	135	56.8
Broken up in Germany	96*	40.3
Surrendered at Sevastopol......	4	1.7
Interned in neutral countries....	2	.8
Sunk after armistice...........	1	.4
Total...................	238	

* Consists of 70 under construction and 26 unseaworthy.

Classification, by Type

		U Sea-going	U B Coastal	U C Mine Layers	
Total built and laid down..	441	169	151	121	
Built during war..........	343	112	136	95	
Lost before armistice.....	200	67	73	60	
Available at armistice.....	168	73	60	35	
Surrendered at Harwich...	135	59	51	25	
Building at armistice*....	70	29		26	
Unseaworthy*...........	26	12			
Surrendered at Sevastopol.	4				
Interned after armistice...	2				
Sunk after armistice......	1				

U Seagoing
U B Coastal
U C Mine Layers

* Broken up in Germany.

STATISTICS BRANCH - GENERAL STAFF
WAR DEPARTMENT

6 - 12 - 20

MERCHANT SHIPPING LOSSES DURING WORLD WAR PERIOD

Comparison of war losses of merchant steamers of the principal maritime countries with losses due to marine risk or non-war causes. Vessels of less than 100 tons are not included.

Source of information: Lloyds' Register.

	GROSS TONS LOST			Per cent	
	War	Non-War	Total	War losses	Non-war losses
France..........	722,939	84,138	807,077	90	10
Holland.........	201,797	27,244	229,041	88	12
Great Britain*...	7,923,023	1,132,645	9,055,668	87	13
Italy...........	745,766	115,669	861,435	87	13
Denmark........	210,880	34,422	245,302	86	14
Greece..........	349,661	65,014	414,675	84	16
Norway.........	976,516	195,244	1,171,760	83	17
Belgium.........	85,842	19,239	105,081	82	18
Sweden.........	180,415	83,586	264,001	68	32
Spain...........	157,527	80,335	237,862	66	34
Brazil..........	20,328	10,951	31,279	65	35
United States**..	343,090	187,948	531,038	65	35
Japan...........	119,764	150,269	270,033	44	56
Total.......	12,037,548	2,186,704	14,224,252	85	15

* Includes dominions.
**Includes Great Lakes.

War losses	12,037,548	
Non-war losses	2,186,704	

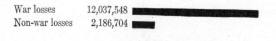

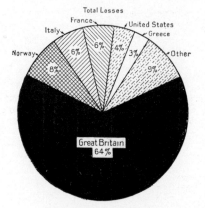

Total Losses

Total 14,224,252 tons

STATISTICS BRANCH - GENERAL STAFF
WAR DEPARTMENT
4 - 24 - 20

a. m. Preparatory measures had already been taken to insure the prompt transmission to the troops of the announcement of an Armistice. However, the advance east of Beaumont on the morning of the 11th had been so rapid and communication across the river was so difficult that there was some fighting on isolated portions of that front after 11 a. m.

Between September 26th and November 11th, 22 American and 4 French divisions, on the front extending from southeast of Verdun to the Argonne Forest, had engaged and decisively beaten 47 different German divisions, representing 25 per cent. of the enemy's entire divisional strength on the western front. Of these enemy divisions 20 had been drawn from the French front and 1 from the British front. Of the 22 American divisions 12 had, at different times during this period, been engaged on fronts other than our own. The First Army suffered a loss of about 117,000 in killed and wounded. It captured 26,000 prisoners, 847 cannon, 3,000 machine guns, and large quantities of material.[2]

The dispositions which the enemy made to meet the Meuse-Argonne offensive, both immediately before the opening of the attack and during the battle, *demonstrated the importance which he ascribed to this section of the front and the extreme measures he was forced to take in its defense.* From the moment the American offensive began until the Armistice, his defense was desperate and the flow of his divisions to our front was continuous. The rate at which German divisions were used up shows an increase of 27 divisions on the American front during the battle.

Under the instructions issued by me on November 5th, for operations by the Second Army in the direction of the Briey Iron Basin, the advance was undertaken along the entire front of the army and continued during the last three days of hostilities. In the face of the stiff resistance offered by the enemy, and with the limited number of troops at the disposal of the Second Army, the gains realized reflected great credit on the divisions concerned.

[2] The figures here apply to the combined battles of the Argonne and of the final drive.

GERMANY DECLARES HERSELF A REPUBLIC

ABDICATION OF THE KAISER

NOVEMBER 9TH

PRINCE MAXIMILIAN   MARSHAL HINDENBURG
THE FORMER EMPEROR WILLIAM II.
THE FORMER CROWN PRINCE FREDERICK WILLIAM
PRESIDENT EBERT   COUNT VON MOLTKE

The leisurely diplomatic progress of the old style German state-craft toward acknowledging defeat in the Great War was given a sudden and disastrous jolting by the Ally drive begun November 1st. This great attack on the very edge of winter was a decidedly American method of "rushing things." For a month Germany had been talking about arbitration and an "equal" peace. Now she was driven by necessity to abandon her last pretenses. Plainly told by President Wilson that the only approach to peace must be by way of surrender to Marshal Foch upon the battlefield, the German Government on November 5th dispatched commissioners to seek the Marshal. These commissioners made a last diplomatic effort to substitute argument for surrender. When Foch refused all parleying, they had no choice but to submit. That submission was the deathblow to the autocratic, militaristic Empire of Germany.

When that Empire surrendered to force it slew itself, and knew itself to be slain. On November 9th the Kaiser's new Chancellor, Prince Maximilian of Baden, published for the Kaiser an "abdication." The only objection to this was that it lacked the signature of William himself. Neither he nor the Crown Prince was yet willing to confess personal guilt and failure by an abdication. Instead father and son, each as he best could, fled to Holland. From that refuge each of them at a later date, when convinced that there was no other hope, issued a signed abdication.

Within the German Empire there were three other "kingdoms" beside Prussia, and each of these lesser kings had thus the opportunity to precede the Prussian monarchs in their haste to abdicate. The King of Wurtemberg abdicated on November 10th, of Saxony on the 11th, and of Bavaria on the 16th. A dozen or so of lesser princes took a similar step. In most cases their wakening people did not wait for them to act, but hastily formed new governments of their own. Bavaria led the way by proclaiming itself a republic on November 8th.

The chief new government, seeking still to keep Germany a unit of some sort, was meanwhile taking shape in Berlin. On November 9th and 10th there was revolution in Berlin, and almost without opposition a Socialistic Republic was proclaimed. Its leaders were the former heads of the Socialist party, most of them members of the Reichstag and skilled parliamentarians. The revolution was indeed typically German in that it was a most orderly transfer of authority from one party to another. Marshal Hindenburg promptly pledged his own allegiance and that of the army to the new government. The retiring Chancellor, Prince Max, announced that the retiring Kaiser authorized the new Chancellor chosen by the Socialists, the former harness-maker, Frederick Ebert.

Ebert thus took over all authority at once, and later was declared by his party to be the provisional President of the new Republic. Thus to William, King of Prussia, head of a long line of princely autocrats, rulers by "divine right," there succeeded Frederick, the harness-maker of Heidelberg, son of a tailor, holding a dubious and unelected presidency in the midst of anarchistic tumult. That was the result which the German aristocracy had brought about by its most stupendous of all efforts at World Dominion.

C. F. H.

BY PRINCE MAXIMILIAN

Proclamation of November 9th, announcing the Kaiser's abdication

THE Kaiser and King has decided to renounce the throne. The Imperial Chancellor will remain in office until the questions connected with the abdication of the Kaiser, the renouncing by the Crown Prince of the throne of the German Empire and of Prussia, and the setting up of a regency have been settled. For the regency he intends to appoint Deputy Ebert as Imperial Chancellor, and he proposes that a bill shall be brought in for the establishment of a law providing for the immediate promulgation of general suffrage and for a constitutional German National Assembly, which will settle finally the future form of government of the German Nation and of those peoples which might be desirous of coming within the empire.

BY THE FORMER KAISER WILLIAM II.

Actual Abdication document, published in Berlin on November 30th

By the present document I renounce forever my rights to the crown of Prussia and the rights to the German imperial crown. I release at the same time all the officials of the German Empire and Prussia and also all officers, non-commissioner officers and soldiers of the Prussian Navy and Army and of contingents from confederated States from the oath of fidelity they have taken to me, as their Emperor, King, and supreme chief.

I expect from them until a new organization of the German Empire exists that they will aid those who effectively hold the power in Germany to protect the German people against the menacing dangers of anarchy, famine, and foreign domination.

Made and executed and signed by our own hand with the imperial seal at Amerongen, November 28 [1918].

WILHELM.

BY MARSHAL HINDENBURG
Statement issued on March 20, 1919

Public opinion has been recently discussing the question why the Kaiser went to Holland. To obviate erroneous judgments, I should like to make the following brief observations. When the Imperial Chancellor, Prince Max of Baden, announced the Kaiser's abdication on November 9th, without the Kaiser's previous declaration of assent, the German Army was not beaten, but its strength had dwindled and the enemy had fresh masses in readiness for a new attack. The conclusion of the armistice was directly impending. At this moment of the highest military tension revolution broke out in Germany, the insurgents seized the Rhine bridges, important arsenals, and traffic centers in the rear of the army, thereby endangering the supply of ammunition and provisions, while the supplies in the hands of the troops were only enough to last for a few days. The troops on the lines of communication and the reserves disbanded themselves, and unfavorable reports arrived concerning the reliability of the field army proper.

In view of this state of affairs the peaceful return home of the Kaiser was no longer to be thought of and could only have been enforced at the head of loyal troops. In that case the complete collapse of Germany was inevitable, and civil war would have been added to the fighting with the enemy without, who would doubtless have pressed on with all his energy. The Kaiser could, moreover, have betaken himself to the fighting troops, in order to seek death at their head in a last attack; but the armistice, so keenly desired by the people, would thereby have been postponed, and the lives of many soldiers uselessly sacrificed. Finally, the Kaiser might leave the country. He chose this course in agreement with his advisers, after an extremely severe mental struggle, and solely in the hope that he could thereby best serve the Fatherland, save Germany further losses, distress, and misery, and restore to her peace and order. It was not the Kaiser's fault that he was of this opinion.

BY COUNT DETLEF VON MOLTKE
Officer on the Kaiser's personal Staff

I come now to the 29th of October, the day of the departure of the Emperor from Potsdam for Spa, the headquarters of the Army in the West. The journey was resolved upon by the General Staff at midday. The suddenness of it did not surprise us soldiers, accustomed as we were to quick movements. It aroused, however, speculation on the part of the public and was commented on from different angles by the press, on the 30th, some of the more radical newspapers even hinting, in guarded language, at flight.

When we examine the reasons for the journey, we must not forget that the Emperor and King was not only Monarch but Commander-in-Chief of the Military Forces of the Empire. We must, therefore, ask ourselves what remained of the Imperial powers after the change to parliamentary government in the first days of the month? The answer is: almost nothing. The hypocritical Wilson had now brought it to pass among his Allies, external and internal to Germany that the Emperor as Monarch, that is as Civil Governor, had but little authority. In the new parliamentary government sat as the Fata Morgana of the new system Erzberger and Scheidemann, the plague and bane of Germany. The Emperor had been obliged to surrender the power over war and peace to the Reichstag. All the appointments of Ministers and of the higher military officials as well as all decisions in regard to military political affairs required the approval of the Cabinet of Ministers. All the powers in these respects formerly exercised by the Emperor had been taken from him and nothing left to him but the powers of administration in detail. This was the aspect of the Emperor's powers in the latter October days. The American Professor had issued his commands and the German Michel had obeyed and fallen from power. Can anyone then blame the Emperor that, having been deprived of all of his powers as Monarch, he betook himself as soldier to his brave, hard-pressed soldiers? This question carries its own answer.

At 4 P. M., October 30th, we arrived in Spa. Two days later, on November 1st, Dr. Drews, Minister of the Interior, presented himself to the Emperor for the purpose of requesting abdication. The Emperor heard him through and then replied: "What, you as a Prussian officer, who have sworn your oath of loyalty to your King, you come before me with such a proposition! I will describe to you then the chaos you invite. I and my house abdicate! Immediately all the German dynasties fall! The army is left without a leader! The front dissolves and the soldiers stream back across the Rhine. The traitors throughout the country get together burning, plundering, murdering and the enemy assists in the nefarious work! I have no idea of abdicating! The King of Prussia dare not betray Germany, least of all in this hour of her greatest need. I also have sworn my oath and I shall keep it!" Has not everything turned out as prophesied by the Emperor?

On the 2nd of November occurred the abdication of Emperor Charles, following the collapse of the Austro-Hungarian front in Upper Italy. On the same day news was brought to the Emperor of the heroic resistance of my old regiment, the Guard Cuirassiers, to the advancing enemy. This report was received by him with joy and gratitude, alas, almost the final joy of his imperial life. On the 3rd of November, the Emperor betook himself by way of Liege and Brussels to the battlefront. Near Ghent representatives from eleven divisions were greeted and decorated. The presence of the Kaiser had not been announced and the fresh and hardy and orderly appearance of the troops was all the more gratifying. The spontaneous enthusiasm of the soldiers on seeing their Commander-in-Chief was also most encouraging.

On the 5th of November in the early morning we arrived in Spa. During the immediately following days we learned of the revolt in Kiel and of the demand of the Social Democrats for the abdication of the Emperor. Railroad connection with Germany began to be irregular and broken. Soon it ceased altogether. No train crossing the Rhine. Telegraphic and telephonic connection with Berlin became difficult. It appeared to be under some sort of censorial control and confidential messages could no longer be trusted. Finally we had to have recourse to air service. Two airships flew to Berlin, but none returned.

I come now to the 9th of November, that day of greatest misfortune to our Fatherland. In the night or early morning the Chancellor, Prince Max, telegraphed that the Emperor must abdicate, otherwise the Cabinet could no longer remain, that the Social revolution was extending on all sides, and that the Social-Democrats could no longer hold the radicals under control. It was also reported that the city and town officials in the large cities on the coast and in the western and southern portions of the Empire had assumed independent authority and that the Rhine and the great magazines of munitions and food along and east of this line had been seized by the Revolutionists. Such was the situation when at 10 A. M. on that fateful day Hindenburg appeared before the Emperor. The matter first considered was whether it were possible to suppress the internal revolt by force of arms. The new Chief of Staff, General Gröner, took the ground that there was in his opinion no prospect of success in such a move. The idea was given up because the Emperor was unwilling to shed the blood of his own countrymen in a fratricidal conflict. There was also the danger that the Revolutionists might stop the supplies to the army. They had threatened it and there were supplies for only a few days at the front. The Emperor inclined to the plan of waiting for the conclusion of the Armistice and then leading the army back in person into Germany, without announcing any purpose of employing it against the revolt. General Gröner considered this idea also unrealizable since the revolt had turned against the Emperor personally. He said that the army would march back peacefully and in order under his (Gröner's) command, but not under the Emperor's command, "Because it no longer stands behind your Majesty!" he exclaimed. In spite of the fact that some of the generals did not agree with Gröner, the plan was abandoned, in deference to his view.

I relate this in all calmness, but I beg my readers to place themselves for a moment in the position of the Emperor, who, as I well know, had never wished the war and had always had in mind the good of his people and consider what must have been his feelings when his own military subordinates now turned the consultation to the question of his abdication.

The Chancellor and his colleagues in the ministry were from Berlin, pressing with increasing earnestness and impatience for the abdication. The Crown Prince, who had been summoned from his headquarters to take part in the deliberations, now arrived on the scene. Under-Secretary von dem Busche telephoned from the Chancellor's office in Berlin that Liebknecht would be proclaimed President of the Republic in case the Emperor did not at once abdicate. It was further reported that Berlin was bathed in blood, that the troops forming the garrison had gone over to the Revolutionists and that only the immediate abdication of the Emperor could save the Fatherland from civil war. After several fruitless attempts to establish telephonic communication with Berlin, the Chief of Staff of the Garrison, Major von Berge, was reached. He reported to the inquiry regarding the situation in Berlin that most of the troops of the garrison had mutinied, that the fighting in the streets was not very considerable and that it was not at all true that Berlin was bathed in blood.

Immediately following this message came another telephoned by His Excellency Wahnschaffe, declaring that civil conflict was no longer a matter of hours but of minutes!

Then the Emperor in great agony of mind declared that if civil war could be prevented in no other way, he would abdicate as Emperor, but would remain King of Prussia.

The Emperor signed this declaration and caused it to be telephoned to Berlin. Immediately the following surprising answer was received: "To late. We can no more make use of that. By order of the Chancellor."

The Wolf Telegraphic Bureau made public the following telegram: "His Majesty, the Emperor and King, has abdicated, the Crown Prince has renounced the succession. Prince Max has been appointed Regent, and representative Ebert, Chancellor."

This telegram had been given to the public at midday, while the telephone message from the Kaiser announcing his decision did not leave Spa until half past one, one hour and a half later. Nothing whatever had been said in the consultation at Spa about the renunciation of the succession by the Crown Prince and, of course, nothing about that was contained in the Emperor's telephonic message. The action of the government in Berlin was thus nothing other or less than a coup d'etat of the most serious and virulent nature.

In the course of the afternoon, reports were received that detachments of the troops not only along the routes to the base of supplies but at the front had mutinied. The garrison at Spa even was said to have become unreliable. It was reported that it would not do anything against the Emperor but would do nothing for him. Nevertheless, the Kaiser said, at 8 o'clock in the evening, in my own hearing, "I do not think of leaving. I shall remain with the army in Spa."

Around ten o'clock the same evening the Emperor was advised by his counsellors to go into neutral territory in order to avoid further shedding of blood and civil war. He was now called upon to make this critical decision under the feeling that he had been abandoned, even thrown overboard by his own people, and betrayed by the highest counsellor of the Crown. What should he do? Which way should he turn after both the front and the Fatherland had been closed to him? After agonizing self-deliberation, he chose Holland as his place of refuge.

I come now to the 10th (November). The night passed quietly but I doubt if a single eye was closed in sleep during its entire course. Soon after 4 a. m. we assembled in the dining car. The Emperor came in apparently self-possessed and calm, gave us all a friendly shake of the hand, as usual. During the breakfast we learned the shameful terms of the armistice. At 5 o'clock a. m. the train started for the Dutch frontier. It had a guard of four soldiers in each car, since it had to pass through places occupied by mutinied troops. Soon ten minutes after we halted at the little station La Reide. In the darkness, the Emperor left the train and stepped, accompanied by a few gentlemen, into the automobile provided to take him across the Dutch frontier.

The rest of us continued in the train. We traveled through Pepinster and Liege and ruined Vise. About 7 a. m. the train stopped. Obliquely across the track was a wire hedge. We had reached the Dutch frontier. As parting greeting the last German sentinel had called after us some coarse words. Our car was uncoupled and we waited for the Dutch engine to take us across the frontier. It came at about 10 o'clock a. m. and drew us into the neutral Kingdom. When we reached the first Dutch station we saw the Emperor, who had preceded us in automobile, walking up and down the platform. In great depression of spirit we presented ourselves before him.

The Dutch Government had been made acquainted with the decision of the Emperor by its Consul in Brussels. The Emperor had also telegraphed to the Queen asking her permission to enter her kingdom as a private gentleman. The Emperor had been received at the frontier by the Dutch Military Commander, Major van Dyl. The Major looked out for our protection against the public, as the place was filled with hostile Belgian deserters. In the course of the forenoon the German Consul at Maastricht had a number of Dutch officers, both civil and military, presented themselves before the Emperor.

We learned that the Queen had placed the Castle Amerongen, property of Count Bentick, at the service of the Emperor. Our departure from the frontier for the Castle was fixed for the next day, the 11th of November. It was a most depression, shameful journey. At every station thousands of people were gathered, greeting us with shouting, whistling, cursing. They threatened us, made signs of choking and hanging us, etc. In such manner was our poor Emperor received on Dutch soil.

BY THE KAISER
Personal letter to his son, Frederick William, dated November 9, 1918

MY DEAR BOY:

After the Court Chamberlain had informed me that he could no longer guarantee my safety at Main Headquarters, and that the troops also were no longer trustworthy, I resolved after a severe mental struggle to leave the army, which has collapsed, and go to Holland. I advise you to stick to your post until the conclusion of the armistice. In Berlin two Governments, under the leadership of Ebert and Liebknecht, are fighting against each other. I hope to see you again in happier times. Your faithful and deeply affected father,

WILHELM.

BY PRINCE FREDERICK WILLIAM
Letter dated November 11, 1918, addressed to "Imperial Chancellor" Ebert, the new head of Socialistic Germany

The Crown Prince urgently desires to remain at his post to do his duty like every other soldier. He will bring his army back home in a well-disciplined and orderly manner, and undertakes to do nothing whatever at this juncture against the present Government. What is the Government's attitude in this matter?

GOVERNMENTAL ANSWER OF NOVEMBER 12TH

After hearing Major Gen. von Wrisberg of the Prussian War Ministry, the Government must give its refusal to the request of the Crown Prince.

BY PRINCE FREDERICK WILLIAM
Letter of November 16, 1918, addressed to Marshal Hindenburg

HIGHLY HONORED FIELD MARSHAL:

In these most grievous days of our life, both for my father and for myself, I too must say good-by to your Excellency. With deep emotion I have been obliged to decide to make use of the authority granted me by your Excellency to lay down my post as chief commander and to take up my residence in the first instance in a neutral country. I have only been able to force myself to this step after hard internal struggles, although it is repugnant to my whole nature not to be able to lead my brave troops home. I desire, however, once again briefly to explain my attitude.

Contrary to many unjust opinions, which have always tried to represent me as a war instigator and a reactionary, I have from the beginning adopted the standpoint that this war was for us a war of defense. Again and again during 1916, 1917, and 1918 I made both oral and written representations to the persons concerned that Germany must endeavor by every means in her power to terminate the war and be glad at maintaining herself against the entire world on the basis of the *status quo*. In many conversations with General Ludendorff I for a long time pleaded for a wise peace by understanding, and expressed the view that the most favorable opportunity for attaining this end was reached when we occupied strong, powerful positions before and also during the spring offensive.

As regards internal politics, I am the last person to oppose the liberal development of our Constitution. Only a few days ago I set forth this view in writing to Prince Max of Baden. Nevertheless, when the weight of events hurled my father from his throne, I was not only not heard, but was simply passed over as Crown Prince and as heir to the throne. No renunciation was either demanded from or made by me. Notwithstanding these facts my standpoint was to persevere at my post, and my ideal was, by holding my army group together, to avoid further causes of damage and disintegration for our Fatherland. The attitude of the present Government, however, was authoritative as to my remaining further at my military post. I had been informed by it that the Government did not count upon further military employment for me.

Your Excellency will kindly also note that copies of this letter have been sent to the Minister of the royal house, the Prussian Ministry, the Vice-Presidents of the lower house, the President of the upper house, the Chairman of the Military Cabinet, and some friends of mine among the military leaders.

FREDERICK WILLIAM.

BY FREDERICK EBERT
Address of November 10, 1918

Citizens: The ex-Chancellor, Prince Max of Baden, in agreement with all the Secretaries of State, has handed over to me the task of liquidating his affairs as Chancellor. I am on the point of forming a new Government in accord with the various parties, and will keep public opinion freely informed of the course of events.

The new Government will be a Government of the people. It must make every effort to secure in the quickest possible time peace for the German people and consolidate the liberty which they have won.

The new Government has taken charge of the administration, to preserve the German people from civil war and famine and to accomplish their legitimate claim to autonomy. The Government can solve this problem only if all the officials in town and country will help.

I know it will be difficult for some to work with the new men who have taken charge of the empire, but I appeal to their love of the people. Lack of organization would in this heavy time mean anarchy in Germany and the surrender of the country to tremendous misery. Therefore, help your native country with fearless, indefatigable work for the future, every one at his post.

I demand every one's support in the hard task awaiting us. You know how seriously the war has menaced the provisioning of the people, which is the first condition of the people's existence. The political transformation should not trouble the people. The food supply is the first duty of all, whether in town or country, and they should not embarrass, but rather aid, the production of food supplies and their transport to the towns.

Food shortage signifies pillage and robbery, with great misery. The poorest will suffer the most, and the industrial worker will be affected hardest. All who illicitly lay hands on food supplies or other supplies of prime necessity or the means of transport necessary for their distribution will be guilty in the highest degree toward the community.

I ask you immediately to leave the streets and remain orderly and calm.

Supplementary Address of November 17th

First, we do not intend to confiscate any bank or savings bank deposits nor any sums in cash or banknotes or other valuable papers deposited in the bank safes.

Secondly, we do not intend to cancel any subscriptions to the Ninth War Loan, or any other war loan, or in any other way to impair the legitimacy of those loans. The Government, however, is determined to enforce the strictest measures that large fortunes and great incomes shall contribute appropriately toward the public expense.

Thirdly, salaries, pensions, and other claims on the State, held by officials, employees, officers, wounded and other soldiers and their relatives, will remain absolutely valid.

THE ARMISTICE

OFFICIAL CORRESPONDENCE OF GENERALS FOCH AND
HINDENBURG
NARRATIVES OF EYE-WITNESSES
WOODROW WILSON

The surrender of Germany was not so complete and unconditional
as had been that of her three partners in crime. As usual, the weaker
criminals had suffered most. Germany had not laid down her arms
until by her preliminary negotiations she had received from the Ally
Governments the assurance that they would base their peace demands
upon President Wilson's "Fourteen Points." Of course general principles, such as the "Fourteen Points" may be twisted by diplomats into
meaning almost anything they wish, as for example in Germany's own
peace with Russia where she had twisted "no annexations" into meaning that she was to be the autocrat over all Russia's richest provinces.
So the German rulers had hoped to argue the "Fourteen Points" into
a very comfortable peace for themselves. In this, however, they had
been sternly checked by the Allies. The latter, under Wilson's lead,
had insisted that the Allies, and not Germany, should decide upon the
meaning and application of the "Fourteen Points." The Ally decision
was to be guided by these because of their righteousness and not to
lighten Germany's retribution. Her part must be simply to accept their
decision and obey it.

To prevent all possibility of Germany's pretending to obey and
afterward refusing, the Allies insisted on such an armistice as should
not only acknowledge their complete military victory but should also
leave Germany completely disarmed and unable to renew the contest.
Hence the armistice must be a wholly one-sided affair. The German
commissioners must come to Foch to ask for it; and they had then
to accept his terms, which would be such as to deprive Germany utterly
of all military or naval strength. These points were clearly stated
to the German Government.

On November 6th the German Government declared that it would
seek such an armistice. On November 7th von Hindenburg got into
telegraphic touch with Marshal Foch, and in the correspondence here
given arranged the necessary visit of submission. The German commissioners, a military chief, a naval one, and three civilians, headed
by the noted Catholic parliamentary leader, Mathias Erzberger, reached
Foch's headquarters on November 8th. Declaring themselves amazed
by the severity of the terms of the armistice, they held off for over
two days. But Marshal Foch refused to argue with them, and the Ally

415

troops continued their successful drive. Of the tumult that ensued in Germany we have already told. So that, fearful of still worse disaster, the German commissioners signed the terms at last, at five in the morning of November 11th.

The terms were arranged to go into effect six hours after the signing; so that the fighting ceased at 11 a. m. On that eleventh hour of the eleventh day of the eleventh month of 1918 a new, and let us trust a better, age was born among men.

C. F. H.

BY MARSHAL HINDENBURG

Telegraphic wireless dispatch received by Marshal Foch at 12.30 a. m. on November 7th

GERMAN General Headquarters to the Allies' General Headquarters; the German Commander-in-Chief to Marshal Foch:

The German Government, having been informed through the President of the United States that Marshal Foch had received powers to receive accredited representatives of the German Government and communicate to them conditions of an armistice, the following plenipotentiaries have been named by it:

Mathias Erzberger, General H. K. A. von Winterfeld, Count Alfred von Oberndorff, General von Grünnel, and Naval Captain von Salow.

The plenipotentiaries request that they be informed by wireless of the place where they can meet Marshal Foch. They will proceed by automobile, with subordinates of the staff, to the place thus appointed.

BY MARSHAL FOCH

Telegraphic wireless response sent out at 1.30 a. m.

To THE GERMAN COMMANDER-IN-CHIEF:

If the German plenipotentiaries desire to meet Marshal Foch and ask him for an armistice, they will present themselves to the French outposts by the Chimay-Fourmies-La Capelle-Guise road. Orders have been given to receive them and conduct them to the spot fixed for the meeting.

BY MARSHAL HINDENBURG
Telegraphic response received at 1 p. m.

The German plenipotentiaries for an armistice leave Spa to-day. They will leave here at noon and reach at 5 o'clock this afternoon the French outposts by the Chimay-Fourmies-La Capelle-Guise road. They will be ten persons in all, headed by Secretary of State Erzberger.

Supplementary telegraphic notice received at 1.50 p. m.

German General Headquarters to the Allied General Headquarters: The Supreme German Command to Marshal Foch: From the German outposts to the French outposts our delegation will be accompanied by a road-mending company to enable automobiles to pass the La Capelle road, which has been destroyed.

Supplementary notice received at 6 p. m.

The German Supreme Command to Marshal Foch: By reason of delay the German delegation will not be able to cross the outpost line until between 8 and 10 o'clock to-night at Haudroy, two kilometers northeast of La Capelle.

BY EYE-WITNESSES
The coming of the first German emissary as reported by the French captain at the outpost at Chimay

Notice had reached me that an envoy might arrive and that fire had ceased in our sector. About 3 o'clock in the afternoon a German lieutenant appeared. He was magnificently turned out and magnificently mounted, and had an escort of two men. I met him about a hundred yards in front of our lines, and he wished me to go back with him to meet the plenipotentiaries. I told him I could not leave my command; and at first he made some demur, the idea of those with him being that a French officer should accompany the plenipotentiaries from the other side of the line. I assured him there would be no firing in the sector, that the plenipotentiaries could cross the line in safety, and that I would receive them at my post of command.

"This gentleman is an officer," he said to the men with him, "and as an officer I can accept and trust his word." Five o'clock was the time fixed for the arrival of the delegates, but at that hour no one arrived, the mission, as is known, actually making their appearance considerably later in the evening, when they at once proceeded on their way.

Arrival of the German Delegates as Seen by a British Correspondent

The roads were a mass of mud, motor-cars of all sorts were ranged by the side of the main street, and the German plenipotentiaries were temporarily halted because of a breakdown to a motor lorry in the road in front of them. There were seven cars in all, two of them belonging to French Headquarters and five being German. The plenipotentiaries must have halted for nearly half an hour, and certain members of the junior staff attached to them got down while the details of a fresh route to be followed were discussed by them with the French officers by whom they were being escorted.

The senior members remained in the cars, invisible in darkness. Those we saw were of the typical officer class, clean-shaven and almost aggressively self-contained. For the most part they were silent, but occasionally they talked in low tones.

On the pavement by the houses there was a continual movement of French soldiers. No guard was round the cars, for any sort of guard was entirely unnecessary. There was not a single individual among the two or three hundred men present who even moved forward to catch a glimpse of the mission. There was no question as to any one doubting their identity, for the cars bore on their panels the crest of the Black Eagle.

The demeanor of the French soldier was typical of the high standard of courtesy set by Marshal Foch. Both army and nation realized that with Marshal Foch in command the terms of the armistice were in absolutely safe hands, as he had abundantly shown that he had taken to the full such measures as the situation required. He insisted, however, that every detail of the transaction should be conducted in absolute privacy, and there was not present at the historic meeting a single representative of the French or allied press.

Statement by One of the German Delegates

When on November 5th we left Spa in motor-cars and reached the French lines we found enemy carriages already waiting to take us to the unknown scene of negotiations. This motor tour with the French officers lasted ten hours, and it appears likely was intentionally prolonged in order to drive us all over the devastated province and prepare us by what we saw for what was shortly to be put before us in the way of hatred and revenge in the extremely severe armistice conditions. Now and again a Frenchman pointed silently to heaps of ruins, or mentioned a name, *"Voilà St. Quentin."* In the evening, wherever it was, a train stood ready for us. The windows of the carriages were curtained, and when we awoke next morning the train stood in the midst of a wood.

We know now that the negotiations took place in the forest of Compiègne, but a week ago we knew nothing. Perhaps it was a measure of precaution, even for our sakes, that we were taken through no town. Perhaps acts of violence were feared on the part of the population, for the hatred for us among them is boundless. The wood was evidently barred by troops to all comers. There were no houses and no tents. On the railway line stood two trains, one occupied by Marshal Foch and his people, the other by ours.

Here for three days we lived, worked, and deliberated. This seems to be the modern form of such negotiations. The castles and fortresses of olden times have gone, even for such purposes. The train with its sleeping, drawing-room, and dining cars was very comfortable, and we were provided with everything we wanted. The officer who had charge of the train had us supplied, and the conduct of the numerous guards who stood around was beyond reproach.

But all the hostility and the fullness of hate for our country that seems now to be cherished in France came to expression in the form of the negotiations, as well as in the terrible nature of the conditions. Those of us who were soldiers wore uniforms and the Iron Cross. The introduction of the half-dozen French officers who conducted the negotiations with us *"in plenum"* and the greetings were of the coldest.

Foch, who showed himself only twice—at the opening and at the end—gave us no word of the particular politeness that in earlier times distinguished the most chivalrous nation in the world, and his officers just as little. He received us with the words, *"Qu'est ceque vous désirez, messieurs?"* and invited us into his business car, furnished with tables and maps. As each was to speak his own language and everything was translated, the reading of the conditions alone occupied nearly two hours. It was moreover a discovery when Foch answered that there were to be no negotiations, and only dictated matter. Altogether, with all his coldness, he was by no means so tactless and brusque as was General d'Esperey at Belgrade.

Then we retired to our train, which stood on the other line. As we had been sent by the old Government, and had certainly not been authorized to sign everything without conditions, we proceeded, at the instance of Erzberger, to divide the various points under three heads, military, naval, and diplomatic, and discussed them separately with the members of the enemy commissions, which consisted only of officers. Military Germany thus, with two civilians, stood face to face with now completely militarized France. The enemy maintained, in the persons of all his representatives, the same objective; their coldness was mitigated by no single word that bordered upon the human, as had marked our reception by the Marshal. The English Admiral adopted the tone of the French, and only from Foch's Chief of the General Staff, who bore the Alsatian name of Weygand, did we perhaps receive any greater politeness.

During our two days' proceedings there was really no negotiation, and we could only try to obtain concessions on various conditions. For when the enemy demanded delivery of 160 U-boats we could only point out the technical impossibility, as we had not 160 to give. This demand had to be changed into the formula, "all U-boats." The chief point was that of food, and of this we were in a certain measure able to obtain assurance.

In the meantime, in this lonely wood, with its two railway trains, we were cut off from all intercourse with the outside world. Foch himself went off twice to Paris, and couriers were able in two hours to arrive with the papers. Thus it was possible for the enemy on Sunday, early, to hand us the Paris newspapers with the abdication of the Kaiser. We read no laughter, no triumph, in their faces. Immediately before the close of the second and last plenary sitting we placed before the enemy in the German language our protest against the treaty, but in the end we had to sign.

THE ARMISTICE

I.—Military Clauses on Western Front

One—Cessation of operations by land and in the air six hours after the signature of the armistice.

Two—Immediate evacuation of invaded countries: Belgium, France, Alsace-Lorraine, Luxemburg, so ordered as to be completed within fourteen days from the signature of the armistice. German troops which have not left the above-mentioned territories within the period fixed will become prisoners of war. Occupation by the allied and United States forces jointly will keep pace with evacuation in these areas. All movements of evacuation and occupation will be regulated in accordance with a note annexed to the stated terms.

Three—Reparation beginning at once to be completed within fifteen days of all the inhabitants of the countries above enumerated (including hostages, persons under trial or convicted).

Four—Surrender in good condition by the German armies of the following war material: Five thousand guns (2,500 heavy, and 2,500 field), 25,000 machine guns, 3,000 minenwerfer, 1,700 airplanes (fighters, bombers—firstly, all of the D 7's and all the night bombing machines). The above to be delivered in situ to the allied and United States troops in accordance with the detailed conditions laid down in the note (annexure No. 1) drawn up at the moment of the signing of the armistice.

Five—Evacuation by the German armies of the countries on the left bank of the Rhine. The countries on the left bank of the Rhine shall be administered by the local troops of occupation. The occupation of these territories will be carried out by allied and United States garrisons holding the principal crossings of the Rhine (Mayence, Coblenz, Cologne), together with the bridgeheads at these points of a thirty-kilometer radius on the right bank and by garrisons similarly holding the strategic points of the regions. A neutral zone shall be reserved on the right bank of the Rhine between the stream and a line drawn parallel to the bridgeheads and to the stream and at a distance of ten kilometers, from the frontier of Holland up to the frontier of Switzerland. The evacuation by the enemy of the Rhinelands (left and right bank) shall be so ordered as to be completed within a further period of sixteen days, in all, thirty-one days after the signing of the armistice. All the movements of evacuation or occupation are regulated by the note (annexure No. 1) drawn up at the moment of the signing of the armistice.

Six—In all territories evacuated by the enemy there shall be no evacuation of inhabitants; no damage or harm shall be done to the persons or property of the inhabitants. No person shall be prosecuted for offenses of participation in war measures prior to the signing of the armistice. No destruction of any kind shall be committed. Military establishments of all kinds shall be delivered intact, as well as military stores of food, munitions, and equipment, not removed during the time fixed for evacuation. Stores of food of all kinds for the civil population, cattle, etc., shall be left in situ. Industrial establishments shall not be impaired in any way and their personnel shall not be removed.

Seven—Roads and means of communication of every kind, railroads, waterways, main roads, bridges, telegraphs, telephones, shall be in no manner impaired. All civil and military personnel at present employed on them shall remain. Five thousand locomotives and 150,000 wagons in good working order, with all necessary spare parts and fittings, shall be delivered to the associated powers within the period fixed in annexure No. 2, and total of which shall not exceed thirty-one days. There shall likewise be delivered 5,000 motor lorries (camion automobiles) in good order, within the period of thirty-six days. The railways of Alsace-Lorraine shall be handed over within the period of thirty-one days, together with pre-war personnel and material. Further, the material necessary for the working of railways in the countries on the left bank of the Rhine shall be left in situ. All stores of coal and material for the upkeep of permanent ways, signals, and repair shops shall be left in situ. These stores shall be maintained by Germany in so far as concerns the working of the railroads in the countries on the left bank of the Rhine. All barges taken from the Allies shall be restored to them. The note, annexure No. 2, regulates the details of these measures.

Eighth—The German command shall be responsible for revealing within the period of forty-eight hours after the signing of the armistice all mines or delayed action fuses on territory evacuated by the German troops and shall assist in their discovery and destruction. It also shall reveal all destructive measures that may have been taken (such as poisoning or polluting of springs and wells, etc.). All under penalty of reprisals.

Nine—The right of requisition shall be exercised by the allied and United States armies in all occupied territories, subject to regulation of accounts with those whom it may concern. The upkeep of the troops of occupation in the Rhineland (excluding Alsace-Lorraine) shall be charged to the German Government.

Ten—The immediate repatriation without reciprocity, according to detailed conditions which shall be fixed, of all allied and United States prisoners of war, including persons under trial or convicted. The allied powers and the United States shall be able to dispose of them as they wish. This condition annuls the previous conventions on the subject of the exchange of prisoners of war, including the one of July, 1918, in course of ratification. However, the repatriation of German prisoners of war interned in Holland and in Switzerland shall continue as before. The repatriation of German prisoners of war shall be regulated at the conclusion of the preliminaries of peace.

Eleven—Sick and wounded who cannot be removed from evacuated territory will be cared for by German personnel, who will be left on the spot with the medical material required.

II.—Disposition Relative to the Eastern Frontiers of Germany

Twelve—All German troops at present in the territories which before belonged to Austria-Hungary, Rumania, Turkey, shall withdraw immediately within the frontiers of Germany as they existed on August First, Nineteen Fourteen. All German troops at present in the territories which before the war belonged to Russia shall likewise withdraw within the frontiers of Germany, defined as above, as soon as the Allies, taking into account the internal situation of these territories, shall decide that the time for this has come.

Thirteen—Evacuation by German troops to begin at once, and all German instructors, prisoners, and civilians as well as military agents now on the territory of Russia (as defined before 1914) to be recalled.

Fourteen—German troops to cease at once all requisitions and seizures and any other undertaking with a view to obtaining supplies intended for Germany in Rumania and Russia (as defined on August 1, 1914).

Fifteen—Renunciation of the treaties of Bucharest and Brest-Litovsk and of the supplementary treaties.

Sixteen—The Allies shall have free access to the territories evacuated by the Germans on their eastern frontier, either through Danzig, or by the Vistula, in order to convey supplies to the populations of those territories and for the purpose of maintaining order.

III.—Clause Concerning East Africa

Seventeen—Evacuation by all German forces operating in East Africa within a period to be fixed by the Allies.

IV.—General Clauses

Eighteen—Repatriation, without reciprocity, within a maximum period of one month in accordance with detailed conditions hereafter to be fixed of all interned civilians, including hostages under trial or convicted, belonging to the Allied or associated powers other than those enumerated in Article Three.

Nineteen—The following financial conditions are required: Reparation for damage done. While such armistice lasts no public securities shall be removed by the enemy which can serve as a pledge to the Allies for the recovery or reparation for war losses. Immediate restitution of the cash deposit in the national bank of Belgium, and in general immediate return of all documents, specie, stocks, shares, paper money, together with plant for the issue thereof, touching public or private interests in the invaded countries. Restitution of the Russian and Rumanian gold yielded to Germany or taken by that power. This gold to be delivered in trust to the Allies until the signature of peace.

V.—Naval Conditions

Twenty—Immediate cessation of all hostilities at sea and definite information to be given as to the location and movements of all German ships. Notification to be given to neutrals that freedom of navigation in all territorial waters is given to the naval and mercantile marines of the allied and associated powers, all questions of neutrality being waived.

Twenty-one—All naval and mercantile marine prisoners of the allied and associated powers in German hands to be returned without reciprocity.

Twenty-two—Surrender to the Allies and United States of all submarines (including submarine cruisers and all mine-laying submarines) now existing, with their complete armament and equipment, in ports which shall be specified by the Allies and United States. Those which cannot take the sea shall be disarmed of the personnel and material and shall remain under the supervision of the Allies and the United

States. The submarines which are ready for the sea shall be prepared to leave the German ports as soon as orders shall be received by wireless for their voyage to the port designated for their delivery, and the remainder at the earliest possible moment. The conditions of this article shall be carried into effect within the period of fourteen days after the signing of the armistice.

Twenty-three—German surface warships which shall be designated by the Allies and the United States shall be immediately disarmed and thereafter interned in neutral ports or in default of them in allied ports to be designated by the Allies and the United States. They will there remain under the supervision of the Allies and of the United States, only caretakers being left on board. The following warships are designated by the Allies: Six battle cruisers, ten battleships, eight light cruisers (including two mine layers), fifty destroyers of the most modern types. All other surface warships (including river craft) are to be concentrated in German naval bases to be designated by the Allies and the United States and are to be completely disarmed and classed under the supervision of the Allies and the United States. The military armament of all ships of the auxiliary fleet shall be put on shore. All vessels designated to be interned shall be ready to leave the German ports seven days after the signing of the armistice. Directions for the voyage will be given by wireless.

Twenty-four—The Allies and the United States of America shall have the right to sweep up all mine fields and obstructions laid by Germany outside German territorial waters, and the positions of these are to be indicated.

Twenty-five—Freedom of access to and from the Baltic to be given to the naval and mercantile marines of the allied and associated powers. To secure this the Allies and the United States of America shall be empowered to occupy all German forts, fortifications, batteries, and defense works of all kinds in all the entrances from the Cattegat into the Baltic, and to sweep up all mines and obstructions within and without German territorial waters, without any question of neutrality being raised, and the positions of all such mines and obstructions are to be indicated.

Twenty-six—The existing blockade conditions set up by the allied and associated powers are to remain unchanged, and all German merchant ships found at sea are to remain liable to capture. The Allies and the United States should give consideration to the provisioning of Germany during the armistice to the extent recognized as necessary.

Twenty-seven—All naval aircraft are to be concentrated and immobilized in German bases to be specified by the Allies and the United States of America.

Twenty-eight—In evacuating the Belgian coast and ports Germany shall abandon in situ and in fact all port and river navigation material, all merchant ships, tugs, lighters, all naval aëronautic apparatus, material and supplies, and all arms, apparatus, and supplies of every kind.

Twenty-nine—All Black Sea ports are to be evacuated by Germany; all Russian war vessels of all descriptions seized by Germany in the Black Sea are to be handed over to the Allies and the United States of America; all neutral merchant vessels seized are to be released; all warlike and other materials of all kinds seized in those ports are to be returned and German materials as specified in Clause Twenty-eight are to be abandoned.

Thirty—All merchant vessels in German hands belonging to the allied and associated powers are to be restored in ports to be specified by the Allies and the United States of America without reciprocity.

Thirty-one—No destruction of ships or of materials to be permitted before evacuation, surrender, or restoration.

Thirty-two—The German Government will notify the neutral Governments of the world, and particularly the Governments of Norway, Sweden, Denmark, and Holland, that all restrictions placed on the trading of their vessels with the allied and associated countries, whether by the German Government or by private German interests, and whether in return for specific concessions, such as the export of shipbuilding materials, or not, are immediately canceled.

Thirty-three—No transfers of German merchant shipping of any description to any neutral flag are to take place after signature of the armistice.

VI.—Duration of Armistice

Thirty-four—The duration of the armistice is to be thirty days, with option to extend. During this period if its clauses are not carried into execution the armistice may be denounced by one of the contracting parties, which must give warning forty-eight hours in advance. It is understood that the execution of Articles 3 and 18 shall not warrant the denunciation of the armistice on the ground of insufficient execution within a period fixed, except in the case of bad faith in carrying them into execution. In order to assure the execution of this convention under the best conditions, the principle of a permanent international armistice commission is admitted. This commission will act under the authority of the allied military and naval Commanders in Chief.

VII.—The Limit for Reply

Thirty-five—This armistice to be accepted or refused by Germany within seventy-two hours of notification.

This armistice has been signed the Eleventh of November, Nineteen Eighteen, at 5 o'clock French time.

> F. FOCH.
> R. E. WEMYSS.
> ERZBERGER.
> A. OBERNDORFF.
> WINTERFELDT.
> VON SALOW.

BY PRESIDENT WILSON
Address to Congress after Announcing the Armistice

The war thus comes to an end; for, having accepted these terms of armistice, it will be impossible for the German command to renew it.

It is not now possible to assess the consequences of this great consummation. We know only that this tragical war, whose consuming flames swept from one nation to another until all the world was on fire, is at an end and that it was the privilege of our own people to enter it at its most critical juncture in such fashion and in such force as to contribute, in a way of which we are all deeply proud, to the great result. We know, too, that the object of the war is attained; the object upon which all free men had set their hearts; and attained with a sweeping completeness which even now we do not realize. Armed imperialism such as the men conceived who were but yesterday the masters of Germany is at an end, its illicit ambitions engulfed in black disaster. Who will now seek to revive it?

The arbitrary power of the military caste of Germany, which once could secretly and of its own single choice disturb the peace of the world, is discredited and destroyed. And more than that—much more than that—has been accomplished. The great nations which associated themselves to destroy it have now definitely united in the common purpose to set up such a peace as will satisfy the longing of the whole world for disinterested justice, embodied in settlements which are based upon something much better and more lasting than the selfish competitive interests of powerful States. There is no longer conjecture as to the objects the victors have in mind. They have a mind in the matter, not only, but a heart also. Their avowed and concerted purpose is to satisfy and protect the weak as well as to accord their just rights to the strong.

The humane temper and intention of the victorious Governments have already been manifested in a very practical way. Their representatives in the Supreme War Council at Versailles have by unanimous resolution assured the peoples of the Central Empires that everything that is possible in the circumstances will be done to supply them with food and relieve the distressing want that is in so many places threatening their very lives; and steps are to be taken immediately to organize these efforts at relief in the same systematic manner that they were organized in the case of Belgium. By the use of the idle tonnage of the Central Empires it ought presently to be possible to lift the fear of utter misery from their oppressed populations and set their minds and energies free for the great and hazardous tasks of political reconstruction which now face them on every hand. Hunger does not breed reform; it breeds madness and all the ugly distempers that make an ordered life impossible.

For with the fall of the ancient Governments, which rested like an incubus on the people of the Central Empires, has come political change not merely, but revolution; and revolution which seems as yet to assume no final and ordered form, but to run from one fluid change to another, until thoughtful men are forced to ask themselves, With what Governments and of what sort are we about to deal in the making of the covenants of peace?

With what authority will they meet us, and with what assurance that their authority will abide and sustain securely the international arrangements into which we are about to enter? There is here matter for no small anxiety and misgiving. When peace is made, upon whose promises and engagements besides our own is it to rest?

Let us be perfectly frank with ourselves and admit that these questions cannot be satisfactorily answered now or at once. But the moral is not that there is little hope of an early answer that will suffice. It is only that we must be patient and helpful and mindful above all of the great hope and confidence that lie at the heart of what is taking place. Excesses accomplish nothing. Unhappy Russia has furnished abundant recent proof of that. Disorder immediately defeats itself. If excesses should occur, if disorder should for a time raise its head, a sober second thought will follow and a day of constructive action, if we help and do not hinder.

The present and all that it holds belong to the nations and the peoples who preserve their self-control and the orderly processes of their Governments; the future to those who prove themselves the true friends of mankind. To conquer with arms is to make only a temporary conquest; to conquer the world by earning its esteem is to make permanent conquest. I am confident that the nations that have learned the discipline of freedom and that have settled with self-possession to its ordered practice are now about to make conquest of the world by the sheer power of example and of friendly helpfulness.

The peoples who have but just come out from under the yoke of arbitrary government and who are now coming at last into their freedom will never find the treasures of liberty they are in search of if they look for them by the light of the torch. They will find that every pathway that is stained with the blood of their own brothers leads to the wilderness, not to the seat of their hope. They are now face to face with their initial test. We must hold the light steady until they find themselves. And in the meantime, if it be possible, we must establish a peace that will justly define their place among the nations, remove all fear of their neighbors and of their former masters, and enable them to live in security and contentment when they have set their own affairs in order. I, for one, do not doubt their purpose or their capacity. There are some happy signs that they know and will choose the way of self-control and peaceful accommodation. If they do, we shall put our aid at their disposal in every way that we can. If they do not, we must await with patience and sympathy the awakening and recovery that will assuredly come at last.

The President's Thanksgiving Proclamation of November 17th

It has long been our custom to turn in the autumn of the year in praise and thanksgiving to Almighty God for His many blessings and mercies to us as a nation. This year we have special and moving cause to be grateful and to rejoice. God has in His good pleasure given us peace. It has not come as a mere cessation of arms, a relief from the strain and tragedy of war. It has come as a great triumph of Right. Complete victory has brought us, not peace alone, but the confident promise of a new day as well, in which justice shall replace force and jealous intrigue among the nations. Our gallant armies have participated in a triumph which is not marred or stained by any purpose of selfish aggression. In a righteous cause they have won immortal glory and have nobly served their nation in serving mankind. God has indeed been gracious. We have cause for such rejoicing as revives and strengthens in us all the best traditions of our national history. A new day shines about us, in which our hearts take new courage and look forward with new hope to new and greater duties.

While we render thanks for these things, let us not forget to seek the Divine guidance in the performance of those duties, and Divine mercy and forgiveness for all errors of act or purpose, and pray that in all that we do we shall strengthen the ties of friendship and mutual respect upon which we must assist to build the new structure of peace and good-will among the nations.